Cracking the
LSAT®

THE PRINCETON REVIEW

Cracking the LSAT®

ADAM ROBINSON AND
ROB TALLIA

2000 EDITION

RANDOM HOUSE, INC.
NEW YORK

Princeton Review Publishing, L.L.C.
2315 Broadway
New York, NY   10024
E-mail: info@review.com

ISBN 0-375-75409-1
ISSN 1062-5542

Editor: Gretchen Feder
Production Editor: Julieanna Lambert
Designer: Illeny Maaza
Production Coordinator: Robert McCormack
Illustrations by: The Production Department of The Princeton Review

Manufactured in the United States of America on partially recycled paper.

9 8 7 6 5 4 3 2 1

2000 Edition

ACKNOWLEDGMENTS

A successful LSAT program is a collaborative effort. We'd especially like to thank our teachers John Sheehan, Lindsey van Wagenen, Mark Sawula, Dave Schaller, Jim Reynolds, Adam Frank, and Adam Landis for their suggestions and contributions. An extra thanks to Karen Lurie for her expertise and for making sure we were on target. Special thanks are owed John Hasnas.

We'd like to thank our agent, Julia Coopersmith, for her tireless help and editorial suggestions. To our editor Diane Reverand, our deep appreciation for her patience with our perfectionist delays and for her sponsorship of the entire *Cracking the System* project.

A very special thanks to Oliver Hart, professor of economics at M.I.T., and to Debora Davies and the folks at *Columbia Law Review* for their generous permission to quote an excerpt from an article by Professor Hart.

Finally, we'd like to thank all those who have taught us everything we know about taking tests—our students.

CONTENTS

1

The LSAT: General Information and Strategies

"CRACKING" THE LAW SCHOOL ADMISSION TEST

In this chapter, we're going to give you an overall preparation plan for the LSAT. Preferably, you've bought this book at least a few months before the date of the LSAT you plan to take, so you'll have time to (a) actually follow the suggestions we make below; (b) work through (at least twice) the specific problems in chapters 2, 3, and 4; and (c) complete both practice tests at the end of this book.

If you've bought this book only a few weeks before the LSAT, read through this chapter and absorb the test-taking tips that we give you, then work through chapters 2, 3, and 4. Finally, try to take at least one of the tests in the back of the book.

If you've bought (or are merely opening) this book for the first time only a few *days* before the LSAT, well, we admire your bravado. Take a complete test to see approximately what you would score on a real LSAT. If it's more than five or six points below where you want to be, consider skipping the test and taking it at a later date. The best way to improve your score dramatically is to work steadily on hundreds of problems throughout the course of a few months. Remember, the title of this book is *Cracking the LSAT*, not *Crashing the LSAT*.

THE STRUCTURE OF THIS CHAPTER

REMINDER: Order the LSAT Registration Bulletin from LSAC—you can get one mailed to you by going to their excellent web site (www.lsac.org) or by calling them at (215) 968-1001

Before we hit you with some general test-taking techniques, we want to make sure that you know all that we know about the LSAT itself. We'll start with a few pages' worth of information on the test—make sure you read all this info carefully so you know exactly what you're up against.

In addition, you'll want to order the *LSAT Registration Bulletin* from the Law School Admissions Council (LSAC)—you can get one mailed to you by going to their very excellent web site (www.lsac.org) or by calling them at (215) 968-1001. The *Bulletin* has much more information than we give you here, order forms for signing up for the LSAT and for the Law School Data Assembly Service (LSDAS), and order forms for obtaining previously released LSATs. It also contains a full-length, previously administered LSAT.

WHAT IS THE LSAT?

The LSAT is a 101-question, heavily speeded multiple-choice test. By *heavily speeded*, we mean that the test is formatted in such a way that the "average" test-taker (whoever that is) would not be able to complete all the questions in the time allotted. The LSAT is required by every single American Bar Association (ABA)-certified law school in the United States—if you want to go to a U.S. law school, you not only have to take the LSAT, but you have to do pretty well on it, too.

WHEN IS THE LSAT GIVEN?

The LSAT is administered four times a year—February, June, September/October, and December. Typically, students applying for regular fall admission to a law program take the test either the previous June or October. You can take the test in December, but many schools will have filled at least a portion of their seats by the time your scores hit the admissions office. See chapter 7 on Law School Admissions for more information about when and how to apply to law school.

HOW IMPORTANT IS THE LSAT?

Not only is the LSAT required by every single ABA-approved U.S. law school, but it is also weighted very heavily in the admissions process. In many schools, it is weighted just as heavily as (or even more heavily than) your undergraduate grade point average (UGPA). That's the number that you worked very hard on for four years in college, remember? The fact that a four-hour, multiple-choice test that has nothing to do with how well you'll do in law school is viewed as equally important as your undergraduate performance makes us angry. It should make you angry, too.

HOW IS THE LSAT SCORED?

The LSAT is scored on a scale of 120 to 180, with the median score being a 150. You need to get about fifty-six questions right to get that median score of 150, which means you need to bat about 55 percent. The curve steepens sharply above a 150, so that to get a 160, you need seventy-three questions, or 72 percent correct. Very few people get a perfect score, mainly because they're not given enough time to answer all the questions.

Along with your LSAT score, you will receive a percentile ranking. This ranking compares your performance with that of everyone else who has taken the LSAT for the previous five years. Since a 150 is the average LSAT score, it would give you a percentile ranking of 50. A score of 155 moves you up to a ranking of 70. A 160 pulls you up to a ranking of 85. And any score over 166 puts you above 95 percent of the LSAT-takers.

As you can see, small numerical jumps (five points or so) can lead to a difference of as much as 20 percentile points. That means you're jumping over 20 percent of all test-takers if, on your first test, you score a 150, but on the real test, you score a 155. Small numbers, big results.

The following table summarizes how many questions you can skip or miss and still reach your LSAT goal. Notice that 93 percent of those taking the test make *more* than nineteen errors. Remember this when you think you should try to answer each and every question.

Approximate Number of Errors (out of 101)	LSAT Score	Percentile Rank
2	180	99++
6	175	99+
11	170	97+
19	165	93+
28	160	84+
36	155	69+
45	150	50+
54	145	31+
62	140	15+
69	135	6+

WHAT IS A GOOD SCORE?

A good score on the LSAT is the one that gets you in to the law school you want to go to. These numbers will be highly useful to you in deciding where you should apply to school.

Many people feel that you have to score at least a 160 to get into a "good" law school. That's pure myth. Remember, any ABA-approved law school has to meet very strict standards in terms of its teaching staff, library, and facilities. Most schools use the Socratic method to teach students basic law. Therefore, a student's fundamental law school experiences can be very similar no matter where he or she went to school—be it NYU or Quinnepeac Law School. Read through chapter 7 for a much more comprehensive discussion of "good" scores and where to go to law school.

WHO'S RESPONSIBLE FOR THIS, ANYWAY?

The LSAT is brought to you by the wonderful folks at the LSAC, based in Newtown, PA. They work with the law schools and the ABA on many facets of the admissions process. When you register for the LSDAS, that too is run by the LSAC. See chapter 7 for a full discussion of this alphabet soup.

WHAT EXACTLY IS ON THE LSAT?

The LSAT is composed of five thirty-five-minute multiple-choice sections and one thirty-minute essay. Two of the five multiple-choice sections will be Arguments, one will be Games, and one will be Reading Comprehension. The fifth (but usually one of the first three to be administered) section will be an experimental section, in which you do thirty-five minutes of unpaid work for LSAC (you can send them a bill after you've passed the Bar). This experimental section can be Arguments, Games, or Reading Comprehension.

A Sample LSAT

As you can see, the LSAT is four hours of pure, unbridled joy—and that's why we tell you to prepare very well for this test—so you only have to take it once.

For instance, your LSAT could look like this:

Section 1:   Games (35 minutes)

Section 2:   Experimental Reading Comprehension (35 minutes)

Section 3:   Arguments (35 minutes)

10-minute Break

Section 4:   Reading Comprehension (35 minutes)

Section 5:   Arguments (35 minutes)

30-minute Essay

As you can see, it's four hours of pure, unbridled joy. And since they finger-print you and check your ID before the test begins, you can add another hour's worth of administrative mumbo-jumbo to that number. That's why we say that you should prepare very well for this test—so you only have to take it once. Then you can go and burn all your LSAT prep materials in the nearest incinerator.

The structure of an Arguments section

There will be two "real" Arguments sections, each lasting thirty-five minutes, on your LSAT. Each section has between twenty-four and twenty-six questions. Sometimes, there will be two questions attached to one argument, or passage, so a section may contain twenty passages but still have twenty-five questions. Typically, the argument passages are no more than three or four sentences in length, but they can still be very dense and every word is potentially important. The arguments themselves are not in order of difficulty.

The structure of a Games section

You will be given four "logic games" in a thirty-five-minute section. Each game will have a setup and a set of conditions or clues that are attached to it. Then five to seven questions will ask you about various possible arrangements of the elements in the game. The four games are not in order of difficulty.

The structure of a Reading Comprehension section

You will be given four Reading Comprehension passages, of about sixty to eighty lines each, in a thirty-five-minute section. Between five and eight questions will be attached to each passage. This is probably something you're familiar with from the SAT, the ACT, the CATs, and other myriad standardized tests you might have taken over the years. Just like Games and Arguments, these passages are not in any order of difficulty.

WHAT DOES ALL THIS TEST?

We're pretty smart at The Princeton Review, but not even *we* know everything. The Arguments and Reading Comprehension sections seem to be testing how well you can *read closely*, i.e., how well you can discern exactly what the author of a particular passage is—and isn't—saying. Games, on the other hand, test absolutely nothing we can see except how well you can do on games. Feel free to go hunt down and read the standard LSAC party line about all the wonderful things it's supposed to test, but it's mainly just blather.

The underlying point is that there are much more creative ways of testing your analytical and verbal skills than plugging your responses into a computer and torturing you in the process. The schools all have access to your complete undergraduate transcript, your academic and professional recommendations, and your essays. They could also ask for some of your undergraduate papers if they wanted to. However, all this reading would take too much time and cost admissions offices too much money—hence they've got a neat little anti-intellectual shortcut in the form of the LSAT.

The overriding point is that it doesn't matter what it's testing—your goal is to do as well as possible on the LSAT. And that's just what we're going to show you how to do.

THE LSAT: GENERAL STRATEGIES

Following are several key things you should do when taking any multiple-choice test, especially the LSAT. Make sure you follow all of these mantras—they are the sum of fifteen years' worth of our experiences with the rather surreal world of the standardized test.

TECHNIQUE #1: SLOW DOWN

Technique #1: Slow Down |

Most LSAT-takers see, for instance, that there are twenty-seven Reading Comprehension questions attached to four fairly long passages. They figure that the best way to attack the section is to make sure that they "get a look at" every one of the questions. Too bad for them. If you do that, you probably won't be spending the amount of time necessary to answer the question correctly (which, after all, *is* the goal). The questions and answer choices on the LSAT require that you *read closely*—you won't be able to "skim" the choices and come up with correct answers. What you need to do is to slow down, and do fewer questions with greater accuracy.

But, you ask, won't that mean that I'll still wind up with the same score? No. It might just be a matter of a few percentage points, but it is common for someone to get only half of the questions correct if he's trying to go too fast. If you slow down and only try to answer 75 percent of the questions, you'll get more questions right. Even if you get only one or two more questions right in a section, and guess randomly on the last half-dozen questions, this means that you're pulling three more questions right per section. Multiply by four sections and you've got twelve more correct answers, which translates into about five or six more points on the LSAT. That's awesome.

Your mantra here is: *I will slow down and answer fewer questions, concentrating on the questions I do choose to answer, thereby being more accurate and getting a higher score.*

TECHNIQUE #2: FILL IN EVERY BUBBLE

Technique #2: Fill in Every Bubble |

Unlike the SAT, for instance, there is no penalty for guessing on the LSAT, meaning that no points are subtracted for wrong answers. Therefore, even if you don't read every question in a section, you want to make sure to fill in the rest of the bubbles before time is called. Even if you get to only 75 percent of the test, you'll be getting an average of five more questions correct by "bubbling in" randomly on twenty-five questions. Make sure you watch your time carefully and fill in answers to any questions that you're not going to get to. Just to be safe, assume the proctor will cut you off two minutes early, so have everything bubbled in by that time.

This is such a key concept that you should remember to do this when you're taking the practice tests in the back of this book and when you're taking previously administered LSATs for practice. Some people want to wait until they get to test day to bubble in questions they don't get to, thinking that they want to see what their "real score" will be on practice tests. However, if you bubble in questions you didn't get to on your practice tests, *that is finding out what your "real" score would be.* And it will ensure that you don't forget to do it on test day—bubbling in randomly could be the difference between a 159 and a 161, for instance.

Your mantra here is: *I will always remember to bubble in all the answers I don't get to, thereby getting a higher score.*

TECHNIQUE #3: USE PROCESS OF ELIMINATION

Technique #3: Use Process of Elimination

One solace (perhaps) on multiple-choice tests is the fact that all the correct answers (*credited responses* in test-speak) will be in front of you. Naturally, they will each be camouflaged by four incorrect answers, some of which will look just as good as, or better than, the credited response. But the fact remains that if you can clear away some of that jungle foliage, you'll be left staring at the credited response. Your goal is to clear away the underbrush and not expect that the correct answers will just leap off the page at you. They won't.

We know you're saying "so what?" to this. The point is that using Process of Elimination is a very different test-taking mindset from what you might be used to. If you look at the answer choices critically, with an eye toward trying to see what's wrong with them, you'll do better on almost any standardized test than if you're always trying to find the right answer. This is because, given enough time and creativity, you can sit there and justify the correctness of any answer choice. You're going to be asked, when you're a lawyer, to connect certain things that may have absolutely no relevance—but on the LSAT, creativity of that sort is worse than dangerous.

Using Process of Elimination will also get you better odds on every question. Every time you cross out an incorrect choice, your chances of answering the question correctly go up. If you can eliminate even two of the choices, your chances have jumped from 20 percent to 33 percent. You'd much rather have 33 percent odds on, let's say, twenty questions that perplex you than 20 percent odds on that same amount. Eliminating two choices on each will get you seven questions right; eliminating none and getting frustrated will only get you four.

Your mantra here is: *I will always look to eliminate answer choices using Process of Elimination, thereby increasing my chances on each question and getting a higher score.*

TECHNIQUE #4: YOUR WILL IS MADE OF IRON

Technique #4: Your Will Is Made of Iron

Yes it is. You might not think so, but it really is. You'll be nervous on test day; a little nervousness is even okay because it will keep you on your toes. But don't let this test psych you out. Remember that when you go into the test, you'll have worked through many LSAT problems and be a lot more prepared than many other people in the room. You'll have absorbed all the techniques we've given you, and you'll be wise to all the nastiness that the LSAT can throw at you.

Therefore, don't let anything get to you. The room is cold, so what. You've brought an extra sweatshirt. You're a genius. The room is hot, so what. You've worn layered clothing so you strip down to a T-shirt. You're a genius. There's a guy next you sneezing and making small clucking noises, so what. You've practiced LSAT questions with the radio on, the TV on, at construction sites, with your roommate snoring, with green eggs and ham. You're a genius. The proctor cuts you short by a minute every time, so what. We warned you about this, and you've already bubbled in answers to the questions you weren't going to be able to get to. You're *really* a genius on that one. There's a combination rap/marching band outside warming up for some football game, so what. Both of these types of music make you do better on LSAT questions. Really they do. You're a genius.

You get the point, right? Don't get distracted or upset, ever. It's not worth it. Your mantra here is: *My will is made of iron. Nothing will distract me on test day. Nothing.*

TECHNIQUE #5: PRACTICE ALL THE TIME, ON REAL STUFF

Technique #5: Practice All the Time, on Real Stuff

We've given you two full sample tests, plus explanations, to work through in the back of this book. Unfortunately, that's just chump change. You should be ordering *at least* four real tests from LSAC (www.lsac.org or 215-968-1001), if not six or more. Here's a little study plan for you, over a two-month period:

Week 1:   Order at least four to six real LSATs (the most recent ones) from LSAC. Take a real LSAT timed. Have a friend proctor the test for you so it's as legitimate as possible.

Week 2:   Work through the Arguments chapter in this book; redo the Arguments questions from the test you took in week 1.

Week 3:   Work through the Games chapter in this book; redo the Games from the test you took in week 1. Take one of the the two practice LSATs in the back of this book.

Week 4:   Work through the Reading Comprehension chapter in this book; redo the Reading Comprehension passages from the test you took in week 1, and from the practice LSAT you took in week 3.

Week 5:   Work untimed through one of the real LSATs you've ordered from LSAC; time yourself on another one.

Week 6:   Review your mistakes in the work you did in week 5 and review the Arguments, Games, and Reading Comprehension chapters in this book. Work the specific problems again. Take the second test in this book.

Week 7:   Work untimed through another real LSAT you've orderded from LSAC; time yourself on another one (this should be the fifth real LSAT you've looked at).

Week 8:   Review all the general techniques in this book, and review any specific problems you might be having in arguments, games, and reading comprehension. Take one more real LSAT timed (using a friend as a proctor again) and analyze the hell out of it.

If you follow the plan above, you'll be extremely prepared for the LSAT when it comes around. Don't worry too much about your scores on any of these practice tests, though. Your performance on the real LSAT should be a bit higher than any of your practice tests if you've been working steadily—you should be taking the LSAT at the culminiation of your studies, and if you follow the plan above, you will be. Never let more than one, or at most two, days pass without looking at LSAT problems once you've started this workout. You'll waste valuable study time relearning techniques that you would have remembered if you had been practicing steadily. The best athletes and musicians are the ones that practice all the time—follow their example and you'll be totally prepared for the LSAT on test day.

Your mantra here is: *I will work steadily and consistently on real LSATs that I've ordered from LSAC.*

TECHNIQUE #6: KEEP YOUR PENCIL MOVING

At almost every standardized testing site you can look in and see people who have just completely lost their concentration. They are either staring at the same problem for five minutes or have let their gaze drift to the cinderblock wall or the asbestos-covered ceiling or something equally riveting. Needless to say, you don't want to join this group of test zombies.

Technique #6: Keep Your Pencil Moving

If a question is giving you trouble, leave it and come back later, if you have time. At some point, continuing to spend time on one question triggers the Law of Diminishing Returns—while you're sitting there obsessing about one question, you could have answered three others correctly. Let it go, and move on.

But what if you never get the chance to come back? So what. The question was putting you in orbit, anyway. The chance of you getting it right was slim. Always go and find problems that you can sink your teeth into immediately. There are plenty of problems to choose from, so make sure you're always on the move.

So what's this about my pencil, then? The best way to attack any standardized test is always to mark the test up with your pencil. You should be constantly crossing out answer choices, circling the right answer, underlining words in the passages, taking notes, drawing diagrams, etc. Don't let the test take you—take the test, attack the test. Making sure your pencil is always moving will help you to do that.

Your mantra here is: *I will attack the test, and not become a zombie, by keeping my pencil moving.*

GENERAL STRATEGIES: SUMMARY

Take these mantras, and learn them well. They are the distilled wisdom of much test-taking expertise. Here they are again:

- I will slow down and answer fewer questions, concentrating on the questions I do choose to answer, thereby being more accurate and getting a higher score.

- I will always remember to bubble in all the answers I don't get to, thereby getting a higher score.

- I will always look to eliminate answer choices using Process of Elimination, thereby increasing my chances on each question and getting a higher score.

- My will is made of iron. Nothing will distract me on test day. Nothing.

- I will work steadily and consistently on real LSATs that I've ordered from LSAC.

- I will attack the test, and not become a zombie, by keeping my pencil moving.

Got 'em? Good. Now let's break the test down section by section.

2
Arguments

ARGUMENTS: HALF OF THE EXAM

That's right—for better or for worse, Arguments (Logical Reasoning in LSAC-speak) questions make up half of the LSAT. For the past six years, there have either been fifty or fifty-one arguments on the LSAT. The good news is that if you can substantially increase your Arguments performance, you've taken a major step toward achieving the LSAT score that you need. How do you go about improving your Arguments score? Well, let's get right to it.

WHAT DOES THIS SECTION TEST?

Arguments test your ability to read closely.

The Arguments section of the LSAT tests a very useful skill to have: the ability to *read closely*. Whether it tests your ability to read closely in the same way that law school will is something that no one knows the answer to (especially not the LSAT writers!). It also tests your ability to break an argument into parts, to identify flaws and methods of reason, and to find assumptions. Each argument is packed with issues that you have to identify to be able to get the correct answer. It's a minefield.

WHY IS THIS SECTION ON THE LSAT?

As we said above, it is testing a skill, or at least part of a skill, that will be useful in law school. Whether this is the best way to test reading closely is questionable—but here it is.

THE SECTION ITSELF

There are two Arguments sections on the LSAT. Each one will have between twenty-four and twenty-six questions, usually for a total of fifty Arguments questions. Some Arguments passages are followed by two questions, and although the test writers could probably generate several questions for each passage, most Arguments passages are followed by a single question. The fact that you are presented with twenty-five or so arguments to do in a thirty-five-minute period highlights the fact that the Arguments section is just as heavily speeded as the Games or Reading Comprehension sections.

If you took the advice in chapter 1, you've already completed a real LSAT (preferably one of the 1997 or 1998 LSATs), and you're familiar with the directions at the start of each Arguments section. Here they are again:

> Directions: The questions in this section are based on the reasoning contained in brief statements or passages. For some questions, more than one of the choices could conceivably answer the question. However, you are to choose the one best answer; that is, the response that most accurately and completely answers the question. You should not make assumptions that are by common-sense standards implausible, superfluous, or incompatible with the passage. After you have chosen the best answer, blacken the corresponding space on your answer sheet.

Fascinating and, of course, almost totally useless. The directions do say, however, that the questions are based on the reasoning behind each argument. As for the part about picking the best answer, we'll get to that a little later on—first let's see how to simply and efficiently understand the reasoning of an LSAT argument.

ARGUMENTS: STRATEGIES

The next few pages talk about the general strategies you need to use during the Arguments sections of the LSAT. These pages contain a few simple rules that you *must* take to heart. We've taught hundreds of thousands of students how to do arguments, and this is the sum of our wisdom.

Always read the question first

Why should you read the question first? Because often the question will tell you what you should be looking for when you read the argument. Reading the question first will tell you that you should be looking for the conclusion of the argument, or looking to weaken the argument in some way, or looking to diagram the argument, or whatever. The question is a tip-off, so use it.

Your mantra: *I will always read the question first.*

Drive 55

You'd better. Reading arguments too fast is a recipe for disaster. They look deceptively simple, right? Usually the arguments are merely three sentences, and the answer choices are just a sentence each. Yes, but many times complex ideas are being presented in these sentences. The answers often hinge on whether you've read one word correctly—like the word *not*, or *but*, or *some*. You should be reading as if you're deconstructing Shakespeare here and not reading some techno-thriller on the beach. So slow down, and pay attention!

Your mantra: *I will do fewer arguments, and get the ones I do right.*

Keep right, pass left

Sorry to harp on this driving thing, but it seems to be working. What should you do if you read the first sentence of the argument and you don't understand what the hell it's saying? Should you read sentence two? The answer is NO. Sentence two is not there to help you understand sentence one. Neither is sentence three. Neither are the answer choices—the answer choices exist to keep you out of law school, not help you get in. If you start reading an argument and you are confused, take a deep breath and read the first sentence again—slower. If this still doesn't help, *skip it*. You've got other fish to fry. There are twenty-four to twenty-six arguments in the section—go do another one! The supercomputer that scores your exam really doesn't care which seventy questions you get right—and neither does anybody else. Don't waste time pounding your head against the desk if you don't understand what the argument is saying—you'll get frustrated, and what's more, you'll get the question wrong.

Your mantra: *If I don't understand the first sentence of an argument, I will move on to another argument I do understand.*

> The supercomputer that scores your exam really doesn't care which seventy questions you get right—and neither does anybody else.

Transfer your answers in groups

A classic question about standardized tests: Should I transfer my answers to the bubble sheet in groups, or transfer each answer after I've solved it? Our response: This section will have two or three arguments on the left-hand page and another two or three arguments on the right-hand page; work on all those questions, and then transfer your answers before you turn the page. If you've left one blank, circle the argument you left blank on your test page, but bubble in an answer on your answer sheet anyway (remember: no guessing penalty). Why should you do this? Because if you don't have time to come back to it, you've still remembered to put an answer on your sheet (most Princeton Review students favor either (B) or (C)—knock yourself out). And if you do have time to go back and work on arguments you skipped the first time around, you've got them handily circled in your test booklet. Then go and change the answer (if necessary) on the answer sheet for that question.

Your mantra: *I will transfer my answers in groups, even bubbling in answers to questions that I'm skipping.*

With five minutes left, transfer answers one at a time

When there are five minutes left, begin to transfer your answers one at a time. You can even skip ahead for a moment and bubble in (B) or (C) (or whatever) for all the remaining questions. That way, if the proctor erroneously calls time before he or she is supposed to, or if you simply know you aren't going to finish in time (these things *can* happen, you know), you've still got an answer on your sheet for every question.

Your mantra here: *When five minutes are left, I will transfer answers singly and make sure I have bubbled in an answer to every question.*

Breathe

Please remember to do this! Some tension in your body will of course exist—some tension is good because it keeps your adrenaline pumping. But don't get so stressed out that you lose the thread of reality. So, after doing each two-page spread of arguments and transferring your answers, take ten seconds, close your eyes, and inhale deeply three times. This will get you ready for the next two-page spread of arguments.

Your mantra: *I will take a ten-second breathing break after every five or six arguments.*

YOUR MANTRAS AND YOU

Here are your Arguments mantras. Feel free to discard them after the LSAT is over.

I will always read the question first.

I will do fewer arguments, and get the ones I do right.

If I don't understand the first sentence of an argument, I will move on to another argument I do understand.

I will transfer my answers in groups, even bubbling in answers to questions that I'm skipping.

When five minutes are left, I will transfer answers singly and make sure I have bubbled in an answer to every question.

I will take a ten-second breathing break after every five or six arguments.

ARGUMENTS-SPECIFIC STRATEGIES

The first step in doing arguments is to make sure you're thinking critically when you read. Maybe you've had a lot of practice reading critically (philosophy and literature majors, please stand up) or maybe you haven't. And if you were a philosophy major in college but your favorite pastime has been watching *The Simpsons* for the past five years, you're probably out of practice. The next few pages show you on what level you need to be reading Arguments to be able to answer questions correctly.

Your goal: issue, point, reasons

Your goal is to understand what each argument is saying (its conclusion) and how the arguer reached that conclusion (the underlying assumptions). If you can understand the reasoning of the person who wrote the Argument, you've won half the battle, since most of the questions in Arguments revolve around the hows and whys of the reasoning of the arguer.

TIP: If you can understand the reasoning of the person who wrote the Argument, you've won half the battle, since most of the questions in Arguments revolve around the hows and whys of the reasoning of the arguer.

Sample Argument #1

Let's start with something fairly simple. Even though this argument is simple, its structure is almost exactly the same as that of any of the "real" LSAT arguments that you will see. Here it is:

> I have to move to Kentucky. I lost my lease on my
> New York apartment and my company is moving to
> Kentucky.

Okay, now what? We've got to make sure we understand the following things about this argument:

- The issue being discussed.

- The point that the author is trying to make.

- The reason or reasons the author gives in attempting to prove his argument.

If we are able to identify the issue, point, and reasons, we are well on our way to understanding what the argument is all about. After reading the argument again, try to identify these three factors.

> I have to move to Kentucky. I lost my lease on my
> New York apartment and my company is moving to
> Kentucky.

- Issue discussed

- Author's point

- Author's reasons

What's the Issue?

The issue here is **moving to Kentucky.** True, the author mentions his New York apartment, his lease, and his company, but what he's talking about is whether or not he is going to move to Kentucky. Plus, "Kentucky" was mentioned twice in the argument—a sure sign that it's important.

What's the Author's Point?

The author's point is that **he has to move to Kentucky**. This is the "big issue." Imagine that this person is your best friend, and he calls you on the phone to tell you this information. Sure, you're interested in the fact that your friend lost his lease, and that his company is moving to Kentucky. But the *big* thing is that your friend is moving! The other facts are just given in support of his conclusion that he has to move to Kentucky.

What Are the Author's Reasons?

The author's reasons for moving to Kentucky are (a) that he lost the lease on his New York apartment and (b) that his company is moving to Kentucky. Each one of these things is a fact, or a premise, given in support of the author's point.

What if I Identified the Wrong Point?

If you had said that the author's point was the fact that his company was moving to Kentucky, or that he had lost his lease, there is a very simple check you can apply to make sure you've got the right point or conclusion. This check is called the Why Test.

The Why Test

The Why Test:

A great way to make sure you've got the right conclusion

The Why Test should be applied every time you state the author's point or conclusion. Let's take the example above and see how it works. If you had said that the author's point was that he had lost his lease, the next step is to ask: *Why did the author lose his lease?* Well, we have no idea why the author lost his lease. We can make a bunch of guesses, but we have no information from the argument that supplies us with this information. Maybe he was putting cockroaches in the walls, like Michael Keaton in *Pacific Heights*. Maybe he played Led Zeppelin at 3 a.m. However, we *don't know* why. Therefore, if there is no answer in the argument itself to the question "Why did the author lose his lease?" it can't be the main point of the argument. Every LSAT argument has at least one reason given in support of the author's point or conclusion. If you can't find one, you don't have the right point!

Now, let's say that you had chosen the fact that the author's company was moving to Kentucky as the author's point. Once again, you would then ask: *Why is the author's company moving to Kentucky?* Once again, we have no idea. Maybe because the state of Kentucky is giving tax breaks to companies; maybe because the president of the company is from Kentucky. But since this type of information is not furnished in the passage, we can't answer the question. The answer to the Why Test will always be in the passage—if you've chosen the correct point or conclusion.

Thus, the only point that works with the Why Test is that the author has to move to Kentucky. *Why does the author have to move to Kentucky?* Because his company is moving to Kentucky, and because he lost his lease on his New York apartment. In this case, the Why Test works perfectly. You have the right point.

Sample Argument #2

Now that we've beaten the Kentucky thing into the ground, let's get a lot more serious. Here's another sample argument:

> The mayor of the town of Shasta sent a letter to the townspeople instructing them to burn less wood. A few weeks after the letter was delivered, there was a noticeable decrease in the amount of wood the townspeople of Shasta were burning on a daily basis. Therefore, it is obvious that the letter was successful in helping the mayor achieve his goal.

Okay, now let's identify the issue, point, and reasons in this argument:

- Issue discussed
- Author's point
- Author's reasons

What's the Issue?

The issue here is the **amount of wood the townspeople of Shasta are burning.** We've got the mayor sending a letter about this issue, and then we are told that the residents of Shasta burned less wood.

What's the Author's Point?

The author's point is that **the mayor's letter was the reason the townspeople burned less wood.** This seems pretty much like a straight cause-and-effect case, doesn't it? We had the townspeople of Shasta burning too much wood, we had the mayor sending a letter, and now we have the townspeople burning less wood! All's well that ends well, right?

What Are the Author's Reasons?

Let's use the Why Test here, shall we? If we've chosen the right point or conclusion, we should be able to figure out the author's reasons in no time. *Why did the author conclude that the letter was successful in convincing the townspeople to burn less wood?* The author's reason is the fact that the mayor sent a letter, and then the townspeople began to burn less wood.

The big secret

What is the big secret here? This seems to be pretty straightforward, doesn't it? We've got straight cause and effect, don't we? But we also have something else in this argument: underlying assumptions. For many arguments on the LSAT, *this* is the key concept you will need to flush out. Sure, we've correctly identified the issue, point, and reasons, but we now have to take a further step—understanding what assumptions the author made in getting to his conclusion. Why? Because many of the questions asked by the LSAT will have something to do with the author's underlying assumptions.

What Is an Assumption?

An assumption, both in life and on the LSAT, is typically a dangerous leap of logic we make to get from one point to another. If you see a friend of yours wearing a yellow shirt, for instance, you can make the assumption that your friend likes yellow. You would also, however, be making the following *extra* assumptions:

- Your friend is not color-blind and does not actually think he's wearing purple.

- Your friend was not threatened by a madman who said that unless he wore a yellow shirt for one month straight, his house would be burned to the ground.

- Your friend was not just attacked by a mustard-squirting mime.

- Your friend...

You get the point. Any time we make an assumption, it's because we've seen a particular effect (in this case, your friend wearing a yellow shirt), and we think we've identified the proper cause (in this case, that your friend likes yellow, and not that he encountered a mime or a madman). Then, for better or for worse, we *connect* the cause and the effect. We've made a leap of logic.

Assumptions on the LSAT

Assumptions on the LSAT are also a leap of logic. Sometimes, it's logic so simple that it looks as if the author has actually stated it—but he really hasn't. The author's assumption is never explicitly stated in the passage. It is always unstated. Let's go back to the wood-burning argument. Here, we have an observed effect—the townspeople of Shasta burning less wood. We have a possible cause—the mayor's letter. In LSAT-land, the arguer will always take this to the bank and attempt to cash it— in this case, that the letter caused the wood-burning decrease. However, as we've seen from the above example, we're also assuming the following:

- That the decrease in the burning of wood was not due to an increase in the price of wood.

- That it did not get warmer, and therefore the people needed to burn less wood to stay warm.

- That the townspeople are able to read.

- That...

Once again, you get the point. The author actually made many assumptions when he made the leap of logic from the letter being sent, to the townspeople burning less wood, to the letter being the reason why the townspeople were burning less wood.

THIS IS ALL REALLY EXCITING, BUT...

Four of the answer choices are going to be wrong, and their purpose is to distract you from the "best" answer choice.

You want to get to the answer choices, don't you? Well, we will—soon. But what has been the point of the last several pages? To show you how to read the argument itself in a critical way. This will help you immensely with the answer choices, because you've already identified the parts of the argument, the conclusion of the argument, and the author's underlying assumptions. This means that many times you'll have the answer to the question written out before you read any answer choices, and you can simply match your answer with the correct choice.

The reason we want you to think so much before going to the answer choices is that the answer choices are not there to help you get a good score on the LSAT. Four of the answer choices are going to be wrong, and their purpose is to distract you from the "best" answer choice. True, many times this choice will merely be the least evil or nonsensical of five evil or nonsensical answer choices. Nonetheless, the more work you put into analyzing the argument before reading the choices, the better your chance of choosing the "credited response."

So why hammer this at you? Because you might or might not have had a lot of practice reading critically. You're not simply reading for pleasure, or reading the newspaper or a menu at a restaurant here—you've got to focus your attention on these short paragraphs. Read LSAT arguments critically, like you're reading a contract you're about to sign (perhaps with the Devil, if you want to be melodramatic). Don't just casually glance over them so you can quickly "get to the answer choices." The answer choices will chew you up and spit you out like that sand-thing in *Return of the Jedi*—we promise you.

WORKING ARGUMENTS: A STEP-BY-STEP PROCESS

The Princeton Review has come up with a four-step process for working arguments. It is a very simple process that will lead you to LSAT nirvana if you follow it for every argument that you do. Here are the steps:

Step 1: Read the question
This is actually one of your mantras. Reading the question first will many times tip you off about what you need to look for in the argument.

Step 2: Work the argument
This is what we've been practicing for the last few pages (it's all about to come together, isn't it?). You're going to read the argument *critically*, looking for the issue that is being discussed and looking also for the author's conclusion.

Step 3: Stop, think, and write
That's right, *write*. Don't think that you can do all of this in your head—identifying the issue, stating the author's point, noting the author's reasons, and coming up with any underlying assumptions. You should write out the issue, and the author's point, and quickly write out any assumptions you've identified. This sounds like it would take a long time, but it really doesn't. Here's the shorthand for the wood-burning argument:

> Issue—burning less wood
>
> Point—letter caused this
>
> Assumptions—nothing else caused it

As you can see, it's a total of about ten words; sometimes it will be less. But now you're ready to go and attack the answer choices.

Step 4: Use Process of Elimination
We first mentioned Process of Elimination (POE) in chapter 1. It's a key component to every section of the LSAT, especially Arguments and Reading Comprehension. Why? Here are the directions for Arguments again:

> <u>Directions:</u> The questions in this section are based on the reasoning contained in brief statements or passages. For some questions, more than one of the choices could conceivably answer the question. However, you are to choose the one <u>best</u> answer, that is, the response that most accurately and completely answers the question. You should not make assumptions that are by common-sense standards implausible, superfluous, or incompatible with the passage. After you have chosen the best answer, blacken the corresponding space on your answer sheet.

Remember, standardized tests are about playing the odds.

As you can see, the point here is that there is no one right answer (as there is in logic games, for instance). Your goal is to pick the "best" answer, which sometimes means that you're picking the least cruddy answer out of five really cruddy answer choices. So it's important to always use POE when you get to the answer choices. What does this mean? It means that your goal should be to *eliminate the four worst answer choices*. Your goal should *not* be to "find the right answer." If you can find a reason to cross off a choice, you've just improved your chances of getting the question right. Remember, standardized tests are about playing the odds.

THE NINE TYPES OF ARGUMENTS QUESTIONS

Almost every question in the Arguments section of the exam will fit into one of the following nine categories: Conclusion, Assumption, Weaken, Strengthen, Paradox, Inference, Reasoning, Principle, and Parallel. Each of these questions has its own set of techniques, which we'll cover on the following pages. At the end of each question type you'll find a chart summarizing the most important techniques. The chart will be repeated in full at the end of the chapter for all nine categories.

SO ARE YOU READY?

Yup. We're finally going to give you an entire LSAT argument. First we'll give you the whole argument, and then we'll break it down into steps. Then, you can compare your answers against ours. Finally, after each argument "lesson," we'll explain some extra techniques that you'll need to absorb. That way, by the end of Lesson 9, you'll know everything we know!

This first lesson is about Conclusion questions. See if the work you do for each step looks like what we have written! Good luck!

LESSON 1: CONCLUSION QUESTIONS

THE ARGUMENT

1. A growing number of ecologists has begun to recommend lifting the ban on the hunting of leopards and on the international trade of leopard skins. Why, then, do I continue to support the protection of leopards? For the same reason that I oppose the hunting of people. Admittedly, there are far too many human beings on this planet to qualify us for inclusion on the list of endangered species. Still, I doubt the same ecologists endorsing the resumption of leopard hunting would use that fact to recommend the hunting of human beings.

    Which of the following is the main point of the argument above?

(A) The ban on leopard hunting should not be lifted.
(B) Human beings are a species like any other animal, and we should be placed on the endangered species list in view of the threat of nuclear annihilation.
(C) Hunting of animals, whether or not an endangered species, should not be permitted.
(D) Ecologists do not consider human beings a species, much less an endangered species.
(E) Ecologists cannot be trusted where emotional issues like hunting are involved.

Always read the question first. Always.

Cracking Conclusion questions

Step 1: Read the Question

Good, you've read the question. Here it is again:

1. Which of the following is the main point of the argument above?

This question is asking for the main point, or *conclusion*, of the argument. Now you're going to work the argument, and your goal is to find your own conclusion.

Step 2: Work the Argument

You read the argument. You read it slowly enough that you know the issue in the argument, and you can identify the author's point and his reasons. Here it is again:

A growing number of ecologists has begun to recommend lifting the ban on the hunting of leopards and on the international trade of leopard skins. Why, then, do I continue to support the protection of leopards? For the same reason that I oppose the hunting of people. Admittedly, there are far too many human beings on this planet to qualify us for inclusion on the list of endangered species. Still, I doubt the same ecologists endorsing the resumption of leopard hunting would use that fact to recommend the hunting of human beings.

Great. It's an argument about leopards. Also, something about whether or not we should hunt them. Keep in mind that we only need to find the main point in a conclusion argument. Finding the assumption won't make these arguments any easier, so don't bother. Let's go to step 3.

Step 3: Stop, Think, and Write

Here's what we got as our issue, point, and reasons:

- Issue discussed: *Whether we should hunt leopards.*

- Author's point: *We should not hunt leopards.*

- Author's reasons: *One, because it would be like hunting human beings, and two, just because a species is not endangered is not a good reason to hunt it.*

Remember, you can use the Why Test to check the author's point if you're not sure.

Step 4: Use Process of Elimination

Okay, now let's look at each of the answer choices. Our goal is to eliminate four of the choices by matching our answer to one of the answer choices. If it doesn't look similar, off with its head!

> (A) The ban on leopard hunting should not be lifted.

Does this sound like what we wrote for the author's point? Yes. Let's leave it.

> (B) Human beings are a species like any other animal, and we should be placed on the endangered species list in view of the threat of nuclear annihilation.

Is this the author's point? No, he never mentions anything about putting human beings on the endangered species list. In fact, he says that human beings are NOT an endangered species. Also, what's this stuff about nuclear annihilation? Was that ever mentioned in the argument? Let's cross it off.

> (C) Hunting of animals, whether or not an endangered species, should not be permitted.

This looks pretty good, except that it's too *general*. The argument is talking about leopards only. This might be a politically correct thought, but it's outside the scope of the argument. Let's cross it off.

> (D) Ecologists do not consider human beings a species, much less an endangered species.

Gee, that's too bad. All along we thought we were a species! However, this doesn't say anything about leopards, which is what this argument is about. Once again, it's outside the scope of the argument. Let's cross it off.

> (E) Ecologists cannot be trusted where emotional issues like hunting are involved.

Absolutely, positively, never trust an ecologist. But seriously, it's got the same problem as (D). It doesn't talk about leopards at all, so once again it is outside the scope. It's also a bit extreme, don't you think? Let's cross it off.

Well, it looks like you've got the right answer (A) here. Nice job!

ARGUMENTS TECHNIQUES: PROCESS OF ELIMINATION

3 ways to eliminate choices:
Scope, Extreme Wording, Opposites

Let's go into a bit more depth with Process of Elimination. Answer choices (B), (C), (D), and (E) above all presented us with specific reasons for crossing them off. Below are ways in which we can analyze answer choices to see if we can eliminate them.

Scope

LSAT arguments have very specific limits. The author of an argument stays within these limits in reaching the conclusion. Anything else is irrelevant. When you read an argument, you must pretend that you only know what is written on that page. Never assume anything else. So, any answer choice that is outside the scope of the argument can be eliminated. We did this for answer choices (B), (C), (D), and (E) above. Most of the time, answer choices will be too *general* in scope.

Arguments are usually about specific things—like leopards, as opposed to just "animals." Also, when a phrase such as "nuclear annihilation" appears in an answer choice, and it was not mentioned in the argument, it's a pretty safe bet that that answer choice is far, far away. Like in another galaxy.

Extreme wording

Pay attention to the wording of the answer choices. For *some* question types (most notably Conclusion, Assumption, and Inference), extreme, absolute language (*never, must, exactly, cannot, always, only*) tends to be wrong, and choices with extreme wording can usually be eliminated. Keep in mind, however, that an argument with extreme language can support an extreme answer choice. Extreme language is another reason that we eliminated answer choice (E). You should always note extreme wording *anywhere*—in the passage, the question, or the answer choices, as it will frequently play an important role in some way.

Opposites

Make sure that you are not choosing the exact *opposite* of the viewpoint asked for. Many times, this type of answer choice will look good because it's talking about the same exact subject matter as the correct answer. However, it will say the opposite thing about it. For some question types, such as Weaken, Strengthen, Conclusion, and Parallel-the-Reasoning, one of the answer choices will almost always be an "opposite." This is one of the reasons we eliminated answer choice (B) above.

CRACKING CONCLUSION QUESTIONS: SUMMARY

Check out the chart below for some quick tips on Conclusion questions. The left column of the chart shows some of the ways in which the LSAT folks will ask for a conclusion. The right column is a brief summary of the techniques you should use when attacking Conclusion questions.

Sample Question Phrasings	Attack! Attack! Attack!
What is the author's main point?	Identify the issue, point, and reasons.
What is the conclusion of the argument above?	Use the Why Test, and then match your point against the five answer choices.
The argument is structured to lead which one of the following conclusions?	The closest one wins.
	When down to two choices, use extreme wording and scope to eliminate one choice.

LESSON 2: ASSUMPTION QUESTIONS

THE ARGUMENT

2. Some people fear that our first extraterrestrial visitors will not be the friendly aliens envisaged in popular science fiction movies, but rather hostile invaders bent on global dictatorship. This fear is groundless. Any alien civilization that makes it to our planet must have acquired the wisdom to control war, or it would have destroyed itself long before contacting us.

The author bases the argument above on which of the following assumptions?

(A) Our planet will have contact with extraterrestrial visitors at some time in the future.
(B) Any developed civilization capable of interstellar travel has the technology to dominate our planet.
(C) Any civilization that has learned to control war on its own planet will not wage war on another.
(D) Alien civilizations are more morally advanced than those on Earth.
(E) Most people are afraid that if extraterrestrials do visit the earth, it will be for the purpose of invasion.

Cracking Assumption questions

Step 1: Read the Question
Good, so you've read the question. Here it is again:

2. The author bases the argument above on which of the following assumptions?

As you can see, it's an Assumption question. With this argument, therefore, we are not only going to have to identify the issue, point, and reasons, but also attempt to identify the underlying assumptions that the author makes to get to her point.

Step 2: Work the Argument

Always read the argument critically, looking for the author's point and reasons.

You read the argument. You read it slowly enough that you know the issue in the argument, and you can identify the author's point and her reasons. Here it is again:

Some people fear that our first extraterrestrial visitors will not be the friendly aliens envisaged in popular science fiction movies, but rather hostile invaders bent on global dictatorship. This fear is groundless. Any alien civilization that makes it to our planet must have acquired the wisdom to control war, or it would have destroyed itself long before contacting us.

Great. Aliens and war. Cool stuff. However, doesn't there seem to be a little break in the logic toward the end of the argument? Hmmm.

Step 3: Stop, Think, and Write

Here's what we got as our issue, point, reasons, and assumption:

- Issue discussed: *Whether aliens will be nice.*

- Author's point: *The aliens will be nice.*

- Author's reasons: *If you can travel through space that well, you're not a warmonger.*

- Author's assumption: *Something about space travel and war, right? Let's see—how about that you can only be that great at science if you are wise enough to realize that war is bad?*

The key thing here is to understand the leap of logic. Here's this nice argument about the nice aliens, and then WHAM! In the last sentence, the author talks about wisdom. That's a *gap* in the argument that we have to notice. And to fill that gap, we're going to bridge it with some thought about science or space travel and wisdom.

Step 4: Use Process of Elimination

Let's go to the answer choices. We know that the credited response is going to have to say something about wisdom *and* something about science or space travel.

> (A) Our planet will have contact with extraterrestrial visitors at some time in the future.

Does this sound like what we wrote for our assumption? Does it mention anything about wisdom or science? Also, be careful of the word *will* here—an answer choice containing extreme language in Assumption questions is very often wrong, though occasionally it can be the correct answer. But let's cross this one off.

> (B) Any developed civilization capable of interstellar travel has the technology to dominate our planet.

Is this the underlying assumption? Well, it does mention technology and travel, so we're on the right track with that (technology can mean applied science). Let's leave it for now.

> (C) Any civilization that has learned to control war on its own planet will not wage war on another.

This doesn't look like our assumption either, but it does talk about controlling war (i.e., having wisdom). Let's leave this one, too.

> (D) Alien civilizations are more morally advanced than those on Earth.

Which alien civilizations? All of them? Remember, we're only talking about alien civilizations that have the capability of interstellar travel. This seems to be out of the scope of the argument. Also, it's a bit extreme. Let's cross it off.

(E) Most people are afraid that if extraterrestrials
do visit the earth, it will be for the purpose of
invasion.

That's too bad. But the author isn't concerned with what most people think—he's arguing against them, in fact. So, whatever "most people" think would never be an underlying assumption of this author's argument. In fact, this is almost opposite to what the author said. Additionally, if you added this statement to the argument, it would destroy the argument, not help it. Let's cross it off.

We're down to two choices—now what?

Well, welcome to the real deal. This is what is going to happen more often than not. You're going to get down to two answer choices on many arguments, especially on many Assumption arguments. And neither of the answer choices is going to look all that much like the assumption that you came up with in your working of the argument. However, you still know what the argument is about. Now it's time to apply some more techniques.

ARGUMENTS TECHNIQUES: NEGATING ASSUMPTION CHOICES

One of the most important things to remember about any assumption is the fact that, when making an argument, your assumptions are *necessary* for your conclusion to be true. Remember your friend with the yellow shirt? It was necessary for all of those assumptions to be true, like the one about your friend not being color-blind. But what if you made that statement false? What if it were true that your friend is color-blind? What would happen to your argument that your friend is wearing that shirt because he likes yellow? *It would fall apart.*

So here's the technique: To see if any answer choice on Assumption questions is really necessary (and therefore the correct answer), make that statement false. Simply negate the language of the choice, and see if the argument falls apart in the process. Let's make (B) from above false:

(B) Any developed civilization capable of
interstellar travel <DOES NOT HAVE> the
technology to dominate our planet.

Does this information now destroy the author's argument? Not really. All it's saying is that interstellar travel technology and world-domination technology are two different things. It really doesn't have much impact one way or the other. Now, let's cross it out, and check by negating our only other choice, (C):

(C) Any civilization that has learned to control
war on its own planet <WILL> wage war on
another.

Oops. Look what happens. If we negate this choice, it totally destroys the author's argument (in no uncertain terms) that if the aliens have acquired the wisdom to control war, they won't attack us. Thus, it's our answer.

As you can see, you've got a lot of techniques to use when dealing with Assumption questions. You can sometimes use *scope* to knock out answers—as in answer choice (D)—since the correct answer will many times link two ideas from the argument. You can watch out for *extreme wording*—as in answer choices

(B) and (D)—though sometimes it may in fact be present in the correct answer choice. You should also cross out anything that says the *opposite* of what the author thinks—as in answer choice (E). And now, you can *negate* an answer choice to see if, when negated, it destroys the argument. Remember, the negation test *only* works for Assumption questions.

ARGUMENTS TECHNIQUES: TYPES OF ASSUMPTIONS

There are many types of assumptions that one can make. However, there are a few classic ones that always show up on the LSAT. You've already learned one, in fact—the wood-burning argument was an example of a *causal* (i.e., cause-and-effect) assumption. Let's review that one first.

Causal assumptions

"Causal" is shorthand for cause and effect. It means making an assumption where you see an observed effect (people burning less wood, for instance) and a possible cause for that effect (the mayor's letter), and then linking the two by saying that the possible cause was *the* cause. When you do that, you're also saying that there was no other cause. Here's another causal argument:

> Every time I walk my dog, it rains. Therefore, walking my dog must be the cause of the rain.

Goofy, right? However, this is classic causality. We see the observed effect (it's raining), we see a possible cause (walking the dog), and then the author connects the two by saying that walking his dog caused the rain. Got it?

So why are causal assumptions so popular on the LSAT? Because you can ask many different types of questions after writing a causal argument. You can ask the test-taker to identify the assumptions, which are:

1. *A* caused *B*.

2. Nothing else besides *A* caused *B* (there are no alternate causes).

You can also ask a *weaken* question, because it's easy to write an answer—the answer will merely state a possible alternate cause. And finally, you can ask a *strengthen* question, because once again it's easy to write an answer—this time, the answer will eliminate a possible weakening cause.

To weaken the dog/raining argument, all we have to do is write an answer choice that says something like "The location of the moon, which has been known to affect weather patterns, was in a position generally associated with rain and snow." Aha! So it's not some dumb guy walking his dog, it's the position of the moon.

To strengthen the dog/raining argument, we can write an answer choice that says something like "The location of the moon, which has been known to affect weather patterns, was not in a position generally associated with rain and snow." Therefore, it wasn't the moon, which in this case (for better or for worse) strengthens the dumb guy's argument that the rain was caused by walking his dog. As you can see, there are good reasons for the popularity of causal arguments.

Statistical assumptions

Statistical Assumptions:

A given statistic or sample proves the conclusion.

Another popular type of assumption on the LSAT is the *statistical* or *sampling* assumption. This assumes that a given statistic or sample proves a conclusion, or that an individual is representative of a group. Here's an example:

> Three out of four lawyers surveyed believe they are underpaid. Therefore, probably all lawyers believe they are underpaid.

What is being assumed here? That the survey is representative. Maybe it is, maybe it isn't. Do we even know how many lawyers were actually surveyed? If you had only surveyed four lawyers, could the first sentence be true? Yes, it could, but it would hardly be a representative sample of *all* lawyers. This is statistics that we're dealing with here; never forget that there are three types of lies in the world: lies, damn lies, and statistics.

So what? Well, once again, you can encounter various types of questions and answer choices after you've read an argument that contains a statistical assumption. You can ask an Assumption question (the correct answer will be that the sample is representative), you can ask a Weaken question (the correct answer will be a fact that in some way shows the sample to be unrepresentative), and you can ask a Strengthen question (the correct answer will provide a fact that shows how the sample is representative).

Analogy assumptions

Analogy Assumptions:

One group is the same as another group.

A third type of assumption on the LSAT is the analogy assumption. This assumes that a given group, idea, or action is logically similar to another group, idea, or action. Read the argument below.

> Overcrowding of rats leads to aberrant behavior.
> Therefore, if people are also overcrowded, they will probably exhibit some aberrant behavior.

What is being assumed here? That in some way, people and rats are *analogous*. If they are, the argument stands up. But if there is no connection whatsoever between rats and people, what happens to the argument? It falls apart. And just like with causal and statistical assumptions, the LSAT writers can ask Assumption, Weaken, and Strengthen questions based on analogy assumptions.

CRACKING ASSUMPTION QUESTIONS: SUMMARY

Whew! We've just covered a ton of information with Assumption questions. We learned more Process of Elimination techniques (specifically, how to negate answer choices to find the most powerful assumption), and then we learned three very popular types of assumptions—causal, statistical, and analogy. Below is a chart that summarizes Assumption questions.

Sample Question Phrasings	Attack! Attack! Attack!
What is an underlying assumption in the above argument? *Which of the following is necessary for the author's point to be valid?* *Which one of the following statements is the author assuming?*	Identify the issue, point, reasons, and assumptions of the author. Use the Why Test, and then match your assumption(s) against those in the answer choices. If you're having trouble finding the assumption, look for a gap between two different ideas in the argument. When down to two choices, negate each statement to see if the argument falls apart. If it does, that's your answer.

LESSON 3: WEAKEN QUESTIONS

THE ARGUMENT

3. A growing number of ecologists has begun to recommend lifting the ban on the hunting of leopards and on the international trade of leopard skins. Why, then, do I continue to support the protection of leopards? For the same reason that I oppose the hunting of people. Admittedly, there are far too many human beings on this planet to qualify us for inclusion on the list of endangered species. Still, I doubt the same ecologists endorsing the resumption of leopard hunting would use that fact to recommend the hunting of human beings.

   Which of the following, if true, would most weaken the author's argument?

   (A) Human beings might, in fact, be placed on the list of endangered species.
   (B) It is impossible to ensure complete compliance with any international hunting ban.
   (C) Leopards, now dangerously overpopulated, cannot be supported by their ecosystems.
   (D) Despite the growing number of ecologists supporting a repeal of the ban on leopard hunting, most still support it.
   (E) The international ban on leopard hunting was instituted before leopards became an endangered species.

Find the assumptions for
weaken questions and attack
them.

Cracking Weaken questions

Step 1: Read the Question
Good, you've read the question. Here it is again:

> 3. Which of the following, if true, would most weaken
> the author's argument?

Cool. This type of question really tips us off as to what we should be doing. We will need to attack this argument as we're reading it. Chances are, the argument is not a very good one and we should be able to find a gap in the author's reasoning. The author probably "went too far" by making a conclusion from not enough information. Let's see if we can nail him.

Step 2: Work the Argument
You read the argument. You read it slowly enough that you know the issue in the argument, and you can summarize the author's point and his reasons. Here it is again:

> A growing number of ecologists has begun to
> recommend lifting the ban on the hunting of
> leopards and on the international trade of leopard
> skins. Why, then, do I continue to support the
> protection of leopards? For the same reason that I
> oppose the hunting of people. Admittedly, there are
> far too many human beings on this planet to qualify
> us for inclusion on the list of endangered species.
> Still, I doubt the same ecologists endorsing the
> resumption of leopard hunting would use that fact to
> recommend the hunting of human beings.

Hey! We've read this argument already, right? It's the one about the leopards. The first time around, all we had to do was get the author's conclusion. Now, however, we have to attack his argument. So we need his underlying assumptions now, too.

Step 3: Stop, Think, and Write
Here's what we got as our issue, point, reasons, and assumption:

- Issue discussed: *Whether we should hunt leopards.*

- Author's point: *We should not hunt leopards.*

- Author's reasons: *One, because hunting leopards is like hunting human beings, and two, just because a species is not endangered is not a legitimate reason to hunt it.*

- Author's assumption: *That in some way, leopards and humans are analogous.*

Cool, right? We just learned about analogy assumptions, and now here is one right off the bat! The author of this argument is saying that hunting leopards would be like hunting humans, and that therefore we shouldn't do it.

Step 4: Use Process of Elimination
Let's go to the answer choices. In order to weaken this argument, the credited response is going to have to attack the assumption by saying that leopards and humans are in some way *dissimilar*.

> (A) Human beings might, in fact, be placed on the
>   list of endangered species.

Aside from the goofiness and wishy-washiness of this answer, does this look like it will damage the author's conclusion that we shouldn't hunt leopards? No, because the goal here is to find ways in which we are *not* like leopards. Let's cross it off.

> (B) It is impossible to ensure complete
>   compliance with any international hunting
>   ban.

Bummer. It'd be nice if everyone obeyed hunting laws. However, does this weaken the argument that we shouldn't hunt leopards? No, because it's merely saying that not everyone would obey the law, not that they would be morally right about it. Let's cross it off.

> (C) Leopards, now dangerously overpopulated,
>   cannot be supported by their ecosystems.

Interesting. This seems to be saying that if we *don't* kill some leopards, they might die out because they "cannot be supported by their ecosystems." Would this call into question the fact that leopards and humans are so similar? Maybe. Let's leave it.

> (D) Despite the growing number of ecologists
>   supporting a repeal of the ban on leopard
>   hunting, most still support it.

Yes, the ecologists are not all in agreement here. However, the opinions of people are not what's important—on Weaken questions, we're looking for facts that overturn or somehow weaken the assumptions the author has made. Whether the number of ecologists supporting the ban is a majority or a minority doesn't matter. Let's cross it off.

> (E) The international ban on leopard hunting was
>   instituted before leopards became an
>   endangered species.

That's nice. We were thinking about leopards even before they were endangered. But does this call into question the author's analogy assumption about humans and leopards? No. Let's cross it off.

Nice job. We stayed focused on the fact that only one piece of information, answer choice (C), somehow showed that humans and leopards aren't all that analogous. It said that leopards are overpopulated, which would weaken the author's argument that we should not hunt them. Now let's take a look at some Weaken question techniques.

ARGUMENTS TECHNIQUES: LOOKING FOR IMPACT AND OPINIONS

The answer to a Weaken question will almost never come out and say the opposite of what the conclusion of the argument said—it's going to be a bit more subtle than that. It will in some way call into question the information or the assumption the author used to get to his conclusion. It's like knocking down a building by sawing off a few key beams, as opposed to blowing it up with half a ton of C-4 explosive.

The correct answer on a Weaken question will work like knocking down a building by sawing off a few key beams.

One key thing to look for when looking at Weaken answer choices, then, is direct impact. Remember how Weaken questions are phrased? The question always contains the phrase, "which of the following, if true, would . . ." What this is telling us to do is treat each answer choice *as if it were hypothetically true*. Basically, then, we have five hypothetical facts in the five answer choices, and one of them, when added to the information in the passage, will have the most negative direct impact on the argument. Answer choices (A), (B), and (E) above had no impact on the fact that we should not lift the ban on hunting leopards. They are all very nice pieces of information that, when applied to the information in the argument, had nothing to do with anything.

Finally, remember answer choice (D), the one about the opinions of the ecologists? Unless the argument is about people's opinions of one thing or another, this type of answer choice is almost always wrong. *So what* if the ecologists, or the head of the World Wildlife Fund, or anyone else for that matter, has an opinion about what is being discussed? Even the opinions of supposed "experts" don't weaken arguments—facts that destroy the arguer's chain of assumptions weaken arguments.

WHAT IF I CAN'T FIND THE ASSUMPTION?

Sometimes, all your hard work looking for an assumption on Strengthen and Weaken questions will be in vain. Either you'll have trouble finding one at all, or the one you've found won't seem to have anything to do with any of the answer choices. Don't despair. Although it's always best to find an assumption, even if you can't, you can still get these questions right.

Focus on the conclusion, and on the idea of direct impact. The correct answer to a Strengthen question will always serve to directly support the conclusion. What do we mean by direct? That means that the answer will almost function like an additional premise, like another reason why (remember the Why Test?) we ought to believe that the conclusion is true. You should never have to make any further assumptions to connect the correct answer to the conclusion. If you find yourself saying "maybe" or "might" or "could," you're not making a connection; you're telling a story. In short, the correct answer to a Strengthen question will be another answer to the question Why? Why should I believe that this conclusion is true?

The same is true for Weaken questions, though, of course, it works the other way around. We don't really have a Why Not Test, but if you were to look at the conclusion and ask, "Why not?" the correct answer to a Weaken question will always provide an answer. It gives you a reason—once again, a direct reason—to believe that the conclusion is *not* true.

CRACKING WEAKEN QUESTIONS: SUMMARY

Well, we're one-third of the way home on Arguments. Remember these two key ideas when doing Weaken questions—the correct answer will most probably destroy one of the author's assumptions, and you should treat each answer choice as hypothetically true, looking for its direct negative impact on the argument. On more difficult Weaken questions there will often be an appealing answer that, with just a little interpretation, looks right. The key is to avoid making any new assumptions when you try to determine the impact of an answer: Look for the *most direct*.

Sample Question Phrasings	Attack! Attack! Attack!
Which one of the following, if true, would most weaken the author's point? *Which of the following statements, if true, would most call into question the results achieved by the scientists?*	Identify the issue, point, reasons, and assumptions of the author. Read critically, looking for where the author made too big a leap in logic. Then, when you go to the answer choices, look for a choice that has the most negative impact on that leap in logic. Assume all choices to be hypothetically true.

LESSON 4: STRENGTHEN QUESTIONS

THE ARGUMENT

4. Most major retail electronic chains experienced a dramatic increase in the amount of merchandise lost to shoplifting during the early 1980s. By 1986, however, all large chains had installed new anti-theft devices in their stores. Since this time, there has been a sharp decline in the number of shoplifting incidents taking place in those stores annually.

Which one of the following, if true, would most strengthen the claim that the antitheft devices were responsible for the decrease in shoplifting?

(A) The average size of electronic merchandise is now small enough to fit into a person's pocket.

(B) The average cost of electronic merchandise decreased since 1986.

(C) Each item in the store was clearly marked with an unremovable security number.

(D) Shoplifting increased at single outlet retail electronics operations since 1986.

(E) Shoplifting increased in the retail industry overall since 1986.

Cracking Strengthen questions

Step 1: Read the Question

Good, you've read the question. Here it is again:

> 4. Which one of the following, if true, would most strengthen the claim that the antitheft devices were responsible for the decrease in shoplifting?

Strengthen questions tip you off that the argument isn't great.

This is a Strengthen question. It is asking us to find a hypothetically true answer that will help the author make her conclusion. Also, it's telling us that the argument isn't all that great, or why would the author need help?

Step 2: Work the Argument

You read the argument. You read it slowly enough that you know the issue in the argument, and you can summarize the author's point and her reasons. Here it is again:

> Most major retail electronic chains experienced a dramatic increase in the amount of merchandise lost to shoplifting during the early 1980s. By 1986, however, all large chains had installed new anti-theft devices in their stores. Since this time, there has been a sharp decline in the number of shoplifting incidents taking place in those stores annually.

We've got retail electronic chains, antitheft devices, and a decline in the number of incidents. Looks like the author is going to try an establish causality, doesn't it?

Step 3: Stop, Think, and Write

Here's what we got as our issue, point, reasons, and assumption:

- Issue discussed: *The number of thefts experienced by retail electronics chains.*

- Author's point: *Decrease in number due to antitheft devices.*

- Author's reasons: *Because the number went down after devices were installed.*

- Author's assumption: *That the devices were the cause, and there were no other causes.*

We're getting the hang of this causal assumption thing, aren't we? Now, let's try to help out the author by finding a fact that strengthens this causality.

Step 4: Use Process of Elimination

Let's go to the answer choices. We know that the credited response is probably going to strengthen the causality of the argument in some way, perhaps by showing us that another possible cause isn't the cause.

> (A) The average size of electronic merchandise is now small enough to fit into a person's pocket.

This looks pretty good. Stuff is smaller (therefore easier to shoplift), yet the number of crimes has decreased over the same period. Maybe it is the antitheft devices, after all. Let's leave it.

(B) The average cost of electronic merchandise decreased since 1986.

Prices of the merchandise have gone down. Perhaps this means that therefore people have less incentive to steal it. Let's leave it.

(C) Each item in the store was clearly marked with an unremovable security number.

Might this mean that the security number acted as a deterrent to stealing the merchandise? Let's leave it, because it is talking about security.

(D) Shoplifting has increased at single outlet retail electronics operations since 1986.

Too bad for the little guy. However, do these folks have the antitheft devices or not? Since we don't know, this answer choice doesn't have too much impact. Let's cross it off.

(E) Shoplifting increased in the retail industry overall since 1986.

Gee, if the industry overall is up, then what is causing the retail electronics chains to be different? Let's leave this one too.

Four answer choices left this time. Phooey!

Here's some more reality for you. But let's take it slow and learn some more Process of Elimination techniques. Let's see how far we can legitimately take our logic to justify a specific answer.

Let's look at answer choice (C) first, which talks about the clearly marked unremovable security number. Perhaps this is the answer, but let's look at how many steps you have to take to rationalize this into being the correct answer. First, you have to assume that people will actually see this number. Then, you have to assume that people understand its purpose. Then, you have to assume that people will actually be deterred by this number. Then, you have to assume that this number triggers some sort of device or something (*not* mentioned in the choice, by the way). Then, you have to assume that people will know that it triggers some device. Then…you see the point. Sure, we can make a case for this choice if given an afternoon or two, but it's not direct enough. Let's cross it off.

Now let's look at answer choice (B), which talks about the average cost of electronic goods decreasing. Maybe people don't bother to steal cheap things, right? But do we have any information on that? No, we don't, so you have to assume it. Also, by what percentage did electronic goods decrease in price? A lot? A little? 0.0000000001 percent? We don't know, so you have to assume that it would be a statistically significant decrease (we don't know how much). See how much you're assuming? Too much. Let's kill it.

Next, we have answer choice (A), which says that many goods are now small enough to fit in one's pocket. This also says (by valid inference), that before, things *weren't* small enough to fit in one's pocket. However, do we have any information about the average size of items shoplifted? We've got the same problem here that we have in answer choice (B). If we were given additional information about the average size of items shoplifted, then we may have found our answer. But, once again, there are too many steps to justify the answer choice.

So we're left with answer choice (E), which tells us that the industry overall has been victimized to a greater degree since 1986. Therefore, there has to be something different about the large retail electronic chains in comparison to the overall industry. What is that? The fact that the large retail electronics chains installed these special security devices.

ARGUMENTS TECHNIQUES: TAKING BABY STEPS

On the LSAT, the correct answers will be direct in terms of impact on the argument.

As we saw from answer choices (A), (B), and (C) from the argument above, you can justify almost any answer choice as long as you have enough time and creativity. Indeed, as a lawyer, you'll be called upon to quite often link two separate and distinct ideas together so well that it looks as if the link can be justified, no matter how ridiculous it might look on the surface. But on the LSAT, the correct answers will be direct in terms of *impact* on the argument. What will be subtle will be what part of the argument it will affect—usually an unstated assumption. So if you find yourself saying, "Well, that could be the answer because if it meant that, then it could mean this, so therefore it could blah blah blah"—too many steps are involved. The correct answer will be a lot less complicated.

CRACKING STRENGTHEN QUESTIONS: SUMMARY

With Strengthen questions, we once again looked for impact on the answer choices—only this time, impact in a favorable way. We also learned that we can justify almost any answer if we have to, but the right answer will be one that takes only one small step from the argument. Here is the chart:

Sample Question Phrasings	Attack! Attack! Attack!
Which one of the following statements, if true, would support the author's conclusion? *Which one of the following statements, if true, would strengthen the author's point?*	Identify the issue, point, reasons, and assumptions of the author. Read critically, looking for where the author made too big a leap in logic. Then, when you go to the answer choices, look for a choice that has the most positive impact on that leap in logic. Assume all choices to be hypothetically true.

LESSON 5: PARADOX QUESTIONS

We've pretty much been cruising up until now, because the process for working the arguments (step 2) has been almost identical for Conclusion, Assumption, Weaken, and Strengthen question types. However, you're about to do something a bit different with this Paradox question. Steps 1 through 4 remain the same, but when you work the Paradox argument (step 2), your goal is to try to spot the apparent paradox or discrepancy. Essentially, the paradox will *be* the issue of the argument. Let's try a sample Paradox question for an argument:

Your goal will be to spot an answer choice that resolves or explains the discrepancy or paradox.

> The ancient Dirdirs used water power for various purposes in the outlying cities and towns in their empire. However, they did not use this technology in their capital city of Avallone.

So here we've got this ancient culture that has this great technology but doesn't use it in the capital city. That's the discrepancy or paradox, right?

Good. Your goal will then be to spot an answer choice that in some way resolves or explains that discrepancy or paradox. You can probably think up a few reasons why the Dirdirs had this technology and didn't use it, such as:

- There were no rivers or other bodies of water in or near Avallone.

- It was too expensive to construct the equipment necessary to harness the water power in Avallone.

- There was no space to put the equipment in Avallone.

That's good for a start. There could actually be a million reasons why they didn't use this technology (the correct answer actually had something to do with the fact that it would have caused social unrest because this technology would have put too many people out of work!). Your goal is to first spot the discrepancy, and then see if you can come up with a fact that would allow both parts of the discrepancy to be true.

THE ARGUMENT

5. A psychologist once performed the following experiment. Subjects were divided into two groups: excellent chess players and beginning chess players. Each group was exposed to a position arising from an actual game. Not surprisingly, when asked to reconstruct the position from memory an hour later, the expert chess players did much better than the beginners. On a board where the pieces were placed in a position at random, however, the expert players were no better able to reconstruct the position from memory than were the beginners.

Which of the following explains the result of the psychologist's experiment above?

(A) Memory is an important part of chess-playing ability.

(B) The beginning chess players as well as the experts were less able to memorize the random position than the "actual" position.

(C) The ability to memorize varies with experience and ability.

(D) Memory is a skill that can be improved with practice.

(E) Being able to make sense of information plays an important role in memorization.

Cracking Paradox questions

Step 1: Read the Question

Good, you've read the question. Here it is again:

> 5. Which of the following explains the result of the psychologist's experiment above?

In Paradox questions, the answer choices are all "hypotheticals."

This question is once again tipping our hand—it's telling us that there is something we need to *explain*. That means that somewhere in the argument is a *discrepancy* or *paradox* and we're going to have to find an answer choice that resolves these seemingly opposing facts.

Step 2: Work the Argument

You read the argument. You read it slowly enough that you can see what the discrepant or paradoxical situation is. Here it is again:

> A psychologist once performed the following experiment. Subjects were divided into two groups: excellent chess players and beginning chess players. Each group was exposed to a position arising from an actual game. Not surprisingly, when asked to reconstruct the position from memory an hour later, the expert chess players did much better than the beginners. On a board where the pieces were placed in a position at random, however, the expert players were no better able to reconstruct the position from memory than were the beginners.

This argument is about chess players and remembering certain positions. What is the apparent paradox?

Step 3: Stop, Think, and Write

Here's what we got as our paradoxical situation:

> The expert players could remember the position of the pieces better than the beginners could when the pieces were placed as they were during an actual game. But, when the pieces were placed at random, the beginners did just as well as the experts.

The arguer seems to find this odd—do you? Well, it really doesn't matter whether you do or not, because the question is telling us that we'd better find something odd or else. So there it is—our big discrepancy. Now our goal will be to find an answer choice that reconciles this oddity.

Step 4: Use Process of Elimination

In Paradox questions, the answer choices are all "hypotheticals," meaning that the five choices will be five facts. One of these facts, when added to the argument, will resolve the apparent paradox, or explain the supposed discrepancy.

Let's see which one of the following choices does this.

> (A) Memory is an important part of chess-playing ability.

That's right, it is. That's why the expert players were able to memorize the first situation better than the beginners were. However, it doesn't explain the second situation—in fact, this worsens the discrepancy. So let's cross it out.

> (B) The beginning chess players as well as the experts were less able to memorize the random position than the "actual" position.

This is good information, but it doesn't explain why the experts did *just as poorly* as the beginners did. So let's cross it out.

> (C) The ability to memorize varies with experience and ability.

This is like answer choice (A), in that it explains the first situation fine, but fails to provide an explanation for the second situation—where the experts did just as poorly as the beginners. Let's kill it.

> (D) Memory is a skill that can be improved with practice.

Again, this is like answer choices (A) and (C). Certainly the experts have practiced more, which is why they're experts to begin with. However, it still doesn't provide an explanation for scenario two. Let's cross it out.

> (E) Being able to make sense of information plays an important role in memorization.

Aha! There is a link between memory and familiarity, i.e., "making sense of information." The expert chess players were able to make sense of the position of the pieces in the first scenario, so they could memorize it more easily. But in the second scenario, there was nothing to make sense of. This is why, when presented with a random pattern of chess pieces, the experts didn't do any better than the beginners!

ARGUMENT TECHNIQUES: PROCESS OF ELIMINATION WITH PARADOX QUESTIONS

A key concept in doing Process of Elimination with Paradox questions is that the correct answer will be some explanation that will allow both of the facts from the argument to be true. In the Dirdir argument, the two facts were: (a) they had water power and (b) they did not use this technology in their capital city. In the chess argument, the facts were (a) that the experts did better than the beginners at memorizing the positions of chess pieces from a previously played position and (b) that the experts did not do any better at memorizing a set of pieces randomly placed on the board. The correct answer in each case allowed each of these facts to be true, and therefore to both exist.

Additionally, note that the phrasing of most Paradox questions contains the clause "if true." Your methodology should be exactly the same here as it is with Weaken and Strengthen questions—you assume each of the five answer choices to be hypothetically true and look for impact on the argument. In the case of Paradox questions, the impact will be about how it will resolve an apparent discrepancy.

CRACKING PARADOX QUESTIONS: SUMMARY

With Paradox questions, the only thing we must find before going to the answer choices is the apparent discrepancy or paradox. Once we're at the answer choices, we have to assume each choice is hypothetically true. Finally, we look to see which one of the answer choices allows both of the facts or sides of the argument to be true. Only one of them will do this.

Sample Question Phrasings	Attack! Attack! Attack!
Which one of the following statements, if true, explains the apparent paradox in the argument? *Which one of the following statements, if true, would explain the discrepancy found by the scientists?*	Identify the apparent discrepancy or paradox. Go to the answer choices and look for a piece of information that, when added to the argument, allows both facts from the argument to be true. Assume all choices to be hypothetically true.

LESSON 6: INFERENCE QUESTIONS

On Inference questions, only one of the choices must be true given the information in the passage.

Inference questions are double-edged swords. On one hand, the techniques for attacking Inference questions are very simple. There are also many Process of Elimination techniques for Inference questions once you get to the answer choices. However, the answer choices are so similar to each other, and the level of close reading you have to perform is so high, that many people only bat about .500 with inference questions.

So here are a few tips right away. First, when you read the argument, the only thing you have to do is get the issue. You don't have to get the author's point, reasons, or assumptions. Second, when you get to the answer choices, only one of the choices *must be true* given the information in the passage. All the other answer choices will be invalid inferences.

THE ARGUMENT

6. Many scientists and researchers equate addiction with physical dependence. This interpretation is fallacious. It fails to account for the most problematic aspect of addiction: drug-seeking behavior. Physical dependence is nothing more than the adaptive result of taking certain chemicals repeatedly. The distinction between dependence and addiction can clearly be seen in the usual failure of detoxification—the supervised gradual withdrawal of the drug—to cure addicted human beings.

   Which of the following can be properly inferred from the statements above?

   (A) Detoxification is usually able to cure human beings of a physical dependence on drugs.
   (B) Addiction is not an adaptive result.
   (C) Addiction, while not completely understood, has nothing to do with physical dependence.
   (D) Drug-seeking behavior is a consequence of physical dependence as well as of addiction.
   (E) It is impossible to completely and permanently cure addicted human beings.

Cracking Inference questions

Step 1: Read the Question
Good, you've read the question. Here it is again:

6. Which of the following can be properly inferred from the statements above?

This question is asking you to *infer* some piece of information from the argument. However, the word *inference* does not mean the same thing on the LSAT as it means in real life. On the LSAT, it means what *must be true* given the statements made in the argument. In life, you make inferences (some bad, some good) based on various pieces of information that that have been presented to you. This is a major distinction.

Step 2: Work the Argument
You read the argument. You read it slowly enough that you know what issue is being discussed. Here it is again:

Many scientists and researchers equate addiction with physical dependence. This interpretation is fallacious. It fails to account for the most problematic aspect of addiction: drug-seeking behavior. Physical dependence is nothing more than the adaptive result of taking certain chemicals repeatedly. The distinction between dependence and addiction can clearly be seen in the usual failure of detoxification—the supervised gradual withdrawal of the drug—to cure addicted human beings.

This argument is about drug addiction, physical dependence, and the failure of detoxification.

Step 3: Stop, Think, and Write

As we said above, there isn't much to do here except review the subject matter of the argument. We've got the difference between drug addiction and physical dependence, drug-seeking behavior, and the failure of detoxification. Now we're going to go to the answer choices and find the one choice that *must be true* given the information in the passage. Ready?

Step 4: Use Process of Elimination

Now we're going to attack the answer choices. We'll only keep the one or ones we think *must be true* given the information presented in the passage. We know you're getting sick of hearing that, but that's the "big money" technique here. Also, we'll look for things with extreme wording or that are out of scope. Hit it, Sam:

> (A) Detoxification is usually able to cure human beings of a physical dependence on drugs.

This looks okay. Note the word "usually" in this case, which is a pretty wishy-washy word. The argument states that the *difference* between dependence and addiction is revealed by the fact that detox *cannot* cure addiction. What does this tell you? That it *can* cure dependence. So let's leave it.

> (B) Addiction is not an adaptive result.

Two things wrong with this one, right? First, it's very strong, unequivocal language "addiction is *not*." Dangerous. Second, all the argument said was that physical dependence is an adaptive result, not that addiction isn't. Let's cross it out.

> (C) Addiction, while not completely understood, has nothing to do with physical dependence.

As in choice (B), note the harshness of the language. Addiction has "nothing to do" with dependence. Where in the argument did it say that? Nowhere. Let's cross it off.

> (D) Drug-seeking behavior is a consequence of physical dependence as well as of addiction.

Well, this certainly hits all the issues mentioned in the argument, right? Drug-seeking behavior, physical dependence, addiction. But we're going to have to go back and read the argument to see if it actually said that drug-seeking behavior is a result (that's what *consequence* means here) of both dependence and addiction. Go back and read the argument now. Got it? As you can see, the argument only talked about drug-seeking behavior being a result of addiction. We don't know anything about the consequences of physical dependence based on the information given to us. No doubt there are consequences of physical dependence, but the argument does not provide us with this information. Let's cross it out.

> (E) It is impossible to completely and permanently cure addicted human beings.

Ouch. Look at the harshness of this answer choice. "It is *impossible*" is not a statement that's very easily proven. Yes, it's probably impossible to climb Mount Everest with your hands tied behind your back, but just to be sure, let's kill this answer choice, too.

Well, we got the right answer, but only after going back and really checking to make sure answer choice (C) was not necessarily true given the information in the passage. So, (A) is a good, and typical, answer to an Inference question. It is based on a specific sentence and *explicitly* states something that is *implicitly* stated in the sentence. Now let's spend some more time with our good friend Process of Elimination.

ARGUMENTS TECHNIQUES: EXTREME WORDING REVISITED

Do you remember the Process of Elimination techniques we used to cross off wrong answer choices in Conclusion questions? They included scope, opposites, and extreme wording. Scope is still certainly an issue with Inference questions, because if there is something in an answer choice that wasn't mentioned in the argument, there's no way you can infer anything about it, can you?

However, when it comes to Inference questions, extreme wording (as you saw in the above example) plays a key role. It is much easier to say that something is *usually* true than to say that something is *always* true. You have to spend a lot more time backing up the second phrase. Let's take a look at another example:

1. Al Gore might be president in the year 2000.

2. Al Gore will be president in the year 2000.

There's only one difference between these two sentences: one has the word "might," the other has the word "will." Yet there is a vast difference between these two statements. Sure, Al Gore might be president in the year 2000—he's over 35 years old and he was born in the United States. That qualifies him for the presidency. Therefore, he might become president. However, saying that he *will* be president in the year 2000 is making a very strong, very unprovable statement. Many things might happen to prevent him from becoming president, even assuming that he will *want* to be president to begin with (he probably does, though). Whatever. The point here is that sentence 1 is a completely valid statement based on what we know right now. Sentence 2, however, can never be proven to anyone's satisfaction, and thus is an example of extreme wording. Take a look at the handy little chart below:

> It's much easier to say that something is usually true than it is to say that something is always true.

Nice and Wishy-Washy	Dangerously Extreme
might	always
could	never
may	at no time
can	must
some	will
possible	all
usually	not
sometimes	positively
at least once	absolutely
frequently	unequivocally

ARGUMENTS TECHNIQUES: THE CONTRAPOSITIVE

To get the contrapositive, reverse the order of the original statements and negate them both.

Do you know what an "if...then" statement is? It's very simple. Read this sentence:

> If you hit a glass with a hammer, it will break.

We can get fancy and diagram this statement as A → B, right? "A" would represent the glass being hit with the hammer, and "B" would represent the glass being broken. Cool.

Chances are, this is a true statement most of the time. In an LSAT argument, if we run across this sentence *in the argument itself*, we have to assume its basic truth. But what if the arguer then made the following conclusion from this information:

> If a glass is broken, it was hit with a hammer.

Not *necessarily*. It could have been thrown out the window, stepped on by a giraffe, shot up with an AK-47, etc. If this were an answer choice on an Inference question, what would you do? Hopefully, you would cross it out, because it doesn't have to be true.

We can diagram the above statement as well, saying it's B → A. However, we now know that if your first statement is A → B, then B → A does not have to be true. What about this statement:

> If you didn't hit a glass with a hammer, it didn't break.

Again, not necessarily. It could have been thrown out the window, run over by a car, dissolved with acid, etc. If this were an answer choice on an Inference question, what would you do? Hopefully, you would cross it out, because it doesn't have to be true.

We can diagram this statement too, by negating the letters, so it looks like this: –A → –B. However, we now know that if your first statement is A → B, then –A → –B does not have to be true either. So how about this statement:

> If the glass isn't broken, it wasn't hit with a hammer.

This *must* be true. How did we get it? We reversed the order of the original statements, and negated both statements. The resulting statement is called the *contrapositive*. So if this were an answer choice in an Inference question and if the first statement was contained somewhere in the argument, it would actually be the right answer.

The diagram for the above statement looks like this: –B → –A. So by reversing the order of the letters *and* negating both letters, we know that –B → –A is a valid inference from A → B.

So what? Well, we're telling you this because sometimes arguments contain "if...then" statements like the one above. Usually the LSAT writers then ask an Inference question. And then what happens is that three of the answer choices will *look like* the contrapositive. However, there will only be one right answer—it'll be the one where the statements have been reversed and negated!

CRACKING INFERENCE QUESTIONS: SUMMARY

With Inference questions, what we must find before going to the answer choices are the issues being discussed. Once we're at the answer choices, our goal is to eliminate the four answer choices that don't have to be true. We're also going to look out for scope and, especially, issues of extreme wording.

The way that Inference questions are phrased can be very tricky. See the Sample Question Phrasings column in the chart below for examples of how Inference questions can be worded.

Sample Question Phrasings	Attack! Attack! Attack!
Which one of the following statements can be validly inferred from the information above?	Identify the issues being talked about in the argument and go to the answer choices.
Which one of the following statements must be true given the information above?	Once there, cross off any answer choices that don' t have to be true—remember, the right answer *must be true* given the information in the passage.
*Which one of the following conclusions can be validly drawn from the passage above?**	Use scope and extreme wording to eliminate answer choices.
Which one of the following conclusions is best supported by the passage above?	Use the contrapositive if there are "if...then" statements contained in the passage and in the answer choices.

*Note the fact that this example says "conclusions" and not "conclusion." "Conclusions" means that it's an Inference question.

LESSON 7: REASONING QUESTIONS

You will probably encounter at least ten, or possibly fifteen, Reasoning questions when you take the LSAT. Why so many? We have no idea. That's just the way it is. So what are they? Reasoning questions want to know one of two things:

1. *How* the author made his or her argument

   or

2. *Why* the author's method of reasoning is bad

Seems pretty simple, right? Well, sometimes it is, and sometimes it's pretty difficult due to very close "second answers" and deliberately inscrutable vocabulary. The answers to reasoning questions will fall into one of two categories: *general* answers that do not actually mention the subject matter of the argument, and *specific* answers that do address the subject matter of the argument. You won't know whether the answer choices will be general or specific until you get them. Occasionally, the answer choices will be a mix of both.

So how do you attack these questions? You know after you've read the question what type of question it is, so that's good. And you know that your step 3 goal will be to describe what is happening in the argument—either how the author made her point (for instance, she gave examples, she used survey results, she inferred causality, etc.) or why the author's conclusion isn't valid (for instance, she misunderstood a statistic, she excludes possible alternate causes, etc.). Got it? Well, let's try one!

THE ARGUMENT

7. Fortunately for the development of astronomy, observations of Mars were not exact in Kepler's time. If they had been, Kepler might not have "discovered" that the planets move in elliptical rather than circular orbits, and he would not have formulated his three laws of planetary motion. There are those who complain that the science of economics is inexact, and that economic theories neglect certain details. That is their merit. Theories in economics, like those in astronomy, must be allowed some imprecision.

    In the passage above, the author reaches his conclusion by

    (A) finding an exception to a general rule.
    (B) drawing an analogy.
    (C) appealing to an authority.
    (D) attributing an unknown cause to a known effect.
    (E) using the word "theory" ambiguously.

Cracking Reasoning questions

Your goal on Reasoning questions is to describe how the author made his argument.

Step 1: Read the Question
Good, you've read the question. Here it is again:

7. In the passage above, the author reaches his conclusion by

This is asking us to describe the author's method of reasoning. So let's read the argument and see how he gets from point A to point B.

Step 2: Work the Argument
You read the argument. You read it slowly enough that you know how the author got from point A to point B. Also it is often useful to find the conclusion and premises; it helps you discern the reasoning. Here it is again:

Fortunately for the development of astronomy, observations of Mars were not too exact in Kepler's time. If they had been, Kepler might not have "discovered" that the planets move in elliptical rather than circular orbits, and he would not have formulated his three laws of planetary motion.

There are those who complain that the science of economics is inexact, that economic theories neglect certain details. That is their merit. Theories in economics, like those in astronomy, must be allowed some imprecision.

This argument is Kepler, astronomy, and economics and imprecision being good. Fascinating stuff.

Step 3: Stop, Think, and Write

Our goal here is simply to describe how the author made his argument. In this case, it looks as if the entire thing about Kepler is an analogy used to say that it's okay that economic theories are imprecise. However, perhaps this analogy isn't a particularly good one. What do you think?

Step 4: Use Process of Elimination

Now we're going to attack the answer choices. Let's see if we can find an answer choice that has something to do with the author making an analogy:

(A)   finding an exception to a general rule.

What does the word "exception" refer to in the argument? Anything? It doesn't look that way, so let's cross it off.

(B)   drawing an analogy.

Looks pretty good—this is exactly what we said. Let's leave it.

(C)   appealing to an authority.

Who does the term "authority" apply to in the argument? Anyone? It doesn't look that way. Let's cross it off.

(D)   attributing an unknown cause to a known effect.

Sounds fancy, but this argument isn't about cause and effect. It's about making an analogy. Let's cross it out.

(E)   using the word "theory" ambiguously.

How is the word "theory" used ambiguously? It looks pretty straightforward to us. Let's cross it off.

Cool, we got the right answer pretty easily here. Note how most of these answer choices sounded really impressive but in the end were just pure garbage. We'll talk more about language and how it relates to Reasoning questions a bit later.

Now let's look at a different type of Reasoning question for the same argument.

8.   A logical critique of the argument above would most likely emphasize that the author

(A)   fails to cite other authorities.
(B)   does not consider nonscientific theories.
(C)   neglects the possibility that there may have been other reasons for Kepler's success.
(D)   assumes the truth of the very proposition he is trying to prove.
(E)   ignores the differences between the sort of imprecision allowed in astronomy and that allowed in economics.

Step 1: Read the Question

Good, you've read the question. Here it is again:

> 8. A logical critique of the argument above would
>   most likely emphasize that the author

So now we're expected to describe *why* the argument above is bad. Remember, this is totally different than "weakening" an argument by assuming the five answer choices to be hypothetically true. Here, all we're looking for is a description of how the argument is bad. Finding assumptions is *very useful* for finding a flaw. Most flaws *are* assumptions.

Step 2: Work the Argument

You've read the argument. You've read it slowly enough that you know how the author got from point A to point B. Here it is again:

> Fortunately for the development of astronomy,
> observations of Mars were not exact in Kepler's
> time. If they had been, Kepler might not have
> "discovered" that the planets move in elliptical
> rather than circular orbits, and he would not have
> formulated his three laws of planetary motion.
> There are those who complain that the science of
> economics is inexact, that economic theories neglect
> certain details. That is their merit. Theories in
> economics, like those in astronomy, must be
> allowed some imprecision.

This argument is Kepler, astronomy, and economics and imprecision being good. Still fascinating stuff.

Step 3: Stop, Think, and Write

Our goal here is simply to describe why the author's argument is faulty in some way. In this case, it looks as if the entire thing about Kepler is an analogy used to say that it's okay that economic theories are imprecise. This might not strike you as a particularly good argument, but all we're concerned with here is how the author reached his conclusion—what tools did he use to get there?

Step 4: Use Process of Elimination

Now we're going to attack the answer choices. Let's see if we can find an answer choice that has something to do with the author making an analogy:

> (A) fails to cite other authorities.

This is almost never the correct answer in a Reasoning question. Usually, the argument is wrong somehow *internally*, not because the author didn't bring in some expert from the big city. Let's cross it off.

> (B) does not consider nonscientific theories.

True, but once again, so what? The author doesn't talk about nonscientific theories, but the analogy is either a good or a bad one on its own. Let's kill it.

> (C) neglects the possibility that there may have
>   been other reasons for Kepler's success.

Aha. This means that Kepler might have been great for other reasons. However, we're not trying to weaken causality here, but show how the analogy is weak. Let's cross it off.

> (D)   assumes the truth of the very proposition he is
>   trying to prove.

This is what we would call "gibberish." Basically, it's saying that he's saying he's right because he thinks he's right. But he's not doing that; he's drawing an analogy. Let's cross it off.

> (E)   ignores the differences between the sort of
>   imprecision allowed in astronomy and that
>   allowed in economics.

Oops, right? The analogy isn't very good between astronomy and economics. Hence, this is our answer.

So we've seen how Reasoning questions can be divided into questions that ask you to describe the author's line of reasoning and questions that ask you to describe why the author's line of reasoning is faulty. Now let's look at some Process of Elimination techniques for Reasoning questions.

ARGUMENTS TECHNIQUES: PROCESS OF ELIMINATION WITH REASONING QUESTIONS

One thing you might have noticed we did when discussing some of the answer choices was to take each word or phrase from the answer choice and ask, "Does this correspond to anything that actually occurred in the argument?" Most of the time, the answer is no. The answer choices might sound fancy ("the author assumes what he sets out to prove," "the author appeals to authority," etc.), but unless you can go back to the argument and say, "Ah, yes, *this* is where the author gives an example, and *this* is where he gives the counterexample," then an answer choice that mentions "examples" and "counterexamples" will be wrong. This technique is HUGE. It will eliminate two or three answer choices every time.

Therefore, take answer choices on Reasoning questions very slowly, and make sure to match each piece of the answer choice to a piece of the argument. Once you come across something in an answer choice that doesn't correspond to anything in the argument, you can get rid of that answer choice. Once it's half bad, it's all bad.

On Reasoning questions, match each piece of the answer choice to a piece of the argument.

CRACKING REASONING QUESTIONS: SUMMARY

As you can see, the goal in Reasoning questions is to come up with your own description of either how the reasoning of the argument proceeds or why the argument is bad. If you are able to come up with a terse, exact description, you can usually match it with one of the answer choices. The vocabulary in the answer choices will no doubt be much more esoteric than the words you used, but as long as the meaning is the same, you're golden.

Sample Question Phrasings	Attack! Attack! Attack!
Which one of the following indicates a flaw in the author's reasoning? *The argument proceeds by...* *Melinda challenges Kim's view by arguing that...* *The point at issue between David and Jocasta is that...* *Which one of the following indicates a weakness in the author's argument?*	Read the argument carefully and then describe what is happening in your own words, or describe why the argument is bad internally. Then, take this description and rigorously apply it to the answer choices. Once you're at the answer choices, use the technique of comparing the words and phrases that appear in the choices against what actually occurred in the argument. Cross out anything that didn't appear in the argument. Lather, rinse, repeat.

LESSON 8: PRINCIPLE QUESTIONS

THE ARGUMENT

Save Principle questions for later on in the section.

We're nearing the home stretch here on arguments. The last two question types we will cover are Principle and Parallel-the-Reasoning. Both of these types of questions should be done last, if at all, for a variety of reasons, the biggest of which is that they waste a lot of time because they take a long time to do. Sure, maybe you can get one right, but in the meantime you could have answered two other arguments correctly. Let's take a look at a Principle question first.

9. It has been suggested that a gift is truly generous only if the giver sacrifices something that is valuable, and does so without expectation of reward; whereas, a gift is self-serving either if the giver receives a benefit from giving the gift or if the giver anticipates that she will receive some benefit.

    Which one of the following situations conforms to the principle described above?

    (A) Kim gave her niece an antique necklace that she herself loved to wear because she expected that her niece would then take her out to dinner. Thus, Kim's act was both generous and self-serving.

(B) In order to promote himself as a philanthropist, Joseph gave $10,000 to a ballet company; Joseph's gift was truly generous because his gift allowed the company to remain financially solvent.

(C) Although she intended to perform the deed anonymously, the multi-millionaire's delivery of a Thanksgiving dinner to a poor family was publicized in a local paper and she was subsequently showered with praise, thus proving that truly generous gifts can reap benefits for the giver.

(D) In an attempt to impress all of her friends, Jill told them about her donation of $50 to an environmental organization; her gift was not self-serving, since many of her friends were not impressed by her generosity.

(E) Michael agreed to give a large sum of money to a public television station. As a result, he was given a set of coffee mugs. Even though he wasn't aware that he would receive them, Michael's gift was self-serving.

Cracking Principle questions

Step 1: Read the Question
Good, you've read the question. Here it is again:

Principle questions are matching questions.

9. Which one of the following situations conforms to the principle described above?

Basically, Principle questions are matching questions. Either you will be given a principle in the argument and then asked to match it with one of five possible examples of that principle from the answer choices, or you will be given an example in the argument and then given five potential principles in the answer choices and be asked to match one of those with the example. This question is an example of the first situation.

Step 2: Work the Argument
You read the argument. To identify the credited response, it's important to make explicit the principles stated in the argument. Here it is again:

> It has been suggested that a gift is truly generous only if the giver sacrifices something that is valuable, and does so without expectation of reward; whereas, a gift is self-serving either if the giver receives a benefit from giving the gift or if the giver anticipates that she will receive some benefit.

This principle is about when a gift is truly generous and when it is not. Generous: Sacrifices something without expectation of reward. Self-serving: Giver receives or expects a benefit. Now let's see if we can come up with an example on our own that illustrates this.

Step 3: Stop, Think, and Write
Our goal here is merely to consider what the most important aspects of the principle are when it comes to looking for an example. We must be clear on what makes a gift generous and what makes a gift self-serving.

Step 4: Use Process of Elimination

Now we're going to match our example with the answer choices and see if anything is similar.

(A) Kim gave her niece an antique necklace that she herself loved to wear because she expected that her niece would then take her out to dinner. Thus, Kim's act was both generous and self-serving.

Because Kim expected a reward (a dinner out), her gift cannot be described as generous. Let's cross it out.

(B) In order to promote himself as a philanthropist, Joseph gave $10,000 to a ballet company; Joseph's gift was truly generous because his gift allowed the company to remain financially solvent.

Because Joseph expected a reward (promoting himself as a philanthropist), his gift cannot be described as generous. So this example is wrong when it says it's a truly generous gift. We'll take the money for the ballet company, though. But let's cross it out.

(C) Although she intended to perform the deed anonymously, Jeanette's delivery of a Thanksgiving dinner to a poor family was publicized in a local paper and she was subsequently showered with praise, thus proving that truly generous gifts can reap benefits for the giver.

Because the gift did not entail a sacrifice and wasn't valuable (a Thanksgiving dinner from a multi-millionaire), the gift cannot be described as generous. Let's nix this one, too.

(D) Jill told all of her friends about her donation of $50 to an environmental organization; her gift was not self-serving, since many of her friends were not impressed by her generosity.

Because Jill expected a reward, her donation was self-serving: The answer choice categorizes her behavior as not self-serving, so this answer is wrong. Let's cross it off.

(E) Michael agreed to give a large sum of money to a public television station. As a result, he was given a set of coffee mugs. Even though he wasn't aware that he would receive them, Michael's gift was self-serving.

This is the credited response. Because Michael got a benefit, no matter how small, his gift is categorized as self-serving. But this statement fits within the parameters of the principle given in the argument: Because he got something, it was self-serving. Therefore, this example is valid.

ARGUMENTS TECHNIQUES: PROCESS OF ELIMINATION WITH PRINCIPLE QUESTIONS

As we saw from the above example, you are looking to find an example that will satisfy the conditions of the principle. In the other type of Principle question, you are given five principles in the answer choices. The actions or examples are given in the argument, and your job is to match the action with the one principle that "justifies" those actions. Either way, your Process of Elimination technique is to match the action or example with the tenets of the principle—if part of the answer choice doesn't match, throw it out.

CRACKING PRINCIPLE QUESTIONS: SUMMARY

Refer to the chart below on how to attack Principle questions.

Sample Question Phrasings	Attack! Attack! Attack!
Which one of the following principles justifies the actions taken by Mia in the argument above? *Which of the following examples conforms to the principle given in the argument above?*	Make sure you're clear in which direction the argument is flowing—are they giving you five principles in the answer choices, or are they giving you five examples of a principle stated in the argument? Once you're sure, come up with either your own example or your own principle and then match that against the answer choices.

LESSON 9: PARALLEL-THE-REASONING QUESTIONS

We're at the end, finally. And there is a reason we saved Parallel-the-Reasoning questions for last—because you should probably avoid them and spend your time doing other questions that will take you less time and therefore get you more points. Most Parallel-the-Reasoning questions can be diagrammed in some fashion. Your job is to then find the answer choice that has the same diagram.

Save Parallel arguments for last.

THE ARGUMENT

10. A full moon is known to cause strange behavior in people. People are behaving strangely today, so there is probably a full moon.

   Which of the following most closely parallels the flawed pattern of reasoning used in the argument above?

   (A) Abnormal sunspot activity causes animals to act strangely. We are experiencing abnormal sunspot activity today, so animals are probably acting strangely.
   (B) Medical reference books often have red covers. This book has a red cover, so it is probably a medical reference work.
   (C) The law of gravity has worked for as long as mankind has been able to observe it. It's working today, and it will probably continue to work tomorrow.
   (D) A mental illness has much in common with a physical illness. Therefore, mental illnesses should probably be treated in much the same way as physical illnesses.
   (E) People with an ear for music often have an equal facility for learning languages. Bill has an ear for music, so he probably has a facility for learning languages.

Cracking Parallel-the-Reasoning questions

Step 1: Read the Question
Good, you've read the question. Here it is again:

10. Which of the following most closely parallels the flawed pattern of reasoning used in the argument above?

Cool. It's a Parallel-the-Reasoning argument, and we know that we have to try and diagram the argument, if possible, and match that diagram against the answer choices. We also know that the reasoning itself is bad, because the question tips us off to that. Let's go to it.

Step 2: Work the Argument
You read the argument. Here it is again:

A full moon is known to cause strange behavior in people. People are behaving strangely today, so there is probably a full moon.

This looks eminently diagrammable. It also sounds like an invalid contrapositive, doesn't it? Let's see....

Step 3: Stop, Think, and Write
Here's what we got as our diagram:

A full moon is known to cause strange behavior in people (A → B); people are behaving strangely today, so there is probably a full moon (B → A). Oops!

The arguer screwed up, didn't he? He used an invalid contrapositive in sentence two. He flipped the elements, but didn't negate them! Now all we have to do is find the same invalid contrapositive in the answer choices.

Step 4: Use Process of Elimination

Now we're going to match our diagram with the answer choices and see if anything is similar.

> (A) Abnormal sunspot activity causes animals to act strangely. We are experiencing abnormal sunspot activity today, so animals are probably acting strangely.

Diagram it: Abnormal sunspot activity causes animals to act strangely (A → B); we are experiencing abnormal sunspot activity today, so animals are probably acting strangely (A → B again). This doesn't match the argument, so this isn't the answer. Cross it off.

> (B) Medical reference books often have red covers. This book has a red cover, so it is probably a medical reference work.

Diagram it: Medical reference books often have red covers (A → B); this book has a red cover, so it is probably a medical reference work (B → A). Bingo! This is the same type of flawed reasoning, another invalid contrapositive.

> (C) The law of gravity has worked for as long as mankind has been able to observe it. It's working today, and it will probably continue to work tomorrow.

Can we even diagram this? It looks like the entire thing is merely saying that if it's working today, it'll work tomorrow. So it's just (A → B) and nothing else. Kill it.

> (D) A mental illness has much in common with a physical illness. Therefore, mental illnesses should probably be treated in much the same way as physical illnesses.

This is (A → B), and then in the second sentence (A → B) again. Nope.

> (E) People with an ear for music often have an equal facility for learning languages. Bill has an ear for music, so he probably has a facility for learning languages.

Again, this is (A → B) in the first sentence, and then (A → B) repeated in the second sentence. It's out.

Nice job! We got the right answer simply by diagramming the statement in the argument, and then diagramming each of the answer choices until we found the one that matched our original diagram.

However, we're sure you noticed that it took you a long time to do this question. Many times, Parallel-the-Reasoning questions are even longer than this one, and will take you three minutes apiece to do. If you spend your time doing these questions, you might only get to half of an Arguments section!

ARGUMENTS TECHNIQUES: PROCESS OF ELIMINATION WITH PARALLEL-THE-REASONING QUESTIONS

Whenever possible, diagram Parallel arguments.

It's pretty straightforward here—if you are able to diagram the argument, then you must go to the answer choices and diagram those as well. You can't tell just by "looking," either. Write it out and then you've got proof that the choice either matches or doesn't match with the argument.

Sometimes you can't diagram Parallel-the-Reasoning questions. In these instances, try to describe the reasoning questions. Especially look for patterns that can be easily summed up (e.g., we have two things that appear to be similar, then we note a difference, or one thing is attributed to be the cause of another). Try to find an answer that could be summed up in the same way.

CRACKING PARALLEL-THE-REASONING QUESTIONS: SUMMARY

Refer to the chart below on how to attack Parallel-the-Reasoning questions.

Sample Question Phrasings	Attack! Attack! Attack!
Which one of the following is most closely similar in reasoning to the argument above? *Which one of the following exhibits a pattern of flawed reasoning similar to the argument above?*	Parallel-the-Reasoning questions will either contain flawed or valid reasoning, and the question will tip you off. Try to diagram the argument and then diagram each of the answer choices, trying to match one of these against the diagram you came up with for the argument itself. Save Parallel-the-Reasoning questions for *last*!!!

CRACKING ARGUMENTS: PUTTING IT ALL TOGETHER

Now you've learned how to attack every type of question they will throw at you in Arguments. How do you integrate this knowledge into working an Arguments section?

DO THE RIGHT ARGUMENTS FOR *YOU*

Your first goal should be to make sure that you are starting off doing the best arguments for *you*. This probably means you should skip the Parallel-the-Reasoning and Principle questions that you encounter. These questions will waste time and they are simply more difficult than other questions. Also, you should skip any arguments where you honestly don't know what they they are talking about. You're not going to get those questions right, or you'll spend seven minutes trying to figure each of them out. In that time, you could have gotten three other arguments correct.

Consequently, you should be skipping at least five to ten Arguments questions on your first pass through the section. Circle the arguments that you've skipped so you know to come back to them if you have time, but remember to bubble in an answer to them anyway in case you don't have the time. The worst that can happen is that you don't get a chance to go back and work the five arguments that you had the least chance of getting correct, so big deal!

YOU AND YOUR CHART

Following is the chart that will lead you to Arguments nirvana. You should probably re-type the chart yourself (it will help you to better remember all the information in it), and then print out a copy for yourself. Then go to your local copy shop and get it laminated, and use it for a placemat until you take the LSAT. We know, we know, you think we're joking. But we're really not.

Recopy this chart and put it
on your refrigerator.

Question Type	Sample Question Phrasings	Attack! Attack! Attack!
Conclusion	*What is the author's main point?* *What is the conclusion of the argument above?* *The argument is structured to lead to which one of the following conclusions?*	Identify the issue, point, and reasons. Use the Why Test, and then match your point against the five answer choices. The closest one wins. When down to two choices, use extreme wording and scope to eliminate one choice.
Assumption	*What is an underlying assumption in the above argument?* *Which of the following is necessary for the author's point to be valid?* *Which one of the following statements is the author assuming?*	Identify the issue, point, reasons, and assumptions of the author. Use the Why Test, and then match your assumption(s) against those in the answer choices. If you're having trouble finding the assumption, look for a gap between two different ideas in the argument. When down to two choices, negate each statement to see if the argument falls apart. If it does, that's your answer.
Weaken	*Which one of the following, if true, would most weaken the author's point?* *Which of the following statements, if true, would most call into question the results achieved by the scientists?*	Identify the issue, point, reasons, and assumptions of the author. Read critically, looking for where the author made too big a leap in logic. Then, when you go to the answer choices, look for a choice that has the most negative impact on that leap in logic. Assume all choices to be hypothetically true.
Strengthen	*Which one of the following statements, if true, would support the author's conclusion?* *Which one of the following statements, if true, would strengthen the author's point?*	Identify the issue, point, reasons, and assumptions of the author. Read critically, looking for where the author made too big a leap in logic. Then, when you go to the answer choices, look for a choice that has the most positive impact on that leap in logic. Assume all choices to be hypothetically true.
Paradox	*Which one of the following statements, if true, explains the apparent paradox in the argument?* *Which one of the following statements, if true, would explain the discrepancy found by the scientists?*	Identify the apparent discrepancy or paradox. Go to the answer choices and look for a piece of information that, when added to the argument, allows both facts from the argument to be true. Assume all choices to be hypothetically true.

Question Type	Sample Question Phrasings	Attack! Attack! Attack!
Inference	*Which one of the following statements can be validly inferred from the information above?* *Which one of the following statements must be true given the information above?* *Which one of the following conclusions can be validly drawn from the passage above?* *Which one of the following conclusions is best supported by the passage above?*	Identify the issues being talked about in the argument and go to the answer choices. Once there, cross off any answer choices that don't have to be true—remember, the right answer MUST BE TRUE given the information in the passage. Use scope and extreme wording to eliminate answer choices. Use the contrapositive if there are "if...then" statements contained in the passage and in the choices.
Reasoning	*Which one of the following indicates a flaw in the author's reasoning?* *The argument proceeds by...* *Melinda challenges Kim's view by arguing that...* *The point at issue between David and Jocasta is that...* *Which one of the following indicates a weakness in the author's argument?*	Read the argument carefully and then describe what is happening in your own words, or describe why the argument is bad internally. Then take this description and rigorously apply it to the answer choices. Once you're at the answer choices, use the technique of comparing the words and phrases that appear in the choices against what actually occurred in the argument. Cross out anything that didn't appear in the argument. Lather, rinse, repeat.
Principle	*Which one of the following principles justifies the actions taken by Mia in the argument above?* *Which of the following examples conforms to the principle given in the argument above?*	Make sure you're clear in which direction the argument is flowing—are they giving you five principles in the answer choices, or are they giving you five examples of a principle stated in the argument? Once you're sure, come up with either your own example or your own principle and then match that against the answer choices.
Parallel-the-Reasoning	*Which one of the following is most closely similar in reasoning to the argument above?* *Which one of the following exhibits a pattern of flawed reasoning similar to the argument above?*	Parallel-the-Reasoning questions will either contain flawed or valid reasoning, and the question will tip you off. Try to diagram the argument and then diagram each of the answer choices, trying to match one of these against the diagram you came up with for the argument itself. Save Parallel-the-Reasoning questions for *last!!!*

3

Games

WHAT IS A GAME?

Games are puzzles. Each game consists of a number of *elements* in an initial situation that we call the *setup*. This situation is incompletely described by a set of conditions or *clues*. Sometimes these clues are modified by a question. If so, the new clues apply to that question only.

WHAT DOES THIS SECTION TEST?

Games test how well you can organize an incomplete set of indirect clues so that you can extract information quickly.

WHY IS THIS SECTION ON THE LSAT?

It beats us. Games test your ability to determine various sorts of spatial relationships. They bear no relation to anything lawyers do.

THE SECTION ITSELF

The Games section contains four sets, or games. Each game includes five to seven questions. The section has a total of 24 questions.

Before we begin, take a moment to read the instructions to this section:

> Directions: Each group of questions in this section is based on a set of conditions. In answering some of the questions it may be useful to draw a rough diagram. Choose the response that most accurately and completely answers each question and blacken the corresponding space on your answer sheet.

These are the directions that will appear on your LSAT. As usual on the LSAT, the official directions are very little help. Review them now. They will not change. Don't waste time reading them in the test room.

THE GOOD NEWS

The good news is that with some rigorous practice diagramming games, you can radically improve your LSAT score. Many students have walked into Princeton Review classes only getting a few Games questions right, but walk out scoring about 75 percent on the section. You can do the same, as long as you follow our step-by-step process.

GAMES: GENERAL STRATEGIES

Following is a list of general strategies that you should use when you are working the Games section. Make sure you take these strategies to heart.

Slow and steady

As in arguments, you want to do fewer games questions, which will enable you to more accurately complete the ones you do. The LSAT writers have put four games in the section to scare you into trying to work too fast, thereby cutting down on your accuracy. If you're able to get to three games in the section, and get all the questions on those three games correct, chances are you'll receive a very good LSAT score.

Your mantra: *I will slow down and do fewer games, thereby increasing my accuracy.*

Survey the field

Remember, every correct answer on the LSAT is worth exactly one point. So it doesn't matter which games you do. It's quite possible that the two games that you should do first in a section may be the third and fourth games presented. Remember, the LSAT questions are not in order of difficulty. Therefore, you should look over all four games when you open to the section, and decide which ones are most attackable. We'll spend time later going more in-depth into what makes a game more attractive as opposed to less attractive.

Your mantra: *I will look over the Games section and make my own order of when I will do each game.*

Transfer your answers after each game

Work all the questions on a particular game; then transfer your answers to the bubble sheet. You need a few seconds to take a deep breath after each game, and transferring your answers allows your brain to do something mindless for a few seconds. When you're down to five minutes, make sure you've got every single question bubbled in. Then, transfer your answers singly, changing whatever you might have bubbled in first. That way, when time is called you'll have an answer for every single question.

Your mantra: *I will transfer my answers after each game until five minutes are left.*

Breathe

After you've completed each game, use ten seconds to take three deep breaths. Transfer your answers from that game, and then start another game. You've cleared your mind and you're ready to push on.

Your mantra: *I will use ten seconds after each game I complete to take some deep breaths.*

YOUR MANTRAS AND YOU

Here they are again:

> *I will slow down and do fewer games, thereby increasing my accuracy.*

> *I will look over the Games section and make my own order of when I will do each game.*

> *I will transfer my answers after each game until five minutes are left.*

> *I will use ten seconds after each game I complete to take some deep breaths.*

GAMES: SPECIFIC STRATEGIES

The directions for the Games section misleadingly state that "it may be useful to draw a rough diagram" when working the section. That's like saying there *may* be snow in Antarctica. Actually, it *is* *necessary* to draw a very *detailed* diagram. Furthermore, you want to "symbolize" all of the clues that you are given.

Get rid of the words

Games are a visual exercise. Games test your ability to mentally imagine how various elements can be arranged in space. Therefore, words don't help you—pictures do. Your goal will be to translate all the words that you are given in the setup and the clues, and sometimes in the questions themselves, into pictures. The LSAT writers will not expect you to take such a rigorous approach to visualizing the infomation that you're being presented with. Therefore, you should do it.

Be consistent

There are various ways you can symbolize and diagram the information that is being presented to you in a game. We're going to show you what we think is the best and most efficient way to diagram and symbolize. Whatever method you choose, be consistent with your symbols and your diagram—don't mix and match. You'll get confused and wonder why you've gotten three answers for half the questions, and no answers for the other half of the questions.

Be careful

Your goal is to transfer all the information that you received in the setup and the clues into some sort of visual symbolization. However, if you don't read the clues carefully enough, you can wind up symbolizing something incorrectly. This will eventually lead to your diagram becoming complete gibberish. So make sure you read the information slowly enough that you don't make mistakes in your symbolization.

Be creative

Just start your pencil moving and begin drawing something.

The four games that you will see on the real LSAT will look slightly different than the games you have practiced with in the past. Under time pressure, they may seem *completely* different. But they really won't be. Just start your pencil moving and begin drawing *something*. At some point during your diagramming or your symbolization, you will realize that this game is similar to something else you've already done. So don't panic—start drawing!

GAMES: A STEP-BY-STEP PROCESS

Just as in Arguments, The Princeton Review has boiled down the Games section into a process. In Games, it's a six-step process as opposed to a four-step process with arguments, but the theory is the same: You will follow this process for every game that you do, and it will help you get correct answers. Sound good? Then let's go to it!

Step 1: Decide on the appropriate diagram and draw it

Your first step will be to determine how to set up the game by drawing a diagram. Typically, various elements are *assigned* relationships to other elements. Your goal is to determine how to best represent this situation visually.

Step 2: Symbolize the clues

After you've drawn the skeleton of a diagram, move on to symbolizing the clues listed below the setup. The clues should be symbolized in a way that is consistent with the diagram you have set up.

Step 3: Double-check your clues and make deductions

Never forget how important it is to symbolize everything correctly. Quickly read over the clues to make sure you've done this. Then, see if your symbols, when compared to the diagram, and compared to each other, yield any other pieces of information that you can either symbolize or take note of.

Step 4: Identify the key

There will always be one element or one very important clue that will limit or otherwise impact the game in some significant way. The key is something that will help you diagram your game faster. If you take a step back and look at all the information you've translated and deduced, you should be able to identify this factor. If not, it will become apparent to you at some point during the game.

Step 5: Attack the questions

Not all games questions are on the same level of difficulty. We'll show you which types of questions to attack first and why. As a rule, you should always look for questions that further limit the initial conditions of the game and provide you with more information. These questions can be done much more quickly than those questions that don't provide you with any information.

Step 6: Use Process of Elimination

We know, you're sick of hearing about Process of Elimination. But get used to it! It will come in handy on Games, just as it did on Arguments. (Oh, and by the way, you'll use it for Reading Comp, too.)

READY FOR SOME GAMES?

Now let's see how the six steps work on a real game. Give yourself fifteen minutes to try the following game—don't worry if you have no idea how to attack it. Use only half a sheet of scratch paper *at most* to work on this game. You will have limited space when you take the real exam, so get used to writing small! Do the best you can, and then see how we worked the game. After each game, we'll give you some extra techniques for attacking this section of the LSAT. You should work through each exercise before going on to the next game. By the end of the chapter, you'll know everything we know.

GAME #1: DAYS AND ENTREES

Just take it slow, folks!

A restaurant must choose its main dinner entree for each night of one week, beginning on Sunday and ending on Saturday. The possible entrees are lamb chops, roast beef, veal, poached salmon, spaghetti, trout, and manicotti. The following conditions must be met when determining the menu:

The lamb chops must be served either the night before or the night after the spaghetti is served.

The roast beef must be served either the night before or the night after either the poached salmon or the trout is served.

The manicotti cannot be served the night before or the night after the veal is served.

The veal must be served on Monday.

1. Which one of the following is a possible menu in order from Sunday to Saturday?

    (A) Lamb chops, spaghetti, roast beef, trout, manicotti, poached salmon, veal
    (B) Roast beef, poached salmon, lamb chops, spaghetti, veal, trout, manicotti
    (C) Spaghetti, veal, lamb chops, manicotti, poached salmon, roast beef, trout
    (D) Trout, veal, roast beef, poached salmon, manicotti, lamb chops, spaghetti
    (E) Trout, veal, manicotti, poached salmon, roast beef, lamb chops, spaghetti

2. If lamb chops are served on Saturday, which one of the following must be true?

    (A) The spaghetti is served on Thursday.
    (B) The roast beef is served on Tuesday.
    (C) The manicotti is served on Thursday.
    (D) The poached salmon is served on Wednesday.
    (E) The trout is served on Sunday.

3. If the trout is served on Thursday, the poached salmon must be served on

    (A) Sunday
    (B) Tuesday
    (C) Wednesday
    (D) Friday
    (E) Saturday

4. If the roast beef is served on Saturday, which one of the following must be true?

    (A) The trout is served on Friday.
    (B) The manicotti is served on Thursday.
    (C) The spaghetti is served on Wednesday.
    (D) The lamb chops are served on Tuesday.
    (E) The poached salmon is served on Sunday.

5. Which one of the following is a night on which the manicotti could be served?

(A) Sunday
(B) Tuesday
(C) Wednesday
(D) Friday
(E) Saturday

Cracking Game #1

Step 1: Decide on the Appropriate Diagram and Draw It

What we have here is seven days of the week and seven entrees. We learned this from the first paragraph, which is called the *setup*. We recommend using a grid in this situation to organize the information. In this case, we need to decide what goes on top of the grid—the days of the week or the entrees. We are assigning elements (entrees) to places (days), so the days go on top of the grid. Also, we have what is called a *one-to-one correspondence* in this game—there are seven places (days) and seven elements (entrees) that correspond to each of the places. This is a good thing, because it will simplify the number of possible places to which the elements can be assigned.

In general, factors with a natural order (days of the week, rooms numbered 1 through 4) should be placed on top of the diagram. Always put what doesn't change on top of the diagram. For example: Nine people ride to work in three cars. The three cars don't change, but who rides with whom will change, depending on the question. So the cars would go on top of the diagram.

Take a look at our diagram for this game:

Su	M	Tu	W	Th	F	Sa

Draw excruciatingly exact
symbols for the information
given to you

Step 2: Symbolize the Clues

The indented information is where we find the *clues*. We need to symbolize these clues so that we never have to go back to this information again, thereby eliminating all the actual *words*. We're going to use some shorthand to represent the clues, so let's take them one by one.

> The lamb chops must be served either the night before
> or the night after the spaghetti is served.

As you can see, we created a shorthand for each of the entrees, denoting them by their first letter (L = lamb chops and S = spaghetti). We then put these two letters next to each other to show that they must be *consecutive*. We put a box around the two letters to show that this is a "block" of information that is fixed. Finally, we put the double-pointed arrow underneath the block to show that it can be either "LS" or "SL."

The great thing about this piece of information is that it will occupy two of the seven possible spaces. Blocks are pieces of information that will make your job easier, so look for them when you are reading over the clues and deciding whether to do a particular game.

> The roast beef must be served either the night before or
> the night after either the poached salmon or the trout
> is served.

This is also good information, but not quite as good as the "LS" block. We do know that R (roast beef) must be next to either P (poached salmon) or T (trout), so we drew two blocks, remembering to put the word " or " in between to show that it can be either of these two drawings. Note the double arrow again, indicating that it could either be "RT" or "TR" if T is next to R, or "RP" or "PR" if P is next to R. The good thing here is that it *must* be one or the other of these two symbols.

> The manicotti cannot be served the night before or the
> night after the veal is served.

As you can see, this clue is telling us what we *can't* have. Here, we can't have the M (manicotti) next to the V (veal). So we drew another block, again with the double arrow underneath, and then we drew a slash through the block itself to indicate that this can never be true. We've just drawn our first *anti-block*.

The veal must be served on Monday.

Su	M	Tu	W	Th	F	Sa
	ⓥ↓					

Not surprisingly, the best piece of information is saved until last. As you can see, this piece of information is so definitive that we were able to put it directly into the diagram. Whenever you have information that places one of the elements in a particular slot, put it directly into the diagram. It will save time and your diagram will be better for it. Additionally, we circled the letter and ran an arrow down the appropriate column to show that it will *always* be served on Monday.

Step 3: Double-Check Your Clues and Make Deductions

As we mentioned, this is the time to read over the clues once more to make sure we have the right letters in the right positions. Have you done that? Good. Now, let's take a look at the clues we've drawn to see what kinds of deductions we might make.

The first thing we notice, perhaps, is that V is fixed on Monday. What else do we know about V? That M cannot be next to it. Therefore, we know that M cannot be Sunday or Tuesday, since V is always on Monday. Look at the diagram below to see how we indicated this.

Su	M	Tu	W	Th	F	Sa
-M	ⓥ↓	-M				

Now, what is our next most definitive piece of information? It is the fact that L and S must always be next to each other. This is good information, because there is one place that neither L nor S can go, since they must be next to each other—that place is Sunday. Why? Because there's no consecutive space next to Sunday for the second letter in this block to go to—V is in Monday. Therefore, *neither* L nor S can go in Sunday.

Next, let's go to our R block. We know that one other thing (either P or T) must go next to R. Therefore, R needs a space next to it just like L and S do. Thus, R can't go in Sunday either, for the same reason that L and S can't. Now let's look at the work we did:

Pay close attention to slots that are very restricted.

Su	M	Tu	W	Th	F	Sa
-M-L -S-R	(V)	-M				

Gee, it looks as if Sunday is a very restricted day, right? Four of our seven letters can't go there. If you count V also (which you should), it's actually five out of seven letters that can't go in Sunday. So what can go in Sunday? Only P or T. Let's plot it:

Su	M	Tu	W	Th	F	Sa
-M-L -S-R P/T	(V)	-M				

Clearly, we've done some good work with the left side of our diagram. We looked at each of the clues against the diagram itself, and came up with some solid information to indicate on our diagram. We know that both blocks will need to go to the *right* of Monday. Where exactly can they go? That's what we'll find out in the next step.

Step 4: Identify the Key

What's the key in this game? Well, we just noted that both blocks (L/S, and R/P or R /T) have to go to the *right* of Monday. There are only five spaces vacant to the right of Monday, and both blocks of two spaces each have to fit within those five consecutive spaces. What's the last letter that must go to the right of Monday? M—that's right. We also know that M must go to the right of Tuesday. *However, M can't be on Wednesday or Friday.* Why not? Because if you put M in either of those places, you don't have room for one of the blocks. So here's your final set of deductions:

Su	M	Tu	W	Th	F	Sa
-M-L -S-R P/T	Ⓥ	-M	-M		-M	

We know that this might be the toughest concept we've thrown at you so far. Below is an illustration of what the possibilities are when you've got two blocks of two spaces each that need to go into a total of only five consecutive slots. Take a look at what happens:

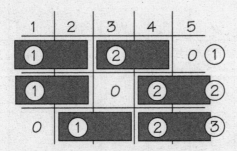

As you can see, the second and fourth spaces are always going to be needed for one half of one of the blocks. In our diagram, we're playing with five spaces—Tuesday, Wednesday, Thursday, Friday, and Saturday. Therefore, M cannot go in either the second (Wednesday) or the fourth (Friday) space, since we have two blocks that we must place in those five spaces. Cool. M seems to be a major key to the diagram, so, if we can place M, which can now only go on Thursday or Saturday, we'll know exactly where our blocks can and can't go!

Step 5: Attack the Questions

There are three words that are almost always used at the beginning of each game question—*if*, *which*, and *suppose*. "If" questions give you an extra piece of information that you can use to further limit the possibilities of your diagram—for that question only. These are the questions you should hunt down and do first. They will be easier than the other questions. If you're given several "If" questions in a game, look for the one that gives you the most information and do that one first—it'll be the easiest question in the set.

"Which" questions, however, don't provide you with any more limiting pieces of information. They are general questions and should be saved for later, after you've answered all the "If" questions. Also "If" questions can help us do later "Which" questions. Finally, "Suppose" questions change one of the original conditions of the game—these questions should be done LAST. They are rare but do show up occasionally.

Let's answer the "If" questions in this game and see how we do.

2. If lamb chops are served on Saturday, which one of the following must be true?

(A) The spaghetti is served on Thursday.
(B) The roast beef is served on Tuesday.
(C) The manicotti is served on Thursday.
(D) The poached salmon is served on Wednesday.
(E) The trout is served on Sunday.

Here's how to crack it

Fill in your diagram:

As you can see, putting L into the Saturday slot forces the S into the Friday slot, since they need to be together. And since M can only go on Saturday or Thursday, we know that M is now in the Thursday slot. L in Saturday, S in Friday, and M in Thursday: these three things MUST be true. We don't know for sure where R, P, or T are. But let's look at the answer choices and see if we can find an answer. We can—it's answer choice (C). None of the other four choices MUST be true, though some of them could be true.

On to our next "If" question:

3. If the trout is served on Thursday, the poached salmon
   must be served on

   (A) Sunday
   (B) Tuesday
   (C) Wednesday
   (D) Friday
   (E) Saturday

Here's how to crack it

Fill in your diagram:

Place all your blocks before looking at the answer choices.

This question tells us to put T into Thursday. This of course will now force M into Saturday. It will also force P into Sunday, since Sunday can be only P or T. Finally, there are only three spaces left, and only two (Tuesday and Wednesday) are consecutive. Thus, the S/L block must go into Tuesday and Wednesday. Now, we've only got R left, and the only place it can go is Friday. What's the question again? P must be where? Sunday, of course. (A) is our answer. On this question, we wound up being able to fill in almost all the slots—and we didn't even need to do that!

Here's our third "If" question:

4. If the roast beef is served on Saturday, which one of the following must be true?

(A) The trout is served on Friday.
(B) The manicotti is served on Thursday.
(C) The spaghetti is served on Wednesday.
(D) The lamb chops are served on Tuesday.
(E) The poached salmon is served on Sunday.

Here's how to crack it
Fill in your diagram:

Su	M	Tu	W	Th	F	Sa
-M-L -S-R P/T	Ⓥ	-M	-M		-M	
				M	S	L ②
P		S/L	S/L	T	R	M ③
P/T	↓	S/L	S/L	M	P/T	R ④

So we've got R in Saturday. We know that M is in Thursday, and that P or T must be in the Friday slot next to R. This once again pushes the S/L block into Tuesday and Wednesday. Therefore, which of the answer choices MUST be true? Only (B). We're really smokin' now, aren't we?

We've got only two questions left now. Both of them begin with the word "Which," indicating that the questions will be general in nature. Typically, this means that you are going to have to use some sort of Process of Elimiation to get the right answer. It won't jump out at you like the answers to the "If" questions did. Therefore, here's step 6.

Step 6: Use Process of Elimination

Process of Elimination in games comes into play when you have not been given any information in the question with which to get your own answers before you read the answer choices. Therefore, you have to attack the choices themselves and get rid of the four that are wrong in some way. Take a look at the following question:

1. Which one of the following is a possible menu in order from Sunday to Saturday?
   - (A) Lamb chops, spaghetti, roast beef, trout, manicotti, poached salmon, veal
   - (B) Roast beef, poached salmon, lamb chops, spaghetti, veal, trout, manicotti
   - (C) Spaghetti, veal, lamb chops, manicotti, poached salmon, roast beef, trout
   - (D) Trout, veal, roast beef, poached salmon, manicotti, lamb chops, spaghetti
   - (E) Trout, veal, manicotti, poached salmon, roast beef, lamb chops, spaghetti

Here's how to crack it

This is the easiest kind of "Which" question to do. It's called a Possible Arrangement question. They are easy because all you have to do is take each clue from the setup and apply it to each answer choice, eliminating any choice that violates a clue. Start with the easiest clue to check:

> The veal must be served on Monday.

Possible Arrangement questions: Apply each clue to each answer choice.

Choices (A) and (B) violate this clue. Eliminate them. Next clue to check:

> The lamb chops must be served either the night before or the night after the spaghetti is served.

Choice (C) violates this clue. Eliminate it. Next clue to check:

> The manicotti cannot be served the night before or the night after the veal is served.

Choice (E) violates this clue. Eliminate it. You're done. The only choice left is choice (D).

Cool, huh? You could have opted to check M's location additionally, since you deduced that it can only go on either Thursday or Saturday. That's another reason why (C) and (E) are wrong.

NOTE: Remember, your process here is to take the clues and apply them to the choices, *not* the other way around. Taking each choice and applying it to each of the clues will take more time. Normally, each clue in a game question will eliminate one of the choices. If you take each clue and apply it to the answer choices, it will be quicker because you only have to read each clue once. Believe it.

Here's our last "Which" question. Go to it:

5. Which one of the following is a night on which the manicotti could be served?

    (A) Sunday
    (B) Tuesday
    (C) Wednesday
    (D) Friday
    (E) Saturday

Here's how to crack it

Well, we deduced that M can only go one of two places—Thursday and Saturday. You can also check back to you previous work and see where M has been placed throughout the game—you'll see that Thursday and Saturday are the only possible answers. Only Saturday is listed in the choices, so (E) is our answer. Cake.

So, what did we just do? Once again, here's the step-by-step approach to all games:

Step 1:   Decide on the Appropriate Diagram and Draw It

Step 2:   Symbolize the Clues

Step 3:   Double-Check Your Clues and Make Deductions

Step 4:   Identify the Key

Step 5:   Attack the Questions

Step 6:   Use Process of Elimination

GAMES TECHNIQUES: GOOD SYMBOLIZATION

Good symbolization is a major key to getting all the questions in a particular game correct. Your symbols should be simple, concise, and, most importantly, in harmony with your diagram and the other symbols for that particular game. Go ahead and symbolize the clues listed below. Symbolize each clue next to the clue itself. Then compare your symbol with the symbol we have. We'll explain how we got to ours, and why you should be symbolizing along the same lines we are.

Anna sits to the east of Bob and to the west of Carol.

This is a very common type of clue. It's testing your ability to read carefully and to recognize the fact that you are being given two separate pieces of information. You can of course consolidate these pieces of information into one symbol, but be careful! Make sure you know which way is east and which way is west—under time pressure, these basic pieces of knowledge do tend to disintegrate.

B ~ A ~ C

As you can see, we've put A in between B and C. "To the east" means "to the right," so the first thing we did was to put A to the right of B. Then, we read that A sits "to the west," i.e., "to the left," of Carol. We didn't put this in a box because we don't know whether or not these people are sitting right next to each other—all we know is "right" and "left." Therefore we used the squiggly line to indicate possible *expansion* of the letters in relation to each other.

The two doctors never sit together.

Too bad for them. This is very similar to a clue we had in the game we just did. We know that there are two Ds and that these two Ds can never be together. It's a simple anti-block:

If the game ever gives us the placement of one of the doctors, we know now that the other doctor can't go immediately to the right or left of the first one. We also know that there are only two doctors from the phraseology, "The two doctors..."

In a five-story building, J lives two floors above W.

Here's a chance to actually draw a diagram. We can draw a five-story building first:

Then, we can symbolize the fact that J lives two floors above W. But be careful here—if you live two floors above your friend, for instance, there is only *one* floor that actually separates you. Take a look at our symbol:

J
I
W

As you can see, the phraseology is meant to lead you astray. Your goal is to visualize the information given, and to read the clues carefully and double-check them before you begin the game. If you had inserted an extra floor, your game would swiftly degenerate into chaos. Also, notice the fact that our symbol was consistent with the flow of the diagram—we drew a vertical diagram, so we drew a vertical symbol.

Reread each clue to see if your visual matches the exact text of the clue!

The three boys are flanked by two girls.

This clue gives you several pieces of information. First, there are three boys. Second, there are two girls. Third, the three boys all sit together. Fourth, one girl sits on either end of the line of boys. Let's put it all together:

G B B B G

Notice how we didn't just write "3B" and "2G." Instead, we wrote three separate B letters and two separate G letters. That's consistent with the information the clue gives. If the clue involves five engines, for instance, draw "EEEEE" and not "5E." The former is much more visual, which is your goal.

Hannah will attend the dance only if David attends the dance.

Here, we have an instance of "if...then" terminology. Remember this from Arguments? As always, we've got to make sure that the correct person is on the left side of our arrow. Here's another tip as to which person should go on the left of the diagram—put the person with the "problem" or "condition" on the left side of the arrow. Who is the restricted person? Here's what we got:

$$H \longrightarrow D$$

Cool. Hannah had the problem; she went on the left side of the arrow. And remember, if you had put David on the left side of the arrow, you wouldn't have been forced to put anything to the right side of the arrow. So what's your contrapositive here, hotshot? Ours is:

$$-D \longrightarrow -H$$

Well, if yours looked like ours, then you remembered that to get the contrapositive, you have to do two things: Flip the letters and negate the letters. So we know not only that Hannah attends the dance only if David attends, but also that if David doesn't go to the dance, neither can Hannah. Too bad for her.

A, B, and C are tuba players; D, E, and F are cellists.

In this case, we are given elements and then told that these elements all have a particular characteristic. We should also probably differentiate, if possible, between the tuba players and the cellists. How can we do that?

$$A_t B_t C_t d_c e_c f_c$$

As you can see, we used the "subscript" method here, merely adding a small "t" or "c" after the elements. We also differentiated the cellists by making them lowercase. This will come in handy for when you have two sets of elements and you need to differentiate between the two in some way. Finally, note that we didn't merely say "A, B, C = t" or something like that. We're going to have to move the elements around during the game; adding the subscripts will give you the added advantage of moving each element's classification automatically with the element itself.

There is at least one fire drill per week.

Yes, we know this stuff is endlessly fascinating. How would you do this one? Well, we really don't know too much about this game yet, so let's make something very basic:

$$F^+$$

We just drew an F, but we did use the superscript of the plus sign to indicate that there may be more than one (i.e., "at least one," as the clue says) fire drill in a given week. Awesome.

Here's a summary chart of how we symbolized each clue:

CLUE	SYMBOL
Anna sits to the east of Bob and to the west of Carol.	$B \sim A \sim C$
The two doctors never sit together.	D/D (crossed out)
In a five-story building, J lives two floors above W.	5 / 4 / 3 / 2 / 1 J / I / W
The three boys are flanked by two girls.	G B B B G
Hannah will attend the dance only if David attends the dance.	$H \longrightarrow D$
[Contrapositive]	$-D \longrightarrow -H$
A, B, and C are tuba players; D, E, and F are cellists.	$A_t B_t C_t d_c e_c f_c$
There is at least one fire drill per week.	F^+

GAMES TECHNIQUES: WHEN NOT TO SYMBOLIZE

Ideally, you should symbolize every clue. Some clues, however, are difficult to symbolize, especially negative clues that do not refer to any specific element. For example, consider the following clues:

If you can't think of a quick and simple way to symbolize a clue, circle it and move on.

> No more than three books of the same subject are put on the shelf.
> Players cannot score more than three points in the first round.

These clues cannot quickly be symbolized in any convenient fashion. The key word, as always, is *quickly*. If you cannot think of a way to symbolize a clue, put an asterick next to it, then put an asterick in your list of clues. Then you won't forget that there was a clue you couldn't symbolize. Now let's try another game.

GAME #2: PICTURE FRAME

Adapt your diagram to the description of the arrangement of elements given to you in the setup.

Not all games will fall into the predictable pattern of a grid. Read the setup slowly to determine what kind of diagram is needed to show the relationship between the "spaces" and the elements that are assigned to those spaces. Typically the description that is given is fairly explicit—if you're reading carefully. Try the game below, giving yourself fifteen minutes. Then see how we attacked it.

Family pictures are displayed in a circular frame that holds six pictures. The pictures to choose from are: aunt, brother, father, mother, sister, uncle. The arrangement of the pictures mmust meet the following conditions:

The uncle must not be displayed next to the brother.
The aunt must not be displayed next to the mother.
The sister must be displayed next to the mother.

1. If the sister is displayed to the immediate right of the aunt, which picture must be displayed to the immediate right of the sister?

   (A) the aunt
   (B) the brother
   (C) the father
   (D) the mother
   (E) the uncle

2. Which one of the following is a possible arrangement of the pictures in the circular frame?

   (A) mother, aunt, sister, uncle, brother, father
   (B) mother, aunt, uncle, brother, sister, father
   (C) uncle, father, brother, aunt, mother, sister
   (D) uncle, sister, mother, brother, aunt, father
   (E) uncle, aunt, sister, mother, father, brother

3. If the mother is displayed next to the brother, which one of the following is a complete and accurate list of the pictures that can be displayed on the other side of the brother?

   (A) the father
   (B) the father, the aunt
   (C) the father, the aunt, the sister
   (D) the sister, the aunt, the uncle
   (E) the father, the sister, the aunt, the uncle

4. If the uncle is displayed next to the mother, and the aunt is displayed next to the sister, which one of the following pictures must be displayed on the other side of the aunt?

   (A) the brother
   (B) the father
   (C) the mother
   (D) the sister
   (E) the uncle

5. If there are two pictures between the uncle and the father, which two pictures must be surrounding the brother?
   - (A) the mother and the father
   - (B) the mother and the aunt
   - (C) the father and the sister
   - (D) the father and the aunt
   - (E) the sister and the uncle

Cracking Game #2

Step 1: Decide on the Appropriate Diagram and Draw It

Are you assigning things to places? Yes. Is there still a one-to-one correspondence between the number of places and the number of elements? Yes. The only difference here is that a circle is being given to you instead of a grid. How do you quickly and efficiently draw a circle with six even spaces? Take a look:

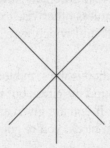

> Redraw non-gridlike diagrams for each question you answer!

Cool, huh? This diagram is three lousy little lines! It will take you nanoseconds to draw it. However, you'll need to re-draw this diagram for each question, because it's not in the form of a grid like the first game. And it's important to write small and redraw so your previous work is saved. Now let's symbolize the clues.

Step 2: Symbolize the Clues

We have blocks and anti-blocks, as follows:

The uncle must not be displayed next to the brother.

As you can see, we're going to draw our clues the same way we drew them in game 1. The fact that it's around a circle doesn't really matter. The positions of the elements next to each other still matter, however, so we've still got the little double arrow underneath the anti-block in this clue.

The aunt must not be displayed next to the mother.

Same as above. You're doing great.

The sister must be displayed next to the mother.

Good! Finally a piece of positive information—by the way, the best clue is very often the last clue given in the list of clues, so don't get discouraged. Now let's see if we can make any deductions.

Step 3: Double-Check Your Clues and Make Deductions
Have you re-read the clues to make sure you've symbolized correctly? Good. Is it possible to make any deductions here? Well, one thing you should remember is that there is no starting point or ending point on a circle. So when you begin to place the elements around the circle, it doesn't matter exactly where on the circle you place those elements. Additionally, always assume that the elements are facing the circle inwards (unless otherwise explicitly stated in the game) so you know which way is "right" and which way is "left" for each element.

Step 4: Identify the "Key"
By far our best piece of information is the s/m block. You could theoretically just place this block somewhere around the circle, but you don't know whether or not m is to the left or the right of s. If you are given any extra information that gives the exact positioning of the s/m block, you're golden. Do those questions first.

Step 5: Attack the Questions
Remember to look for questions that begin with the word "If." These questions will give you information. And remember that the key to this game is the s/m block, so look for questions that contain more information about either s or m. Let's hit it:

1. If the sister is displayed to the immediate right of the aunt, which picture must be displayed to the immediate right of the sister?

   (A) the aunt
   (B) the brother
   (C) the father
   (D) the mother
   (E) the uncle

Here's how to crack it
We're going to draw another diagram. We will put s at the end of one of the spokes of our six-pointed wheel, facing inward. Then, we will put a to the left of s, and then we'll see what else we can figure out.

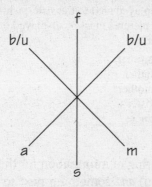

As you can see, we were able to get pretty far here. We were able to place a and s, and then we were able to place m on the other side (the right side) of s. Additionally, we were able to definitively place f as well, because b and u cannot be together, and there were only three consecutive places remaining to place b, u, and f. However, we didn't even need to get that far—all we needed to know was who is to the immediate right of the sister—m. This is a Must-Be-True question, and the only thing that must be true is (D).

Let's do the next question:

You should always attack "If...must be true" questions FIRST.

3. If the mother is displayed next to the brother, which one of the following is a complete and accurate list of the pictures that can be displayed on the other side of the brother?

(A) the father
(B) the father, the aunt
(C) the father, the aunt, the sister
(D) the sister, the aunt, the uncle
(E) the father, the sister, the aunt, the uncle

Here's how to crack it

Fill in your diagram, and don't forget the blocks and antiblocks:

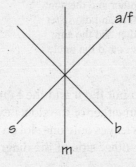

The first thing we must do is put m and b next to each other. Next, we have to put s on the other side of m. This leaves only three possible elements that can go on the other side of b. And finally, we know that u can never be next to b, so we're down to two elements—a and f. What answer choice contains these and only these letters? (B).

4. If the uncle is displayed next to the mother, and the aunt is displayed next to the sister, which one of the following pictures must be displayed on the other side of the aunt?

(A) the brother
(B) the father
(C) the mother
(D) the sister
(E) the uncle

Here's how to crack it

We've been given a nice string of information for this question. We have something next to m (element u) *and* something next to s (element a). This means we've got an a-s-m-u block that we can place around the diagram. Let's do it:

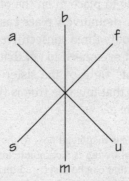

As you can see, the a-s-m-u block forces both b and f into specific slots. Therefore, the picture displayed on the other side of the aunt is the brother, so the answer is (A). Let's go to another "If" question:

5. If there are two pictures between the uncle and the father, which two pictures must be surrounding the brother?

(A) the mother and the father
(B) the mother and the aunt
(C) the father and the sister
(D) the father and the aunt
(E) the sister and the uncle

Here's how to crack it

This information tells you to put the u and the f on opposite ends of the circle. You know that b cannot be in either of the slots next to u, so it has to go in one of the two slots next to f. This leaves only one slot on one side of the diagram, and two consecutive slots on the other side of the diagram.

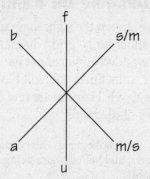

As you can see, the s/m block had to go where the two consecutive slots were, so therefore the last open slot is for a. Thus, a and f must be the two pictures surrounding the brother—answer choice (D).

Step 6: Use Process of Elimination

The final question in this game is a "Which" question. Fortunately, it's also a Possible Arrangement question. All we need to do is apply each of the clues to the answer choices, and see which ones are eliminated. Go to it:

2. Which one of the following is a possible arrangement of the pictures in the circular frame?

   (A) mother, aunt, sister, uncle, brother, father
   (B) mother, aunt, uncle, brother, sister, father
   (C) uncle, father, brother, aunt, mother, sister
   (D) uncle, sister, mother, brother, aunt, father
   (E) uncle, aunt, sister, mother, father, brother

Here's how to crack it

That was cool, right? The first clue (the u/b antiblock) knocked out (A), (B), and (E)—(E) because the frame is a circle, so the first and sixth positions are next to each other. The second clue (the a/m antiblock) knocked out (C). We're done. The answer is (D).

Nice job—you've completed another whole game!

GAMES TECHNIQUES: DRAWING THE RIGHT DIAGRAM

How do you know if you've drawn the right diagram? Well, the first thing you should try to do is always shoot for a "grid" diagram. These will be the easiest to draw, and you'll have the added bonus of not having to re-draw the diagram for each question. However, sometimes you will have to approach the drawing of a diagram as in the game above. Here are are few more scenarios that indicate how to draw different types of diagrams:

Eight dishes—artichoke, beef, celery, danish, eggplant, fennel, grapes, and halibut—are being placed around a circular table.

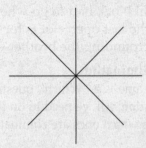

This is very similar to what you just did, only now you have to draw an eight-pointed wheel.

There are six houses—A, B, C, D, E, and F—on a street. Three houses are on the north side of the street and three houses are on the south side of the street. House 1 faces house 4, house 2 faces house 5, and house 3 faces house 6.

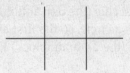

This sounds complex but as you can see, the diagram turns out to be three very simple lines again. This diagram showed up on the real LSAT very recently.

Eight animals—A, B, C, D, E, F, G, and H—are in eight cages. Cage 1 faces cage 5, cage 2 faces cage 6, cage 3 faces cage 7, and cage 4 faces cage 8.

All that's different about this one is that you have to draw a total of four lines. This, too, showed up on the LSAT.

Occasionally, the LSAT folks will be given to a fit of generosity and will provide you with a diagram. By all means, use their diagram. Copy it as many times as you need to. Draw it a bit more simply if necessary. Don't look a gift horse in the mouth.

Games Techniques: Question Strategy

Here are some general strategies for dealing with the different types of games questions:

Make sure you've got this question strategy down COLD. Put it next to your Arguments chart on your refrigerator.

- On Must-Be-True questions, try to disprove each answer choice. The choice that's always true is the right answer. The wrong answers could be false. These questions are looking for the only possible answer; therefore, you should do these first when you encounter an "If...must be true" question.

- On Could-Be-True questions, try the answer choices. When you find a choice that's possible, that's the correct answer. The wrong answers cannot be true. These questions usually will require more work than Must-Be-True questions.

- On Must-Be-False questions, try each answer choice. The answer choice that cannot be true is the right answer. The wrong answers could be true. Very similar to Must-Be-True questions.

- On Could-Be-False questions, try to disprove each answer choice. The choice that's not always true is the right answer. The wrong answers must be true.

- On Possible-Arrangement questions, use Process of Elimination. Start with the most definite clue and eliminate all answer choices that violate it. Do this with each clue.

- On questions that start with the word "Suppose," either a new clue is added to the original clues or one of the original clues is removed. Do these questions last, because the change in the rules applies only to this question. Always remember to check all the original clues that are not changed. Chances are at least one of your deductions will no longer be valid for this question.

- On Except/Cannot questions, circle the "except/cannot" to help you remember, then do the question in reverse. For example, if the question asks, "All of the following could be true EXCEPT," eliminate every answer choice that could be true. Check every answer choice; the one that is not like the others is the correct answer.

GAME #3: TENANTS AND APARTMENTS

You will be able to use a grid diagram with many types of games. However, at times you'll manage two or more sets of elements within this grid diagram. Not to worry—it's very approachable. Give yourself another 15 minutes to do this question.

Eight tenants—J, K, L, M, N, O, P, and Q—live in a five-story building. On each floor, there is one studio apartment and one one-bedroom apartment. From the ground floor up, the floors are numbered one through five. The following is known about the tenants' living arrangements:

No tenant shares an apartment with any other tenant.
No one lives in the fifth-floor studio.
No one lives in the third-floor one-bedroom.
M lives in the second-floor studio.
P lives in the fourth-floor studio.
M and O each live on a higher floor than Q.
K, N, and Q live in one-bedroom apartments.

1. If K lives on a lower floor than P, then who must live in the second-floor one-bedroom?

    (A) J
    (B) K
    (C) L
    (D) N
    (E) Q

2. What is the maximum number of tenants any one of whom could be the one who lives in the fifth-floor one-bedroom?

    (A) 1
    (B) 2
    (C) 3
    (D) 4
    (E) 5

3. If J lives on a lower floor than L, then which of the following statements must be false?

    (A) J lives in the second-floor one-bedroom.
    (B) K lives in the fourth-floor one-bedroom.
    (C) L lives in the third-floor studio.
    (D) N lives in the fourth-floor one-bedroom.
    (E) O lives in the fifth-floor one-bedroom.

4. If P lives on the floor above O, and O lives on the floor above N, then what is the maximum number of possible living arrangements for all eight tenants?

    (A) 1
    (B) 2
    (C) 3
    (D) 4
    (E) 5

5. Suppose that M moves from the second-floor studio into the second-floor one-bedroom, but all the other conditions remain the same. Which of the following statements could be false?

   (A) J lives on a floor below K.
   (B) K lives on a floor below N.
   (C) L lives on a floor below K.
   (D) O lives on a floor below N.
   (E) O lives on a floor below K.

Cracking Game #3

Step 1: Decide on the Appropriate Diagram and Draw It

This looks a bit more complex than the first two diagrams, but we still have a one-to-one correspondence with elements to places. We know there are eight non-empty apartments, and eight people that will live in them. The only difference here is that we have two types of apartments: studios and one-bedrooms. Here's how we drew our diagram:

	S	1B	S	1B	S	1B
5						
4						
3						
2						
1						

We're back to a grid here— now it's just two columns for each question.

First, we drew a vertical grid because it will mimic the same design as an apartment building. The clues and questions will be using words like "above" and "below" when referring to the relationship between the elements, so a vertical diagram will keep us in line with that. Second, notice the fact that we really had to make two columns for the grid—a studio apartment column and then a one-bedroom column. We showed the difference between the columns by making dashed lines. We're using solid lines to indicate when we've changed to a new question. Now let's look at the clues.

Step 2: Symbolize the Clues

The first four clues are all things we can put directly into our diagram. Here they are:

> No one lives in the fifth-floor studio.
> No one lives in the third-floor one-bedroom.
> M lives in the second-floor studio.
> P lives in the fourth-floor studio.

We'll get to these clues in a minute. The fifth clue is this:

M and O each live on a higher floor than Q.

This clue is giving us two pieces of information, that both M and O live on a higher floor than Q. Here are our symbols for this clue:

As you can see, all we did was show how M and O are both "above" Q. We used the squiggly line because we don't know how far above Q they are. Here's the sixth and final clue:

K, N, and Q live in one-bedrooms.

Now we know that K, N, and Q all have to be in the one-bedroom column. We made a quick notation of that:

K,N,Q = 1B

However, we'll probably wind up integrating this information directly into the diagram before we go to the questions. Now, here are the first four clues again—and then our diagram that shows how we added the information.

No one lives in the fifth-floor studio.
No one lives in the third-floor one-bedroom.
M lives in the second-floor studio.
P lives in the fourth-floor studio.

	S	1B	S	1B	S	1B	S	1B
5	✕							
4	P							
3		✕						
2	M							
1								

So we've put Xs through the two empty apartments and then put the P and the M directly into the diagram. Now we're ready for step 3.

Step 3: Double-Check Your Clues and Make Deductions

Did you reread the clues to make sure you symbolized correctly? Good. As for deductions, if M lives on the second floor and must live above Q, then Q must live on the first floor. Since Q must live in a one-bedroom, Q lives in the first-floor one-bedroom. That's our first major deduction. There are several more deductions that we can make. Take a look at the diagram to see how many other deductions you got. Remember also that we wanted to indicate that K, N, and Q all had to be in one-bedrooms. Here is our diagram:

Make sure your diagram clearly indicates any spaces that won't have elements in them.

	S 1B	S 1B	S 1B	S 1B
5	✕			
4	P			
3	-N -K ✕			
2	M			
1	-O -N -K J/L Q			

There are only two studios that remain open. Both are limited because neither N nor K can go in them. Furthermore, O cannot go in the first-floor studio either, because O must be higher than Q. Therefore, the first-floor studio is an extremely limited space, and the only remaining elements than can go in it are J or L.

Step 4: Identify the Key

Make sure you always go back and refer to all the wonderful deductions you made. The first-floor studio is a restricted space, so always attempt to fill that space if possible. The key here is that studios are much more restricted than one-bedrooms. You've got a lot going on in this game, so make sure to go slow enough when filling in all the letters. You've done great work so far—don't go too fast and get twisted around.

Step 5: Attack the Questions

Here's our first "If" question.

1. If K lives on a lower floor than P, then who must live in the second-floor one-bedroom?

    (A) J
    (B) K
    (C) L
    (D) N
    (E) Q

Here's how to crack it

Great. This "If" question is giving you more information. It's telling you that K must live on a lower floor than P. So take a look at our diagram:

	S	1B	S	1B	S	1B	S	1B
5	X							
4	P							
3	-N -K	X						
2	M							
1	-O -N -K J/L	Q						

That's right! K is forced into the second-floor one-bedroom, and hence it's our answer. Circle (B). Let's hit the next "If" question.

3. If J lives on a lower floor than L, then which of the following statements must be false?

(A) J lives in the second-floor one-bedroom.
(B) K lives in the fourth-floor one-bedroom.
(C) L lives in the third-floor studio.
(D) N lives in the fourth-floor one-bedroom.
(E) O lives in the fifth-floor one-bedroom.

Here's how to crack it

Well, this settles the question about the first-floor studio, doesn't it? If J is lower than L, that means that J must live on the first-floor studio and L must be somewhere above the first floor. Take a look at our diagram:

	S	1B	S	1B	S	1B	S	1B
			①		③			
5	X		X		X			
4	P		P		P			
3	-N -K	X	X	-N -K	X			
2	M		M	K	M			
1	-O -N -K J/L	Q	J/L	Q	J	Q		

The question is asking which one choice must be false. Your goal here is to cross out any choices that can be true. You do this by reading each choice and looking at your diagram. So let's do that. (A) cannot be true because we've already definitively placed J on the first floor. So it's our answer. (B), (C), (D), and (E) can all be true since those spaces are still open on the diagram! Let's move on.

4. If P lives on the floor above O, and O lives on the floor above N, then what is the maximum number of possible living arrangements for all eight tenants?

    (A) 1
    (B) 2
    (C) 3
    (D) 4
    (E) 5

Here's how to crack it

This question contains two very good pieces of information. Let's put the information in first and then talk about exactly what information the question wants from you.

	S	1B	S	1B	S	1B	S	1B
			①		③		④	
5	X	X	X	X	X	X	X	X
4	P		P		P		P	
3	-N -K	X	X	X	-N -K	X	O	X
2	M		M	K	M		M	N
1	-o -n -K J/L	Q	J/L	Q	J	Q	J/L	Q

Keep everything neat so you can quickly refer back to your previous work.

Cool. We've definitively placed two other elements. However, the question is asking us about how many ways the full diagram can look. The manner in which the question is phrased ("the maximum number of possible living arrangements for all eight tenants") is confusing and pretentious. So translate it! Then, write out the actual possibilites to the side of your diagram. The only open spaces are the first-floor studio, the fourth-floor one-bedroom, and the fifth-floor one-bedroom. Additionally, the first-floor studio can only be one of two possible elements—J or L. So break it down like this:

WHEN J IS IN 1S:

1S	41B	51B
J	K	L

OR

1S	41B	51B
J	L	K

WHEN L IS IN 1S:

1S	41B	51B
L	J	K

OR

1S	41B	51B
L	K	J

So we've got two possibilities for each of the two scenarios—when J is in the first-floor studio, and when L is in the first-floor studio. Hence, a total of four possibilities, so the answer is (D). Let's move on.

Step 6: Use Process of Elimination

The final two questions in this game are a "Which" question and a "Suppose" question. Let's take care of the "Which" question first.

2. What is the maximum number of tenants any one of whom could be the one who lives in the fifth-floor one-bedroom?

    (A) 1
    (B) 2
    (C) 3
    (D) 4
    (E) 5

Here's how to crack it

This is an overly complex way of asking how many different people can be in the fifth-floor one-bedroom. You know it can't be P, M, or Q. Now check your previous work and see who we've placed there before: on question 4, we put K, J, and L there. This leaves us with O and N. Can we put them there without breaking any rules? Try and you'll find you can. So the correct answer is (E).

Now let's knock out the last question, the "Suppose" question. You can use your original diagram for this question, but you must review all the clues before you can begin to definitively place things again.

5. Suppose that M moves from the second-floor studio into the second-floor one-bedroom, but all the other conditions remain the same. Which of the following statements could be false?

    (A) J lives on a floor below K.
    (B) K lives on a floor below N.
    (C) L lives on a floor below K.
    (D) O lives on a floor below N.
    (E) O lives on a floor below K.

Here's how to crack it

Well, we have to shift M over to the second-floor one-bedroom. Do that, and then make sure that this doesn't screw up any of your original deductions. Does it?

	S	1B	S	1B	S	1B	S	1B	S	1B
		①		③		④		⑤		
5	X	X	X	X	X		X		X	K/N
4	P		P		P		P		P	K/N
3	-N -K	X	X		-N -K	X	O	X	X	
2	M		M	K	M		M	N	M	
1	-O -N -K J/L	Q	J/L	Q	J	Q	J/L	Q	J/L	Q

Fortunately, it doesn't. In fact, it further limits the diagram (as we've indicated) because now K and N only have two places to go. So now let's attack the answer choices, and we'll do that by eliminating anything that must be true. (A) must be true, since K, N, P, and an empty apartment take up the entire fourth and fifth floors. Cross it out. (B) does not have to be true—K could also live above N. Therefore, it "could be false" and it's our answer. (C), (D), and (E) all must be true, if you feel like checking.

GAMES TECHNIQUES: MAKING DEDUCTIONS

We've worked through three games now and it's probably obvious that if you can make deductions before you go and work the questions, the questions become much easier. And you can't make deductions by glancing briefly at your diagram and clues in your haste to get to the questions. You have to look carefully at the diagram and the symbols you've drawn from the clues. There's a quick three-step process you should use :

Three ways to make deductions: Learn them.

- Take each symbol and apply it to the diagram. Write in any deductions.

- Take each symbol and apply it to all the other symbols. Combine if appropriate, or write a new symbol. Write in any deductions.

- Take a step back and look at your entire diagram. Notice any spaces that are extremely "limited," i.e., have lots of minuses in them. See if there are only one or two remaining choices for that space. Write in any deductions.

These three steps should take you at least thirty to forty-five seconds. This is time well spent; you'll spend much less time on the questions, since you won't have to "test" all of the answer choices to see if they work. Some answer choice "testing" will always occur, but the less of that you have to do, the better! It's a time-waster.

Wow. We're about halfway through the Games chapter—you're doing great!

GAME #4: HATS AND SCARVES

A few tips before we start this game: One, reread the section on "making deductions"; two, remember our old friend the contrapositive. Give yourself fifteen minutes and then all will become clear to you.

A window display is being created featuring four hats and three scarves. The only hats being considered are A, B, C, D, E, and F, and the only scarves being considered are J, K, L, M, and N.

If A is displayed, then neither B nor L can be displayed.

B is displayed only if D is displayed.

C cannot be displayed unless J is displayed.

D can only be displayed if K is displayed.

If L is displayed, then M must be displayed.

F cannot be displayed unless D is not displayed.

1. Which one of the following is a possible display of hats in the window?

   (A) A, B, C, F
   (B) A, C, D, E
   (C) A, D, E, F
   (D) B, C, D, F
   (E) B, C, E, F

2. If F is displayed, which one of the following must be true?

   (A) A is not displayed.
   (B) B is not displayed.
   (C) K is not displayed.
   (D) L is displayed.
   (E) M is displayed.

3. If both B and E are displayed, then which one of the following CANNOT be a partial list of items displayed?

   (A) C, D, E
   (B) C, J, M
   (C) C, D, F
   (D) C, J, K
   (E) D, K, M

4. Each of the following could be displayed together EXCEPT

   (A) B and K
   (B) B and F
   (C) B and M
   (D) E and F
   (E) E, J, and M

5. If B is displayed, which one of the following is a list of items that could also be displayed?
   (A)   A, M, N
   (B)   C, E, F
   (C)   C, L, M
   (D)   E, F, M
   (E)   E, J, M

Cracking Game #4

Step 1: Decide on the Appropriate Diagram and Draw It

Well, you've got a lot going on here—first of all, you've got two sets of elements (hats ABCDEF and scarves JKLMN). Next, it doesn't seem as if all the elements will be used, because only four out of the six hats are being displayed, and only three out of the five scarves are being displayed. However, we think it's important to keep track of all the elements. How would you do that? Here's what we did:

```
IN (4+3)          OUT (2+2)
_ _ _ _ / _ _ _   _ _ / _ _
```

> When elements are either "in or out," or "selected or not selected," draw a two-column diagram.

As you can see, we created an "in" column and an "out" column. We've indicated the number of hats and the number of scarves in each column. This will allow us to keep track of all the elements, so if we are given information about whether something is in or whether something is out, we'll be able to use it. Now let's hit the clues.

Step 2: Symbolize the Clues

We've got a whole mess of conditional clues here. Remember that every time you have a conditional clue, you also can deduce the contrapositive. So here's what we have so far:

> Go slowly with "if...then" clues and making contrapositives.

CLUE	CONTRAPOSITIVE
B → D	-D → -B
C → J	-J → -C
D → K	-K → -D
L → M	-M → -L

ANTI-BLOCKS

AB̶

AJ̶

ED̶

> You can save a lot of time and effort by making anti-blocks.

All right. Now let's look a little more closely at these clues. Consider the first clue:

$$A \rightarrow -B \qquad B \rightarrow -A$$

So if A is displayed, B cannot be displayed, and if B is displayed, A cannot be displayed. The end effect is that there is no way both A and B can be displayed at the same time. That means that this is identical to AB̶ because the AB̶ is also telling that A and B cannot be displayed at the same time. So rather than writing out the clue and its contrapositive, we can save a lot of time and effort by just making anti-blocks whenever we have a conditional clue like this one $A \rightarrow -B$.

Step 3: Double-Check Your Clues and Make Deductions

Did you go back and re-read all your clues, making sure that you diagrammed properly? You'd better! Okay, now for the deductions. How can you make deductions with a string of "If...then" statements? By linking similar clues together. Do you see any two clues that can be linked? Take a look below:

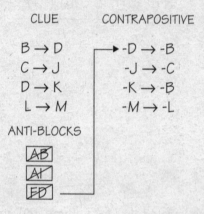

As you can see, there is one point of commonality—D is involved in both an F/D anti-block and a conditional clue. So what does that mean? Well, it means that you can make the following deduction:

$$F \rightarrow -B$$

Why? Because if you have F, you cannot possibly have D, since they are involved in an anti-block. You further know that without D, you cannot possibly have B. Thus, if you have F, you cannot possibly have B. Now, what have we just learned about conditional clues that are formatted like this? That they are actually anti-blocks in disguise. So this clue should read:

$$\boxed{B\cancel{F}}$$

So now we have a fourth anti-block to work with. Notice the fact that two of the elements (E and N) are not restricted at all. But if you get information about any of the other letters, you can begin to fill in pieces of your diagram. And by the way, a minus sign next to a letter in this game means that it goes in the "out" column.

Step 4: Identify the Key

What do you think will most help you with this game? The out column. And what is most useful in dealing with the out column? Anti-blocks. Any time you have an anti-block, you know for certain that one of those two elements must go in the out column. It's possible that both will be there—remember, your clues are about what can and cannot be selected together, not what can and cannot be in the out column together. But if you focus on anti-blocks, you will quickly be able to determine that certain elements will be in the out column.

Step 5: Attack the Questions

Here is our first "If" question. Let's see what we can do with this one.

2. If F is displayed, which one of the following must be true?

   (A) A is not displayed.
   (B) B is not displayed.
   (C) K is not displayed.
   (D) L is displayed.
   (E) M is displayed.

Here's how to crack it

We only seem to have received one piece of information with this question. But remember that one of our deductions was about F, so now that we know where F is, we should know where several other elements can go:

IN (4+3)	OUT (2+2)
_ _ _ _ / _ _ _	_ _ / _ _
F A C E / J _ _	B D / L _ ②

Wow, right? We knew from the question that F was "in." That meant that both B and D are "out." Therefore, we know the exact composition of all of the "in" hats—A, C, E, and F. Once we know that, we can also run through and see that l must be the "out" and that j must be "in." We've filled in almost the entire diagram! So what's our answer? (A) can't be true, because A is "in." (B) must be true, because if F is "in," B is "out." Bingo! Let's go on to the next question.

Did we go too fast for you on that one? Take a look below to see exactly how we got from start to finish:

Notice how it's like falling dominoes...and how whether knowing that something is "out" is just as valuable as knowing that something is "in."

IN (4+3)	OUT (2+2)
_ _ _ _ / _ _ _	_ _ / _ _
F	
F	B _ /
F	BD /
FA	BD /
FA	BD /L_
FAC	BD /L_
FAC / J_ _	BD /L_
FACE / J_ _	BD /L_

Now let's hit the next question.

3. If both B and E are displayed, then which one of the following CANNOT be a partial list of items displayed?

    (A) C, D, E
    (B) C, J, M
    (C) C, D, F
    (D) C, J, K
    (E) D, K, M

Here's how to crack it

We've got two pieces of information in this question. Let's see what that gives us:

IN (4+3)	OUT (2+2)	
_ _ _ _ / _ _ _	_ _ / _ _	
FACE / J_ _	BD /L_	②
CDBE / JK_	FA /L_	③

Once again, we are able to fill in quite a lot here. Since the question tells us that four of the answer choices are correct (remember, we're looking for the one partial list that is invalid), take a look at the letters you placed in your "out" column (A, F, and L), and see if they appear in any of the choices. Choice (C) has F, doesn't it? It's our answer. Let's move on.

5. If B is displayed, which one of the following is a list
   of items that could also be displayed?

   (A) A, M, N
   (B) C, E, F
   (C) C, L, M
   (D) E, F, M
   (E) E, J, M

Here's how to crack it

Only one piece of information again, but that doesn't seem to be stopping us,
does it?

IN (4+3)	OUT (2+2)	
_ _ _ _ / _ _ _	_ _ / _ _	
FACE / J _ _	BD /L _	②
CDBE / JK _	FA /L _	③
CDBE / JK _	FA /L _	⑤

In composition, the arrangement of the letters looks suspiciously like #3,
doesn't it? Only now, we're looking for the only possibility that can work. Any
answer choice that contains something in the "out" column should now be
crossed off. (A), (B), (C), and (D) all contain an element that has been definitively
placed in the "out" column. The answer is (E).

We're in the home stretch. Let's knock out the "Which" questions.

Step 6: Use POE

The final two questions in this game are general questions. The first one is a
partial Possible-Arrangement question. You know how to attack it—so go to it!

1. Which one of the following is a possible display of
   hats in the window?

   (A) A, B, C, F
   (B) A, C, D, E
   (C) A, D, E, F
   (D) B, C, D, F
   (E) B, C, E, F

Here's how to crack it

Take each of the clues from your list of symbols that have to do with the hats,
and apply the clue to each answer choice, eliminating any choice that violates the
clue. "If A then no B" knocks out (A). "If B then D" knocks out (E). "If F then no
D" knocts out (C) and (D). The answer is (B). Sweet. Here's your final question:

4. Each of the following could be displayed together
   EXCEPT

   (A) B and K
   (B) B and F
   (C) B and M
   (D) E and F
   (E) E, J, and M

Here's how to crack it

Well, there are several ways to attack this question. The first is to check your deductions and see if you know anything about any of these choices. In answer choice (B), we've got F and B together, which we know can't be true. If you didn't see that, you can look at your previous work to cross off answer choices you know can work. That would eliminate (A) and (D). You could then "test" answer choice (B) to see if it works or not. It doesn't—so it's our answer.

GAMES TECHNIQUES: GETTING THE CONTRAPOSITIVE

You can't practice enough with "if...then" clues.

The game you just completed required several skills, none more important than being able to symbolize "If...then" clues and then getting the contrapositive of those clues. Below is a little chart that is going to drill you on just these skills. It's a five-column chart. Column 1 has clues. Put your symbols in column 2. The answers are in column 3, so cover it up with a piece of paper. Put the contrapositive of the clues in column 4. Column 5 contains our contrapositives, so cover it up when you're working out the contrapositives. Got it? Go!

CLUE	YOUR SYMBOL	OUR SYMBOL	YOUR CONTRAPOSITIVE	OUR CONTRAPOSITIVE
If Jack attends, Mark must attend.	J M	J → M	-M → -J	-M → -J
Ann will work only if Kate works.	A →K	A → K	-K → -A	-K → -A
Bob cannot work unless Gary is working.	B →G	B → G	-G → B	-G → -B
If Will goes to the party, Cam won't go.*	W → -C	W → -C	C W	C → -W
Doug will not drive unless May also drives.	D →M	D → M	-M → -D	-M → -D
If Harry is invited, both Charles and Linda must be invited.	H → CL	H → [CL]	-CL → -H	-[CL] → -H

* This could be summed up as an antiblock [WC] .

Nice job on the chart. Ready for the next game? Take a break, will ya?

GAME #5: THREE BUSES

Not all games will fit nicely into a one-to-one or two-to-one relationship between slots and elements. Some games will involve the distribution of elements between various slots. You might have twelve animals to place in four cages, or ten people to place in seven houses, for instance. Your first goal is to attempt, if possible, to figure out what the exact distribution is. If you can do that, the game becomes much easier. Look for distribution clues in the information that's presented to you. On this game, give yourself twenty minutes or so—try figuring out the distribution for five minutes. If you get stuck, our solution is at the end! *Bon chance*, as they say in Paris.

Five girls—Fiorenza, Gladys, Helene, Jocelyn, and Kaitlin—and four boys—Abe, Bruce, Clive, and Doug—ride to school each day in three separate buses.

Abe and Fiorenza always ride together.
Gladys and Helene always ride together.
Jocelyn and Kaitlin never ride together.
Doug always rides in the bus with the fewest children.
Boys cannot outnumber girls in any bus.
The maximum number of children in any bus is four.

1. The bus in which Doug rides can hold how many children?

   (A) 1
   (B) 2
   (C) 3
   (D) 4
   (E) 5

2. Bruce can ride with each of the following EXCEPT

   (A) Abe
   (B) Clive
   (C) Doug
   (D) Fiorenza
   (E) Helene

3. If Bruce and Clive ride in the same bus, which one of the following must also be in the bus?

   (A) Abe
   (B) Fiorenza
   (C) Gladys
   (D) Jocelyn
   (E) Kaitlin

4. Which of the following could be a list of all the passengers in one bus?

   (A) Doug, Gladys
   (B) Fiorenza, Abe, Bruce
   (C) Jocelyn, Kaitlin, Clive, Bruce
   (D) Fiorenza, Gladys, Bruce, Clive
   (E) Abe, Bruce, Fiorenza, Jocelyn

5. Abe can NEVER ride with which one of the following?

   (A) Bruce
   (B) Clive
   (C) Gladys
   (D) Jocelyn
   (E) Kaitlin

6. If Bruce rides with Fiorenza, Gladys must ride with which one of the following?

   (A) Clive
   (B) Doug
   (C) Fiorenza
   (D) Jocelyn
   (E) Kaitlin

Cracking Game #5

Step 1: Decide on the Appropriate Diagram and Draw It

First draw the diagram, then worry about distribution.

So we've got a total of nine children to place in three buses. Our diagram will be a simple grid—the only thing missing will be the exact number of children to be placed in each bus:

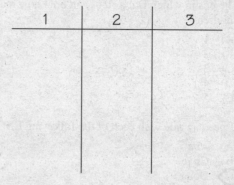

Step 2: Symbolize the Clues

We've got several clues here, and they fit into two categories—relationship clues and distribution clues. The relationship clues are the normal ones we've been seeing up until now—things like blocks and anti-blocks. Distribution clues give you information about how the elements will be distributed throughout the slots. Let's symbolize the relationship clues first:

The first three clues are all pretty straightforward, right? Cool. Now let's briefly symbolize our distribution clues to see if they make any sense:

$$D = \text{fewest}$$

$$\text{Boys} \le \text{Girls}$$

$$\text{Bus} \le 4 \text{ children}$$

Well, we did symbolize this stuff, but it's not exactly setting us on fire, is it? Let's go to step 3 to see how we should be attacking the game at this point.

Step 3: Double-Check Your Clues and Make Deductions

Did you read over the clues to make sure that you've symbolized correctly? Good. Now let's take a look at the game from a bird's-eye view—you've got a bunch of children, a few of whom you don't know anything about (B and C), and you want to know how these children are distributed throughout the buses. If you can figure that out, the questions should be a lot easier, right?

So what's your best distribution clue? The fact that there can't be more than four children in any one bus, right? Let's make a little distribution chart to see what the possibilities are. Remember that buses 1, 2, and 3 represent no particular buses, so it doesn't matter if the bus with four children is the first or second or third bus, or if there even will be a bus with four children. Check out our possibilities below:

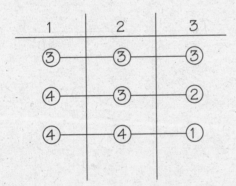

As you can see, this first distribution clue narrows the possibilities to three separate distributions: 3-3-3, 4-3-2, and 4-4-1. Let's take a look at our second clue, the fact that boys cannot outnumber girls in any bus. Does this clue do anything to limit the number of distributions? Yep, you're right. Take a look below:

Yep, that's right. If boys cannot outnumber girls in any bus, and there are four boys, that means that the 3-3-3 distribution cannot be valid for this game. Why not? Because if the distribution is 3-3-3, then in one of the buses, there must be two boys and one girl, which we can't have. Cool. Now what about the final clue, that Doug must ride in the bus with the fewest children? Take a look below:

Spend a few minutes trying to narrow down the possible distributions—it's worth it!

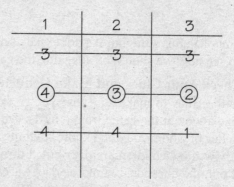

Neat, huh? If Doug must ride in the bus with the fewest children, then the 4-4-1 distribution possibility can't be valid for this game either. Doug would have to go in bus 1, and since Doug is a boy, he can't be the only rider on a bus, since boys cannot outnumber girls in any bus. Therefore, we know that our diagram will look like this:

```
  1   (4)    2   (3)    3   (2)
 _ _ _ _    _ _ _      _ D
```

Since buses 1, 2, and 3 represent no particular buses, as we just said, let's put four children in bus 1, three children in bus 2, and two children in bus 3. Any other deductions? Take a look at the diagram above for a few minutes, and now go back to your relationship clues. Anything click? Check this out:

```
     1          2            3
                          -G-H-F
                           J/K
  B̄ B̄ Ḡ Ḡ    B̄ Ḡ Ḡ        ─    D
                            G    B
```

Yes, we've spent some quality minutes figuring out all this stuff. However, we now know the exact distribution of the children, how many of each gender are in every bus, the definitive placement of one child, and several other limiting factors—such as the fact that neither the G/H block nor the A/F block can go in bus 3, leaving D to go with either J or K only.

Step 4: Identify the Key

As you've probably suspected from the deductions involved, understanding the distribution of elements is the key to this game. In this particular game, we were able to find out the exact distribution. If you get a distribution game where you're not able to figure out the exact distribution, keeping track of the distribution of elements for each question will be your "key." Now, let's hit it.

Step 5: Decide Question Order

As always, let's start with our "If" questions.

2. If Bruce and Clive ride in the same bus, which one of the following must also be in the bus?

(A) Abe
(B) Fiorenza
(C) Gladys
(D) Jocelyn
(E) Kaitlin

Here's how to crack it

Well, you know where B and C have to go if they're together, right? Let's check it out:

1	2	3
$\overline{B}\ \overline{B}\ \overline{G}\ \overline{G}$	$\overline{B}\ \overline{G}\ \overline{G}$	$\frac{J/K}{G}\ \frac{D}{B}$
♭C G H	A F _	_ D ③

As you can see, B and C in the first slot puts the A/F block in the second slot. This then forces the G/H block into slot 1 along with B and C. Looks like (C) is our answer. Now try this one:

3. If Bruce rides with Fiorenza, Gladys must ride with which one of the following?

(A) Clive
(B) Doug
(C) Fiorenza
(D) Jocelyn
(E) Kaitlin

Here's how to crack it

Well, you know that a always comes with F, so you've once again got two boys (A and B) to place. Take a look below:

1	2	3
$\overline{B}\,\overline{B}\,\overline{G}$	$\overline{B}\,\overline{G}\,\overline{G}$	$\dfrac{J/K}{G}$ $\dfrac{D}{B}$
B C G H	A F _	_ D ③
B A F _	C G H	_ D ⑤

So we've got B, A, and F all in bus 1, which means that the G/H block must go in bus 2. A boy must also go in bus 2, and the only one left is C. It's our answer—choice (A).

Never forget that blocks are your best pieces of information—always remember to place them in the diagram.

Step 6: Use Process of Elimination

The final four questions in this game are general. However, you were able to deduce so much that they probably won't present too much of a problem. Let's do this one first:

4. Which of the following could be a list of all the passengers in one bus?

    (A) Doug, Gladys
    (B) Fiorenza, Abe, Bruce
    (C) Jocelyn, Kaitlin, Clive, Bruce
    (D) Fiorenza, Gladys, Bruce, Clive
    (E) Abe, Bruce, Fiorenza, Jocelyn

Here's how to crack it

This is a simple Possible-Arrangement question. Just grab your clues and deductions and apply them to the answer choices. The G/H block eliminates (A) and (D), the boys not being able to outnumber the girls eliminates (B), and the J/K anti-block eliminates (C). We're left with (E). Cool.

5. The bus in which Doug rides can hold how many children?

    (A) 1
    (B) 2
    (C) 3
    (D) 4
    (E) 5

Here's how to crack it

We've answered this one already because we made the proper deductions. It's (B), two children.

1. Bruce can ride with each of the following EXCEPT

   (A) Abe
   (B) Clive
   (C) Doug
   (D) Fiorenza
   (E) Helene

Here's how to crack it

Look at your diagram and your previous work. Is there anywhere B can't go? It can't go with D in bus 3, so (C) is our answer. Also note that you had B with A, C, F, and H in previous questions. Let's kill the last question:

6. Abe can NEVER ride with which one of the following?

   (A) Bruce
   (B) Clive
   (C) Gladys
   (D) Jocelyn
   (E) Kaitlin

Here's how to crack it

We can attack this in several ways, of course—using our previous work is one way. We've had A with both B and C in the past, so (A) and (B) are gone. And since J and K are interchangeable, neither (D) nor (E) can be the answer either. It's (C), Gladys, because you can't have a situation where both blocks are in the same diagram. Try it if you need to, but it won't work because that leaves three boys left to place between buses 2 and 3, which we can't have. So you're done.

Games Techniques: Identifying Difficulty

How can you tell whether a game is "easy" (can be totally worked out in twelve to fifteen minutes) or "hard" (a time-waster that takes you twenty or more minutes)? There are several things you can *look* for, but perhaps the two most important questions to ask are:

1. Can I draw a diagram to illustrate the relationship between slots and elements?

2. Do the clues give me good information that I can plug into this diagram?

If the answers to both of these questions aren't yes, you might want to look around for other games to do. Remember that the questions and answer choices aren't there to increase your understanding of the game. If you're able to draw a diagram and put information into this diagram, the questions should go much faster.

Another key factor to look for is the number of sets of elements. (Is it one set of elements, like children, or two or more, such as children and dogs and scarves?) The more sets of elements you have to deal with, the more time-consuming the game will be. You probably shouldn't start off with a game that has more than two sets of elements.

Finally, always take a look at the questions. If there is a good ratio of "If" to "Which" questions, that's a good thing. If most of the questions are providing you with more information, the game will almost always go much faster. So to recap: Look for games that are easily diagrammable, have good clues, have one or two sets of elements, and have lots of "if" questions. Now let's hit another game.

The order in which you decide to do the games can make or break your LSAT score.

GAME #6: BIRDS AND ANIMALS

Now we think you're ready to handle something a bit more complex. Remember that not all games will have just one of each type of element. Sometimes you will not know how many times a given element might be used. However, your process remains exactly the same for these games as for all other games. Give yourself twenty minutes on this one and see how you do. We're almost there.

Elements used more than once? No big deal.

A zoomaster is deciding which birds and animals will go in five consecutive cages, numbered 1 through 5, left to right. Each cage will contain one of three species of birds—egret, finch, or parrot—and one of three species of animals—antelope, giraffe, or otter. The zoomaster must abide by the following conditions:

If finches are in a given cage, antelopes must also be placed in that cage.

If otters are in a given cage, egrets cannot be in that same cage.

In at least one cage, parrots and antelopes are together.

Parrots are never in consecutive cages.

If egrets and finches are both exhibited, the egrets must always be in lower-numbered cages than the finches.

The second cage contains otters.

1. Which one of the following must be true?

   (A) Egrets are exhibited in the first cage.
   (B) Parrots are exhibited in the second cage.
   (C) Parrots are exhibited in the third cage.
   (D) Antelopes are exhibited in the fourth cage.
   (E) Antelopes are exhibited in the fifth cage.

2. Each of the following is a possible line-up of animals in the five cages EXCEPT

   (A) antelope, otter, antelope, giraffe, otter
   (B) antelope, otter, giraffe, antelope, antelope
   (C) antelope, otter, antelope, antelope, antelope
   (D) giraffe, otter, giraffe, giraffe, antelope
   (E) giraffe, otter, antelope, antelope, antelope

3. Which one of the following is not possible when both egrets and finches are exhibited?

   (A) Antelopes are exhibited in two consecutive cages.
   (B) Finches are exhibited in two consecutive cages.
   (C) Giraffes are not exhibited.
   (D) Otters are exhibited in the third cage.
   (E) Parrots are exhibited in two different cages.

4. If egrets are exhibited in the fifth cage, which one of the following must be true?

   (A) Antelopes are exhibited in the third cage.
   (B) Egrets are exhibited twice.
   (C) Finches are exhibited twice.
   (D) Giraffes are not exhibited in consecutively numbered cages.
   (E) If giraffes are exhibited, then they are exhibited in the fifth cage.

5. If egrets are exhibited twice, each of the following must be true EXCEPT:

   (A) Antelopes are exhibited in the fourth cage.
   (B) Antelopes are exhibited in the fifth cage.
   (C) Egrets and finches are exhibited in consecutively numbered cages.
   (D) If antelopes are exhibited in as many cages as possible, then they are exhibited four times.
   (E) Giraffes cannot be exhibited in consecutively numbered cages.

6. If finches are exhibited twice, it is possible to determine the types of animals and birds for how many of the 10 slots?

   (A) 7
   (B) 6
   (C) 5
   (D) 4
   (E) 3

Cracking Game #6

Step 1: Decide on the Appropriate Diagram and Draw It

Well, the diagram is pretty well laid out for you, isn't it? Five cages, with a bird and an animal in each cage. Here's what we got:

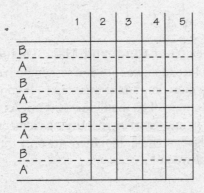

There you go. Now let's hit the clues.

Step 2: Symbolize the Clues

We've got lots of different types of clues, don't we? Clues 1, 2, and 5 are conditional; clue 3 is a block; clue 4 is an anti-block; and clue 6 definitively places something into our diagram. Remember when you have a conditional clue like $O \rightarrow -E$, it's faster to write it as anti-block so $O \rightarrow -E/E \rightarrow -O$ is better written as

Here's what we got for the conditional clues:

$$F \rightarrow A \qquad -A \rightarrow -F$$

$$E + F \rightarrow E \sim F$$

Looks okay, right? Of course, we've added the contrapositives where we could. Here are the other two clues:

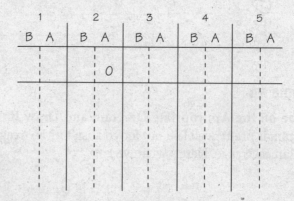

There's a small wrinkle to the block, the fact that we know that there might be more than one of them. So we've added a little "+" after the block to indicate that there might be more than one. Finally, we've got a diagram that has an O placed in the animal slot for cage 2.

Step 3: Double-Check Your Clues and Make Deductions

Spending time making deductions will make doing the questions much easier.

Have you re-read the clues to make sure you've symbolized correctly? The more complex the game, the more important this step is. If you've got one thing even slightly wrong, everything will be totally messed up! As for deductions, there's a major one that you can find. Start by identifying elements that aren't able to go in certain cages, and also remember that there are only three possibilities for any given slot. Here's what we got:

Cool, right? We were able to definitively place P along with O in cage 2, because neither F nor E can go with O—because if you have O, you can't have E, and if you have F, you have to have a with it. Take note of the other "minuses" in the diagram—these will all be very helpful because you've only then got at most two different elements that can go in those slots!

Now, let's consider our conditional clue about finches a little more carefully. If finches are placed in a cage, antelopes must also be placed in that cage. So suppose I have an otter in a cage. Could I have finches? No. What about a giraffe? Again, no. So ultimately, I can also conceive of this clue as two separate anti-blocks: Finches can be with neither giraffes nor otters, because that can be only with antelopes, and each bird can only be with one animal. I could write these deductions thusly:

This is just another way to think of that clue, but it's a useful one. It makes it clear just how restricted F is.

Step 4: Identify the Key

In almost all games that contain two sets of elements, one set will be more restricted than the other. You will have more information on that set of elements, and when answering questions, that set of elements is *the* set you should focus on first. In this game, there are more restrictions and information about the birds than the animals. Additionally, note the fact that you do have a block to place—the P/A block. Where can this block go? It can't go in cage 1, 2, or 3 any more, right? Placing the P/A block is a major key to this game, then. Let's see how we do on the questions.

Step 5: Decide Question Order

We've got three "If" questions to attack, so let's get to 'em!

4. If egrets are exhibited in the fifth cage, which one of the following must be true?

(A) Antelopes are exhibited in the third cage.
(B) Egrets are exhibited twice.
(C) Finches are exhibited twice.
(D) Giraffes are not exhibited in consecutively numbered cages.
(E) If giraffes are exhibited, then they are exhibited in the fifth cage.

Here's how to crack it

Well, we've got an E in the fifth cage, so where does that force our P/A block? Here's what we got:

1		2		3		4		5	
B	A	B	A	B	A	B	A	B	A
-P		-F-E		-P					
		P	O						
E	-O	P	O	E	-O	P	a	E	-O ④

As you can see, putting E into the fifth slot forces our P/A block into cage 4. The other piece of information we want to focus on is the clue "If egrets and finches are both exhibited, egrets must always be in lower-numbered cages than the finches." Since we've got an egret in cage 5, that means that no finches can be exhibited, because if you put a finch in a lower-numbered cage than an egret, it would violate this clue. Hence, we've got egrets in cages 1, 3, and 5. We've wound up filling in seven out of our ten spaces. When we check the answer choices, the only thing that must be true is (D), the fact that giraffes can't be exhibited in consecutively numbered cages, since we've got an O in cage 2 and an A in cage 4. So it's our answer. Here's the next "If" question:

5. If egrets are exhibited twice, each of the following must be true EXCEPT:

   (A)   Antelopes are exhibited in the fourth cage.
   (B)   Antelopes are exhibited in the fifth cage.
   (C)   Egrets and finches are exhibited in consecutively numbered cages.
   (D)   If antelopes are exhibited in as many cages as possible, then they are exhibited four times.
   (E)   Giraffes cannot be exhibited in consecutively numbered cages.

Here's how to crack it

You now know from the question the exact number of times each type of bird is exhibited—you've probably already figured out that P is always exhibited twice, since you need a P/A block and P/O is in cage 2. This question tells us that E is exhibited twice also, so you know that there is one F. Here's our diagram:

So we've got the Es definitively in cages 1 and 3. This means that P and F must be in cages 4 and 5—you don't know exactly where the two go. Either way, however, an A must be in both cage 4 and cage 5, since A must always go with F and A has to go with the P. This means that the animal slots for cages 1 and 3 must either be giraffes or antelopes. Thus, (A), (B), (D), and (E) must all be true. Only (C) can be false, so it's our answer. Let's hit the next question.

6. If finches are exhibited twice, it is possible to determine the types of animals and birds for how many of the 10 slots?

(A) 7
(B) 6
(C) 5
(D) 4
(E) 3

Get the answer first, then look at the choices.

Here's how to crack it

As with the last question, the information provided tells us the exact number of each type of bird. Since we always have two of P, and now we have two of F, we've got one E. That E must be in the first cage, since it has to go in a lower-numbered cage than any and all Fs. So here's our diagram:

We've wound up being able to definitively place only three birds, but since cages 4 and 5 contain either an F or a P, we know that the animal exhibited must be an antelope. So we've got four animals definitively placed as well, giving us 7 total. Our answer here is (A).

Step 6: Use POE

The final three questions are all "Which" questions. Let's take a look at number 1.

1. Which one of the following must be true?

(A) Egrets are exhibited in the first cage.
(B) Parrots are exhibited in the second cage.
(C) Parrots are exhibited in the third cage.
(D) Antelopes are exhibited in the fourth cage.
(E) Antelopes are exhibited in the fifth cage.

Here's how to crack it

We've done a lot of work on this game, so chances are that something that we've already done will tell us what the answer is here. We don't know if (A) has to be true, so let's leave it in for the moment. We know for sure that (B) must be true (it's our deduction) so it's our answer. We're done with this question!

2. Each of the following is a possible line-up of animals in the five cages EXCEPT

(A) antelope, otter, antelope, giraffe, otter
(B) antelope, otter, giraffe, antelope, antelope
(C) antelope, otter, antelope, antelope, antelope
(D) giraffe, otter, giraffe, giraffe, antelope
(E) giraffe, otter, antelope, antelope, antelope

Here's how to crack it

On this question, you're merely looking for the one line-up that can't work. You can still use the Possible-Arrangement technique of applying the clues to the answer choices. Your two best clues are of course: (1) an otter must be in cage 2 and (2) there is a P/A block in either cage 4 or cage 5. The P/A block in cage 4 or cage 5 means that line-up (A) can't work, so it's our answer. Here's the final question:

3. Which one of the following is not possible when both egrets and finches are exhibited?

(A) Antelopes are exhibited in two consecutive cages.
(B) Finches are exhibited in two consecutive cages.
(C) Giraffes are not exhibited.
(D) Otters are exhibited in the third cage.
(E) Parrots are exhibited in two different cages.

Here's how to crack it

Take a look at previous scenarios where you've had both egrets and finches exhibited. Then, run through the answer choices and see if you've already drawn any of them. You've had (A) in question 5, (B) in question 6, (C) in question 6, and (E) in all previous questions. The only thing you haven't had is (D), so it's our answer. Nice job! We're almost at the end!

GAMES TECHNIQUES: FLEXIBILITY

As you can see, the last game required a lot of flexibility to get through. It had several types of clues, required that you keep track of ten slots, and didn't have a fixed number of each type of element. The key thing to remember, however, is that the process in attacking this game is exactly the same process as in every other game. Here's a brief run-down of some LSAT curve-balls, and how to hit them:

How not to freak out

- If you have many more elements than spaces, focus on distribution. Chances are you'll be given distribution clues that may determine exactly how many elements will go in each space. This will make the game much easier because the number of possibilities will be greatly reduced.

- If you don't know the exact number of all types of elements, focus on making deductions and filling in slots. Typically, these types of games will provide you with spaces that can only have one of two or three types of elements anyway, so the number of possibilities for any one slot will be quite low. The more slots you're able to either definitively fill in or reduce to only one of two choices, the easier the game will be.

- If you have all conditional clues and no definitive information, focus on making sure you've diagrammed everything correctly and have gotten all the contrapositives possible. Then, look to link these conditional clues to see if you can make any deductions. Many times the questions will be mainly "If" questions, which will provide you with more concrete information, which will in turn trigger many of the conditional clues.

- If you have more than two types of elements per slot, focus on finding and creating more blocks of information. These types of games will pair different types of elements together, so the more precisely you draw your blocks, the clearer the potential placement of these blocks will be. Also, many times the extra sets of elements will be binary and very tangential to the bulk of the questions.

Ready for the last game? We hope so, because it's about time to tackle Reading Comprehension.

GAME #7: COOKING CONTEST

Some games, like the game you're about to try, don't really require a complex diagram. What you'll see are a set of rules (usually two or three) for either mixing or combining or switching a group of elements from one position to another. Your goal here is to go slowly, making sure you understand the rules given. You can still use your pen by drawing the "movements" the rules denote to make sure you can see what's going on. Give yourself only ten minutes for the game below, because it's always going to be the hardest game in the section—so do it last, if at all.

Billy, Carly, Debbie, and Ethan are competing in a cooking contest. In each round of the contest, different dishes are prepared. A contestant is eliminated the first time he or she fails to prepare a dish properly. The contestants will be reordered between rounds according to one of the following rules:

Rule X: Whoever was in third place moves in front of the contestant who was previously in second place.

Rule Y: Whoever was in third place moves in front of the contestant who was previously in first place.

Rule Z: Whoever was in last place moves into the first place position.

If reordering involves a place where a contestant has been eliminated, that reordering cannot occur.

If none of the reorderings can occur, the contestants will remain in the same order as they were in the preceding round.

You'd want to save this game until last, right?

1. If the order in one round is Ethan, Billy, Carly, Debbie, and if Carly alone is eliminated in that round, which one of the following must be the order of the contestants for the next round?

    (A) Billy, Debbie, Ethan
    (B) Billy, Ethan, Debbie
    (C) Debbie, Billy, Ethan
    (D) Debbie, Ethan, Billy
    (E) Ethan, Billy, Debbie

2. If the order in one round is Carly, Billy, Debbie, Ethan, and if no one is eliminated in that round, it must be true that in the next round

    (A) Billy is third
    (B) Carly is second
    (C) Debbie is first
    (D) Ethan is first
    (E) Ethan is fourth

3. If the order in a round is Billy, Debbie, Ethan, Carly, and no one is eliminated, which one of the following could be the order in the next round?

    (A) Billy, Carly, Ethan, Debbie
    (B) Carly, Billy, Ethan, Debbie
    (C) Carly, Ethan, Billy, Debbie
    (D) Debbie, Billy, Ethan, Carly
    (E) Ethan, Billy, Debbie, Carly

4. If two rounds go by with no eliminations, and if the order of contestants in the third round is the same as it was in the first round, which one of the following represents the reorderings taking place so far?

    (A) X, followed by Y
    (B) X, followed by X
    (C) Y, followed by X
    (D) Z, followed by Y
    (E) Z, followed by Z

Cracking Game #7

Step 1: Decide on the Appropriate Diagram and Draw It

We don't really have a diagram here, so all we should do is note the "contestants"—B, C, D, and E. Let's see what the rules are.

Step 2: Symbolize the Clues

We can draw the three rules to see who goes where after a "round." Take a look at the diagram below:

$$\text{RULE X: BCDE}$$

$$\text{RULE Y: BCDE}$$

$$\text{RULE Z: BCDE}$$

The final two clues talk about whether or not a reordering can occur based on the number of contestants left. Make sure you understand what this means before going to the questions!

Step 3: Double-Check Your Clues and Make Deductions

Have you symbolized the rules correctly? Good. You want to look for questions that will tell you definitively whether someone has been eliminated and what the exact positions of the contestants are. That way, you'll be able to properly manipulate the rules and the contestants.

Step 4: Identify the Key

The key to this game is really not doing it at all, or at the very least, doing it last. Make sure you understand how this type of game doesn't allow for a standard diagram and avoid it on the real test!

Step 5: Attack the Questions

Fortunately there are only four questions and they are all "If" questions. Let's see how you do:

1. If the order in one round is Ethan, Billy, Carly, Debbie, and if Carly alone is eliminated in that round, which one of the following must be the order of the contestants for the next round?

   (A) Billy, Debbie, Ethan
   (B) Billy, Ethan, Debbie
   (C) Debbie, Billy, Ethan
   (D) Debbie, Ethan, Billy
   (E) Ethan, Billy, Debbie

Here's how to crack it

If Carly is eliminated, and she was in the third position, no reordering that involves a contestant in the third position can take place, since all we have left is EBD. That means no Rule X and no Rule Y. So, we execute Rule Z, which puts our last contestant, Debbie, into the first position. Ethan and Billy don't move. The new order is Debbie, Ethan, Billy, or choice (D).

2. If the order in one round is Carly, Billy, Debbie, Ethan, and if no one is eliminated in that round, it must be true that in the next round that

   (A) Billy is third
   (B) Carly is second
   (C) Debbie is first
   (D) Ethan is first
   (E) Ethan is fourth

Here's how to crack it

Try each move and see what happens. Executing Rule X produces the order Carly, Debbie, Billy, Ethan. Executing Rule Y produces the order Debbie, Carly, Billy, Ethan. Executing Rule Z produces the order Ethan, Carly, Billy, Debbie. In all three of those situations, Billy is third, so the answer is (A).

When you work out each possibility, you'll notice that there are fewer outcomes than you think.

3. If the order in a round is Billy, Debbie, Ethan, Carly, and no one is eliminated, which one of the following could be the order in the next round?

(A) Billy, Carly, Ethan, Debbie
(B) Carly, Billy, Ethan, Debbie
(C) Carly, Ethan, Billy, Debbie
(D) Debbie, Billy, Ethan, Carly
(E) Ethan, Billy, Debbie, Carly

Here's how to crack it

Try each move and see what happens. Executing Rule X produces the order Billy, Ethan, Debbie, Carly. There is no answer choice with that order. Executing Rule Y produces the order Ethan, Billy, Debbie, Carly, which appears in choice (E). That's our answer.

4. If two rounds go by with no eliminations, and if the order of contestants in the third round is the same as it was in the first round, which one of the following represents the reorderings taking place so far?

(A) X, followed by Y
(B) X, followed by X
(C) Y, followed by X
(D) Z, followed by Y
(E) Z, followed by Z

Here's how to crack it

Start with a random order: Billy, Carly, Debbie, Ethan. Now try the answers. We have to make sure that we end up with the same order in the third round that we have in the first round. Choice (A) suggests X, then Y. So if we started with B, C, D, E, Rule X produces B, D, C, E. Then execute Rule Y. That produces C, B, D, E. We do not have the same order in the third round as we did in the first round, do we? On to choice (B). If we started with B, C, D, E, Rule X produces B, D, C, E. Then execute Rule X again. That produces B, C, D, E. We have the same order in the third round as we did in the first round. (B) is our answer.

Why do we leave games like this until last in the section? They can often be complicated and time-consuming, because we can't really make any deductions before the game. In all the other games, there is a system: a diagram, clues, deductions. The worst thing about these games is that you usually have to test the answer choices, which is the biggest time-waster of all.

GAMES TECHNIQUES: ORDERING THE SECTION

Putting the games in a "workable" order is your most powerful tool for doing well on the Games section. You must read all four setups first, always thinking, "Do I know what to do here?" Rank the games in order from easier to harder, and then do them in that order. That way, if you don't finish the section (which is true of most people), you will run out of time on the harder ones, but you can make sure you answer the easier ones, the ones you know you can get right. For example, the "cooking contest" game should have been the game ranked last in a section. Here are some criteria you should use when ranking games:

- A one-to-one correspondence between elements and space…is good.

- Lots of blocks and definitive placements of elements in the clues…is good.

- A lot of "If" questions that provide you with concrete information to plug in…is good.

- More than two sets of elements in the game…isn't so hot. Look for another game to do first.

- Many more elements than spaces with no clearly defined distribution…isn't so hot. Look for another game to do first.

- Many conditional clues paired with many "Which" questions…isn't so hot. Look for another game to do first.

These rules are very basic. To see how they play out, when you work the two tests in the back of this book, look at our explanations to see what our section order was. Doing the easiest games first will get you at least two or three more points on the LSAT—so it's clearly worth it to hunt those games down. If you can average each game in about eleven or twelve minutes, you're doing very well, because you should get about eighteen or nineteen questions right on test day by doing the three easiest games and getting all of the questions right, and skipping the toughest game altogether.

Playing the percentages

GAMES TECHNIQUES: PRACTICING ON YOUR OWN

- Do everything in pencil, and don't erase your work.

- Work and write small—you will not be given a lot of space to draw your diagram.

- If a particular symbol isn't working, or is even causing mistakes, stop using it. Try something else.

- Do games over and over. If you had trouble with one, go back to it later and try it again until you get it.

- Practice games only when you are able to give them your full attention.

- *Very important:* Rework all the games (including the games in this chapter) at least twice.

- Always keep in mind which games go the fastest for you. Look for those games and do those first on the real LSAT.

SUMMARY

Here's the step-by-step approach to ALL games:

Step 1:   Decide on the Appropriate Diagram and Draw It

Step 2:   Symbolize the Clues

Step 3:   Double-Check Your Clues and Make Deductions

Step 4:   Identify the Key

Step 5:   Attack the Questions

Step 6:   Use Process of Elimination

Below is a summary chart of the games that you did in this section. When you rework the games, note those that took you the least amount of time and analyze why that was. Also look at the games that took you the longest to do, and work on those skills that seem to be slowing you down. Find similar games in the two tests in the back of this book and on the real LSATs you've ordered and work those games over and over. There's no substitute for practice. The chart is designed to give you a map of the games from this section, showing the basic characteristics of each game and how to attack it. Refer to the chart when working out games from previously released LSATs. We'll see you in Reading Comprehension.

Game Name	Characteristics	How to Crack It
Days & Entrees	• one-to-one correspondence • blocks • grid format	Make sure you've drawn your blocks correctly, make deductions, and use the information provided to you in the "if" questions.
Picture Frame	• one-to-one correspondence • antiblocks • circle format	Be flexible with how you draw your diagram, and draw a new diagram for each question in the game.
Tenants & Apartments	• two tiers • empty spaces • one-to-one correspondence	Remind yourself that the process is exactly the same for two tiers as for one. Keep your diagram very neat and very specific.
Hats & Scarves	• two columns only—In and Out • all clues "if...then" format • using the contrapositive	Make sure you've diagrammed all the contrapositives correctly, try to link clues together, and keep track of each "In" space and each "Out" space.
Three Buses	• distribution—many more elements than spaces • blocks and anti-blocks • distribution clues	Spend a minute or two trying to work out the distribution of elements to space—this will make the game go much smoother if you see it.
Birds & Animals	• two tiers • multiple use of elements • antiblocks • some "if...then" clues	This is testing your ability to pull several different types of clues together. Spend some time trying to link these clues up with each other—you'll get more deductions that way.
Cooking Contest	• no standard diagram • a set of rules to keep track of • fixed number of elements	Something you probably want to steer away from. Keep track of the rules and draw out the changes whenever you can.

Another chart for your refrigerator!

4

Reading Comprehension

WHAT IS READING COMPREHENSION?

It's dull. Dull as dirt. There are of course other definitions, but the fact that Reading Comprehension is dull is probably the most accurate description we can think of. Why is it dull? For several reasons, but probably the most compelling is the fact that *no one actually writes like that*. It's true—you're not just being anti-intellectual when you're thinking these passages are boring.

So why are the passages written like that? Well, most of the time they are culled from much longer passages. The LSAT writers then delete much of the introductory material. They also delete examples, illustrations, charts, pictures, transitions, and conclusions. What we're left with is information, and lots of it.

Thus, when you're reading a Reading Comprehension passage (like you've been doing since seventh grade on tests such as the SAT, the PSAT, the CAT, the Ohio tests, the ACT, the Regents, etc.), you probably do the following:

1. Read the first sentence of the passage.

2. Read the second sentence of the passage.

3. Read the third sentence of the passage.

4. Begin reading the fourth sentence of the passage, then realize that you've forgotten the information from the first sentence.

5. Go back and reread the first two sentences of the passage.

6. Push on toward the middle of the passage, now both bored and frustrated out of your mind, thinking that you're stupid because you've once again forgotten the information in the first sentence of the passage.

7. Quickly finish reading the passage and start doing the questions in order, getting frustrated because you always have to go back to the passage to find the answers even though you just read the damn thing fifteen seconds ago.

> There's no way that you can retain sixty or seventy lines' worth of information for even five seconds let alone five minutes.

Sound familiar? Well, since the passage is usually all information, that's about what *should* be happening. There's no way that you can retain sixty or seventy lines' worth of information for even five seconds. We just can't do it. Especially when we've got no personal interest in the information being presented. You probably don't care about steel mills or water bugs or the painter Watteau, and you certainly wouldn't be reading a passage like the one on the LSAT if you were interested. You'd buy a book, or read an article in a magazine, or go to a museum, or whatever.

Naturally, we're going to provide you with a method to attack this heinous section of the LSAT. We just wanted to let you know that you weren't crazy.

WHAT DOES THIS SECTION TEST?

More than anything, Reading Comprehension tests your ability not to rip up the test into little pieces and fling them at the proctor. Since the passages are presented in such a way as to prevent comprehension, this section also tests your ability to play cards with the deck stacked against you.

WHY IS THIS SECTION ON THE LSAT?

Reading Comprehension is on the LSAT because the LSAT writers are just as sadistic as the SAT and ACT and GMAT and GRE and MCAT writers.

The section itself

The Reading Comprehension section contains four passages and each passage has five to eight questions attached to it, for a total of twenty-seven questions. The passages are all typically between fifty-five and sixty-five lines.

Before we begin, take a moment to read the instructions to this section:

> <u>Directions:</u> Each passage in this section is followed by a group of questions to be answered on the basis of what is <u>stated</u> or <u>implied</u> in the passage. For some of the questions, more than one of the choices could conceivably answer the question. However, you are to choose the <u>best</u> answer, that is, the response that most accurately and completely answers the question, and blacken the corresponding space on your answer sheet.

These are the directions that will appear on your LSAT. As usual on the LSAT, the official directions provide very little help. Review them now. They will not change. Don't waste time reading them in the test room.

DON'T DESPAIR

We're about to give you a very simple four-step process for attacking the Reading Comprehension section of the LSAT. It's a bit radical, but with practice, you'll be able to increase your Reading Comprehension score. And anyway, what's the fun in learning standardized-test techniques that aren't radical?

READING COMPREHENSION: GENERAL STRATEGIES

Following is a list of general strategies that you should use when you are working the Reading Comprehension section. Make sure you take these strategies to heart, O LSAT Pilgrim.

Take your time

This is the third time we're telling you this, right? If you rush through the Reading Comprehension section of the LSAT, you're going to make several mistakes. The questions and answer choices are just as difficult as in the Arguments section, and you've got more of them, too. So if you've been getting to all four Reading Comprehension passages but you're only getting 60 percent of the questions correct, slow down! Only do three passages and see how your accuracy will increase!

Your mantra: *I will slow down and do fewer Reading Comprehension passages, thereby increasing my accuracy.*

Pick your passages

As in Games, you don't want to open up the Reading Comprehension section and just start doing the first passage. Look at all four passages—see which one or ones look easier to you, and start there. There are several criteria—organization of the passage, subject matter of the passage, number of questions, types of questions, length of the questions and answer choices, etc. We'll talk more about how to choose Reading Comprehension passages, but the point here is to find the passages that you think you'll be more effective on and do those first.

Your mantra: *I will look over the Reading Comprehension section and put the passages in my own order.*

Transfer your answers after each passage

Work *all* the questions on a particular passage; then transfer your answers to the bubble sheet. You need a few seconds to take a deep breath after each passage, and transferring your answers allows your brain to do something mindless for a few seconds. When you're down to five minutes, make sure you've got every single question bubbled in. Then, transfer your answers singly, changing whatever you might have bubbled in first. That way, if time is called early (remember, assume ineptitude on the part of all proctors), you've got an answer for every single question.

Your mantra: *I will transfer my answers after each passage until five minutes are left.*

Breathe

After you've completed each passage, use ten seconds to take three deep breaths. Transfer your answers from that passage, and then go and start another passage. You've cleared your mind and you're ready to push on.

Your mantra: *I will use ten seconds after each passage I complete to take some deep breaths.*

YOUR MANTRAS AND YOU

Here they are again:

> *I will slow down and do fewer Reading Comprehension passages, thereby increasing my accuracy.*
>
> *I will look over the Reading Comprehension section and put the passages in my own order.*
>
> *I will transfer my answers after each passage until five minutes are left.*
>
> *I will use ten seconds after each passage I complete to take some deep breaths.*

READING COMPREHENSION: A STEP-BY-STEP PROCESS

We're about to give you a four-step process that will help you attack the Reading Comprehension section of the LSAT. Whenever you do a passage, follow these steps exactly. This process is designed to help you read the passage actively, searching for what you'll need to answer the questions. That's the key to working efficiently and effectively through this section of the LSAT.

Step 1: Read the questions

When you read a book, do you just open it up to page one and begin reading? Hardly. You first read the back cover, the front cover, the blurbs, the paragraph about the author, etc. You also look to see how long the book is, and maybe see how it's organized—how long the chapters are, for instance, or how small the typeface is. Yet, in Reading Comprehension, we're asked to just begin reading with absolutely no idea of what we're going to encounter in the next sixty lines.

So what can you do to solve this problem? Simple—read the questions first. By reading the questions, you'll know what the subject matter is in the passage, and you'll also know what specific issues are going to be important for you to know about. For instance, if there is a passage about the poet James Merrill, and a question asks about his home in Stonington, Connecticut, you'll know in advance that the part of the passage that talks about this will be important. In addition, you'll know that anything about his apartment in New York City probably won't be important—unless another question asks about that.

Even knowing the general questions in a Reading Comprehension exercise can help—you'll know, for instance, that you will be asked about the author's tone or primary purpose, or the structure of the passage. Therefore, you can be reading with a specific goal in mind. This process of reading the questions and then noting what each one is asking (either by circling or underlining or re-writing) should really only take you a minute or so. Then, you can go to the passage.

A Step-by-Step Process

The big money technique: Read the questions first.

Step 2: Attack the passage

Great. You've read the questions, so now you can read the passage. However, most students try to memorize the passage. As we've already discussed, the passage contains too many facts to be able to memorize them, even for five minutes. So how should you read this passage? Should you just skim it? Or just read the first few sentences of each paragraph?

Here's your answer: try to get through the passage fairly quickly—for fast readers, ninety seconds, and for slower readers, three minutes at most. You'll read every word of the passage, but you're only looking to do a few things in this time. Here they are:

1. Underline, circle, or star any word, phrase, or section of the passage that was mentioned in one of the questions.

2. Look for the underlying structure of the passage: Is the passage a description of three theories? Or is it merely mentioning one theory, and then refuting it?

3. Get the main idea of the passage—if four of the questions asked about the poet James Merrill, chances are he is part of the main idea of the passage—for instance, that James Merrill was a good poet although he could have been better, or that James Merrill was a great poet because he broke away from convention, etc.

Don't try to find the actual answers to any of the specific questions—you're going to have to go back and re-read those parts anyway. Just find out and note where the information is—so you can go back to the passage efficiently. While this process may take you more than three minutes the first few times around, you'll be able to pick up speed the more you practice it. So, you can now finally go to the questions, and you've only spent three to five minutes on the first two steps.

Step 3: Answer the questions in your own words

This step should really read as follows: Answer the questions in your own words *before you read the answer choices*. How are you able to do this? Simple. You read the question, go back to the passage, and then, for the first time, read the appropriate part of the passage *slowly* and *for content*.

Most of the time in reading comprehension questions, you should be able to know at least one word or idea that needs to be in the correct answer. You will see how this works in the passage below—how, by going back and reading the appropriate part of the passage carefully, you'll be able to come up with your own answer to each question.

Step 4: Match your answers and use POE

So now that you've got this wonderful answer, what do you do with it? You match it against the answer choices. The key here is to remain confident of what *you* said needs to be in the correct answer. Remember that four of the answer choices are wrong!

Something you'll notice about the wrong answer choices is that many of them will reference information contained in a different part of the passage. So the answer will look good because it's mentioning specific content from the passage, but in reality it's mentioning information that answers a totally different question. If you've come up with your own answer in step 3, you won't be misled by these answer choices.

LET'S DO A READING COMPREHENSION PASSAGE

Okay, those are the steps. Now let's see how they work on a real Reading Comprehension passage. Notice how the next several pages are formatted—first, you get only the questions themselves. This is where you should do step 1. Then, you get the passage and the questions—this is where you should do steps 2 and 3. Do not go to the last version of the passage—the one with the passage, questions, and answer choices—until you've generated an answer for each of the questions. Then, compare those answers with the choices given to you in the final version of the passage, using Process of Elimination when necessary. Try to complete all of this in about fifteen minutes the first time around—don't worry if it takes you longer than that. With practice, you can get your speed down to twelve or even nine minutes (i.e., three or four passages completed).

After the passage we'll give you some extra techniques for attacking this section of the LSAT, just as we did in the Arguments and Games discussions.

READING COMPREHENSION PASSAGE: *THE FIRM*

Step 1: Read the Questions

Any discussion of theories of the firm must start with the neoclassical approach, the staple diet of modern economists. Developed over the last one hundred
(5) years or so, this approach can be found in any modern-day textbook on microeconomics; in fact, in most textbooks it is the *only* theory of the firm presented.
(10) Neoclassical theory views the firm as a set of feasible production plans. A manager presides over this production set, buying and selling inputs and outputs in a spot market and choosing the plan
(15) that maximizes owners' welfare. Welfare is usually represented by profit, or by the firm's market value.

To many economists, this is a caricature of the modern firm; it is
(20) rigorous but rudimentary. At least three reasons help explain its prolonged survival. First, the theory lends itself to an elegant and general mathematical formalization. Second, it is useful for
(25) analyzing how a firm's production choices respond to exogenous change in the environment, such as an increase in wages or sales tax. Finally, the theory is also useful for analyzing the consequences of
(30) strategic interaction between firms under conditions of imperfect competition; for example, it can help us understand the relationship between the degree of concentration in an industry and that
(35) industry's output and price level.

Granted these strengths, neoclassical theory has some clear weaknesses. It does not explain how production is organized within a firm, how conflicts of interest
(40) between the firm's various constituencies—its owners, managers, workers, and consumers—are resolved, or, more generally, how the manager achieves the goal of profit-maximization. More subtly,
(45) neoclassical theory begs the question of what defines a given firm or what determines its boundaries. Since the theory does not address the issue of each firm's size or extent, it cannot explain, for
(50) example, the consequences of two firms choosing to merge. Neoclassical theory describes in rudimentary terms how firms function but contributes little to any meaningful picture of their structure.

(55) Principal-agent theory, an important recent development, addresses some of the weaknesses of the neoclassical approach. Principal-agent theory now recognizes conflicts of interest between
(60) different economic actors. The theory still views the firm as a production set, but now a professional manager makes production choices—such as investment or effort allocations—that the firm's
(65) owners do not observe. Also, because the manager deals with the day-to-day operations of the firm, she is presumed to have information about the firm's profitability that the owners lack. In
(70) addition, the manager has other goals in mind beyond the owners' welfare, such as on-the-job perks, an easy life, empire-building, and so on.

Under these conditions, principal-
(75) agent theory argues that it will be impossible for the owners to implement their own profit-maximizing plans directly, through a contract with the manager; in general, the owners will not
(80) even be able to tell *ex post facto* whether the manager has chosen the right plan. Instead, the owners will try to align the manager's objectives with their own by putting the manager on an incentive
(85) scheme such as profit-sharing. Even under an optimal incentive scheme, however, the manager will put some weight on her own objectives at the expense of those of the owners, and
(90) conflicting interests remain. Hence, we have the beginnings of a managerial theory of the firm.

1. It can be inferred from the passage that the neoclassical view, despite its weaknesses, would be most useful in analyzing which one of the following types of firm?

   (A) a one-person entrepreneurial venture
   (B) a nonprofit foundation
   (C) a multinational corporation
   (D) a tightly held partnership
   (E) an absentee-owned service franchise

2. According to the information presented in the passage, the neoclassical and principal-agent theories of the firm hold which of the following premises in common?

(A) The manager of a firm must address conflict-of-interest issues as they arise.
(B) The owner of a firm seeks to directly implement a plan to maximize profits.
(C) A firm's production decisions are determined by a production set made up of the owner and a professional manager.
(D) A firm's owner is responsible for making decisions regarding investment and effort allocations.
(E) A firm can be viewed as a set of production choices.

3. According to the passage, the major contribution of the principal-agent theory of the firm is the insight that

(A) a firm's manager is not concerned with profit-maximization.
(B) the owners of a firm view their welfare in terms of profits.
(C) the manager of a firm is not motivated solely by monetary reward.
(D) the manager of a firm makes production choices.
(E) the neoclassical theory begs the question of what defines a firm.

4. It can be inferred from the information in the passage that all of the following would be examples of production decisions the manager of a firm might make EXCEPT

(A) offering sales discounts
(B) initiating an overtime shift
(C) investing in new equipment
(D) selling a division of the firm
(E) introducing a new product

5. In this passage the author is primarily concerned with

(A) outlining the evolution of the principal-agent theory of the firm.
(B) laying the groundwork for a comprehensive theory of the firm.
(C) demonstrating the need for a valid theory of the firm.
(D) showing how an elegant and mathematically formalized theory of the firm is not possible.
(E) discussing the weaknesses of the neoclassical theory of the firm.

6. Which one of the following phrases could replace the phrase "a caricature" (line 19) without changing the author's meaning in that sentence?

(A) an hypothesis
(B) an abstraction
(C) an oversimplification
(D) a satire
(E) a prediction

7. Which one of the following titles best summarizes the main idea of the passage?

(A) The Neoclassical Economic Theory: A Caricature of the Modern Firm
(B) The Development of the Principal-Agent Theory of the Firm
(C) Managers: Can They Be Trusted?
(D) Toward a Complete Theory of the Firm
(E) Conflicts of Interest Within a Firm

Step 2: Attack the Passage
Step 3: Answer the Questions in Your Own Words

Any discussion of theories of the firm must start with the neoclassical approach, the staple diet of modern economists. Developed over the last one hundred
(5) years or so, this approach can be found in any modern-day textbook on microeconomics; in fact, in most textbooks it is the *only* theory of the firm presented.
(10) Neoclassical theory views the firm as a set of feasible production plans. A manager presides over this production set, buying and selling inputs and outputs in a spot market and choosing the plan
(15) that maximizes owners' welfare. Welfare is usually represented by profit, or by the firm's market value.

To many economists, this is a caricature of the modern firm; it is
(20) rigorous but rudimentary. At least three reasons help explain its prolonged survival. First, the theory lends itself to an elegant and general mathematical formalization. Second, it is useful for
(25) analyzing how a firm's production choices respond to exogenous change in the environment, such as an increase in wages or sales tax. Finally, the theory is also useful for analyzing the consequences of
(30) strategic interaction between firms under conditions of imperfect competition; for example, it can help us understand the relationship between the degree of concentration in an industry and that
(35) industry's output and price level.

Granted these strengths, neoclassical theory has some clear weaknesses. It does not explain how production is organized within a firm, how conflicts of interest
(40) between the firm's various constituencies—its owners, managers, workers, and consumers—are resolved, or, more generally, how the manager achieves the goal of profit-maximization. More subtly,
(45) neoclassical theory begs the question of what defines a given firm or what determines its boundaries. Since the theory does not address the issue of each firm's size or extent, it cannot explain, for
(50) example, the consequences of two firms choosing to merge. Neoclassical theory describes in rudimentary terms how firms function but contributes little to any meaningful picture of their structure.

(55) Principal-agent theory, an important recent development, addresses some of the weaknesses of the neoclassical approach. Principal-agent theory now recognizes conflicts of interest between
(60) different economic actors. The theory still views the firm as a production set, but now a professional manager makes production choices—such as investment or effort allocations—that the firm's
(65) owners do not observe. Also, because the manager deals with the day-to-day operations of the firm, she is presumed to have information about the firm's profitability that the owners lack. In
(70) addition, the manager has other goals in mind beyond the owners' welfare, such as on-the-job perks, an easy life, empire-building and so on.

Under these conditions, principal-
(75) agent theory argues that it will be impossible for the owners to implement their own profit-maximizing plans directly, through a contract with the manager; in general, the owners will not
(80) even be able to tell *ex post facto* whether the manager has chosen the right plan. Instead, the owners will try to align the manager's objectives with their own by putting the manager on an incentive
(85) scheme such as profit-sharing. Even under an optimal incentive scheme, however, the manager will put some weight on her own objectives at the expense of those of the owners, and
(90) conflicting interests remain. Hence, we have the beginnings of a managerial theory of the firm.

Economics! Fascinating!

1. It can be inferred from the passage that the neoclassical view, despite its weaknesses, would be most useful in analyzing which one of the following types of firm?

   (A) a one-person entrepreneurial venture
   (B) a nonprofit foundation
   (C) a multinational corporation
   (D) a tightly held partnership
   (E) an absentee-owned service franchise

2. According to the information presented in the passage, the neoclassical and principal-agent theories of the firm hold which of the following premises in common?

(A) The manager of a firm must address conflict-of-interest issues as they arise.
(B) The owner of a firm seeks to directly implement a plan to maximize profits.
(C) A firm's production decisions are determined by a production set made up of the owner and a professional manager.
(D) A firm's owner is responsible for making decisions regarding investment and effort allocations.
(E) A firm can be viewed as a set of production choices.

3. According to the passage, the major contribution of the principal-agent theory of the firm is the insight that

(A) a firm's manager is not concerned with profit-maximization.
(B) the owners of a firm view their welfare in terms of profits.
(C) the manager of a firm is not motivated solely by monetary reward.
(D) the manager of a firm makes production choices.
(E) the neoclassical theory begs the question of what defines a firm.

4. It can be inferred from the information in the passage that all of the following would be examples of production decisions the manager of a firm might make EXCEPT

(A) offering sales discounts
(B) initiating an overtime shift
(C) investing in new equipment
(D) selling a division of the firm
(E) introducing a new product

5. In this passage the author is primarily concerned with

(A) outlining the evolution of the principal-agent theory of the firm.
(B) laying the groundwork for a comprehensive theory of the firm.
(C) demonstrating the need for a valid theory of the firm.
(D) showing how an elegant and mathematically formalized theory of the firm is not possible.
(E) discussing the weaknesses of the neoclassical theory of the firm.

6. Which one of the following phrases could replace the phrase "a caricature" (line 19) without changing the author's meaning in that sentence?

(A) an hypothesis
(B) an abstraction
(C) an oversimplification
(D) a satire
(E) a prediction

7. Which one of the following titles best summarizes the main idea of the passage?

(A) The Neoclassical Economic Theory: A Caricature of the Modern Firm
(B) The Development of the Principal-Agent Theory of the Firm
(C) Managers: Can They Be Trusted?
(D) Toward a Complete Theory of the Firm
(E) Conflicts of Interest Within a Firm

Step 4: Match Your Answers and Use Process of Elimination

Any discussion of theories of the firm must start with the neoclassical approach, the staple diet of modern economists. Developed over the last one hundred
(5) years or so, this approach can be found in any modern-day textbook on microeconomics; in fact, in most textbooks it is the *only* theory of the firm presented.

(10) Neoclassical theory views the firm as a set of feasible production plans. A manager presides over this production set, buying and selling inputs and outputs in a spot market and choosing the plan
(15) that maximizes owners' welfare. Welfare is usually represented by profit, or by the firm's market value.

To many economists, this is a caricature of the modern firm; it is
(20) rigorous but rudimentary. At least three reasons help explain its prolonged survival. First, the theory lends itself to an elegant and general mathematical formalization. Second, it is useful for
(25) analyzing how a firm's production choices respond to exogenous change in the environment, such as an increase in wages or sales tax. Finally, the theory is also useful for analyzing the consequences of
(30) strategic interaction between firms under conditions of imperfect competition; for example, it can help us understand the relationship between the degree of concentration in an industry and that
(35) industry's output and price level.

Granted these strengths, neoclassical theory has some clear weaknesses. It does not explain how production is organized within a firm, how conflicts of interest
(40) between the firm's various constituencies— its owners, managers, workers, and consumers—are resolved, or, more generally, how the manager achieves the goal of profit-maximization. More subtly,
(45) neoclassical theory begs the question of what defines a given firm or what determines its boundaries. Since the theory does not address the issue of each firm's size or extent, it cannot explain, for
(50) example, the consequences of two firms choosing to merge. Neoclassical theory describes in rudimentary terms how firms function but contributes little to any meaningful picture of their structure.

(55) Principal-agent theory, an important recent development, addresses some of the weaknesses of the neoclassical approach. Principal-agent theory now recognizes conflicts of interest between
(60) different economic actors. The theory still views the firm as a production set, but now a professional manager makes production choices—such as investment or effort allocations—that the firm's
(65) owners do not observe. Also, because the manager deals with the day-to-day operations of the firm, she is presumed to have information about the firm's profitability that the owners lack. In
(70) addition, the manager has other goals in mind beyond the owners' welfare, such as on-the-job perks, an easy life, empire-building, and so on.

Under these conditions, principal-
(75) agent theory argues that it will be impossible for the owners to implement their own profit-maximizing plans directly, through a contract with the manager; in general, the owners will not
(80) even be able to tell *ex post facto* whether the manager has chosen the right plan. Instead, the owners will try to align the manager's objectives with their own by putting the manager on an incentive
(85) scheme such as profit-sharing. Even under an optimal incentive scheme, however, the manager will put some weight on her own objectives at the expense of those of the owners, and
(90) conflicting interests remain. Hence, we have the beginnings of a managerial theory of the firm.

1. It can be inferred from the passage that the neoclassical view, despite its weaknesses, would be most useful in analyzing which one of the following types of firm?

   (A) a one-person entrepreneurial venture
   (B) a nonprofit foundation
   (C) a multinational corporation
   (D) a tightly held partnership
   (E) an absentee-owned service franchise

When you're down to two choices, go back to the passage for more information.

2. According to the information presented in the passage, the neoclassical and principal-agent theories of the firm hold which of the following premises in common?

   (A) The manager of a firm must address conflict-of-interest issues as they arise.
   (B) The owner of a firm seeks to directly implement a plan to maximize profits.
   (C) A firm's production decisions are determined by a production set made up of the owner and a professional manager.
   (D) A firm's owner is responsible for making decisions regarding investment and effort allocations.
   (E) A firm can be viewed as a set of production choices.

3. According to the passage, the major contribution of the principal-agent theory of the firm is the insight that

   (A) a firm's manager is not concerned with profit-maximization.
   (B) the owners of a firm view their welfare in terms of profits.
   (C) the manager of a firm is not motivated solely by monetary reward.
   (D) the manager of a firm makes production choices.
   (E) the neoclassical theory begs the question of what defines a firm.

4. It can be inferred from the information in the passage that all of the following would be examples of production decisions the manager of a firm might make EXCEPT

   (A) offering sales discounts
   (B) initiating an overtime shift
   (C) investing in new equipment
   (D) selling a division of the firm
   (E) introducing a new product

5. In this passage the author is primarily concerned with

   (A) outlining the evolution of the principal-agent theory of the firm.
   (B) laying the groundwork for a comprehensive theory of the firm.
   (C) demonstrating the need for a valid theory of the firm.
   (D) showing how an elegant and mathematically formalized theory of the firm is not possible.
   (E) discussing the weaknesses of the neoclassical theory of the firm.

6. Which one of the following phrases could replace the phrase "a caricature" (line 19) without changing the author's meaning in that sentence?

   (A) an hypothesis
   (B) an abstraction
   (C) an oversimplification
   (D) a satire
   (E) a prediction

7. Which one of the following titles best summarizes the main idea of the passage?

   (A) The Neoclassical Economic Theory: A Caricature of the Modern Firm
   (B) The Development of the Principal-Agent Theory of the Firm
   (C) Managers: Can They Be Trusted?
   (D) Toward a Complete Theory of the Firm
   (E) Conflicts of Interest Within a Firm

Cracking "The Firm"

How do you think you did on the passage? Well, let's walk through it step-by-step. Note what we did on each step of the process and compare it to your work.

Step 1: Read the Questions

Here we're going to reprint each question and then tell you what it told us. Take a look at question 1:

> 1. It can be inferred from the passage that the neoclassical view, despite its weaknesses, would be most useful in analyzing which one of the following types of firm?

This question mentions two specific issues—*neoclassical view* and *firm*. We don't yet know what either thing is yet, except to note how there seem to be *types* of *firms*, and perhaps *views* other than *neoclassical*. Let's move on to question 2.

> 2. According to the information presented in the passage, the neoclassical and principal-agent theories of the firm hold which of the following premises in common?

Cool. Now we know that the *neoclassical view* from question 1 is a theory, and we know that there's at least one more theory—the *principal-agent theory*. We also know that the passage is probably about something called *the firm*.

> 3. According to the passage, the major contribution of the principal-agent theory of the firm is the insight that

Great. A question specifically related to the *principal-agent theory*. And *the firm* is mentioned again.

> 4. It can be inferred from the information in the passage that all of the following would be examples of production decisions the manager of a firm might make EXCEPT

This question asks about the decisions of a production manager. This question will be a bit tougher to answer than the others because it is an EXCEPT question, but it again tells us something specific to look for in the passage.

> 5. In this passage the author is primarily concerned with

This is a general question asking us to state what the author is primarily concerned with. Just from reading the other questions, it's pretty clear that it's something about *firms* and perhaps the various theories relating to them.

> 6. Which one of the following phrases could replace the phrase "a caricature" (line 19) without changing the author's meaning in that sentence?

This is a specific question relating to one phrase of one sentence of the passage. Even if we don't know what the word *caricature* means, we should be able to figure it out using context clues. Let's read the last question.

7. Which one of the following titles best summarizes the main idea of the passage?

The words in the correct answer here should be very similar to those in number 5. We know already that something about *firms* should be in the title of this passage.

Great! We've read the questions, so now we can go back and read the passage. We're going to look for the following specific pieces of content and note their location:

Neoclassical theory (questions 1 and 2)

Principal-agent theory (questions 2 and 3)

Production manager (question 4)

Step 2: Attack the Passage

Break the passage up into little chunks of information—remember, it's easier to swallow a fly than an elephant.

We're not going to reprint the passage, but below is a list of what each paragraph of the passage told us, and what we felt was important from it. Then, we'll show you what we thought were the main idea and structure of the passage as a whole. Here we go:

Paragraph 1: Something about **firms** and **neoclassical theories**

Paragraph 2: Something about **neoclassical theory** and **production managers**

Paragraph 3: Reasons why **neoclassical theory** has survived

Paragraph 4: Reasons why **neoclassical theory** is inadequate

Paragraph 5: Something about **principal-agent theory** and **production managers**

Paragraph 6: More about **principal-agent theory**, **production managers**, **owners**, and **managerial theory**

As you can see, we've retained no information about any of the bolded text; all we've done is to note what is mentioned where. However, we should be able to come up with a main idea for the passage, and to note the structure of the passage:

Main idea: Something about how there are **two main theories of firms** and how **neither is perfect**

Structure: One theory of firms is presented, then another theory of firms is presented, then it is suggested that there may need to be a third theory.

That's it. There's no need to go more in-depth than that now. We'll save that for when we actually come up with our own answers to the questions. And now that we know where the information is in the passage, we should be able to do that with efficiency. So let's go to step 3.

Step 3: Answer the Questions in Your Own Words

Now let's look at the questions again and come up with our own answers for them—before we look at the answer choices.

> 1. It can be inferred from the passage that the neoclassical view, despite its weaknesses, would be most useful in analyzing which one of the following types of firm?

Let's go back to the passage and find out the *strengths and weaknesses* of the neoclassical theory—i.e., paragraphs 3 and 4. Our answer: we want to look for a type of firm that is *simple* and *profit-driven*.

> 2. According to the information presented in the passage, the neoclassical and principal-agent theories of the firm hold which of the following premises in common?

We know that we should go back to where the passage begins to talk about principal-agent theory—i.e., paragraph 5. Our answer: something about how both theories view the firm as a *production set* (lines 62–63).

> 3. According to the passage, the major contribution of the principal-agent theory of the firm is the insight that

Let's go back and read paragraph 5, about principal-agent theory, and see what the author thinks is the best thing about it. Our answer: something about how the *manager has other goals.*

> 4. It can be inferred from the information in the passage that all of the following would be examples of production decisions the manager of a firm might make EXCEPT

Let's make a quick list here, even though we might not get everything in. But whatever we've written down can be crossed out if it's in an answer choice. We get: *investments, allocations, day-to-day operations.*

> 5. In this passage the author is primarily concerned with

Our answer: *explaining two theories of firms and showing strengths and weaknesses of each.*

> 6. Which one of the following phrases could replace the phrase "a caricature" (line 19) without changing the author's meaning in that sentence?

From context clues, it seems that the word *caricature* is referring to how the neoclassical model isn't complete—that it's too simple. Our answer: something *too simple* or *too basic.*

> 7. Which one of the following titles best summarizes the main idea of the passage?

Our answer: *Two theories of firms and how neither is perfect.* This answer should be similar to the answer for number 5, since they are asking very similar questions.

Step 4: Match Your Answers and Use Process of Elimination

Here are, finally, the answer choices. Let's see how we did when we compare our answers to the choices.

1. It can be inferred from the passage that the neoclassical view, despite its weaknesses, would be most useful in analyzing which one of the following types of firm?

    (A) a one-person entrepreneurial venture
    (B) a nonprofit foundation
    (C) a multinational corporation
    (D) a tightly held partnership
    (E) an absentee-owned service franchise

Our answer was: *something simple and profit-driven.* (A) looks pretty good, since a one-person firm is pretty simple. (B) won't work, since a nonprofit organization isn't profit-driven. (C) is too complex—a multinational corporation isn't simple. (D) is also too complex—a partnership isn't simple. (E) is also too complex—a service franchise isn't simple. So our best answer is (A), which is the correct answer.

2. According to the information presented in the passage, the neoclassical and principal-agent theories of the firm hold which of the following premises in common?

    (A) The manager of a firm must address conflict-of-interest issues as they arise.
    (B) The owner of a firm seeks to directly implement a plan to maximize profits.
    (C) A firm's production decisions are determined by a production set made up of the owner and a professional manager.
    (D) A firm's owner is responsible for making decisions regarding investment and effort allocations.
    (E) A firm can be viewed as a set of production choices.

Our answer was: *something about production sets.* (A), (B), and (D) don't mention production sets, so eliminate them. (C) talks about owners and managers and production sets, which is too complex based on our answer. (E) is the most basic choice here, and it's the correct answer.

Note that so far on these first two questions, we kept it simple. We had gone back and found specific answers, and as long as we stuck to our guns and didn't try to choose "fancy" answers, we did fine. Let's keep going.

3. According to the passage, the major contribution of the principal-agent theory of the firm is the insight that

    (A) a firm's manager is not concerned with profit-maximization.
    (B) the owners of a firm view their welfare in terms of profits.
    (C) the manager of a firm is not motivated solely by monetary reward.
    (D) the manager of a firm makes production choices.
    (E) the neoclassical theory begs the question of what defines a firm.

Our answer was: *something about how the manager has other goals.* (A) is too extreme. (B) doesn't talk about managers. (C) talks about how the manager has more than one motivation or goal. Let's leave it. (D) is true, but the paragraph doesn't say it is the *major* contribution. (E) doesn't talk about either managers or goals. (C) is the correct answer. Once again, we kept it simple and focused and we got the right answer.

4.   It can be inferred from the information in the passage
     that all of the following would be examples of
     production decisions the manager of a firm might
     make EXCEPT

   (A)   offering sales discounts
   (B)   initiating an overtime shift
   (C)   investing in new equipment
   (D)   selling a division of the firm
   (E)   introducing a new product

Our answer was: *investments, allocations, day-to-day operations.* (A) looks like a day-to-day operation decision. (B) also looks like an operating decision. (C) is an investment. (D) doesn't look like any of these things, so let's keep it. (E) doesn't look like any of these things either. So we're down to two—which one of these two things looks like something a production manager would have control over—selling a part of the business or introducing a new product? Looks like (E) would be closer, since it's simpler and less complex a move than selling a division. It also talks about "products," which is something a production manager would be concerned about. So we chose (D), "selling a division."

5.   In this passage the author is primarily concerned with

   (A)   outlining the evolution of the principal-agent
         theory of the firm.
   (B)   laying the groundwork for a comprehensive
         theory of the firm.
   (C)   demonstrating the need for a valid theory of
         the firm.
   (D)   showing how an elegant and mathematically
         formalized theory of the firm is not possible.
   (E)   discussing the weaknesses of the neoclassical
         theory of the firm.

Our answer was: *explaining two theories of firms and showing strengths and weaknesses of each.* (A) is too specific, since it only mentions one theory. (B) looks a bit broad, but it's better than (A), so let's leave it. (C) is also a bit broad, but let's leave that too. (D) is too specific. (E) only mentions one theory. So we're down to (B) and (C), and neither one looks all that much like our answer. Oh well…let's use process of elimination. Could it be possible that by mentioning two flawed theories you're laying the groundwork for a new one? Is there any evidence of this? Sure…in the last sentence of the passage, which talks about a new theory, the managerial one. So (B) might be okay. What about (C)? Does the author anywhere mention that these theories are needed, or who needs them, or why? You can look, but you won't find it. (B) is the better answer.

6. Which one of the following phrases could replace the phrase "a caricature" (line 19) without changing the author's meaning in that sentence?

   (A) an hypothesis
   (B) an abstraction
   (C) an oversimplification
   (D) a satire
   (E) a prediction

Our answer: *something too simple or too basic*. (C) just kind of jumps out at us, the word "oversimplification." Nothing else is all that close. It's our answer.

7. Which one of the following titles best summarizes the main idea of the passage?

   (A) The Neoclassical Economic Theory: A Caricature of the Modern Firm
   (B) The Development of the Principal-Agent Theory of the Firm
   (C) Managers: Can They Be Trusted?
   (D) Toward a Complete Theory of the Firm
   (E) Conflicts of Interest Within a Firm

We said: *Two theories of firms and how neither is perfect*. However, we saw that the answer to question 5 didn't really conform to our answer, and we've noted how the answers for these two questions should be similar. So let's also keep in mind the answer for question 5, which was "laying the groundwork for a comprehensive theory of the firm." (A) is too specific—there are two theories to the passage. (B) is also too specific, for the same reason as (A). (C) doesn't even talk about firms, so that's out. (D) looks a lot like our answer for question 5, so let's leave it. (E) is too specific, merely referencing one of many issues that firms have to deal with. So it's (D).

Cool. You've gotten through your first reading comprehension passage. Now you've got to go and apply these techniques to as many reading comprehension practice passages as you can get your hands on. Below are some major techniques and processes that you should be using when you work through the Reading Comprehension section of the exam.

READING COMPREHENSION TECHNIQUES: PROCESS OF ELIMINATION

As you can see from the passage above, coming up with your own answers helped you on many of the questions. You will still have to use Process of Elimination, however, in many instances. Just like in arguments, you can use several Process of Elimination techniques when working Reading Comprehension passages. The three most important ones are described below.

Wrong part of the passage

As we mentioned earlier in the chapter, many of the wrong answer choices do contain content from the passage. The problem is that this information is from a different part of the passage. For instance, if a passage is describing the properties of three different kinds of acids, and a question asks about the properties of the second acid, many of the wrong choices will be properties of the first and third acids. But as long as you focus on the information about the second acid only, you'll be able to eliminate any choices that talk about the first and third acids.

In the passage above, question 3, answer choice (B), was a perfect example of this. The question asked about the principal-agent theory, yet answer choice (B), "the owners of a firm view their welfare in terms of profits," is something that was a property of neoclassical theory. But if you focus only on the text that relates to principal-agent theory, you won't be misled by this answer choice.

Extreme language

Here's a familiar technique from arguments. And as we mentioned in the arguments chapter, extreme language is usually very difficult to prove, so it's rarely contained in correct answers. The same rule applies to Reading Comprehension—if you're down to two choices, and one is wishy-washy and one is extreme, pick the wishy-washy choice.

In the passage above, question 3, answer choice (A), is an excellent example of extreme wording. Answer choice (A) says that "a firm's manager is not concerned with profit-maximization," which is too extreme. Choice (C) was much better here, because it said that a manager is not motivated solely by monetary reward. That is nice and wishy-washy, saying that the manager has at least one other motive. The addition of the word "solely" in this instance made choice (C) very different from choice (A).

Scope

Here's another familiar technique from Arguments. Many answer choices in Reading Comprehension will either be too general or too specific. If the passage is about the poet James Merrill, and you're asked to come up with the main idea of the passage, the answer will not be that the passage is about "poetry," nor will it be that the passage is about "James Merrill's house in Connecticut."

In the passage above, question 7, answer choices (A), (B), and (C) are all good examples of scope. Choice (A) only mentions neoclassical theory; choice (B) only mentions principal-agent theory; and choice (C) only mentions managers and no theories at all. While all this content was mentioned in the passage, all of it is too specific to be the correct answer to a main idea question.

READING COMPREHENSION TECHNIQUES: QUESTION TYPES

Reading Comprehension questions fit into two main categories—general questions and specific questions. In the passage above, questions 5 and 7 were general questions because they asked about the author's purpose and the main idea of the passage. All of the other questions were specific in nature, because they asked about a specific part of the passage or about a specific idea from the passage. Here's a chart showing the various types of Reading Comprehension questions and how you should attack each one:

Surely you knew you'd get another chart, right?

General Questions	
Question Type	**Technique**
Main Idea	Come up with your own main idea—what you think the passage is about. Be critical; any word or phrase or idea that you think is an essential part of the passage MUST be the answer you choose.
Structure of the Passage	Write out what you think is the general flow of the passage. Did the author introduce three theories and then refute them all? If so, look for a similar choice. If any part of the choice is wrong, it's all wrong—cross it off.
Primary Purpose	Decide what you feel the author was attempting to do in the passage. For example, was he debunking a myth, showing how a well-accepted theory is correct, introducing a new theory? Then match your decription to the answer choices.
Author's Tone/Attitude	Come up with your own description of what you felt was the author's attitude towards his subject. Typically, it's something pretty wishy-washy—LSAT Reading Comprehension authors don't tend to get too worked up one way or the other. Words like "balanced" and "objective" are usually right; words like "enthusiastic" and "derogatory" are usually wrong. Words like "dispassionate" and "apathetic" are usually wrong, too—why would an apathetic person write something to begin with?

Specific Questions	
Question Type	**Technique**
Specific Word/Phrase	Go back to the passage, find the paragraph that contains the information or the specific word or phrase in the question, and read it carefully. Then answer the question in your own words before going to the choices.
Line Reference	Go back to the passage and read five lines above and five lines below the line reference given to you in the uestion. If it says "line 56," read lines 51–61. This should help you find out the purpose of the author's ord or phrase—then match your answer to the choices.
Paragraph Reference	Go back to the passage and read the paragraph referenced in the question. Also, note how that paragraph fits into the passage as a whole by checking what you said was the structure of the passage. Then, come up with your own answer and match it to the choices.

READING COMPREHENSION TECHNIQUES: PASSAGE SELECTION

Reading Comprehension passages can pretty much be put into four broad content categories: artistic/literary criticism; science; history/political science; and legal/social science. Well, so what? Exactly. While you might have been an art major in college, it's not necessarily a certainty that if you get a passage about Michelangelo, you'll get all the answers right. You might do better on the science passage about water bugs, where you have no personal involvement, previous knowledge, or theories of your own.

The point here is: Look at the passages you've done in practice tests and see which ones you got the most questions right on. The answer might surprise you. So while passage content is a factor in deciding whether or not to do a passage, it's not the only factor. Below is a list of the most important factors:

1. The number of questions for a passage

2. The number of *specific* questions for a passage

3. The number of paragraphs in a passage

4. The length of each paragraph in a passage

5. The length of each question for a passage

6. The length of the answer choices for a passage

7. The subject matter of a passage

Consequently, you should base your decision not just on one of the above factors, but on a combination of several factors. If you decide to do the first passage in a section, for instance, it should be because it has seven questions, four even-sized paragraphs, and you are comfortable with the content. Choosing the best Reading Comprehension passages for you is just as important as choosing the best games for you—these decisions can affect your overall score by several points, so make wise decisions.

SUMMARY

Here's our step-by-step approach to the Reading Comprehension section:

Step 1:   Read the Questions

Step 2:   Attack the Passage

Step 3:   Answer the Questions in Your Own Words

Step 4:   Match Your Answers and Use Process of Elimination

5

The Writing Sample

The Writing Sample is a thirty-minute ungraded essay whose topic is assigned. Your essay is supposed to be an argument supporting either of two given positions. You'll receive a booklet containing both the topic and the space in which to write your essay. You will also receive scratch paper.

Before we begin, take a moment to read the instructions to this section:

Don't devote too much study time to the Writing Sample.

General Directions: You are to complete the brief writing exercise on the topic inside. You will have 30 minutes in which to plan and write the exercise. Read the topic carefully. You will probably find it best to spend a few minutes considering the topic and organizing your thoughts before you begin writing. **Do not write on a topic other than the one specified. Writing on a topic of your own choice is not acceptable.**

There is no "right" or "wrong" position on the writing sample topic. Law schools are interested in how skillfully you support the position you take and how clearly you express that position. How well you write is much more important than what you write. No special knowledge is required or expected. Law schools are interested in organization, vocabulary, and writing mechanics. They understand the short time available to you and the pressure under which you are writing.

Confine your writing to the lined area following the writing sample topic. You will find that you have enough space in this booklet if you plan your writing carefully, write on every line, avoid wide margins, and keep your handwriting a reasonable size. Be sure your writing is legible.

Scratch paper is provided for use during the writing sample portion of the test only. Scratch paper cannot be used in other sections of the LSAT.

The writing sample is photocopied and sent to law schools to which you direct your LSAT score. A pen will be provided at the test center, which must be used (for the writing sample only) to ensure a photocopy of high quality.

These are the instructions that will appear on the cover of your LSAT Writing Sample booklet. You'll be given a chance to read them before you write your essay.

THE WRITING TOPIC

Inside the booklet you'll find the assigned topic and about thirty blank lines on which to write your essay. You'll also get scratch paper on which to organize your essay. The assigned topics are innocuous. Expect a topic something like this:

Karen Stratton is looking into buying a property with the plan to turn it into an animal-supply store. Write an essay in support of one of two proposed properties, the cost of which would be almost exactly the same, keeping in mind Karen's needs:

- Karen needs to establish a market and begin making back her investment rather quickly, since she will be putting most of her money into buying the property.

- Karen wants her store to be different and memorable, so she can cultivate a loyal clientele.

Property One is a storefront in the middle of the main drag of the bustling downtown area. The outside of the storefront looks like the fronts of most of the other stores on the block. The central location would make shopping there convenient for people who work in the downtown area, and is accessible by all forms of public transportation.

Property Two is an old, renovated Victorian house on the outskirts of town. The design of the house is unique. It is six miles from the nearest public transport, making it accessible only by car and cab. It is closer to the farm country and has space for a garden, which Karen can use to grow organic products for her store.

_____

_____

_____

_____

_____

_____

_____

_____

_____

_____

_____

_____

_____

Fill up the page when writing your LSAT essay.

_____

_____

_____

_____

_____

_____

_____

_____

_____

_____

_____

_____

_____

_____

_____

_____

_____

_____

_____

_____

_____

How Much Will My Essay Affect My LSAT Score?

Not one bit.

Only four sections contribute to your LSAT score: one Games section, two Arguments sections, and one Reading Comprehension section. An unmarked photocopy of your essay will be sent to the law schools to which you apply.

Who Will Read My Essay?

Possibly no one.

How well or poorly you do on the Writing Sample will almost certainly not affect your admissions chances.

Then Why Do Law Schools Require It?

Law schools feel guilty about not being interested in anything about you other than your grades and LSAT scores. Knowing that you have spent thirty minutes writing an essay for them makes them feel better about having no interest in reading what you have written.

IF THE WRITING SAMPLE IS SO UNIMPORTANT, WHY DISCUSS IT?

Just for your own peace of mind. Once you have the rest of the test under control, look over the rest of this chapter. If you are short on time, you'd be better off practicing Arguments.

There's also the possibility that a bored admissions officer will accidentally pass his eyes over what you have written. If your essay is ungrammatical, riddled with misspellings, off the topic, and wildly disorganized, the admissions officer will think somewhat less of you.

So we're going to assume that the Writing Sample counts a wee bit. You should assume the same thing, but don't lose sleep over it. No one ever got into law school because of the LSAT Writing Sample; and it's doubtful that anyone ever got rejected because of it, either. Besides, good writing requires surprisingly few rules, and the rules we'll review will help your writing in general.

WHAT ARE THEY LOOKING FOR?

The general directions to the Writing Sample mention that law schools are interested in three things: essay organization, vocabulary, and writing mechanics. Presumably, writing mechanics covers grammar and style.

What they're *really* looking for

Researchers at the Educational Testing Service once did a study of essay-grading behavior. They wanted to find out what their graders really responded to when they marked papers, and which essay characteristics correlated most strongly with good scores.

The researchers discovered that the most important characteristic, other than "overall organization," is "essay length." Also highly correlated with good essay scores are the number of paragraphs, average sentence length, and average word length. The bottom line? **Students who filled in all the lines, indented frequently, and used big words earned higher scores than students who didn't.**

We will discuss these points in more detail later. Since organization is the most important characteristic, let's start with that.

ESSAY ORGANIZATION

Your essay should contain five paragraphs (remember high school?). In the first you state your opinion. In the last you restate your opinion. The three middle paragraphs form the body of your argument.

Indent often—four or five times is best.

State your actual argument in three paragraphs. Three paragraphs demonstrate that your argument is concise as well as organized. Of course, if you find that one of your major ideas has secondary ideas, you may have to subdivide one of the middle paragraphs.

So your essay should consist of an introduction paragraph, a conclusion paragraph, and three main paragraphs for your argument. The more you stick with a formula outline, the less thinking you'll have to do when you actually write.

What Am I Trying to Do?

You're trying to persuade your reader that one of two given alternatives is better. You cannot *prove* that one side is better; you can only make a case that it is. The test writers deliberately come up with boringly balanced alternatives so that you can argue for either one of them.

So choose a side and justify your choice.

Picking Sides

The directions stress that neither alternative is "correct." It doesn't matter which side you choose. Pick the alternative that gives you more to work with.

List pros and cons.

Another way to decide is to compile a little list of the pros and cons on your scratch paper. Then simply pick the alternative whose list of pros is longer. Let's see how you'd do this with the sample topic we've given you.

First, list each alternative (Property One, Property Two) as a heading. Underneath each heading draw two columns, one for the pros and one for the cons. Spend the first couple of minutes brainstorming the advantages and disadvantages of each choice. The key to brainstorming is *quantity*, not quality. You can select and discard points later.

Having brainstormed for pros and cons, select the ones you intend to keep and arrange them in order of importance, from *least* to *most* important.

For the purposes of this chapter, let's assume that we intend to give the nod to Property Two.

Don't forget the cons

Some students believe that if you're trying to make a case for something, you should bring up the advantages only. This is wrong.

To persuade readers that Property Two is the better choice, you must show that you have considered every argument that could be made for Property One, and found each one unconvincing.

Your argument, in other words, must show that you have weighed the pros and cons of *both* sides. The more forceful the objections you counter, the more compelling your position becomes.

Evaluating the pros and cons: the criteria

As you think of pros and cons for each position, keep in mind the given criteria. Here you have two considerations—getting money back and establishing a unique business. You must build your essay around these criteria, so don't ignore them. They give you the structure to follow: One bullet equals one paragraph.

The criteria may not be compatible. If so, weigh the pros and cons in light of this situation. In our example, an innovative personality might not get along well with other people. You may want to rank the two criteria in terms of importance. Perhaps getting money back is more important than establishing a unique business. Perhaps not. Decide which consideration is more important. If you cannot decide, state so explicitly.

CAN I RAISE OTHER ISSUES?

You *must* weigh the two stated considerations, but nothing prevents you from introducing additional considerations.

You need not raise additional considerations, but if one occurs to you, and you have the time, mention it in passing. If none occurs to you, mention in the conclusion that you have evaluated the two options in view of the two stated considerations only, acknowledging that other considerations may be important.

PROPERTY ONE VERSUS PROPERTY TWO:
BRAINSTORMING THE PROS AND CONS

Remember: Brainstorm first. Next, select the issues you intend to raise. Then rank the final issues, beginning with the least important.

To organize your brainstorming, use a rough chart like this one:

	quick money	unique business	other factors
Property One	possible; central location good for exposure and quick purchases	looks like every other store front	size? use of space and light?
Property Two	possible, but it might take a while. Harder to get to, but could be a "specialty" shop	probably; unique-looking store, customers would have to be loyal since it's farther away	size? use of space and light?

BEGINNING YOUR ESSAY: RESTATING THE PROBLEM

Having brainstormed the pros and cons of each choice in light of the considerations, you are ready to start writing your essay.

Your first paragraph should do little more than produce your argument. Try not to use a tedious grade school opening like "The purpose of the essay I am about to write is to...."

There are several more interesting ways to introduce an argument. Which one you choose will influence how you organize the rest of your essay. Keep this in mind as you sketch your outline. We'll tell you more about this as we go along.

One possibility for an opening is simply to restate concisely the problem you are to address. Here's an example:

Karen Stratton needs to buy a property for her animal-supply business.
She must turn a profit quickly, but wants to establish a unique business.
The two properties both have positive and negative aspects. We must
weigh their respective strengths and weaknesses in light of Karen's needs.

This type of introduction sets up the conflict rather than immediately taking a side. The second, third, and fourth paragraphs are then devoted to weighing the specific advantages and disadvantages of each candidate. The author's preference isn't stated explicitly until the final paragraph, although a clear case for one should emerge as the essay progresses.

An essay like this is really just an organized written version of the mental processes you went through in deciding which candidate to choose. In the first paragraph you say, in effect, "Here are the problems, the choices, and my decision." In the second, third, and fourth paragraphs you say, "Here are the pros and cons I weighed." In the fifth and final paragraph you say, "So you can see why I decided as I did."

Your hope is that the reader, by following your reasoning step by step, will decide the same thing. The great advantage of this kind of organization is that it *does* follow your mental processes. That makes it a natural and relatively easy method.

BEGINNING YOUR ESSAY: PUTTING YOUR CARDS ON THE TABLE

It's also possible to write an essay in which you begin by announcing your decision. You state your preference in the first paragraph, back it up in the middle paragraphs, and then restate your preference with a concluding flourish in the final paragraph.

Here's an example of such an opening paragraph:

Property One is a centrally located storefront in a busy downtown area, which would probably bring in a lot of quick business. However, it looks like every other storefront, so it wouldn't stand out. Property Two, by contrast, would afford Karen Stratton an opportunity to create a unique-looking store that could be treated as a specialty shop that people would be willing to travel to. I believe that Karen should buy Property Two for her animal-supply store because it suits her needs.

By introducing your argument in this way, you leave yourself with a great deal of latitude for handling the succeeding paragraphs. For example, you might use the second paragraph to discuss both candidates in light of the first consideration, the third paragraph to discuss both candidates in light of the second consideration, the fourth paragraph to weigh the considerations themselves, and the fifth and final paragraph to summarize your argument and restate your preference.

THE BODY OF YOUR ARGUMENT

We've discussed the introductory and concluding paragraphs. Depending on your preference, and depending on the essay topic you actually confront, we recommend three variations for the middle paragraphs:

Variation 1

Paragraph 2:   Both sides in light of the first consideration

Paragraph 3:   Both sides in light of the second consideration

Paragraph 4:   Weighing the two considerations (and other considerations?)

Variation 2

Paragraph 2:   Everything that can be said about Property One

Paragraph 3:   Everything that can be said about Property Two

Paragraph 4:   A sentence or two for Property One, followed by three or four sentences for Property Two

Variation 3

Paragraph 2:   A sentence or two for Property One, followed by three or four sentences for Property Two

Paragraph 3:   A sentence or two for Property One, followed by three or four sentences for Property Two

Paragraph 4:   A sentence or two for Property One, followed by three or four sentences for Property Two

Again, if necessary, you can divide any one of the three middle paragraphs into two paragraphs.

All three variations do the job. Choose a variation you feel comfortable with and memorize it. The less thinking you have to do on the actual exam, the better.

THE PRINCETON REVIEW THESAURUS OF PRETTY IMPRESSIVE WORDS

The following list of words is not meant to be complete, nor is it in any particular order. Synonyms or related concepts are grouped where appropriate.

Use ten-dollar words if you can use and spell them correctly.

- example, instance, precedent, paradigm, archetype
- illustrate, demonstrate, highlight, acknowledge, exemplify, embody
- support, endorse, advocate, maintain, contend, espouse, champion
- supporter, proponent, advocate, adherent
- dispute, dismiss, outweigh, rebut, refute
- propose, advance, submit, marshal, adduce
- premise, principle, presumption, assumption, proposition
- advantages, merits, benefits
- inherent, intrinsic, pertinent
- indisputable, incontrovertible, inarguable, unassailable, irrefutable, undeniable, unimpeachable
- unconvincing, inconclusive, dubious, specious
- compelling, cogent, persuasive
- empirical, hypothetical, theoretical

A note on diction

Make sure you don't spoil your display of verbal virtuosity by misusing or misspelling these or any other ten-dollar words. Also, get your idioms straight.

A final note on a common diction error. If, as in our Writing Sample, your choice involves only two options, *former* refers to the first and *latter* refers to the second. You cannot use these words to refer to more than two options.

Another common diction error occurs when comparing two or more things. The first option is *better* than the second, but it is not the *best*, which is used when discussing three or more options.

RULES TO WRITE BY

1. Write as if you were actually making the recommendation.
2. Write naturally, but don't use abbreviations or contractions.
3. Make sure your position is clear.
4. Write as neatly as possible.
5. Indent your paragraphs.

One Final Reminder

Write legibly! If you can't, *print* legibly!

A Sample Essay

Karen Stratton is looking for a property to buy for her animal-supply store, and has narrowed her search to two. Property One is centrally located and would allow Karen to make money quickly. Property Two is not centrally located, but would allow Karen to cultivate a special business. In view of those considerations, I recommend she buy Property Two.

Property One would certainly be convenient for shoppers. It is also accessible by all forms of public transportation, making it even easier to get to. Karen could certinly make back some money quickly by the location alone. But her store would not be unique; it would look like every other store in the area. People wouldn't be going there for any reason but its location, which means they might not be loyal customers. Also, being in the downtown area, the store might not be big enough for Karen to feature all of the items that would make her store unique, and the outside would not suggest uniqueness either.

Property Two, on the other hand, is certainly unique-looking. It's true that people would have to travel to get there, but Karen could make it into a specialty shop, growing her own products in the garden, etc., and make her store worth the trip. These types of stores inspire loyalty for customers looking for hard-to-find items, and though Karen might not make back her investment right away, she would over time. Her store could also serve the farm community, whose residents might not want to travel downtown.

Another thing Property Two has in its favor is that it is probably bigger than Property One, or if not, it at least would afford Karen creative ways to use space and natural light that a downtown storefront would not. If Karen can afford to be a little patient money-wise, she could end up with a memorable, unique, lucrative business for herself.

Both properties have strengths and deficiencies as far as meeting Karen's needs. I recommend that Karen buy Property Two for her animal-supply store because its strengths outweigh its deficiencies.

SUMMARY

1. Write as if you were actually making the recommendation.

2. Write naturally, but don't use abbreviations or contractions.

3. Make sure your position is clear.

4. Write as neatly as possible.

5. Indent your paragraphs.

6

Putting It All Together

Well, you've worked through four pretty arduous chapters of *Cracking the LSAT*. How should you feel? Answer: CONFIDENT. Why? Because you've been given a specific process for each section of the LSAT. You've got a good game plan—and the team with the good game plan usually wins the game. So here's a quick review of your game plan for each section of the exam:

ARGUMENTS

Step 1:   Read the Question

Step 2:   Work the Argument

Step 3:   Stop, Think, and Write

Step 4:   Use Process of Elimination

Pretty simple, right? Well, many people begin to get anxious and they tend to skip step 3. They want to get right to the answer choices so they can start getting confused and frustrated. However, step 3 is the most important step in this process. If you come up with your own ideas about what should be the right answer before looking at any of the choices, you'll be misled less often by those half-good answer choices.

GAMES

You should have these steps down cold by now.

Step 1:   Decide on the Appropriate Diagram and Draw It

Step 2:   Symbolize the Clues

Step 3:   Double-Check Your Clues and Make Deductions

Step 4:   Identify the Key

Step 5:   Attack the Questions

Step 6:   Use Process of Elimination

As in arguments, many students tend to skip an essential step in the games process. That step is step 3 (again). Students usually see how necessary it is to draw a diagram and symbolize the clues, but then get nervous that they've spent so much time drawing and symbolizing that they go straight to the questions. However, looking at the diagram and the symbols you've drawn for 30 seconds before going to the questions will invariably make the game easier—any deduction you make can save you up to five minutes by eliminating the need to test answer choices.

READING COMPREHENSION

Step 1:   Read the Questions

Step 2:   Attack the Passage

Step 3:   Answer the Questions in Your Own Words

Step 4:   Match Your Answers and Use Process of Elimination

Well, here we've once again highlighted step 3, because it's the most important step and it's the one students tend to skip. Nervousness about time is again the culprit. But as you learned in the Reading Comprehension chapter, pinpointing the correct answer choice becomes much easier when you've already got an idea of what you should be looking for. Don't wait for the answer choices to confuse you—attack the test questions by being ready before you go wallow in the mire of the answer choices.

PACING

The pace at which you work through each section of the LSAT will be a very big key to your success. Many students have not realized that to be effective, you need to slow down a bit and not try to maniacally jam through each section of the test. If you get to every question but have forgotten to read the word "EXCEPT" or you missed the word "however," you're not going to get the question right. Below is a chart that will help pace you on each section of the exam, based on the percentage correct you received on each section of the test the first time you did it.

This is a general chart. Don't worry about being so exact here.

Pacing Yourself			
If You Received...	**Your First Goal Is...**	**Your Intermediate Goal Is...**	**Your Final Goal Is...**
25–45% correct on Arguments	Work 12–15 arguments and try to get 10–12 right in 35 minutes	Work 15–18 arguments and try to get 12–15 right in 35 minutes	Work 18–21 arguments and try to get 15–18 right in 35 minutes
45–65% correct on Arguments	Work 15–18 arguments and try to get 12–15 right in 35 minutes	Work 18–21 arguments and try to get 15–18 right in 35 minutes	Work 21–24 arguments and try to get 18–21 right in 35 minutes
65–85% correct on Arguments	Work 18–21 arguments and try to get 15–18 right in 35 minutes	Work 21–24 arguments and try to get 18–21 right in 35 minutes	Work all the arguments and try to get 20–23 right in 35 minutes
25–45% correct on Games	Do two games correctly in 35 minutes	Get through two full games and halfway through a third one in 35 minutes	Do three games correctly in 35 minutes
45–65% correct on Games	Do two games correctly in 35 minutes	Get through three complete games in 35 minutes, missing only one or two questions	Get through three full games and half of a fourth game in 35 minutes
65–85% correct on Games	Get through two full games and half of a third game in 35 minutes	Do three complete games in 35 minutes and get halfway through the fourth game	Get through the entire section only missing a few questions in 35 minutes
25–45% correct on Reading Comprehension	Do two reading comprehension passages in 35 minutes, trying only to miss one question per passage	Do two full reading comprehension passages and get halfway through a third passage in 35 minutes	Do three full reading comprehension passages in 35 minutes
45–65% correct on Reading Comprehension	Do two full reading comprehension passages and get halfway through a third passage in 35 minutes	Do three full reading comprehension passages in 35 minutes	Do three full reading comprehension passages and get halfway through the fourth passage in 35 minutes
65–85% correct on Reading Comprehension	Do three reading comprehension passages in 35 minutes, trying only to miss one question per passage	Do three full reading comprehension passages and get halfway through the fourth passage in 35 minutes	Do four full reading comprehension passages in 35 minutes

THE DAY OF THE TEST

There is probably just as much bad advice as good advice dispensed about what to do on test day. A lot of the good advice is just common sense, but we're going to give it to you here just in case you're a bit distracted. Here we go:

Visit your test center before test day

Why worry on test day about the best way to get to the test center? Visit the test center a few weeks or days before the test so you know exactly where to go on test day. Better yet, go there with a practice LSAT and try to get into the room where you're going to take the LSAT. Work the test in that room, if possible, so you're on familiar ground the day of the test. This will do wonders for your comfort and confidence. You'll know if the room is hot or cold, whether there's a gaping hole in the roof, if it's lit with black light and fireflies, etc. Use the boy scout motto here: Be prepared.

Eat and drink what you normally eat and drink

We've heard lots of crazy stuff about what people should eat the day of the test—three cups of coffee! Steak and eggs! A box of bon-bons! Folks, if you don't normally drink coffee, the day of the LSAT is not the day to discover the wonders of mochaccino. Eat and drink what you normally eat and drink in the morning—don't all of a sudden introduce anything into your body that it's not used to ingesting at 8 a.m.

Bring some quiet and unassuming snacks

Maybe your proctor won't let you munch on anything during the break, but maybe he or she will. If so, be prepared by bringing a bottle of water and some granola bars or something. If you're subtle about it, chances are no one will care one way or the other. Bringing the martini shaker and the industrial-size bag of pork rinds is not recommended.

Bring a nonbeeping digital watch or timepiece

Once again, "unassuming" is the key here. You want to be able to keep track of the time, so go digital—you can put on your Movado when you go out partying after the LSAT. If your watch tends to beep, buy a $10 digital travel alarm clock from Radio Shack and remove the beep speaker. And with some practice, you can quickly reset your digital clock to the top of the hour at the start of each section, which will make it clear how much time you've spent on each section when you look at it. And make sure to have everything bubbled in by minute 33, so if you haven't finished the section, you'll still have an answer for every question.

Bring lots of pencils and forms of ID

Yep, you're going to be fingerprinted and asked for identification. So bring at least two forms of ID and plenty of pencils for the exam. Also, for what it's worth, highlighters are now allowed. We know you know this. Just do it.

Get there nice and early and warm up your brain

You're going to be stressed out enough on test day without worrying that you'll be late for the test. Get there nice and early (for you New Yorkers, this does *not* mean eight seconds before the test) and warm up your brain by working out a game that you've already done and perhaps running through a few arguments. That way, you'll already be in gear by the time you open up section 1. Plus, it'll make everyone else paranoid as hell.

Some stress good, much stress bad

We know you're going to be stressed the day of the exam, and a little stress is not a bad thing—it will keep you on your toes. But if you tend to get *really* stressed by standardized tests, try a yoga or meditation class, or some other type of relaxation therapy, preferably a month before the test. This way, you'll have some techniques to calm you down, taught to you by people who know what they're doing. One Princeton Review student had a dream about test day—she went into the test, and the bubbles were about five feet in diameter. She hadn't even finished bubbling in one bubble before the proctor called time. If you're having dreams like this, relaxation therapy might help.

Wear layered clothing

Who knows how cold or how warm the test center will be on test day. Wear your most comfortable layered clothing, so you can put more layers on if you're cold or take layers off if you're hot.

Confidence, my dear folks, confidence

Be confident, be aggressive, never say die

Sometimes we'll talk to students after they've taken the LSAT and they'll say: "By the time I got to section 5, I just didn't care anymore. I just filled in whatever." Don't say that, don't think that—section 5 will probably count, because the experimental section is usually in the first three sections of the exam. So when you open up your test to section 5, keep in mind that it's most likely a real section that will count toward your score. Your goal is to take three deep breaths and to fight your way through that last section, and attack it just as aggressively as you attacked the other sections of the exam. It's going to count—don't lose your confidence and your energy here, because it's almost over!

Here is another problem students have reported: "I was doing fine until I hit section 3, I didn't know how to do any of the games and I couldn't concentrate on the last two sections of the test." Well, guess what? That was probably the experimental section! Don't let a weird or tough section get you down, especially if it's early in the test. Remember, they are using the experimental sections to test new questions—some of them invariably will be bad or strange. And even if it is a section that ultimately counts toward your score, if you do well on all the other real sections, you can still get a good score.

Always keep your pencil moving

We all love to daydream. Right before the test begins, daydream about all the time you'll have to daydream after the test is over. During the test, however, keep yourself focused on the test. If you find yourself losing your concentration, take three deep breaths and move on to a different question to clear your head. Then, go back to that the question that started you daydreaming later on.

Most important, you should be using your pencil at all times during the test. Cross off all the wrong answer choices; circle and underline key words in reading comprehension and arguments passages; always diagram and symbolize in games. By constantly keeping your pencil moving, you'll be keeping your brain moving as well.

YOUR TEST DAY "TOP TEN"

Here are the tips mentioned above in a handy numbered list. Pass this on to your grandchildren—they'll be sure to treasure it.

1. Visit your test center before test day.

2. Eat and drink what you normally eat and drink.

3. Bring some quiet and unassuming snacks.

4. Bring a nonbeeping digital watch or timepiece.

5. Bring lots of pencils and forms of ID.

6. Get there nice and early and warm up your brain.

7. Some stress good, much stress bad.

8. Wear layered clothing.

9. Be confident, be aggressive, never say die.

10. Always keep your pencil moving.

Good luck on test day!

7

Law School Admissions

INTRODUCTION

LSAC, LSAT, LSDAS

The Law School Admission Council (LSAC), headquartered in Newtown, Pennsylvania, is the governing body that oversees the creation, testing, and administration of the LSAT (Law School Admission Test). The LSAC also runs the Law School Data Assembly Service (LSDAS), which provides information (in a standard format) on law school applicants to the schools themselves. All American Bar Association (ABA)-approved law schools are members of LSAC. Fascinating.

The process of applying to law school, while simple enough in theory, is viewed by many to be about as painful as a root canal. The best way to avoid the pain is to start early. If you're reading this in December and hope to get into a law school for the following year and haven't done anything about it, you're in big trouble. If you've got an LSAT score that you're happy with, you're in less trouble. However, your applications will get to the law schools after the optimum time and the applications themselves, even with the most cursory glance by an admissions officer, may appear rushed. The best way to think about applying is to start early in the year, take care of one thing at a time, and be totally finished by December.

This chapter will be mainly a nuts-and-bolts manual on what to do when applying to law school and when to do it. There will be a checklist, information about Law School Forums, fee waivers, the Law School Data Assembly Service (LSDAS), and several admissions calendars, which will show you when you need to take which step.

TRENDS

Currently, law schools are experiencing a drop in the number of students that are considered "ABA applicants." At the same time, LSAC is experiencing a drop in the number of students who take the LSAT.

Testing Year	1st Year Enrollment	Total LSAT Administrations	Est. ABA Applicants	% of Takers Applying
1981–82	42,521	119,291	72,912	61
1982–83	42,034	112,125	71,755	64
1983–84	41,159	105,076	63,801	61
1984–85	40,747	95,563	60,338	63
1985–86	40,796	91,848	61,304	67
1986–87	40,195	101,235	65,145	64
1987–88	41,055	115,988	74,938	65
1988–89	42,860	137,088	82,741	60
1989–90	43,826	138,865	88,303	64
1990–91	44,104	152,685	94,026	62
1991–92	44,050	145,567	91,954	63
1992–93	42,793	140,054	86,104	61
1993–94	43,644	132,028	84,574	64
1994–95	44,298	128,553	78,821	61
1995–96	44,000	119,186	70,899	59
1996–97	44,000	105,315	63,500	60
1997–98	42,186	104,000	67,100	65

While there is some talk about certain schools cutting back on the number of seats, there are also fewer people who are applying overall (even though the number of first-year law students has remained much more constant than either the number of LSAT takers or the number of ABA applicants). What does this mean? It might mean that there is slightly less competition for those 1L positions, even though the percentage of students who are applying to schools after they've taken the LSAT has remained fairly constant.

LSAT SCORE DISTRIBUTION

Most test-takers are interested in knowing where there LSAT scores fall within the distribution of all scores. This chart, which comes directly from LSAC, should help you determine how well you did in comparison to fellow test-takers over the last few years. Please be aware, however, that percentiles are not fixed values that remain constant overtime. Unlike an LSAT score, a percentile rank associated with a given test score may vary slightly depending on the year in which it is reported. This is just to give you a roughly accurate idea where you rank compared to those competing for the same spot in law school.

LAW SCHOOL ADMISSION TEST*

Score Distribution
June '95–February '98

Score	Percent Below	Score	Percent Below	Score	Percent Below
180	99.9	158	77.7	136	8.0
179	99.9	157	74.4	135	7.0
178	99.9	156	71.1	134	5.5
177	99.8	155	67.8	133	4.6
176	99.7	154	63.9	132	4.0
175	99.6	153	60.0	131	3.1
174	99.4	152	56.3	130	2.6
173	99.2	151	52.0	129	2.2
172	98.9	150	47.8	128	1.7
171	98.5	149	44.4	127	1.5
170	98.0	148	40.4	126	1.2
169	97.5	147	36.6	125	1.0
168	96.6	146	33.3	124	0.8
167	95.8	145	29.8	123	0.7
166	94.7	144	26.4	122	0.6
165	93.3	143	23.3	121	0.5
164	91.9	142	20.7	120	0.0
163	90.0	141	18.0		
162	88.3	140	15.3	# Scores	319,870
161	85.8	139	13.4	Mean	149.71
160	83.7	138	11.4	Std. Dev.	10.05
159	80.6	137	9.8		

* Scores earned under nonstandard conditions are not included.

Source: Law School Admission Council

When to Apply

Consider these application deadlines for fall admission: Yale Law School, on or about January 10; New York University (NYU) Law School, on or about February 1; Loyola University Chicago School of Law, on or about April 1. While some of this information may make starting the application process in December seem like a viable option, remember that law schools don't wait until they've received every application to start selecting students. In fact, the longer you wait to apply to a school, the worse your chances are of getting into that school. Maybe your chances will go only from 90 percent to 85 percent, but you shouldn't risk it if you don't have to.

Additionally, some schools have "early admissions decisions" options, so that you may know by December if you've been accepted (for instance, NYU's early admission deadline is on or about October 15). This option is good for a few reasons: It can give you an indication of what your chances are at other schools; it can relieve the stress of waiting until April to see where you're going to school; and, if you're waitlisted the first time around, you might be accepted a bit later on in the process—i.e., when everyone else is hearing from law schools for the first time. However, not every school has an early admission option, and not every school's option is the same, so check with your prospective institutions' policies before you write any deadlines on your calendar.

Let's take a look at the major steps in the application process:

Take the LSAT. All ABA-approved and most non-ABA-approved law schools in the United States and Canada require an LSAT score from each applicant. The LSAT is given in February, June, October (occasionally very late September), and December of each year.

Register for LSDAS. You can register for the Law School Data Assembly Service at the same time you register to take the LSAT—both forms are contained in the *LSAT & LSDAS Registration Information Book* (hence the name).

Select at least seven schools. After you've selected your schools, you'll be able to see which schools want what types of things on their applications—though almost all of them will want three basic things: a personal statement, recommendations, and a résumé. Why seven schools? Better safe than sorry. Each applicant should be thinking about putting law schools into three categories: (1) "reach" schools, (2) schools where you've got a good chance of being accepted, and (3) "safety" schools. As a minimum, each applicant should apply to two to three schools in each category. (Most admissions experts will say either 2-2-3 or 2-3-2; to play it safe, apply to three in each category.) It is not uncommon for those with extremely low grades or low LSAT scores (or both) to apply to fifteen or twenty schools.

Write your personal statement(s). It may be that you'll only need to write one personal statement (many schools will ask that your personal statement be about why you want to obtain a law degree), but you may need to write several—which is why you need to select your schools fairly early.

Obtain two or three recommendations. Some schools will ask for two recommendations, both of which must be academic. Others want more than two recommendations and want at least one of your recommenders to be someone who knows you outside traditional academic circles.

Law School Forums

Law School Forums are an excellent way to talk with representatives from and gather information on almost every law school in the country simultaneously. More than 150 schools send admissions officers to these forums, which take place around the country between July and November. If possible, GO:

Atlanta, GA   9/24–9/25
Grand Hyatt Atlanta
3300 Peachtree Road

Bay Area, CA   11/8
Oakland Marriott City Center
1001 Broadway

Boston, MA   10/29–10/30
Marriot Copley Place,
110 Huntington Ave.

Chicago, IL   11/12–11/13
Chicago Marriott Downtown,
540 N. Michigan Ave.

Houston, TX   10/23
JW Marriott
5150 Westheimer Road

Los Angeles, CA   11/15
Los Angeles Airport Marriott
5855 West Century Boulevard

New York, NY   9/17
New York Marriott
World Trade Center,
Three World Trade Center

Washington, DC   7/17
Omni Shoreham Hotel
2500 Calvert Street, NW

Update/create a résumé. Most law school applications ask that you submit a résumé. Make sure yours is up to date and suitable for submission to an academic situation.

Get your academic transcripts sent to LSDAS. A minor administrative detail, seemingly, but then again, if you forget to do this, LSDAS will not send your information to the law schools. LSDAS helps the law schools by acting as a clearinghouse for information—LSDAS, not you, sends the law schools your undergraduate and graduate school transcripts, your LSAT score(s), and an undergraduate academic summary.

Those are the major steps in applying to law school. From reading this chapter, or from reading the *LSAT & LSDAS Registration Information Book*, you might discover that there are other steps you need to take—such as preparing an addendum to your application, asking for application fee waivers, applying for a special administration of the LSAT, etc. If you sense that you might need to do anything special, start your application process even earlier than what is recommended in the *LSAT & LSDAS Registration Information Book*, which is unquestionably the most useful tool in applying to law school. This information book not only contains the forms to apply for the LSAT and LSDAS, but also has a sample LSAT, admissions information, the Law School Forum schedule, and two sample application schedules. These schedules are very useful. For instance, one sample schedule recommends taking the June LSAT for fall admission. This schedule allows you to focus on the LSAT in the spring and early summer and then start the rest of your application process rolling. That's good advice—as mentioned in the LSAT chapter in this book, the LSAT is the most important factor in getting into the best law school possible.

The sample schedule also indicates that you should research schools in late July/early August. While you are doing this, go ahead and subscribe to LSDAS and send your transcript request forms to your undergraduate and any other educational institutions—there's no reason to wait until September to do this (you should pay LSDAS for nine law school applications, unless you're positive you want to apply to only a few schools). Why do this? Because undergraduate institutions can and will screw up and delay the transcript process—even when you go there personally and pay them to provide your records. This is essential if you're applying for early decision at some law schools—the transcript process can be a nightmare. Your undergraduate institution already has all your money; why should they care about administrative matters like transcripts?

Finally, you should be sending your applications to law schools between late September and early November. Naturally, if you bombed the LSAT the first time around, you're still in good shape to take the test again in October. Another good piece of news on that front is that more and more law schools are now just simply taking the highest LSAT score that each applicant has, rather than averaging multiple scores. If you've got to take the LSAT again, this is good news—but with proper preparation (see the LSAT chapter) you can avoid having to spend too much quality time with the LSAT.

Law Schools that Look at Highest LSAT Scores First

Baylor University
Benjamin Cordozo School of Law
Cleveland State University
University of Colorado
University of Denver
Golden Gate University
Gonzaga University
Hamline University
University of Illinois
University of Indiana—
     Indianapolis
University of Kansas
University of Kentucky
Lewis and Clark College
Louisiana State University
Loyola University—
     New Orleans
Marquette University
Mississippi College
University of Missouri—
     Kansas City
University of North Carolina
Northwestern University
University of Notre Dame
University of Pittsburgh
Quinnipiac College
University of Richmond
Roger Williams University
     School of Law
St. Louis University
University of San Diego
Santa Clara University
Seattle University
St. John's University
Suffolk University
Texas Southern University
Thomas M. Cooley Law School
Tulane University
Wake Forest University
Washburn University
Whittier Law School
Willamette University
William Mitchell College of Law
University of Wyoming

A simple checklist

The following is a simple checklist for the major steps of the application process. Each shaded box indicates the recommended month during which you should complete that action.

	Jan.	Feb.	Mar.	Apr.	May	June	July	Aug.	Sept.	Oct.	Nov.	Dec.
Take practice LSAT	▓											
Research LSAT prep companies		▓										
Obtain *Registration Information Book**			▓									
Register for June LSAT				▓								
Take LSAT prep course					▓							
Take LSAT						▓						
Register for LSDAS							▓					
Research law schools								▓				
Obtain law school applications								▓				
Get transcripts sent to LSDAS								▓				
Write personal statement(s)									▓			
Update/create résumé									▓			
Get recommendations									▓			
Send early decision applications										▓		
Finish sending all applications											▓	
Chill												▓

*The *LSAT & LSDAS Registration Information Book* is traditionally published in March of each year. Call 215-968-1001 to order your materials.

HELPFUL HINTS ON PERSONAL STATEMENTS, RECOMMENDATIONS, RÉSUMÉS, AND ADDENDA

While your LSAT score is the most important factor in the admissions process, you should still present a professional résumé, get excellent recommendations, and hone your personal statement when preparing your law school applications. Many law schools still employ the "three-pile" system in the application process:

Pile 1 contains applicants with high enough LSAT scores and GPAs to admit them pretty much automatically.

Pile 2 contains applicants who are "borderline"—decent enough LSAT scores and GPAs for that school, but not high enough for automatic admission. Admissions officers look at these applications thoroughly to sort out the best candidates.

Pile 3 contains applicants with "substandard" LSAT scores and GPAs for that school. These applicants are usually rejected without much further ado. There are circumstances in which admissions officers will look through pile 3 for any extraordinary applications, but it doesn't happen very often.

What does this mean? Well, if you're lucky, you are in pile 2 (and not pile 3!) for at least one of your "reach" schools. And if you are, there's a good possibility that your application will be thoroughly scrutinized by the admissions committee. Consequently, make sure the following four elements of your application are as strong as you can possibly make them:

Personal statement

Ideally, your personal statement should be two pages long. Often, law schools will ask you to identify exactly why you want to go to law school and obtain a law degree. "I love 'L.A. Law' reruns" is not the answer to this question. There should be some moment in your life, some experience that you had, or some intellectual slant that you are interested in that is directing you to law school. Identify that, write about it, and make it compelling. Then you should have three or four people read your personal statement and critique it. You should select people whom you respect intellectually, not people who will merely say, "Gee, that looks cool." Also, your personal statement is not the place to make excuses, get on your soapbox, or try your hand at alliterative verse. Make it intelligent, persuasive, short, and powerful—those are the writing and analytical qualities law schools are looking for.

> Make it intelligent, persuasive, short, and powerful—those are the writing and analytical qualities law schools are looking for.

Recommendations

Most law schools ask for two or three recommendations. Typically, the longer it has been since you've graduated, the tougher it is to obtain academic recommendations. However, if you've kept your papers and if your professors were tenured, chances are you'll still be able to find them and obtain good recommendations—just present your selected prof with your personal statement and a decent paper you did in their course. That way, the recommender has something tangible to work from. And that's the simple secret to great recommendations— if the people you're asking for recommendations don't know anything specific about you, how can the recommendation possibly be compelling? Getting the mayor of your town or a state senator to write a recommendation only helps if you have a personal and professional connection to them in some way. That way, the recommender will be able to present to the admissions committee actual qualities and accomplishments you have demonstrated. If you've been out of school for some time and are having trouble finding academic recommendations, choose people from your workplace, from the community, or from any other area of your life that is important to you. You should respect the people you choose—you should view them as quality individuals who have in some way shaped your life. If they're half as good as you think they are, they will know, at least intuitively, that they in some way were responsible for part of your development or education, and they will then be able to talk intelligently about it. Simply put, these people should know who you are, where you live, what your background is, and what your desires and motivations are—otherwise, your recommendations will not distinguish you from the ten-foot-high pile that's on the admissions committee desk.

Résumés

Résumés are a fairly simple part of your application, but make sure yours is updated and proofed correctly. Errors on your résumé (and, indeed, anywhere on your application) will make you look as if you don't really care too much about going to law school. Just remember that this should be a more academically oriented résumé, since you are applying to an academic institution. Put your academic credentials and experiences first—no matter what they are.

Addenda

If your personal and academic life has run fairly smoothly, you shouldn't need to include any addenda with your application. Addenda are brief explanatory letters written to explain or support a "deficient" portion of your application. Some legitimate addenda topics are: academic probation, low/discrepant GPA, low/discrepant LSAT score, arrests/convictions, DUI/DWI suspensions, a leave of absence or other "time gap," etc. The addenda is not the place to go off on polemics about standardized testing—if you've taken the LSAT two or three times and simply did not do very well, after spending time preparing with a test prep company or private tutor, merely tell the admissions committee that that's what you've done—you worked as hard as you could to achieve a high score and explored all possibilities to help you achieve that goal. Then let them draw their own conclusions. Additionally, addenda should be brief and balanced—do not go into detailed descriptions of things. Explain the problem and state what you did about it. Simply put, do not whine.

GATHERING INFORMATION AND MAKING DECISIONS

There are some key questions that you should ask before randomly selecting law schools around the country or submitting your application to someone or other's list of the "top ten" law schools and saying, "If I don't get in to one of these schools, I'll go to B-school instead." Here are some questions to think about:

Where would you like to practice law?

For instance, if you were born and bred in the state of Nebraska, care deeply about it, wish to practice law there, and want to someday be governor, then it might be a better move to go to the University of Nebraska School of Law than, say, University of Virginia, even though UVA is considered a "top ten" law school. A law school's reputation is usually greater on its home turf than anywhere else (except for Harvard and Yale). Apply to the schools in the geographic area where you wish to practice law. You'll be integrated into the community, you may gain some experience in the region doing clinics during law school, and it should be easier for you to get more interviews and position yourself as someone who already knows, for instance, Nebraska.

What type of law would you like to practice?

Law schools *do* have specialties. For instance, if you are very interested in environmental law, it might be better to go to the University of Vermont School of Law than to go to NYU. The University of Vermont is one of the most highly regarded schools in the country when it comes to environmental law. So look at what you want to do in addition to where you want to do it.

Can you get in?

Many, many people apply to Harvard. Very, very few get in. Go right ahead and apply, if you wish, but unless you've got killer scores and/or have done some very outstanding things in your life (it's okay if you haven't; really it is) your chances are, well, *slim*. Apply to a few reach schools, but make sure they are schools you really want to go to.

Did you like the school when you went there?

What if you decided to go to Stanford, got in, went to Palo Alto, California, and decided that you hated it? The weather was horrible! The architecture was mundane! There's nothing to do nearby! Well, maybe Stanford wasn't the best example—but you get the point. Go to the school and check it out. Talk to students and faculty. Walk around. Kick the tires. *Then* make a decision.

CONCLUSION

The application process is pretty darned simple. It's a lot easier than taking the extremely stressful LSAT, which in turn will be a lot easier than your first year of law school—no matter where you go. However, you've still got to want to go to law school. Otherwise, your applications will be sloppy and late, and you won't get accepted by the schools that you really want to go to. If all this administrative stuff seems overwhelming (i.e., you're the type of person who dreads filling out a deposit slip), the major test-prep companies have designed law school application courses that force you to think about where you want to go and make sure you've got all your recommendations, résumés, personal statements, addenda, and everything else together.

Whatever your level of administrative facility, the choice of where you want to go to school is yours. You'll probably be paying a lot of money to go, so you should really make sure you go to the place that's best for you. Take the time to do research on the schools, because you'll be paying for law school for a long, long time.

Applying on Computer

Almost all law schools want their applications typed. Although this is not exactly an insurmountable hurdle, there are two services that can help you simplify the process. One, law Multi-App, has more than sixty leading law school applications on computer. With Law Multi-App you enter 80 percent of your data only once—then the software bounces it out to each school's unique form. You can quickly download the package from their web site www.multi-app.com or call (800) 51-LAW-AP and have it shipped. Mention The Princeton Review when ordering Multi-App and get 10 percent off the price of the software (don't say we never did anything for you). The other software package, *LSACD*, has almost all the accredited schools on the CD-ROM and contains a searchable database to help you find the best schools for you. You can order the LSAC CD-ROM from the *LSAT & LSDAS Registration Information Book* or from the Law Services web site at www.lsac.org.

8

The Princeton Review
LSAT Diagnostic Test I

ABOUT OUR PRINCETON REVIEW LSAT DIAGNOSTIC

If you can't get your hands on some actual LSATs, our diagnostic test is the next best thing. As we said in chapter 1, you should practice on real LSATs only. Don't be fooled by the sample questions in the other books, which are only superficially similar to actual LSAT questions.

We have constructed our diagnostic test using the same sophisticated procedures and statistical methods used in creating actual LSATs. Thousands of Princeton Review students have taken this test, so we know it is an excellent predictor of LSAT scores. It includes the four sections that contribute to your LSAT score; we have spared you the trouble of taking the unscored experimental section and Writing Sample.

How to Take This Test

Be sure to review the chapters in this book before sitting down to take this test. Clear some table space, take your phone off the hook, and try to complete these sections in one sitting. You may want to take a break after completing the first two sections. If possible, have a friend time you. Trust us: Timing yourself is not nearly the same experience.

THE
PRINCETON
REVIEW

L S A T

Law School Admission Test

SECTION I

Time—35 minutes

24 Questions

Directions: Each group of questions in this section is based on a set of conditions. In answering some of the questions, it may be useful to draw a rough diagram. Choose the response that most accurately and completely answers each question and blacken the corresponding space on your answer sheet.

Questions 1–5

R, S, T, U, V, X, Y, and Z are the only buildings in an urban development.

Building X has more stories than both building T and building Z.

Building Z has more stories than both building T and building Y.

Building T has more stories than building R.

Building R has more stories than building V.

Building Y has more stories than building V.

Building U has more stories than building R but fewer than building S.

1. Which one of the following can be false?

   (A) Building T has more stories than building V.
   (B) Building U has more stories than building V.
   (C) Building X has more stories than building S.
   (D) Building Z has more stories than building R.
   (E) Building Z has more stories than building V.

2. Which one of the following must be false?

   (A) Building R has more stories than building Z.
   (B) Building S has more stories than building X.
   (C) Building S has fewer stories than building Y.
   (D) Building U has more stories than building Z.
   (E) Building Y has more stories than building T.

3. If building S has the same number of stories as building Y, then which one of the following must be true?

   (A) Building T has more stories than building U.
   (B) Building V has more stories than building S.
   (C) Building Z has more stories than building U.
   (D) Building Z has fewer stories than building U.
   (E) Building Z has fewer stories than building S.

4. If building U has more stories than building Z, how many of the buildings could be the third tallest?

   (A) 1
   (B) 2
   (C) 3
   (D) 4
   (E) 5

5. If it is true that the building with the fewest stories is eleven stories tall and the building with the most stories is fifteen stories tall, then which one of the following buildings could have twelve stories?

   (A) building S
   (B) building T
   (C) building U
   (D) building Y
   (E) building Z

GO ON TO THE NEXT PAGE.

Questions 6–12

In a four-floor college dormitory, there are exactly three student resident advisors—Ruiz, Smith, and Turner—who each have graduate or undergraduate status. They are assigned to floors according to the following restrictions:

Each floor of the dormitory can have only one resident advisor.
Ruiz is assigned to the fourth floor.
Smith has graduate status.
Smith is assigned to a floor above Turner.
If there is a resident advisor on the third floor, then that advisor is of the same status as the resident advisor on the fourth floor.
The resident advisors are not all of the same status.

6. Which one of the following statements must be false?

   (A) Smith is on the second floor.
   (B) Smith is on the third floor.
   (C) Turner is on the first floor.
   (D) Turner is on the second floor.
   (E) Turner is on the third floor.

7. Which one of the following statements could be true?

   (A) Ruiz is an undergraduate student, and Turner is a graduate student who is on the second floor.
   (B) Ruiz is an undergraduate student, and Turner is an undergraduate student who is on the second floor.
   (C) Smith is on the third floor, and Turner is a graduate student who is on the first floor.
   (D) Smith is on the third floor, and Turner is an undergraduate student who is on the first floor.
   (E) Smith is on the third floor, and Turner is a graduate student who is on the second floor.

8. If Ruiz is an undergraduate student, which one of the following statements could be true?

   (A) Smith is on the first floor.
   (B) Smith is on the third floor.
   (C) Turner is a graduate student who is on the first floor.
   (D) Turner is a graduate student who is on the second floor.
   (E) Turner is an undergraduate student who is on the second floor.

9. If neither Smith nor Turner is on the third floor, then which of the following must be true?

   (A) There is a graduate student on the first floor.
   (B) There is a graduate student on the fourth floor.
   (C) There is a graduate student on the second floor.
   (D) There is an undergraduate student on the fourth floor.
   (E) There is an undergraduate student on the second floor.

10. Which one of the following statements must be true?

   (A) Ruiz and Smith are both the same status.
   (B) Ruiz and Turner are both the same status.
   (C) Smith and Turner are both the same status.
   (D) Either Ruiz or Turner or both have undergraduate status.
   (E) Either Ruiz or Turner or both have graduate status.

11. If neither Smith nor Turner lives on the first floor, which one of the following statements must be true?

   (A) Ruiz is an undergraduate student.
   (B) Turner is a graduate student.
   (C) Neither Smith nor Turner is a graduate student who lives on the second floor.
   (D) Neither Smith nor Turner is an undergraduate student who lives on the second floor.
   (E) Neither Smith nor Turner is a graduate student who lives on the third floor.

12. Which one of the following CANNOT be true?

   (A) There is an advisor with graduate status who lives on the fourth floor.
   (B) There is an advisor with graduate status who lives on the third floor.
   (C) There is an advisor with undergraduate status who lives on the fourth floor.
   (D) There is an advisor with undergraduate status who lives on the second floor.
   (E) There is an advisor with undergraduate status who lives on the third floor.

GO ON TO THE NEXT PAGE.

Questions 13–18

A track and field coach must assign eight athletes—A, B, C, D, R, S, T, and U—into two groups of four athletes each, one group assigned to compete in events, one athlete at a time, on Saturday, and the other group to compete, also one athlete at a time, on Sunday. All events will be scheduled for the same amount of time, and every event on Sunday is scheduled for exactly the same time slot as an event that takes place on Saturday. The assignments must also conform to the following conditions:

> A must compete on one of the days in the same time slot that C competes on the other day.
> B must compete on one of the days in the same time slot that D competes on the other day.
> R must compete on the same day as A.
> S must compete on the same day as D.
> T must compete in the second time slot on Sunday.

13. Which one of the following, without regard to the order in which they will compete, could be the group of athletes to be assigned to the events on Saturday?

    (A) A, B, C, and S
    (B) A, B, D, and R
    (C) B, C, D, and S
    (D) C, D, S, and U
    (E) D, R, S, and U

14. If athlete S competes on Saturday, which one of the following athletes must compete on Sunday?

    (A) A
    (B) B
    (C) C
    (D) R
    (E) U

15. If athlete R must compete on one of the days in the same time slot that athlete S competes on the other day, which one of the following must be the second athlete to compete on Saturday?

    (A) A
    (B) B
    (C) C
    (D) D
    (E) U

16. If the order, from first to last, of athletes to compete on Sunday is D, T, S, C, which one of the following is an acceptable order of athletes on Saturday, also from first to last?

    (A) A, R, B, U
    (B) B, U, A, R
    (C) B, U, R, A
    (D) U, B, A, R
    (E) U, R, B, A

17. If athlete A must compete between athlete T and athlete R on Sunday, which one of the following must be the first athlete to compete on Saturday?

    (A) B
    (B) C
    (C) D
    (D) S
    (E) U

18. If athlete S must compete on Saturday immediately after athlete A and immediately before athlete R, which athlete must be the third to compete on Sunday?

    (A) B
    (B) C
    (C) D
    (D) S
    (E) U

GO ON TO THE NEXT PAGE.

Questions 19–24

A senior partner of a large law firm is assigning lawyers to each of three of the firm's cases: Case 1, Case 2, and Case 3. Exactly two of the following lawyers must be assigned to each case: Ayala, Bloom, Carpenter, Duggan, Emerson, and Fong. Each lawyer will be assigned to exactly one case. Ayala, Bloom, and Carpenter are senior associates at the firm; Duggan, Emerson, and Fong are not. Ayala, Duggan, and Emerson are corporate tax attorneys; Bloom, Carpenter, and Fong are not. The senior partner must assign the lawyers to the three cases according to the following requirements:

At least one senior associate must be assigned to each case.

At least one corporate tax attorney must be assigned to each case.

Duggan must be assigned to either Case 1 or Case 2.

19. Which one of the following is a possible list of assignments of lawyers to cases according to the requirements?

	Case 1	Case 2	Case 3
(A)	Duggan	Emerson	Ayala
	Fong	Bloom	Carpenter
(B)	Duggan	Emerson	Ayala
	Bloom	Fong	Carpenter
(C)	Emerson	Duggan	Ayala
	Carpenter	Bloom	Fong
(D)	Emerson	Ayala	Duggan
	Carpenter	Bloom	Fong
(E)	Ayala	Duggan	Bloom
	Fong	Emerson	Carpenter

20. Which one of the following must be true?

(A) Ayala and Carpenter will be assigned to the same case.
(B) Ayala and Fong will be assigned to the same case.
(C) Duggan and Bloom will be assigned to the same case.
(D) Duggan and Fong will be assigned to the same case.
(E) Emerson and Bloom will be assigned to the same case.

21. Which one of the following is a complete and accurate list of the lawyers whom the senior partner can assign to the same case as Carpenter?

(A) Bloom
(B) Duggan
(C) Emerson
(D) Bloom and Fong
(E) Duggan and Emerson

22. If Emerson is assigned to Case 2, which one of the following must be true?

(A) Bloom is assigned to Case 1.
(B) Carpenter is assigned to Case 2.
(C) Carpenter is assigned to Case 3.
(D) Fong is assigned to Case 1.
(E) Fong is assigned to Case 3.

23. The senior partner CANNOT make an acceptable assignment of lawyers to cases by assigning

(A) Ayala to Case 1 and Bloom to Case 2
(B) Ayala to Case 2 and Carpenter to Case 3
(C) Duggan to Case 2 and Emerson to Case 3
(D) Emerson to Case 1 and Carpenter to Case 3
(E) Fong to Case 1 and Duggan to Case 2

24. If Bloom is assigned to Case 3, which one of the following must be true?

(A) Ayala is assigned to Case 2.
(B) Carpenter is assigned to Case 1.
(C) Emerson is assigned to Case 1.
(D) Duggan is assigned to the same case as Bloom.
(E) Duggan is assigned to the same case as Carpenter.

S T O P

IF YOU FINISH BEFORE TIME IS CALLED, YOU MAY CHECK YOUR WORK ON THIS SECTION ONLY. DO NOT WORK ON ANY OTHER SECTION IN THE TEST.

SECTION II

Time—35 minutes

27 Questions

Directions: Each passage in this section is followed by a group of questions to be answered on the basis of what is <u>stated</u> or <u>implied</u> in the passage. For some questions, more than one of the choices could conceivably answer the question. However, you are to choose the <u>best</u> answer, that is, the response that most accurately and completely answers the question, and blacken the corresponding space on your answer sheet.

It is commonly asserted that an ideology is powerless against political interest groups and against the unflagging tendency of established social institutions to expand. To dispute this claim, however,
(5) we need only look to the present day political situation. There is, at the present time, an unfortunate political revolution under way among Western countries that is occurring in spite of potent political opposition.

For most of the postwar period, there was a
(10) proliferation of government social welfare programs designed to raise the income share of the poor. Such programs serve, in various forms, to redistribute wealth among the population at large, generally taking from those who are better situated and giving to those who
(15) are economically disadvantaged. As a result of their implementation, the plight of the poor was ameliorated to an even greater degree than was expected.

Despite these positive advances, one school of ideology, known as *redistributional retrenchment,* has
(20) long argued that the gains from redistribution programs are far outweighed by adverse economic side effects. In the wake of the worldwide slowdown in economic growth following the first oil embargo of 1973, these arguments have been treated with increasing respect,
(25) resulting in deliberate government curtailing of social welfare spending. As a consequence, in the United States, England, Germany, and even in the Netherlands and Scandinavia, public income transfer programs have been or are being cut back. On the face of it, only
(30) France and Italy seem to be resisting the trend; Switzerland, though it partook in the rapid expansion of the earlier period, has temporarily reached a plateau in spending. The political mentality that supports redistributional retrenchment now holds considerable
(35) sway. As a consequence of the deliberate government curtailment of social welfare spending, the Western poor are measurably worse off today than they were just a decade ago.

In addition, every dollar cut from the budget of such
(40) programs reduces the government payroll by twenty cents. Thus, the curtailment of social welfare programs has caused a decrease in the number of government jobs. The resulting unemployment has not been fully absorbed by the private sector. There is, then, in

(45) addition to the many poor whose benefits have been cut, a large number of middle-income citizens who oppose redistributional retrenchment.

Given those facts, one would expect everyday political forces to reverse this trend of social welfare
(50) cutbacks. Yet no reversal has occurred. Counting on fundamental principles of democracy and the ultimate power of the vote, political hopefuls have sought to attain office by appealing to such people and addressing the genuine economic distress they are
(55) experiencing. Their efforts have, for the most part, failed. Indeed, those government legislators, administrators, and executives who felt confident that they would succeed in abating the trend, simply because the number of voting citizens who stood to
(60) suffer was so large, underestimated the power of the redistributional-retrenchment ideology. It continues to advance notwithstanding the adverse effect it has had on huge sectors of the population.

1. Which one of the following best states the <u>main idea</u> of the passage?

(A) We must determine whether redistribution offers more benefit than cost.
(B) For a number of reasons, political pressures have failed to slow government redistribution programs.
(C) The ideology behind redistributional retrenchment is currently more powerful than the political forces opposing it.
(D) Governments have curtailed social welfare spending deliberately in order to worsen the plight of the poor.
(E) Redistributional retrenchment is contrary to democratic ideals.

GO ON TO THE NEXT PAGE.

2. According to the passage, which one of the following was most important in creating the modern trend toward redistributional retrenchment?

   (A) arguments that suggest that redistribution programs have negative economic consequences

   (B) the fact that most social welfare programs did not actually serve society's welfare

   (C) the unexpected discovery that redistribution programs raised the income share of the poor

   (D) the tendency of institutions and procedures to maintain themselves

   (E) the fact that most industrialized nations have reached a permanent plateau in their ability to spend

3. In the fourth paragraph of the passage, the author attempts to

   (A) prove that democracy is more potent than any individual ideology

   (B) indicate that not only poor citizens are harmed by redistributional retrenchment

   (C) argue that in a democracy the vote is not as powerful as it is thought to be

   (D) illustrate that government officials do not always understand the political process

   (E) highlight the failure of ordinary political forces to overcome redistributional retrenchment

4. It can be inferred from the passage that the author

   (A) favors redistributional retrenchment but is concerned about its effect on the poor

   (B) opposes redistributional retrenchment because of its effect on the poor and working class

   (C) does not believe democracy can effectively represent the interests of the poor

   (D) thinks redistributional retrenchment is appropriate to some nations but not to others

   (E) believes that redistributional retrenchment was a hasty reaction to a temporary economic slowdown

5. The phrase "potent political opposition" (line 8) refers to

   (A) the ideology that favors taking wealth from the more fortunate and distributing it to the less fortunate

   (B) the political view that opposes redistribution on a large scale

   (C) the adverse effects of redistribution programs on international economic transactions

   (D) the large number of eligible voters who benefit from the existence of social welfare programs

   (E) the large number of political officials who support redistributional retrenchment

6. It can be inferred from the information in the passage that the author believes that redistributional retrenchment

   (A) has reduced profits for private industry

   (B) exerts its most serious effects on public employees

   (C) has produced only 20 percent of the savings its supporters expected

   (D) has left private industry unable to find qualified workers to fill its needs

   (E) has caused unemployment among some citizens who would otherwise have jobs

GO ON TO THE NEXT PAGE.

A fundamental element of the American criminal justice system is trial by an impartial jury. This constitutionally protected guarantee is made meaningful by allowing the defendant to challenge and

(5) have removed from the panel those prospective jurors who are demonstrably prejudiced in the case. Such prejudice may be based on a juror's having some tangible interest in the case or on his relationship to the participants. Beyond this, a juror may be challenged if

(10) the defendant can show that the juror has preconceptions about the issues or parties that would prevent him from rendering a verdict based solely on the law and the evidence put forth at trial. In order to enable the defendant to discover these disqualifying factors,

(15) prospective jurors are subjected to questioning by the court or counsel or both. This interrogation is known as the *voir dire* examination.

Generally, the courts have recognized that any prejudice affecting the ability of a juror to decide a

(20) case fairly is a sufficient ground for a challenge. Such prejudices can be categorized in two basic ways: as a bias implied as a matter of law and as actual bias. The former may include such objective factors as a juror's relationship to a participant in the trial, whereas the

(25) latter may involve such subjective characteristics as racial, religious, economic, social, or political prejudices that would prevent the juror from trying the case fairly.

There is, however, a fundamental disagreement as to

(30) the extent to which the *voir dire* examination does, in fact, uncover juror prejudice. It has been suggested that once the prospective jurors are in the courtroom, they feel that disqualification for bias would impugn their integrity and may, therefore, be willing to lie to avoid

(35) removal from the panel.

While it may be true that people will not invariably answer truthfully on *voir dire*, the same may be said of other stages of the trial. That witnesses do not always testify truthfully at trial compels neither the conclusion

(40) that it is useless to examine or cross-examine them nor the conclusion that the trial process itself is invalid. Similarly, the recognition that prospective jurors may at times suppress what they know to be their own weaknesses need not lead to the determination that the

(45) *voir dire* process itself is worthless.

There is, for the most part, an absence of both explicit statutory guidelines and clear Supreme Court rulings indicating what specific inquiries must be made if *voir dire* is to fulfill its constitutional function. What

(50) the Constitution requires, and will be held to require, of juror interrogation as to, for example, racial prejudice is unclear. Recent case law suggests, however, that policy considerations and perhaps the Constitution itself call for some degree of direct and specific

(55) questioning as to not only racial bias, but also as to other common sources of prejudice as well.

7. The primary purpose of this passage is to

(A) criticize a constitutionally guaranteed right
(B) show how the Constitution fails to protect racial minorities
(C) examine the problems inherent in a legal process
(D) illustrate the weakness that qualifies an otherwise flawless process
(E) compare two criteria that define a legal process

8. The passage suggests that *voir dire* fails in regard to which one of the following issues?

(A) whether counsel or the court should conduct interrogations
(B) determining whether a juror is actually prejudiced with regard to a certain case
(C) the lack of specific statutory guidelines that designate when inquiries should be made
(D) the need to keep issues of law free of social, religious, racial, or economic issues
(E) the objectivity of counsel when interrogating potential jurors

GO ON TO THE NEXT PAGE.

9. The author states that "witnesses do not always testify truthfully" (lines 38–39) in order to highlight the fact that

    (A) lying on the part of trial participants is inevitable
    (B) distinguishing what is true from what is false is one of a juror's duties
    (C) *voir dire* is yet another opportunity for citizens to suppress their prejudices
    (D) witness testimony should not represent the exclusive premise upon which a defendant rests his case
    (E) many levels of the judicial process can be marred by suppression of the truth

10. It can be inferred from the passage that *voir dire*, while possessing specific flaws, is designed to

    (A) aid the defendant by providing him with a trial by an impartial jury
    (B) weed out jurors who do not support the defendant's point of view
    (C) reveal a potential juror's racist inclinations
    (D) convince a prospective juror that his or her duty is to reach a verdict based on the law
    (E) interrogate potential jurors and make them testify to their own prejudices

11. With which one of the following statements would the author be most likely to agree?

    (A) Prospective jurors should be subjected to rigorous questioning regarding their feelings towards specific social, ethnic, and economic groups.
    (B) The virtues of *voir dire* need to be carefully weighed against the limitations before the process is constitutionally mandated.
    (C) Because people can be depended upon to lie during a *voir dire* interrogation, the process itself should be deemed unconstitutional by the Supreme Court.
    (D) Courts should clarify which prejudices constitute sufficient grounds for a challenge.
    (E) While a trial by an impartial jury is a fundamental element of the criminal justice system, the *voir dire* process is the most limited way of approaching the idea.

12. Based on the information in the passage, in which one of the following circumstances might a defendant effectively challenge a prospective juror?

    (A) the prosecutor and the juror share the same racial background
    (B) the juror is ignorant of the laws applicable to the case
    (C) the juror is shown to be a habitual liar
    (D) the juror is casually acquainted with the prosecuting party
    (E) the juror has been disqualified from previous *voir dire* examinations

13. The author states that which one of the following might be a prospective juror's reason for suppressing information that might prejudice him or her from participating in a trial?

    (A) the prospective juror's actual bias with regard to issues such as race, economics, and religion
    (B) the desire to avoid maligning one's own reputation as an objective, bias-free citizen
    (C) the need to feel accepted by an institution of the U.S. government
    (D) the truth is considered less dangerous outside of an actual trial situation
    (E) the prospective juror's desire to mask his or her relationship to trial participants

GO ON TO THE NEXT PAGE.

Late in the nineteenth century, land reform emerged as a dominant concern of the Liberal Party in England. During this time, many prominent thinkers dissented from mainstream liberal ideology by questioning the
(5) justification of individual ownership. To John Stuart Mill, Henry George, and Herbert Spencer, for example, land represented something unique among ownable goods as "a thing not made by man, a thing necessary to life, and of which there is not enough for all." With
(10) these attributes—naturalness of origin, absolute scarcity, and centrality to all productive life-sustaining activity—land and land ownership, it was asserted, could be considered indefensible rights based upon personal labor or achievement.

(15) Prior to the emergence of these political analysts, the *laissez-faire* views of Adam Smith were the dominant liberal position. Smith asserted that "the interests of the state require that land should be as much in commerce as any other good." The "new
(20) liberal" thinking, however, rejected this traditional notion and attacked the institutions of primogeniture and strict family settlement that enabled the landed class to maintain their estates from one generation to the next. The new liberal ideology encompassed both
(25) economic and social goals. They envisioned a break with the static conditions of primogeniture and its replacement with a more egalitarian and morally vigorous society of peasant proprietors.

In addressing the dilemma of land ownership,
(30) proponents of the new liberal thinking offered several different strategies. Herbert Spencer's proposal sought to make land the joint property of society in which all land would be confiscated by the (democratic) state. Individuals might then lease parts of it through
(35) competitive bidding. By paying rent, tenants would thus compensate all non-owners for having relinquished their claim.

John Stuart Mill employed the law of rent to show that increased land values cannot be attributed to the
(40) exertions undertaken by owners; most often, rather, such increases are the function of the "mere progress of wealth and population." In his *Political Economy*, Mill held that private property is justified only insofar as the proprietor of land is its improver. Some policies
(45) advocated by Mill included a special tax on rent, the protection of tenants' rights, state land purchases, and the prohibition of any further enclosures of common lands. While supporting some land reform measures, however, Mill insisted that present owners were owed
(50) compensation. His proposal of a special tax on land pertained to future unearned income without disturbing past acquisitions.

According to Henry George, another prominent new liberal, virtually all social and moral ills of modern
(55) society could be traced to private ownership of land. In *Progress and Poverty*, George rejects the inevitability of poverty and deprivation as remedial defects of society. In his view, rent represented not only unearned income, but a deleterious drain on much of
(60) society's earned income that absorbed the disposable surplus created by society's cooperative efforts. George's solution lay in the socialization of rent. He proposed that the community recapture its entitlement through a special tax on the rental value of land; a
(65) levy—known as the "single tax"—would eliminate the need for taxing productive enterprises and would eventually replace all other taxes.

14. The primary purpose of the passage is to
(A) discuss contrasting views on land reform among nineteenth-century English liberals
(B) trace the development of land ownership laws in England
(C) describe a current debate on land ownership
(D) prove that Adam Smith was not truly a *laissez-faire* liberal
(E) suggest a new political approach to the problem of land scarcity

15. According to the passage, all of the following characteristics were ascribed to land as justification for its special treatment EXCEPT
(A) the limited availability of land as a resource
(B) its nonartificial essence
(C) the integral nature of the commodity to human existence
(D) the effort required to increase its value
(E) the historical precedent for private property

GO ON TO THE NEXT PAGE.

16. According to the passage, Henry George considered economic deprivation to be

(A) an unfortunate but necessary global condition
(B) a temporary state that would inevitably be reversed
(C) a condition that varied according to the policies of the ruling elites
(D) a situation that could be rectified by employing certain policies
(E) a condition that was unlikely to be alleviated

17. In addressing the issue of land reform, Mill prescribed that the unearned benefits accrued to landowners from prior transactions should be

(A) unlike future transactions in that they should not be taxed
(B) considered invalid and used for the benefits of all citizens
(C) left undisturbed by the society at large
(D) confiscated and distributed to the neediest members of society
(E) dealt with on a case-by-case basis in determining their disposal

18. The author introduces the term "new liberal" (lines 19–20) in order to

(A) delineate the dominant political parties of the time
(B) compare the views of Adam Smith to conservative land theories
(C) present a view that differed from traditional liberal thinking
(D) differentiate between U.S. liberals and English liberals
(E) explain the traditional opposition to the institution of primogeniture

19. According to the passage, Mill believed that a landowner would be entitled to profit from his holdings as long as he

(A) did so without taking unfair advantage of the less fortunate
(B) offered some of the profits to be used for the public betterment
(C) was prepared to pay substantial taxes on his past and present holdings
(D) was directly responsible for improving the condition of the land
(E) supplied parts of the land for communal use

20. Based on the content of the passage, one can infer that, according to the traditional liberal outlook prior to the late nineteenth century, land was viewed as

(A) an entity that should be used for the benefit of the entire society
(B) a means by which wealth could be redistributed
(C) a valid, but potentially deleterious, means of producing wealth
(D) a private commodity to be bought and sold without outside interference
(E) an area that developed mysteriously even without human interference

GO ON TO THE NEXT PAGE.

[This passage was written in 1983.]

In both developed and developing nations, governments finance, produce, and distribute various goods and services. In recent years, the range of goods provided by the government has extended broadly, (5) encompassing many goods that do not meet the economic purist's definition of "public goods." As the size of the public sector has increased steadily, there has been a growing concern about the effectiveness of the public sector's performance as producer.

(10) Critics argue that the public provision of certain goods is inefficient and have proposed that the private sector should replace many current public sector activities, that is, these services should be privatized. During the Reagan administration, greater privatization (15) efforts have been pursued in the United States. Concurrent with this trend has been a strong endorsement by international bilateral donor agencies for heavier reliance on the private sector in developing countries. The underlying claim is that the private (20) sector can improve the quality of outputs and deliver goods more quickly and less expensively than the public sector in these countries.

This claim, however, has mixed theoretical support and little empirical verification in the Third World. The (25) political, institutional, and economic environments of developing nations are markedly different from those of developed countries. It is not clear that the theories and empirical evidence that purport to justify privatization in developed countries are applicable to (30) developing countries. Often policy makers in developing nations do not have sufficient information to design effective policy shifts to increase efficiency of providing goods through private initiatives. Additionally, there is a lack of basic understanding (35) about what policy variables need to be altered to attain desired outcomes of privatization in developing countries.

A recent study of privatization in Honduras examined the policy shift from "direct administration" (40) to "contracting out" for three construction activities: urban upgrading for housing projects, rural primary schools, and rural roads. It tested key hypotheses pertaining to the effectiveness of privatization, focusing on three aspects: cost, time, and quality.

(45) The main finding was that contracting out in Honduras did not lead to the common expectations of its proponents because institutional barriers and limited competitiveness in the marketplace have prevented private contractors from improving quality and (50) reducing the time and cost required for construction.

Privatization in developing countries cannot produce goods and services efficiently without substantial reform in the market and regulatory procedures. Policy makers interested in privatization as (55) a policy measure should consider carefully the multiple objectives at the national level.

21. The author's primary purpose in the passage is to

(A) outline some of the shortcomings of privatization in developing nations
(B) contrast the public sector's performance as producer in the United States and Honduras
(C) explain the conditions that are necessary for privatization in Third World nations
(D) justify heavier reliance on the private sector in developing countries
(E) offer a solution for the future course of Honduran economic policy

22. It can be inferred by the author's assessment of the Honduras study that a problem with introducing privatization in developing nations is that

(A) most leaders of developing nations do not concur with the policies of the Reagan administration
(B) the direct administration of services requires more capital than contracting out does
(C) many developing nations lack the necessary competition between contractors in the marketplace
(D) privatization of services is not politically acceptable in the struggling economies of Third World nations
(E) contracting out is limited to upgrading facilities and most developing nations need to concentrate on constructing new facilities

GO ON TO THE NEXT PAGE.

23. Which one of the following would weaken the author's statements about privatization in developing nations?

   (A) The leading industrial nations have all benefited from the improved efficiency of privatization.
   (B) International bilateral donor agencies have endorsed privatization efforts in developing nations.
   (C) Many international economists favor the policies of the Reagan administration.
   (D) A recent study of ten Third World nations found evidence contrary to the Honduran example.
   (E) The citizens of developing nations use the term "public goods" differently than Americans.

24. It could be inferred from the passage that which one of the following groups would most likely have an increased role in the privatized Honduran economy?

   (A) U.S. banks
   (B) Honduran entrepreneurs
   (C) U.S. corporations
   (D) international bilateral donor agencies
   (E) Honduran economists

25. Based on the passage, it can be inferred that economic purists

   (A) have a strict interpretation of what constitutes public goods
   (B) endorse privatization only in developed nations
   (C) are proponents of Honduran efforts to privatize
   (D) feel that contracting out in Honduras has not led to diminished expectations
   (E) disapprove of the shifting of responsibility for providing public services from the public to the private sector

26. "Desired outcomes" (line 36) partially refers to which one of the following?

   (A) effective policy shifts
   (B) urban upgrading
   (C) political stability
   (D) improved quality of outputs
   (E) greater reliance on the public sectors

27. According to the passage, since the Reagan Administration, there has been

   (A) broad international support for privatization
   (B) demand from U.S. banks for diversification of Third World debt
   (C) encouragement for privatization of international donor agencies
   (D) a greater privatization effort pursued in Honduras
   (E) much evidence justifying privatization in developing nations

S T O P

IF YOU FINISH BEFORE TIME IS CALLED, YOU MAY CHECK YOUR WORK ON THIS SECTION ONLY.
DO NOT WORK ON ANY OTHER SECTION IN THE TEST.

SECTION III

Time—35 minutes

25 Questions

Directions: The questions in this section are based on the reasoning contained in brief statements or passages. For some questions, more than one of the choices could conceivably answer the question. However, you are to choose the best answer; that is, the response that most accurately and completely answers the question. You should not make assumptions that are by common sense standards implausible, superfluous, or incompatible with the passage. After you have chosen the best answer, blacken the corresponding space on your answer sheet.

1. The best professors never tell their students what to write. They strive instead to establish an intellectually critical environment conducive to thorough and creative scholarship, because training a student through indoctrination is never as effective as encouraging a student to develop his faculties independently. Truly impressive scholarly work can be produced only by the student who feels that he is breaking new ground, or at least treating familiar ground in a fresh and original manner.

Which one of the following statements is assumed by the argument above?

(A) Most students who are not told what to write produce great scholarly work.

(B) Professors who do not enjoy the security of tenure have no incentive to teach in the fashion described above.

(C) A student cannot create impressive scholarly work if he has been instructed on what he should write.

(D) Many great professors do not use an authoritative and dogmatic style of teaching.

(E) Many good students prefer being told what to write to the pressure of being encouraged to formulate their own, however original, ideas.

2. Although all prisons have some system of social hierarchy among prisoners, there are some social hierarchies in prisons that are based neither on physical strength nor on length of incarceration. However, there is no such thing as a system of social hierarchy in which no distinction is made between those who have influence over the actions of others and those who do not.

Which one of the following can be inferred from the passage above?

(A) The ability to measure personal influence is derived from the need for social hierarchy.

(B) All prison hierarchies have a system with which to identify whether a given individual has influence over the actions of another.

(C) Each individual prison community has its own unique set of criteria by which to measure social status.

(D) There are certain aspects of social status that are common among all social hierarchies.

(E) There are certain aspects of social status that are common among all hierarchies.

GO ON TO THE NEXT PAGE.

3. Early in this century Heisenberg stated that it is impossible to know with certainty both the position and the velocity of an electron at any specific instant. Initially, this theory was rejected by the scientific community because there was no accurate way to measure the movement of electrons. Now, however, the theory is accepted as true, not because we can measure the movement of electrons, but because no other theory of merit has been able to explain the myriad observable inconsistencies of electron behavior.

    The author appeals to which one of the following principles in establishing his conclusion?

    (A) The goal of science is to conscribe the vast variation apparent in nature in one comprehensive theory.

    (B) Through the acceptance of mathematical models that describe observable phenomena, scientists have come to a greater understanding of the uncertainties of nature.

    (C) Standard scientific method is to accept the best known explanation for an observable phenomenon regardless of its inconsistencies.

    (D) Science, through the study of probabilistic phenomena, transforms the complexities of nature into easily quantifiable terms.

    (E) A theory need not be supported by observational data to be accepted by the scientific community.

4. Concerned citizen: The county government's new ordinance limiting the types of materials that can be disposed of in trash fires violates our rights as citizens. The fact that local environmental damage results from the burning of certain inorganic materials is not the primary issue. The real concern is the government's flagrant disregard for the right of the individual to establish what is acceptable on his or her own property.

    Which one of the following principles, if accepted, would enable the concerned citizen's conclusion to be properly drawn?

    (A) Legislative violation of an individual's right to privacy is not justifiable unless the actions of that individual put others at risk.

    (B) The right of an individual to live in a safe environment takes precedence over the right of an individual to be exempt from legislative intrusion.

    (C) An individual's personal rights supersede any right or responsibility the government may have to protect a community from harm.

    (D) An individual has a moral obligation to act in the best interest of the community as a whole.

    (E) A compromise must be found when the right of an individual to act independently conflicts with the responsibility of the government to provide protection for the local environment.

GO ON TO THE NEXT PAGE.

5. As part of a new commitment to customer satisfaction, an electronics company sent a survey to all customers who had purchased its electronic personal organizer in the previous month. The survey, which was sent through the mail, asked customers to give personal information and to rate their satisfaction with the product. Of customers who returned the survey, more indicated that they had a negative opinion of the product's performance than indicated a neutral or positive opinion. On the basis of these results, the company, hoping to increase customer satisfaction, decided to allocate a large amount of capital to redesigning the product.

    Which one of the following, if true, indicates the most serious flaw in the method of research used by the company?

    (A) The company relied on a numerical system of rating responses rather than on open-ended questions that allow for more detailed feedback.
    (B) Customers who were dissatisfied with the information display of the organizer outnumbered customers who were dissatisfied with the variety of functions offered by the organizer.
    (C) Studies show that customer dissatisfaction with a new product is highest during the first year of the product's release and gradually decreases over the following years.
    (D) The marketing division has found that responses to their mail-in surveys are generally accurate.
    (E) People who are satisfied with a product or have no strong opinion about it are less likely to be motivated to return a mail-in questionnaire.

6. In an attempt to restructure the city's transit system, the head of the Mass Transit Authority has announced plans to cut services substantially and to increase fares on the subway and bus systems. He stated that the proposed changes represent the only means available to increase revenue and allow the Transit Authority to serve citizens better.

    Opponents of the head of the Mass Transit Authority's plan would be best served if which one of the following were shown to be true?

    (A) The installation of a new, more efficient turnstile system would eliminate fare evasion, saving more money than the proposed changes would raise.
    (B) The revenue from the proposed changes would not be sufficient to prevent further fare increases in the future.
    (C) The financial problems faced by the Mass Transit Authority were caused by a variety of factors, many of them legal as well as financial.
    (D) A planned conversion from old, heavy steel cars to newer, lighter alloy cars has been factored into the Mass Transit Authority's budget, but has yet to be approved by the city council.
    (E) The citizens of the city would be better served if people relied more on other means of transportation such as walking and biking.

    GO ON TO THE NEXT PAGE.

7. If the water level of the reservoir falls below the "safe line," then either the amount of water being consumed has increased or the amount of rainfall in the area has been below normal. If the amount of rainfall has been below normal, then the native plant life cannot be perfectly healthy.

Assume that the reservoir level falls below the safe line. According to the passage, which one of the following statements cannot be true?

(A) The amount of water being consumed has decreased.

(B) The amount of rainfall has been below normal, and the native plant life is not perfectly healthy.

(C) The amount of water being consumed has increased, the amount of rainfall has been below normal, and some of the native plant life is perfectly healthy.

(D) The amount of water being consumed has decreased, the amount of rainfall has been below normal, and the native plant life is perfectly healthy.

(E) The amount of water being consumed has increased, the amount of rainfall has been higher than normal, and the native plant life is not perfectly healthy.

8. If we are to improve the status of our college in the public's perception, our next promotional campaign should appear in the form of full-page advertisements placed in nationally circulated magazines, rather than in radio advertisements broadcast to a variety of stations. Although advertising fees for both campaigns are roughly equivalent, the production costs of the print advertisement campaign are nearly half those of the radio campaign. Therefore, our next promotional campaign should be a print advertisement campaign.

Which one of the following, if true, would most help to explain the difference in production costs of the two campaigns?

(A) More man-hours would be required in the preparation of the magazine advertisement than in the preparation of the radio advertisement.

(B) The number of people involved in the creation of a national ad campaign is greater than the number of people involved in the creation of a local ad campaign.

(C) The layout of the print ad campaign could potentially be reused in another campaign at a later date.

(D) The perceived impact of a magazine advertisement is greater than that of a radio advertisement.

(E) The creation of the layout for the magazine advertisement can be done in house at no extra cost to the college, whereas the creation of a radio advertisement requires scheduling many hours of expensive time at a recording studio.

GO ON TO THE NEXT PAGE.

9. Schools that train students in technical skills for a specific field of work are more successful, as measured by the percentage of students that gain employment in full-time jobs in the six-month period following graduation, than are institutions that teach a liberal arts curriculum. Technical schools have a student employment rate of approximately 65 percent, whereas liberal arts schools have a rate of only 56 percent. This difference reveals that technical schools are more effectively meeting the challenge of providing education than are liberal arts schools.

Which one of the following is an assumption on which the above argument rests?

(A) Schools will not accurately report information if they believe that information will reflect poorly on them.
(B) The curriculum of a school can be evaluated by examining the number and types of job placements achieved by its students.
(C) The percent of students that gain employment following graduation is a measurement of that school's ability to provide education.
(D) The sole function of education is to help students gain employment.
(E) Technical schools and liberal arts schools serve different educational purposes.

10. Scientists have long dreamed of the technological possibilities of nuclear fusion, a process in which the nuclei of two atoms are fused together. The energy that would be generated by this process would far surpass that of nuclear fission. However, years of research have failed to produce any tangible results and, as a result, funding for fusion projects has been drastically reduced. Nonetheless, some scientists continue to believe that fusion is possible. Unfortunately, the one team that claimed to have achieved "cold" fusion failed to replicate its experimental results, and scientists believe that other explanations can be found for the results the team initially observed. Therefore, it is unwise to conclude that nuclear fusion will be achieved in the immediate future.

In the passage above, the author reaches his conclusion by

(A) criticizing the premises on which the opposing side bases its view
(B) basing his conclusion upon experimental results
(C) drawing a conclusion based on a lack of evidence for the opposing view
(D) questioning the opposing view's use of the indefinite term "cold"
(E) reaching a conclusion that is incompatible with his premises

11. At one time, nutritionists fervently advocated the consumption of large quantities of vitamins to correct certain minor health problems. They justified these claims by citing the negative effects of vitamin deficiency and by pointing out that the Recommended Daily Allowance specifies only the minimum amount of a vitamin required for normal health rather than the amount that would lead to optimal health. Recent studies, however, have discredited those recommendations by showing that high dosages can have detrimental effects.

The argument above best supports which one of the following claims?

(A) A person suffering from a minor ailment will always benefit from medical attention.
(B) Ingesting large doses of vitamins is the best way to treat minor ailments.
(C) A person suffering from a minor health problem would probably do best to avoid excessive doses of vitamins.
(D) Nutritionists were more motivated by their opposition to the Recommended Daily Allowance than by evidence of medical benefit.
(E) All minor health problems should be treated promptly, regardless of the method by which they are treated.

12. Recent studies of preventive dental care have clearly established the positive effects of regular dental care. While the frequency of visits to the dentist varies throughout the population, a general trend has emerged: Those who visit the dentist at least twice a year have significantly fewer dental problems than those who do not.

Which one of the following is most clearly implied in the argument above?

(A) An individual with few dental problems is likely to have recently visited the dentist.
(B) If one has a significant number of dental problems, it is likely that one has visited the dentist fewer than two times a year.
(C) Most people visit their dentists semiannually, and thus have little reason to worry about cavities.
(D) In order to have fewer dental problems, one need only visit the dentist twice a year.
(E) Frequency of dental care can affect the number of dental problems experienced by an individual.

GO ON TO THE NEXT PAGE.

13. In recent years, the number of reported cases of ethical misconduct in the telemarketing of stocks, securities, and other investments has risen dramatically. In answer to the growing demand for regulation of this industry, federal agencies are formulating an approach to the problem that would entail close supervision of the activities of the investment houses that use telemarketing. Such government involvement in private industry is, however, antithetical to private industry and would surely dampen the spirit of free enterprise. Clearly, in order to prevent government interference, investment houses should cease the practice of paying telemarketers on commission.

Which one of the following is an assumption upon which the argument above is based?

(A) Successful capitalism is dependent upon a governmental policy of noninterference and furthered by pro-business regulations.

(B) The government's ability to detect misconduct, even with close supervision, is minimal, and therefore useless.

(C) If judged by contemporary standards, many of these so-called violations are considered ethical.

(D) Earning a high commission as a telemarketer is not proof of one's abilities as an investment broker.

(E) The incidence of ethical misconduct is directly related to the telemarketers' desire for larger commissions.

14. A study of former college athletes revealed that, as a group, they are five times less likely to die before the age of fifty than are members of the population at large. The advice to derive from this is clear: colleges should vastly expand their athletic departments so as to allow a greater proportion of all students to participate in athletics, thereby increasing the overall life expectancy of their student population.

Which one of the following, if true, most seriously weakens the argument above?

(A) Since participation in college athletics requires tremendous academic discipline, college athletes are better suited to succeed in society than are students who do not participate in college athletics.

(B) The students who voluntarily compete in college athletics are more predisposed to good health than are those who do not.

(C) Few colleges have the resources to increase spending on athletics, a nonessential university program.

(D) People who become active after leading sedentary lives can remarkably decrease their chances of contracting heart disease.

(E) Women, whose average life expectancies exceed men's by seven years, have traditionally had fewer opportunities to participate in college athletics than have men.

GO ON TO THE NEXT PAGE.

Questions 15–16

Dear Sirs,

In your letter, which detailed the many reasons you were not able to offer me the position at this time, you mentioned that my color-blindness was the central factor in your decision. In the hope that you may reconsider, I am writing to explain that my overall vision is actually quite good. Enclosed you will find three different optometrists' records confirming that I have never required any kind of corrective eyewear whatsoever.

Mark Furnace

15. Which one of the following would best highlight the flaw in Mr. Furnace's logic?

   (A) Mr. Furnace had not been administered a complete eye examination before he wrote the letter.
   (B) The evidence that Mr. Furnace mentions is not relevant to the decision made.
   (C) In addressing only one of the many reasons why he was rejected, Mr. Furnace undermines his own intentions.
   (D) The extent to which his color-blindness was responsible for his being rejected is not made clear.
   (E) Doctors' records are not considered official documentation of a person's well-being.

16. Which one of the following is an assumption upon which Mr. Furnace's letter is based?

   (A) A deal can be struck with his potential employers.
   (B) A person wearing corrective eyewear should not be hired for certain positions.
   (C) Color-blindness is not a fair criterion upon which to base hiring decisions.
   (D) A note from a doctor can be sufficient to change a potential employers' opinion.
   (E) His color-blindness is not affected by corrective eyewear.

17. An airline representative announced the introduction of a new pricing system that uses sophisticated computer technology. Based on up-to-the-minute information on sales, the system identifies and continually updates peak times of high demand and off-peak times of low demand, keeping prices high when demand is high and lowering prices to attract customers when demand is low. As a result, the airline anticipates that large numbers of customers will choose to travel off-peak in order to experience savings, while those who wish to travel at peak times will enjoy greater availability due to higher prices. The airline therefore anticipates that the majority of customers will experience significant benefits as a result of the new system.

Which one of the following indicates an error in the reasoning on the part of the airline?

   (A) The airline's conclusion is based on an unproven premise.
   (B) The airline displays a naive trust in the possibilities of technology.
   (C) The airline fails to factor in the cost of implementing the new system.
   (D) The airline's conclusion rests on a result that would necessarily cancel out the anticipated benefit.
   (E) The airline fails to establish the percentage of customers who would benefit from the change.

GO ON TO THE NEXT PAGE.

Question 18

Kristen:

Compared to a direct business tax cut, a personal income tax cut is a better way to stimulate our state's economy. A personal income tax cut would give residents greater in-pocket income. With this increase in income, individuals will be encouraged to start their own businesses. In addition, individuals will be more likely to spend more money at existing businesses.

Mark:

A personal income tax cut is not the most effective way to help business. There is no guarantee that individuals will in fact start new businesses, and the additional income may be used to purchase products from a different state or even a different country.

18. Mark objects to Kristen's argument by

(A) suggesting that a personal income tax cut is no more important than a direct business tax cut

(B) claiming that Kristen has reached a premature conclusion based on an inadequate understanding of the consequences of a business tax cut

(C) demonstrating that the negative impact of a personal income tax outweighs the positive effects

(D) questioning Kristen's use of the ambiguous phrase "in-pocket income"

(E) indicating that the positive consequences that Kristen predicts may not occur

19. Observation reveals that as children become physically exhausted, they become more prone to crying and temper tantrums. Thus, an occurrence of screaming or yelling in a small child is best remedied by providing physical rest.

Which one of the following uses the same pattern of reasoning as the argument above?

(A) People who feel insecure often compensate by acting in an aggressive manner. A person who is not acting in an aggressive manner is therefore unlikely to be insecure.

(B) Scientists establish the validity of their theories by conducting meticulously controlled experiments. Thus, a scientist who is conducting a meticulously controlled experiment is well on his way to establishing the validity of his theory.

(C) Completion of a four-year college program leads to an improvement in standard of living. A person who has not attended a four-year college program will not experience a comparable improvement in standard of living.

(D) The best way to avoid the common cold is to observe simple rules of hygiene, like wasing one's hands. After all, people who don't wash their hands are far more likely to contract a cold.

(E) Habitual lack of sleep leads to a condition known as "chronic exhaustion." A person who is not chronically exhausted is likely to get regular and sufficient sleep.

GO ON TO THE NEXT PAGE.

20. Statistics show that there is a direct correlation between the ammonia content and the cleaning power of industrial-strength floor and tile cleaners; simply stated, the more ammonia, the better the cleaner. However, in a nationwide survey of commercial food services, cleaning supervisors uniformly replied that in order for any floor and tile cleaner to be effective, it must be used on a given surface twice a day with the right proportion of cleaner to water, and must be applied with well-maintained mops. The survey thus proves that ammonia content is not relevant to the efficacy of floor and tile cleaners after all.

Which one of the following best identifies the flawed reasoning in the passage above?

(A) There is no reason to assume that effective floor and tile cleaning is the only use for floor and tile cleaner.

(B) It cannot be assumed that industrial-strength floor and tile cleaners contain comparable levels of ammonia.

(C) It is unreasonable to conclude that the ammonia content is not relevant to a cleaner's efficacy just because there are requirements for the proper use of industrial-strength floor and tile cleaners.

(D) It cannot be assumed that the efficacy of all industrial-strength floor and tile cleaners depends on the same procedures for use.

(E) It is unreasonable to assume that the makers of industrial-strength floor and tile cleaners are unaware that food services don't always use them properly.

21. Products containing naproxen sodium produce relief from pain and fever by blocking prostaglandins. As a consequence of recent technological advances, production costs for pain and fever medications containing naproxen sodium, allowing for both packaging and marketing costs, are one-fifth of what they were ten years ago, while the corresponding cost for medications using the ingredient ibuprofen, which is produced by different means, has increased. Therefore, naproxen sodium is a less costly ingredient to use in medication for the prevention of pain and fever relief than ibuprofen.

The conclusion of the argument is properly drawn if which one of the following is assumed?

(A) The cost of producing pain and fever medication containing ibuprofen has increased over the past ten years.

(B) Ten years ago, ibuprofen was used more than five times as often as naproxen sodium.

(C) None of the recent technological advances in producing pain and fever medication with naproxen sodium can be applied to the production of medication using ibuprofen.

(D) Ten years ago, the cost of producing pain and fever medication with the ingredient naproxen sodium was less than five times the cost of producing medications with ibuprofen.

(E) The cost of producing pain and fever medication with naproxen sodium is expected to decrease further, while the cost of producing similar medications using ibuprofen is not expected to decrease.

22. Below is an excerpt from a letter that a medical school sent to an applicant:

We regret that we will not be offering you a position at our school. The committee has been forced to reject many highly qualified applicants because we must restrict our class size to fewer than two hundred students.

Which one of the following can be logically inferred from the information in the letter above?

(A) Only highly qualified applicants were accepted by the medical school.

(B) The applicant was considered to be highly qualified.

(C) The school had already taken its maximum number of students.

(D) Most of the applicants were highly qualified.

(E) The qualifications of applicants were not the only factor affecting admissions.

GO ON TO THE NEXT PAGE.

23. Many Americans are required to spend at least two years studying a foreign language as part of their high school or college education. As a result of this classroom study, students are usually able to conjugate verbs, define words, and write simple sentences. Yet since even those students who received good grades during their foreign language training find themselves unable to hold a brief, unrehearsed conversation in that language, classroom training is clearly insufficient in transmitting the essential principles of another language.

Which one of the following principles, if accepted, would provide the most justification for the conclusion?

(A) If a student cannot adequately conjugate verbs or write simple sentences in a foreign language, he has not grasped the essential principles of that language.

(B) Anyone who can converse fluently in another language is likely to have the ability to conjugate verbs and define words in that language.

(C) Students grasp the essential principles of a foreign language by living in the country where that language is spoken, not by studying it in the classroom.

(D) Someone can be said to understand the basic principles of a foreign language only when he is able to converse spontaneously in that language.

(E) Any person who has not grown up speaking a given language will never truly grasp the essential principles of that language.

24. Jane Anne: Feeling frightened and delighted are mutually exclusive. Therefore, a person's behavior cannot both strike fear and evoke delight simultaneously.

Clive: That's not true. Many people love to go to horror movies. The movies frighten them and amuse them. They simultaneously cringe and laugh.

Clive has weakened Jane Anne's argument by

(A) showing that Jane Anne's argument is based on circular reasoning

(B) demonstrating that two feelings are not mutually exclusive

(C) qualifying Jane Anne's usage of the term "simultaneously"

(D) pointing out the inherent ambiguity in the relationship between "fear" and "delight"

(E) changing an argument by analogy into one based on a more reliable sample

25. Journalistic criticism of literature is falling victim to its own efforts to justify its existence. Critics believe that they garner respect from their readers by ignoring objective description in favor of opinionated commentary. Any new work is given the briefest of summaries and then mercilessly carved up in an effort to divine its deeper meaning. But the best journalist simply presents facts and allows his audience to decide their meanings independently. Critics should convey the truest possible form of the works in question; let the art, and not the art critic, speak to us.

Which one of the following statements best lends support to the argument presented above?

(A) Libraries make all new work available to the interested public without regard to critical opinions.

(B) Because space is limited, it is not practical to reproduce completely every work that is criticized in print.

(C) Writers would likely alter their style if they knew that their works would simply be read rather than criticized.

(D) Since most people have the capacity to appreciate art to some degree, it is superfluous to criticize art and a mistake not to allow people to decide for themselves.

(E) In the context described, only parts of a work could be presented, and this would lead to an increased role for the critic, who would have to decide which parts would be shown.

S T O P

IF YOU FINISH BEFORE TIME IS CALLED, YOU MAY CHECK YOUR WORK ON THIS SECTION ONLY.
DO NOT WORK ON ANY OTHER SECTION IN THE TEST.

SECTION IV

Time—35 minutes

25 Questions

Directions: The questions in this section are based on the reasoning contained in brief statements or passages. For some questions, more than one of the choices could conceivably answer the question. However, you are to choose the best answer; that is, the response that most accurately and completely answers the question. You should not make assumptions that are by common sense standards implausible, superfluous, or incompatible with the passage. After you have chosen the best answer, blacken the corresponding space on your answer sheet.

1. In France, children in preschool programs spend a portion of each day engaged in a program of stretching and exercise. Preschool programs in the United States, however, seldom devote time to a daily stretching and exercise program. In tests designed to measure cardiovascular fitness, children in the United States were outperformed by their French counterparts. It can therefore be determined that children attending preschool programs in the United States can achieve cardiovascular fitness only by engaging in a daily school program of stretching and exercise.

Which one of the following is an assumption on which the argument depends?

(A) A daily program of stretching and exercise will allow all children to achieve cardiovascular fitness.
(B) Cardiovascular fitness is integral to one's overall health.
(C) It has been proven that children who participate in stretching and exercise programs in preschool have better cardiovascular fitness as adults.
(D) Stretching and exercise are necessary components of French children's superior cardiovascular fitness programs.
(E) United States preschool children could make healthful dietary changes as well as changes to their daily fitness regimens.

2. In an effort to lessen the risk of liability, fertility clinics are seeking new methods of record keeping and storage that would help avoid donor sperm that might contain dangerous genes. Toward this end, a database is being developed to aid the clients in their screening of donor sperm. The database is exhaustively thorough, containing the medical histories of more than twenty thousand people, approximately half of them men.

Which one of the following, if true, best explains why the database contains the records of almost ten thousand women?

(A) Small fertility clinics, located in remote areas, wish to have access to a large selection of donor sperm.
(B) Keeping genetic information on women is a standard procedure for many scientific clinics.
(C) Some genetic disorders are not expressed until the onset of puberty.
(D) Some genetic disorders may be carried by, but not manifested in, men who inherited the dangerous gene from their mothers.
(E) Some genetic disorders are due to the effects of drugs and alcohol during puberty.

GO ON TO THE NEXT PAGE.

3. If the Food and Drug Administration (FDA) does not relax some of its regulations governing the testing of experimental drugs, tens of thousands of U.S. citizens are sure to die as a result of certain diseases before an effective treatment is found and made generally available.

It follows logically from the statement above that if the FDA does relax some of its regulations governing the testing of experimental drugs, then tens of thousands of U.S. citizens

(A) will definitely die of certain diseases
(B) will probably die of certain diseases
(C) will probably not die of certain diseases
(D) will not die of certain diseases
(E) may still die of certain diseases

4. The level of blood sugar for many patients suffering from disease Q is slightly higher than the level of blood sugar in the general population. Nonetheless, most medical professionals believe that slightly increasing blood sugar levels is a successful means by which to treat disease Q.

This apparently contradictory argument can best be resolved by which one of the following statements?

(A) Blood sugar levels for patients who have been cured of disease Q are virtually identical to the levels of blood sugar found in the general population.
(B) Many of the symptoms associated with severe cases of disease Q have been recognized in laboratory animals with experimentally induced high blood pressure, but none of the animals developed disease Q.
(C) The movement from inactive to advanced states of disease Q often occurs because the virus that causes Q flourishes during periods when blood sugar levels are slightly low.
(D) The blood sugar level in patients with disease Q fluctuates abnormally in response to changes in blood chemistry.
(E) Low levels of blood sugar are symptomatic of many other diseases that are even more serious than disease Q.

Questions 5–6

Many people, in the wake of an exceedingly large number of deaths in the United States caused by handguns, have argued for a federal law making handguns illegal for ordinary citizens anywhere in the United States. However, it is clear that any such proposal would be completely counterproductive. For instance, when handguns were outlawed in the city of Clarksville in 1990, the number of handgun deaths actually increased by 10 percent by 1991. Furthermore, such a proposal clearly violates the Second Amendment, which ensures every citizen's right to bear arms.

5. The above argument is vulnerable to criticism on the grounds that it

(A) fails to consider the fact that other cities may have had different results with handgun bans
(B) fails to define precisely the ambiguous term "handgun"
(C) assumes that the aim of the Clarksville handgun ban was to reduce the number of handgun deaths
(D) assumes that the Clarksville police were not responsible for a larger number of handgun deaths in 1991 than in previous years
(E) fails to cite a legitimate authority in support of its interpretation of the Second Amendment

6. Which one of the following, if true, would most strongly support the conclusion above?

(A) The number of handgun deaths in Clarksville increased by 20 percent from 1989 to 1990.
(B) The number of handgun deaths in the United States increased by two percent from 1990 to 1991.
(C) The number of handgun deaths in Clarksville in 1991 was not as great as the number of handgun deaths in the entire country.
(D) The attempt to ban handguns in Brazil in 1985 also led to a drastically increased number of handgun deaths.
(E) Canada, which has a handgun ban, has a faster growing rate of deaths from firearms than does the United States.

GO ON TO THE NEXT PAGE.

7. For our protein needs, sea plankton has none of the drawbacks that meat has. Plankton contains neither the high levels of saturated animal fat nor the dangerous hormones that commercially available meats do, and its harvest does not require the massive waste of natural and agricultural resources that meat production does. In light of these facts, it is clear that people must stop getting their protein from meat and start getting it from plankton.

Which one of the following statements, if true, most seriously weakens the argument above?

(A) Relatively few scientific studies have been done on people's willingness to make radical changes in their dietary habits.

(B) The only reports containing information on the drawbacks of plankton as a meat substitute have been funded by the United States Department of Agriculture.

(C) Greater governmental regulation of the meat industry could significantly reduce the use of dangerous chemicals and hormones in meat production.

(D) The costs incurred in the harvest of sea plankton in amounts large enough to meet the average person's annual protein needs exceed the costs incurred in the production of a similar amount of meat.

(E) As of yet, no effective means of making sea plankton commercially available for consumption have been developed.

8. Tenant Representative: Residents of units in the West Building of the Fife Arms apartment complex were recently subjected to rent increases averaging 12.5 percent, while residents of identical apartments in the East Building were given increases of, on the average, only seven percent. Do our landlords really think that the residents of Fife Arms will believe that the maintenance costs on units in the West Building have risen more than one and a half times as quickly as the maintenance costs on units in the East Building? It seems to us that these identical units, which were built at the same time, have deteriorated equally, and we certainly haven't seen any better service here in the West Building than they have in the East Building.

Which one of the following statements would most seriously weaken the tenant representative's argument that the recent rent increases are inequitable?

(A) Before the recent increases were announced, residents of units in the West Building, who were the first to occupy Fife Arms, were not sharing the burden of the cost of maintenance of the entire complex equally with the residents of units in the East Building.

(B) Before the recent increases were announced, residents of units in the West Building, who were the first to occupy Fife Arms, were paying substantially less for the cost of the maintenance of the entire complex than were the residents of the units of the East Building.

(C) Although the units are identical in age, the rate of occupancy for units in the West Building has been higher than that for units in the East Building, resulting in more wear and tear on units in the West Building.

(D) The increases in rent were not determined by the landlords, but imposed by changes in the city regulations regarding landlord-owned residences.

(E) An independent appraiser judged units in the West Building in the Fife Arms to be one and a half times more valuable than units in the East Building.

GO ON TO THE NEXT PAGE.

9. It has long been thought that the ancestors of the human race who lived prior to the Ice Age did not have the aid of the many useful inventions characteristic of post–Ice Age humans. In particular, it has long been believed that they did not have the advantages of sharp cutting tools. Such people supposedly had to manage by tearing things, such as the animal skins that they needed for warmth, with their teeth and fingernails. However, the recent discovery of the well-preserved remains of a pre–Ice Age woman has shown this to be false. The woman was wearing a number of animal skins and carried in her hand a number of sharp-edged stones, which scientists discovered could cut through animal skins remarkably well.

A flaw in the above argument is that it

(A) makes an appeal to the authority of scientists, without giving sufficient justification for that appeal

(B) assumes that the stones were sharpened by the woman herself

(C) assumes that if a thing can be used for a certain purpose, then that purpose must be what the thing in fact was used for

(D) ignores the fact that many pre–Ice Age people used skins for other reasons besides warmth

(E) assumes that any object that could be used for cutting animal skins would be good for cutting all kinds of things

10. The accountant for a large retail store warned that over half of the accounts receivable for the previous quarter were delinquent. He suggested that the store hire a collection agency to collect the debt immediately. His suggestion was not followed, however, when it was noted that the store had already received over two-thirds of the total dollar amount of the outstanding accounts.

If the statements above are true, they most strongly support which one of the following?

(A) The store had already collected on twice as many accounts as remained unpaid.

(B) At least one-third of the accounts had been paid before the beginning of the last quarter.

(C) Two-thirds of the total number of delinquent accounts must have been collected by the store.

(D) The total dollar amount and the total number of delinquent accounts are not necessarily proportional.

(E) If each account paid in installments, then all the accounts paid at least two-thirds of the individual bill.

GO ON TO THE NEXT PAGE.

11. Statistics recently compiled from Fortune 500 companies seem to suggest that, in the top levels of management, those with a Masters in Business Administration (MBA) face fewer obstacles than do non-MBAs in becoming vice presidents and thus positioning themselves for further advancement. Fully seven percent of all MBAs within the companies surveyed are vice presidents, while only two percent of all non-MBAs have achieved that status. Anyone planning a career in top-level management would be wise to go to graduate school for an MBA.

Information about which one of the following would be most helpful in evaluating the validity of the argument above?

(A) the percentages of eligible MBAs and eligible non-MBAs who have recently become corporate vice presidents

(B) the percentage of vice president positions in non–Fortune 500 companies that are held by non-MBAs

(C) whether other opportunities for advancement below the rank of vice president exist in Fortune 500 companies

(D) the actual number of non-MBAs who have recently become vice presidents in Fortune 500 companies versus the actual number of MBAs who have recently become vice presidents in those companies

(E) the percentage of people with MBAs versus the percentage of people without MBAs who seek employment in Fortune 500 companies

12. Concerns about the quality of domestic cars drove many consumers to purchase foreign cars in the 1970s through the late 1980s. But here is a car that will change all that. According to the J.P.R. Glowers customer satisfaction survey, a survey that asks car owners how they feel about their car after the first year of ownership, the Acme Roadster scored highest of all cars in quality for the second year in a row. It also scored very high in safety features, look and feel, and overall driveability. It is clear that this is a car that represents the new domestic standard: high quality for many years of enjoyable driving.

Which one of the following arguments contains a flaw that is most similar to the one in the argument above?

(A) There is no doubt that these are the finest roses in the country. Eight out of nine growers surveyed rated these the most colorful in their class.

(B) This house paint will last for decades. When it was tested on several houses it showed barely a crack after 10 years.

(C) This new skyscraper will be one of the sturdiest buildings ever built. It has three separate stabilization systems, which will allow it to withstand even significant earthquakes.

(D) Even though the domestic tea market has been depressed for years, it should be coming out with some better teas soon, which will increase its market share dramatically.

(E) The best boats in the world are built by domestic boat manufacturers. We know they are the best because they last the longest of any boats in the world.

GO ON TO THE NEXT PAGE.

Questions 13–14

For many years, skeptics scoffed at the idea that plants respond to environmental stimuli other than those that directly affect the process of photosynthesis. Recent studies, however, offer contradictory evidence that seems to suggest that music, for instance, can have a direct and positive effect on plant development. Plants that were kept in the presence of music during the first six weeks of development grew considerably faster and showed fewer signs of disease than those plants developed in silence. The "music-advantaged" plants were also 35 percent more likely to survive the process of transplantation initially than were the "music-disadvantaged" plants.

13. Which one of the following is an assumption upon which the above argument is based?

(A) Many skeptics still do not believe that music is beneficial to plant development.
(B) Plants that do not thrive have been deprived of music during the first six weeks of their development.
(C) Plants that were exposed to music for longer periods of time were healthier and grew faster than those with less exposure.
(D) Some kinds of music are more beneficial to plants than others.
(E) Music does not significantly damage a plant's ability to photosynthesize.

14. A logical critique of the study cited above would most likely raise which one of the following questions?

(A) Was the type of music used during the experiment consistent over time?
(B) Were both plant groups raised in the same quality soil?
(C) Did the "music-advantaged" plants that survived transplantation live longer than the "music-disadvantaged" plants that survived transplantation?
(D) Is the idea that plants respond to environmental stimuli other than those traditionally accepted as aiding growth now accepted by the scientific community?
(E) What types of plants were used in the experiment?

15. Max: It's a travesty that our government gives away billions of dollars every year to foreign countries while people in this country are poor, starving, and living in inadequate housing. Many foreigners now live far better than the majority of our own people, courtesy of our leaders. This is clearly wrong. A government is obligated to serve its own citizens' interests first, before trying to further the interests of other people in other countries.

Alex: But that is precisely what our government is doing in giving large amounts of foreign aid. Giving such money to foreign countries ensures their loyalty to us, so that we will have their help in furthering our international goals. Thus, even though the poor people in this country may not believe that the government is serving them, it most certainly is.

Which one of the following is the point at issue between Max and Alex?

(A) whether or not foreign governments ought to give money away to other countries
(B) what should be considered in the citizens' interests, when judging the actions of a government
(C) whether or not the government should consider the interests of foreign people before the interests of its own citizens
(D) whether or not providing food and adequate housing are important functions of a government
(E) how much of the government's money should be allowed to go to foreign aid

GO ON TO THE NEXT PAGE.

16. Excessive logging has led to a sharp drop in the available supply and an increase in the price of hardwood lumber such as oak and maple. This same pattern has occurred with far too many of our scarce and vital natural resources, resulting in high prices for many products. It is likely, then, that the prices of new hardwood furniture will rise in the near future.

In making the argument above, the author relies on all of the following assumptions EXCEPT:

(A) The price of raw materials is a determining factor in the cost of new furniture.
(B) An increase in the price of lumber usually leads to an increase in the price of newly produced furniture.
(C) There will not be any substantial decrease in other costs to furniture producers that could keep the price of newly produced furniture from increasing.
(D) The cost of new hardwood furniture is affected by an increase in the price of hardwood lumber.
(E) Logging practices can substantially influence the demand for wooden manufactured goods.

Questions 17–18

Dr. Ronson: These animal tracks exhibit some interesting and strange characteristics. This first footprint appears to have two toes, whereas this second footprint appears to have three. And while this first footprint is facing north, this second footprint is facing east. Due to the weight of this evidence, we can safely conclude that these prints were made by two different animals.

Dr. Martinson: These tracks may indeed have been made by two different animals, but your evidence does not conclusively demonstrate that fact. A slight twist of the foot can make a print that seems to have extra toes. And some animals have feet that are oriented at right angles to one another, such that when they walk, their footprints face different directions. Now, if one footprint had claws while the other one did not, I would find your case more persuasive.

17. Drs. Ronson and Martinson disagree about which of the following?

(A) Any group of tracks can be determined as having been made by a single animal or more than one animal, based on the shapes of the footprints and the directions that they are facing.
(B) Any group of tracks made by a single individual would have similarly shaped footprints and would be facing in the same direction.
(C) Each kind of animal leaves a distinct kind of footprint by which it can be uniquely identified.
(D) The shapes and directions of the footprints in groups of tracks can be used to determine the number of animals who made them.
(E) It is not possible for a single animal to leave both a two-toed and a three-toed footprint.

18. Dr. Martinson does which one of the following?

(A) argues that one can never conclusively determine how many animals made a given group of tracks
(B) criticizes Ronson's conclusion based on other known facts about footprints and the properties of some animals' feet
(C) attacks Ronson's authority as a scientist
(D) disputes Ronson's reasoning by giving an explanation of the facts
(E) states an alternative criterion that would conclusively determine whether one or more animals made a given group of tracks

GO ON TO THE NEXT PAGE.

19. At current rates of emission, a tax of one cent per pound of pollutant released into the air or water would raise $15 billion. This seems to be an ideal way to pay for the new environmental cleanup program that was recently instituted by the government. Not only that, but this tax would also help prevent further need for such cleanup efforts by encouraging companies to install more modern, less environmentally damaging equipment, and in the future, the money collected from the tax could support programs such as the National Park Service.

Which one of the following most clearly identifies a flaw in the author's reasoning?

(A) The author makes a generalization based on insufficient data.
(B) The author fails to consider other possible ways to accomplish the same end.
(C) The author mistakes an effect for a cause.
(D) The author makes incompatible assumptions.
(E) The author fails to consider a possible result of his plan.

20. Vaccines have allowed us to eradicate diseases such as smallpox, polio, and diptheria. Vaccines work by the injection of a weak or harmless version of a certain virus or bacteria in order to allow the body to learn to recognize it and build a defense against it, so that if a full-strength version of the virus ever enters the body, it will be recognized and attacked before it can do serious damage. In the last 10 years, vaccine therapy itself has undergone a major change. The old polio vaccine, for instance, actually required the injection of live (although severely weakened) polio virus into the subject, thereby causing polio in about 3 percent of the subjects. However, today's more modern polio vaccine works by administering a completely crippled polio vaccine: one that has had its genetic information removed so that it can never reproduce itself or cause polio. This new vaccine is at least as effective as the old one, and it has not caused polio in a single patient since it began to be used nearly a decade ago.

If all of the above statements are true, which one of the following must also be true?

(A) Aside from the few cases of polio caused by the administration of the old vaccine, the old vaccine was completely effective in preventing polio.
(B) The body must learn to recognize viruses by some other factor than their genetic information.
(C) Once we are able to manufacture a vaccine for a certain virus, the disease caused by that virus will be eradicated within a period of years.
(D) Vaccines will only work if your body's own immune system is in perfect shape.
(E) Except for cases of polio caused by the administration of the old vaccine, the old polio vaccine was no less effective than the new one.

GO ON TO THE NEXT PAGE.

21. In order to lose body fat, you have to raise your metabolism. If you run six hours per week, you'll be able to lose body fat. Therefore, if you lose body fat, you must be running six hours per week.

Which one of the following best describes the flaw in the argument?

(A) Some people might not want to run six hours per week.

(B) Although running six hours per week may be sufficient to raise your metabolism, it may not be necessary.

(C) If you don't run at least six hours per week, you will not raise your metabolism.

(D) Some people may want to run more than six hours per week in order to get in shape more quickly.

(E) Some people are not marathon runners and may take years to lose a significant amount of body fat.

22. The current notion of corporate liability holds that no corporate head can be sued unless criminal misconduct is established. Thus the corporate head cannot be held individually responsible but is viewed simply as a part of the corporate body, rather than as a distinct entity. This makes it difficult to recover compensation for corporate negligence from corporate heads who may ultimately have been responsible for their company's negligence, and may very well be directly responsible for implementation of the negligent act.

Which one of the following best supports the argument that corporate liability should be extended to corporate heads?

(A) The assets of negligent small corporations are often sufficient to compensate for damages awarded in negligence suits.

(B) The assets of heads of small corporations are often insufficient to compensate for damages awarded in negligence suits.

(C) The threat of personal liability will dissuade corporate heads from discharging their duties improperly.

(D) Threats of corporate liability are necessary in order to recover compensation for corporate negligence.

(E) Statistics indicate that where threats of personal liability are present, corporations are more likely to violate regulations that could lead to liability disputes.

23. Sarah, a surgeon at a large hospital, asked a hospital administrator for permission to take the vital organs from a man who had just died in an accident, in order to use his organs to save the lives of several other people who needed immediate organ transplants to survive. The man carried neither identification with which to attempt to contact his family, nor anything that specifically authorized the use of his organs, such as an organ donor card. But the man did have a Goose Lodge lapel pin, and the Goose Lodge had long been in favor of encouraging its members to be organ donors.

Which one of the following principles, if accepted, would determine either that the man's organs should be used or that they should not be used?

(A) If using parts of a dead body can save people's lives, and if members of the dead person's family are notified and do not object, then those parts can be used.

(B) The fact that someone belongs to a group that encourages organ donations does not constitute consent on the part of that person to have his organs used.

(C) Authorization from a person's family, an organ donor card, or other authorizing document signed by that person is always sufficient to give permission to take that person's vital organs.

(D) If no relatives can be found after a period of 30 days, then a dead body can be used for whatever purposes its possessors see fit.

(E) Only if members of a dead person's family consent can that person's organs be used to save other lives.

GO ON TO THE NEXT PAGE.

24. A survey of urban middle-class citizens revealed some inconsistencies in their attitudes towards the homeless. Over 75 percent of those who responded said that they believed the general public to be sympathetic toward the plight of the homeless. Ironically, an overwhelming majority of the respondents confessed to going to great lengths to avoid homeless people on the street.

Which one of the following, if true, would explain the apparent paradox in the results reported in the passage above?

(A) Having sympathy for homeless people and wanting to avoid them on the street are not necessarily incompatible positions.

(B) Sympathizing with one person who has no home is easier than dealing with homelessness as an abstract concept.

(C) There was a wide variety of sentiment regarding homelessness among the respondents themselves.

(D) Many of the respondents had once been homeless people themselves.

(E) The general public is not aware of government programs designed to implement low-income housing.

25. As a result of recent studies that successfully established that drinking a glass of red wine with dinner can reduce the risk of heart disease, doctors have begun to recommend that their patients consume red wine with their evening meals. Surprisingly, according to research intended to track the effectiveness of such recommendations, many patients who followed these recommendations continued to be vulnerable to heart disease.

Which one of the following, if true, would explain the unexpected result described above?

(A) Many patients ignore their doctors' recommendations to drink wine with meals.

(B) A greater number of people are likely to drink red wine than did before the results of the study were known.

(C) The high cost of red wine has discouraged many people from consuming it regularly.

(D) Red wine is not believed to prevent all types of diseases, so it is to be expected that people will continue to have some types of diseases.

(E) The beneficial effects of drinking red wine are incurred only when the wine is drunk in moderation, which many patients fail to do.

S T O P

IF YOU FINISH BEFORE TIME IS CALLED, YOU MAY CHECK YOUR WORK ON THIS SECTION ONLY.
DO NOT WORK ON ANY OTHER SECTION IN THE TEST.

THE PRINCETON REVIEW

Completely darken bubbles with a No. 2 pencil. If you make a mistake, be sure to erase mark completely.

1. YOUR NAME:
(Print)
Last   First   M.I.

SIGNATURE: _____ DATE: ___ / ___ / ___

HOME ADDRESS: _____
(Print)
Number

_____
City   State   Zip Code

PHONE NO.: _____
(Print)

5. YOUR NAME

First 4 letters of last name				FIRST INIT	MID INIT
Ⓐ	Ⓐ	Ⓐ	Ⓐ	Ⓐ	Ⓐ
Ⓑ	Ⓑ	Ⓑ	Ⓑ	Ⓑ	Ⓑ
Ⓒ	Ⓒ	Ⓒ	Ⓒ	Ⓒ	Ⓒ
Ⓓ	Ⓓ	Ⓓ	Ⓓ	Ⓓ	Ⓓ
Ⓔ	Ⓔ	Ⓔ	Ⓔ	Ⓔ	Ⓔ
Ⓕ	Ⓕ	Ⓕ	Ⓕ	Ⓕ	Ⓕ
Ⓖ	Ⓖ	Ⓖ	Ⓖ	Ⓖ	Ⓖ
Ⓗ	Ⓗ	Ⓗ	Ⓗ	Ⓗ	Ⓗ
Ⓘ	Ⓘ	Ⓘ	Ⓘ	Ⓘ	Ⓘ
Ⓙ	Ⓙ	Ⓙ	Ⓙ	Ⓙ	Ⓙ
Ⓚ	Ⓚ	Ⓚ	Ⓚ	Ⓚ	Ⓚ
Ⓛ	Ⓛ	Ⓛ	Ⓛ	Ⓛ	Ⓛ
Ⓜ	Ⓜ	Ⓜ	Ⓜ	Ⓜ	Ⓜ
Ⓝ	Ⓝ	Ⓝ	Ⓝ	Ⓝ	Ⓝ
Ⓞ	Ⓞ	Ⓞ	Ⓞ	Ⓞ	Ⓞ
Ⓟ	Ⓟ	Ⓟ	Ⓟ	Ⓟ	Ⓟ
Ⓠ	Ⓠ	Ⓠ	Ⓠ	Ⓠ	Ⓠ
Ⓡ	Ⓡ	Ⓡ	Ⓡ	Ⓡ	Ⓡ
Ⓢ	Ⓢ	Ⓢ	Ⓢ	Ⓢ	Ⓢ
Ⓣ	Ⓣ	Ⓣ	Ⓣ	Ⓣ	Ⓣ
Ⓤ	Ⓤ	Ⓤ	Ⓤ	Ⓤ	Ⓤ
Ⓥ	Ⓥ	Ⓥ	Ⓥ	Ⓥ	Ⓥ
Ⓦ	Ⓦ	Ⓦ	Ⓦ	Ⓦ	Ⓦ
Ⓧ	Ⓧ	Ⓧ	Ⓧ	Ⓧ	Ⓧ
Ⓨ	Ⓨ	Ⓨ	Ⓨ	Ⓨ	Ⓨ
Ⓩ	Ⓩ	Ⓩ	Ⓩ	Ⓩ	Ⓩ

IMPORTANT: Please fill in these boxes exactly as shown on the back cover of your test book.

2. TEST
_____

3. TEST CODE   **4. REGISTRATION**

Ⓐ Ⓑ Ⓒ Ⓓ Ⓔ Ⓕ Ⓖ

6. DATE OF

Month	Day	Year
◯ JAN		
◯ FEB		
◯ MAR	◯ ◯	◯ ◯
◯ APR	◯ ◯	◯ ◯
◯ MAY	◯ ◯	◯ ◯
◯ JUN	◯ ◯	◯ ◯
◯ JUL	◯ ◯	◯ ◯
◯ AUG	◯ ◯	◯ ◯
◯ SEP	◯ ◯	◯ ◯
◯ OCT	◯ ◯	◯ ◯
◯ NOV	◯ ◯	◯ ◯
◯ DEC		

7. SEX
◯ MALE
◯ FEMALE

THE PRINCETON REVIEW

© 1996 Princeton Review L.L.C.
FORM NO. 00001-PR

Section ①

Start with number 1 for each new section.
If a section has fewer questions than answer spaces, leave the extra answer spaces blank.

Questions 1–30, each with answer choices Ⓐ Ⓑ Ⓒ Ⓓ Ⓔ, repeated across four columns.

Computing Your Score

Directions

1. Use the Answer Key on the next page to check your answers.

2. Use the Scoring Worksheet below to compute your raw score.

3. Use the Score Conversion Chart to convert your raw score into the 120–180 LSAT scale.

Your scaled score on this virtual test is for general guidance only.

Scores obtained by using the Score Conversion Chart can only approximate the score you would receive if this virtual test were an actual LSAT. Your score on an actual LSAT may differ from the score obtained on this virtual test.

In an actual test, final scores are computed using an equating method that makes scores earned on different editions of the LSAT comparable to one another. This virtual test has been constructed to reflect an actual LSAT as closely as possible, and the conversion of raw scores to the LSAT scale has been approximated.

What this means is that the Conversion Chart reflects only an estimate of how raw scores would translate into final LSAT scores. Your score on an actual LSAT may differ from the score range obtained on this virtual test.

Scoring Worksheet

1. Enter the number of questions you answered correctly in each section.

	Number Correct
Section I	_____
Section II	23
Section III	20
Section IV	13

2. Enter the sum here: _____

   This is your raw score.

SCORE CONVERSION CHART

For Converting Raw Scores to the 120–180 LSAT Scaled Score

Reported Score	Raw Score Lowest	Raw Score Highest
180	99	101
179	—*	—*
178	98	98
177	97	97
176	96	96
175	95	95
174	94	94
173	93	93
172	92	92
171	91	91
170	90	90
169	89	89
168	88	88
167	86	87
166	85	85
165	84	84
164	82	83
163	81	81
162	79	80
161	77	78
160	76	76
159	74	75
158	72	73
157	71	71
156	69	70
155	67	68
154	65	66
153	63	64
152	61	62
151	59	60
150	58	58
149	56	57
148	54	55
147	52	53
146	50	51
145	48	49
144	46	47
143	44	45
142	43	43
141	41	42
140	39	40
139	37	38
138	36	36
137	34	35
136	32	33
135	30	31
134	29	29
133	27	28
132	26	26
131	24	25
130	23	23
129	22	22
128	20	21
127	19	19
126	18	18
125	17	17
124	16	16
123	15	15
122	14	14
121	13	13
120	0	12

*There is no raw score that will produce this scaled score for this form.

SECTION I

1.	C	7.	D	13.	D	19.	C
2.	A	8.	C	14.	B	20.	B
3.	C	9.	C	15.	E	21.	E
4.	B	10.	D	16.	C	22.	E
5.	D	11.	C	17.	C	23.	D
6.	E	12.	E	18.	E	24.	E

SECTION II

1.	C	8.	B	15.	E	22.	C
2.	A	9.	E	16.	D	23.	D
3.	B	10.	A	17.	A	24.	B
4.	B	11.	A	18.	C	25.	A
5.	D	12.	D	19.	D	26.	D
6.	E	13.	B	20.	D	27.	A
7.	C	14.	A	21.	A		

SECTION III

1.	C	8.	E	15.	B	22.	E
2.	E	9.	C	16.	D	23.	D
3.	E	10.	C	17.	D	24.	B
4.	C	11.	C	18.	E	25.	D
5.	E	12.	E	19.	D		
6.	A	13.	E	20.	C		
7.	D	14.	B	21.	D		

SECTION IV

1.	D	8.	A	15.	B	22.	C
2.	D	9.	C	16.	E	23.	E
3.	E	10.	D	17.	A	24.	A
4.	C	11.	A	18.	B	25.	E
5.	D	12.	B	19.	E		
6.	B	13.	E	20.	B		
7.	E	14.	B	21.	B		

9

Answers and Explanations to Diagnostic Test I

Questions 1–5

R, S, T, U, V, X, Y, and Z are the only buildings in an urban development.
   Building X has more stories than both building T and building Z.
   Building Z has more stories than both building T and building Y.
   Building T has more stories than building R.
   Building R has more stories than building V.
   Building Y has more stories than building V.
   Building U has more stories than building R but fewer than building S.

less   more
```
 T...X
 Z...X
 T...Z
 Y...Z
 R...T
 V...R
 V...Y
 R...U
 U...S
```

```
                  U—S
       less              more
      ◄—V—R—T—Z—X—►
            └—Y—┘
```

1. Which one of the following can be false?

    (A) Building T has more stories than building V.
    (B) Building U has more stories than building V.
    (C) Building X has more stories than building S.
    (D) Building Z has more stories than building R.
    (E) Building Z has more stories than building V.

1. (A) This must be true. Check the diagram.
    (B) This must be true. Check the diagram.
    (C) Right.
    (D) This must be true. Check the diagram.
    (E) This must be true. Check the diagram.

2. Which one of the following must be false?

    (A) Building R has more stories than building Z.
    (B) Building S has more stories than building X.
    (C) Building S has fewer stories than building Y.
    (D) Building U has more stories than building Z.
    (E) Building Y has more stories than building T.

2. (A) Right.
    (B) This could be true. We don't know exactly where S is.
    (C) This could be true. We don't know exactly where S is.
    (D) This could be true. We don't know exactly where U is.
    (E) This could be true. We don't know exactly where Y is.

SECTION I

3. If building S has the same number of stories as building Y, then which one of the following must be true?

   (A) Building T has more stories than building U.
   (B) Building V has more stories than building S.
   (C) Building Z has more stories than building U.
   (D) Building Z has fewer stories than building U.
   (E) Building Z has fewer stories than building S.

3. (A) We don't know exactly where U is in relation to T.
   (B) This can never be true.
   (C) Right. Y has fewer stories than Z, S has the same number as Y, and U has fewer than S.
   (D) S must have fewer stories than Z, so U must also have fewer stories.
   (E) Y must be less than Z, so S must be, too.

4. If building U has more stories than building Z, how many of the buildings could be the third tallest?

   (A) 1
   (B) 2
   (C) 3
   (D) 4
   (E) 5

4. (A) Only U and X can be the third tallest.
   (B) Right.
   (C) Only U and X can be the third tallest.
   (D) Only U and X can be the third tallest.
   (E) Only U and X can be the third tallest.

5. If it is true that the building with the fewest stories is eleven stories tall and the building with the most stories is fifteen stories tall, then which one of the following buildings could have twelve stories?

   (A) building S
   (B) building T
   (C) building U
   (D) building Y
   (E) building Z

5. (A) If V has eleven stories, then R would have twelve, and Y can tie with R, so the answer is Y.
   (B) If V has eleven stories, then R would have twelve, and Y can tie with R, so the answer is Y.
   (C) If V has eleven stories, then R would have twelve, and Y can tie with R, so the answer is Y.
   (D) Right.
   (E) If V has eleven stories, then R would have twelve, and Y can tie with R, so the answer is Y.

Questions 6–12

In a four-floor college dormitory, there are exactly three student resident advisors—Ruiz, Smith, and Turner—who each have graduate or undergraduate status. They are assigned to floors according to the following restrictions:

Each floor of the dormitory can have only one resident advisor.

Ruiz is assigned to the fourth floor.

Smith has graduate status.

Smith is assigned to a floor above Turner.

If there is a resident advisor on the third floor, then that advisor is of the same status as the resident advisor on the fourth floor.

The resident advisors are not all of the same status.

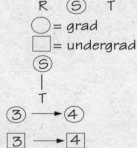

SECTION I

QUESTIONS	EXPLANATIONS

6. Which one of the following statements must be false?

   (A) Smith is on the second floor.
   (B) Smith is on the third floor.
   (C) Turner is on the first floor.
   (D) Turner is on the second floor.
   (E) Turner is on the third floor.

6. (A) This could be true. See the setup for question 8.
   (B) This could be true. See the setup for question 11.
   (C) This could be true. See the setup for question 8.
   (D) This could be true. See the setup for question 11.
   (E) Right. We know that S is above T, and R is already on 4.

7. Which one of the following statements could be true?

   (A) Ruiz is an undergraduate student, and Turner is a graduate student who is on the second floor.
   (B) Ruiz is an undergraduate student, and Turner is an undergraduate student who is on the second floor.
   (C) Smith is on the third floor, and Turner is a graduate student who is on the first floor.
   (D) Smith is on the third floor, and Turner is an undergraduate student who is on the first floor.
   (E) Smith is on the third floor, and Turner is a graduate student who is on the second floor.

7. (A) This can't happen. It would put S on 3, and R and S would have different statuses.
   (B) This can't happen. It would put S on 3, and R and S would have different statuses.
   (C) This can't happen. All three advisors would have the same status.
   (D) Right.
   (E) This can't happen. All three advisors would have the same status.

8. If Ruiz is an undergraduate student, which one of the following statements could be true?

   (A) Smith is on the first floor.
   (B) Smith is on the third floor.
   (C) Turner is a graduate student who is on the first floor.
   (D) Turner is a graduate student who is on the second floor.
   (E) Turner is an undergraduate student who is on the second floor.

8. (A) This can never be true.
   (B) The advisor on the third floor must have the same status as the one on the fourth floor.
   (C) Right.
   (D) This puts S on the third floor, but the advisor on the third floor must have the same status as the one on the fourth floor.
   (E) This puts S on the third floor, but the advisor on the third floor must have the same status as the one on the fourth floor.

SECTION I

9. If neither Smith nor Turner is on the third floor, then which of the following must be true?

   (A) There is a graduate student on the first floor.
   (B) There is a graduate student on the fourth floor.
   (C) There is a graduate student on the second floor.
   (D) There is an undergraduate student on the fourth floor.
   (E) There is an undergraduate student on the second floor.

9. (A) Not necessarily; T could be an undergrad.
   (B) Not necessarily; R could be an undergrad.
   (C) Right. If no one is on the third floor, S, a grad advisor, must be on the second floor.
   (D) Not necessarily; R could be a grad.
   (E) If no one is on the third floor, S, a grad advisor, must be on the second floor.

10. Which one of the following statements must be true?

    (A) Ruiz and Smith are both the same status.
    (B) Ruiz and Turner are both the same status.
    (C) Smith and Turner are both the same status.
    (D) Either Ruiz or Turner or both have undergraduate status.
    (E) Either Ruiz or Turner or both have graduate status.

10. (A) Not necessarily; see the setup for question 8.
    (B) Not necessarily; see the setup for question 11.
    (C) Not necessarily; see the setup for question 11.
    (D) Right, otherwise all three advisors would have the same status.
    (E) This is not necessarily true; only one graduate, S, is required.

SECTION I

QUESTIONS	EXPLANATIONS

11. If neither Smith nor Turner lives on the first floor, which one of the following statements must be true?

   (A) Ruiz is an undergraduate student.

   (B) Turner is a graduate student.

   (C) Neither Smith nor Turner is a graduate student who lives on the second floor.

   (D) Neither Smith nor Turner is an undergraduate student who lives on the second floor.

   (E) Neither Smith nor Turner is a graduate student who lives on the third floor.

11.

   (A) This forces T on the second floor, and S, a grad, on the third floor. Because the advisor on the third floor must be the same as the one on the fourth floor, R is a grad.

   (B) This forces T on the second floor, and S, a grad, on the third floor. Because the advisor on the third floor must be the same as the one on the fourth floor, R is a grad, and since they all can't have the same status, T must be an undergrad.

   (C) Right. This forces T on the second floor, and S, a grad, on the third floor. Because the advisor on the third floor must be the same as the one on the fourth floor, R is a grad, and since they all can't have the same status, T must be an undergrad.

   (D) This forces T on the second floor, and S, a grad, on the third floor. Because the advisor on the third floor must be the same as the one on the fourth floor, R is a grad, and since they all can't have the same status, T must be an undergrad.

   (E) This forces T on the second floor, and S, a grad, on the third floor. Because the advisor on the third floor must be the same as the one on the fourth floor, R is a grad, and since they all can't have the same status, T must be an undergrad.

12. Which one of the following CANNOT be true?

   (A) There is an advisor with graduate status who lives on the fourth floor.

   (B) There is an advisor with graduate status who lives on the third floor.

   (C) There is an advisor with undergraduate status who lives on the fourth floor.

   (D) There is an advisor with undergraduate status who lives on the second floor.

   (E) There is an advisor with undergraduate status who lives on the third floor.

12.

   (A) Sure, R could be a grad (see setup for 11).

   (B) Sure, S could be on the third floor (see setup for 11).

   (C) Sure, R could be an undergrad (see setup for 8).

   (D) Sure, T could be an undergrad on the second floor (see setup for 11).

   (E) Right. Only S can live on the third floor, and S is a grad.

SECTION I

Questions 13–18

A track and field coach must assign eight athletes—A, B, C, D, R, S, T, and U—into two groups of four athletes each, one group assigned to compete in events, one athlete at a time, on Saturday, and the other group to compete, also one athlete at a time, on Sunday. All events will be scheduled for the same amount of time, and every event on Sunday is scheduled for exactly the same time slot as an event that takes place on Saturday. The assignments must also conform to the following conditions:

A must compete on one of the days in the same time slot that C competes on the other day.
B must compete on one of the days in the same time slot that D competes on the other day.
R must compete on the same day as A.
S must compete on the same day as D.
T must compete in the second time slot on Sunday.

	Saturday				Sunday			
	1	2	3	4	1	2	3	4
⑭	S		D			T	B	
⑯	B	R/U	U/R	A	D	T	S	C
⑰	D	S/U	C	U/S	B	T	A	R
⑱	A	S	R	D	C	T	U	B
						T		
						T		

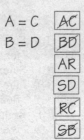

A = C AC
B = D BD
       AR
       SD
       RC
       SB

13. Which one of the following, without regard to the order in which they will compete, could be the group of athletes to be assigned to the events on Saturday?

(A) A, B, C, and S
(B) A, B, D, and R
(C) B, C, D, and S
(D) C, D, S, and U
(E) D, R, S, and U

13. (A) A and C can't be on the same day.
     (B) B and D can't be on the same day.
     (C) B and D can't be on the same day.
     (D) Right.
     (E) A and R must be on the same day.

14. If athlete S competes on Saturday, which one of the following athletes must compete on Sunday?

(A) A
(B) B
(C) C
(D) R
(E) U

14. (A) We don't know where A goes yet.
     (B) Right, see deduction. S has to be on the same day as D, and D can't be on the same day as B.
     (C) We don't know where C goes yet.
     (D) We don't know where R goes yet.
     (E) We don't know where U goes yet.

SECTION I

QUESTIONS	EXPLANATIONS

15. If athlete R must compete on one of the days in the same time slot that athlete S competes on the other day, which one of the following must be the second athlete to compete on Saturday?

   (A) A
   (B) B
   (C) C
   (D) D
   (E) U

15. Because R and S must be in the same time slot, B and D must be in the same time slot, and A and C must be in the same time slot, that means only U is left to be in the same time slot as T. Therefore, U must be the second athlete to compete on Saturday, and the correct answer is (E).

16. If the order, from first to last, of athletes to compete on Sunday is D, T, S, C, which one of the following is an acceptable order of athletes on Saturday, also from first to last?

   (A) A, R, B, U
   (B) B, U, A, R
   (C) B, U, R, A
   (D) U, B, A, R
   (E) U, R, B, A

16. (A) If D is first on Sunday, B must be first on Saturday.
   (B) If C is last on Sunday, A must be last on Saturday.
   (C) Right.
   (D) If D is first on Sunday, B must be first on Saturday.
   (E) If D is first on Sunday, B must be first on Saturday.

17. If athlete A must compete between athlete T and athlete R on Sunday, which one of the following must be the first athlete to compete on Saturday?

   (A) B
   (B) C
   (C) D
   (D) S
   (E) U

17. (A) The TAR block on Sunday puts B in Sunday's first position.
   (B) C has to be third on Saturday, because A is in the third position on Sunday.
   (C) Right. The TAR block on Sunday puts B in Sunday's first position, which forces D in the first position on Saturday.
   (D) S must be second or fourth on Saturday.
   (E) U must be second or fourth on Saturday.

18. If athlete S must compete on Saturday immediately after athlete A and immediately before athlete R, which athlete must be the third to compete on Sunday?

   (A) B
   (B) C
   (C) D
   (D) S
   (E) U

18. (A) The ASR block on Saturday puts D in the fourth position on Saturday, which puts B in the fourth position on Sunday.
   (B) The ASR block puts C first on Sunday, because C must compete in the same time slot as A.
   (C) The ASR block on Saturday puts D in the fourth position on Saturday.
   (D) We already know that S is on Saturday.
   (E) Right. The ASR block on Saturday puts D in the fourth position on Saturday, which puts B in the fourth position on Sunday, and C in the first position on Sunday. That leaves U for the third position on Sunday.

Questions 19–24

A senior partner of a large law firm is assigning lawyers to each of three of the firm's cases: Case 1, Case 2, and Case 3. Exactly two of the following lawyers must be assigned to each case: Ayala, Bloom, Carpenter, Duggan, Emerson, and Fong. Each lawyer will be assigned to exactly one case. Ayala, Bloom, and Carpenter are senior associates at the firm; Duggan, Emerson, and Fong are not. Ayala, Duggan, and Emerson are corporate tax attorneys; Bloom, Carpenter, and Fong are not. The senior partner must assign the lawyers to the three cases according to the following requirements:

    At least one senior associate must be assigned to each case.
    At least one corporate tax attorney must be assigned to each case.
    Duggan must be assigned to either Case 1 or Case 2.

19. Which one of the following is a possible list of assignments of lawyers to cases according to the requirements?

	Case 1	Case 2	Case 3
(A)	Duggan Fong	Emerson Bloom	Ayala Carpenter
(B)	Duggan Bloom	Emerson Fong	Ayala Carpenter
(C)	Emerson Carpenter	Duggan Bloom	Ayala Fong
(D)	Emerson Carpenter	Ayala Bloom	Duggan Fong
(E)	Ayala Fong	Duggan Emerson	Bloom Carpenter

19.
(A) If there has to be a senior and a tax attorney assigned to each case, then A and F must be assigned to the same case.
(B) If there has to be a senior and a tax attorney assigned to each case, then A and F must be assigned to the same case.
(C) Right. If there has to be a senior and a tax attorney assigned to each case, then A and F must be assigned to the same case.
(D) Duggan can't be assigned to Case 3.
(E) Case 2 has no senior attorney; Case 3 has no tax attorney.

SECTION I

QUESTIONS	EXPLANATIONS

20. Which one of the following must be true?

    (A) Ayala and Carpenter will be assigned to the same case.

    (B) Ayala and Fong will be assigned to the same case.

    (C) Duggan and Bloom will be assigned to the same case.

    (D) Duggan and Fong will be assigned to the same case.

    (E) Emerson and Bloom will be assigned to the same case.

20.   (A) If there has to be a senior and a tax attorney assigned to each case, then A and F must be assigned to the same case, so A can't be with C.

    (B) Right. If there has to be a senior and a tax attorney assigned to each case, then A and F must be assigned to the same case.

    (C) This doesn't have to be true; see the setup for question 24.

    (D) If there has to be a senior and a tax attorney assigned to each case, then A and F must be assigned to the same case, so F can't be with D.

    (E) This doesn't have to be true; see the setup for question 22.

21. Which one of the following is a complete and accurate list of the lawyers whom the senior partner can assign to the same case as Carpenter?

    (A) Bloom

    (B) Duggan

    (C) Emerson

    (D) Bloom and Fong

    (E) Duggan and Emerson

21.   (A) C can't be with B because they're both seniors.

    (B) What about Emerson? See the setup for question 22.

    (C) What about Duggan? See the setup for question 24.

    (D) C can't be with B because they're both seniors, and can't be with F because F must be with A.

    (E) Right. C can't be with A or B, because they're both seniors, and can't be with F because F must be with A. That leaves D and E.

22. If Emerson is assigned to Case 2, which one of the following must be true?

    (A) Bloom is assigned to Case 1.

    (B) Carpenter is assigned to Case 2.

    (C) Carpenter is assigned to Case 3.

    (D) Fong is assigned to Case 1.

    (E) Fong is assigned to Case 3.

22.   (A) We don't know where B is yet.

    (B) We don't know where C is yet.

    (C) We don't know where C is yet.

    (D) E on 2 puts D on 1 (D can't be on 3). That puts the AF block on 3.

    (E) Right. E on 2 puts D on 1 (D can't be on 3). That puts the AF block on 3.

23. The senior partner CANNOT make an acceptable assignment of lawyers to cases by assigning

    (A) Ayala to Case 1 and Bloom to Case 2

    (B) Ayala to Case 2 and Carpenter to Case 3

    (C) Duggan to Case 2 and Emerson to Case 3

    (D) Emerson to Case 1 and Carpenter to Case 3

    (E) Fong to Case 1 and Duggan to Case 2

23.   (A) Sure, this is possible.

    (B) Sure, this is possible.

    (C) Sure, this is possible.

    (D) Right. E on 1 and C on 3 forces the AF block on 2, which forces D on 3, which is a violation of the rules.

    (E) Sure, this is possible.

24. If Bloom is assigned to Case 3, which one of the following must be true?

    (A) Ayala is assigned to Case 2.

    (B) Carpenter is assigned to Case 1.

    (C) Emerson is assigned to Case 1.

    (D) Duggan is assigned to the same case as Bloom.

    (E) Duggan is assigned to the same case as Carpenter.

24.   (A) A could be on 1.

    (B) D could be on 2.

    (C) E must be on 3 with B.

    (D) D can't be on 3.

    (E) Right. If B is on 3, and D can't be there, and F can't be there because he has to be with A, E must be on 3 with B. That means the AF block goes on either 1 or 2, and wherever that doesn't go, the only two left, D and C, do go.

SECTION II

<u>Questions 1–6</u> are based on the following passage:

It is commonly asserted that an ideology is powerless against political interest groups and against the unflagging tendency of established social institutions to expand. To dispute this claim, however,
(5) we need only look to the present day political situation. There is, at the present time, an unfortunate political revolution under way among Western countries that is occurring in spite of potent political opposition.

For most of the postwar period, there was a
(10) proliferation of government social welfare programs designed to raise the income share of the poor. Such programs serve, in various forms, to redistribute wealth among the population at large, generally taking from those who are better situated and giving to those who
(15) are economically disadvantaged. As a result of their implementation, the plight of the poor was ameliorated to an even greater degree than was expected.

Despite these positive advances, one school of ideology, known as *redistributional retrenchment,* has
(20) long argued that the gains from redistribution programs are far outweighed by adverse economic side effects. In the wake of the worldwide slowdown in economic growth following the first oil embargo of 1973, these arguments have been treated with increasing respect,
(25) resulting in deliberate government curtailing of social welfare spending. As a consequence, in the United States, England, Germany, and even in the Netherlands and Scandinavia, public income transfer programs have been or are being cut back. On the face of it, only
(30) France and Italy seem to be resisting the trend; Switzerland, though it partook in the rapid expansion of the earlier period, has temporarily reached a plateau in spending. The political mentality that supports redistributional retrenchment now holds considerable
(35) sway. As a consequence of the deliberate government curtailment of social welfare spending, the Western poor are measurably worse off today than they were just a decade ago.

In addition, every dollar cut from the budget of such
(40) programs reduces the government payroll by twenty cents. Thus, the curtailment of social welfare programs has caused a decrease in the number of government jobs. The resulting unemployment has not been fully absorbed by the private sector. There is, then, in

(45) addition to the many poor whose benefits have been cut, a large number of middle-income citizens who oppose redistributional retrenchment.

Given those facts, one would expect everyday political forces to reverse this trend of social welfare
(50) cutbacks. Yet no reversal has occurred. Counting on fundamental principles of democracy and the ultimate power of the vote, political hopefuls have sought to attain office by appealing to such people and addressing the genuine economic distress they are
(55) experiencing. Their efforts have, for the most part, failed. Indeed, those government legislators, administrators, and executives who felt confident that they would succeed in abating the trend, simply because the number of voting citizens who stood to
(60) suffer was so large, underestimated the power of the redistributional-retrenchment ideology. It continues to advance notwithstanding the adverse effect it has had on huge sectors of the population.

SECTION II

QUESTIONS	EXPLANATIONS

Main idea: The ideology of redistributional retrenchment is mightier than anything opposing it.

1. Which one of the following best states the main idea of the passage?

    (A) We must determine whether redistribution offers more benefit than cost.
    (B) For a number of reasons, political pressures have failed to slow government redistribution programs.
    (C) The ideology behind redistributional retrenchment is currently more powerful than the political forces opposing it.
    (D) Governments have curtailed social welfare spending deliberately in order to worsen the plight of the poor.
    (E) Redistributional retrenchment is contrary to democratic ideals.

1. This is a MAIN IDEA question. Come up with your own main idea before you go to the answer choices.

    (A) No, it's pretty clear that the author thinks redistribution is a good thing and that redistributional retrenchment is a bad thing. If you're not convinced, re-read the last paragraph.
    (B) No, they have failed to slow redistributional retrenchment.
    (C) Yes. Redistributional retrenchment is still plowing away even though it's bad.
    (D) The author doesn't say that governments deliberately hurt the poor.
    (E) Maybe, but the author doesn't mention democratic ideals—he just thinks that redistributional retrenchment is a bad idea.

2. According to the passage, which one of the following was most important in creating the modern trend toward redistributional retrenchment?

    (A) arguments that suggest that redistribution programs have negative economic consequences
    (B) the fact that most social welfare programs did not actually serve society's welfare
    (C) the unexpected discovery that redistribution programs raised the income share of the poor
    (D) the tendency of institutions and procedures to maintain themselves
    (E) the fact that most industrialized nations have reached a permanent plateau in their ability to spend

2. This is a SPECIFIC question. Find the part of the passage that first mentions redistributional retrenchment.

    (A) Yes, this is mentioned in lines 18–21.
    (B) They do serve society's welfare—see lines 15–17.
    (C) It was hardly unexpected—it was the goal of the redistribution programs.
    (D) This has nothing to do with anything. Classic LSAT gibberish.
    (E) This is referencing the wrong part of the passage. It's referring to the part about Switzerland. Eliminate it.

SECTION II

QUESTIONS	EXPLANATIONS

QUESTIONS

3. In the fourth paragraph of the passage, the author attempts to

    (A) prove that democracy is more potent than any individual ideology
    (B) indicate that not only poor citizens are harmed by redistributional retrenchment
    (C) argue that in a democracy the vote is not as powerful as it is thought to be
    (D) illustrate that government officials do not always understand the political process
    (E) highlight the failure of ordinary political forces to overcome redistributional retrenchment

4. It can be inferred from the passage that the author

    (A) favors redistributional retrenchment but is concerned about its effect on the poor
    (B) opposes redistributional retrenchment because of its effect on the poor and working class
    (C) does not believe democracy can effectively represent the interests of the poor
    (D) thinks redistributional retrenchment is appropriate to some nations but not to others
    (E) believes that redistributional retrenchment was a hasty reaction to a temporary economic slowdown

EXPLANATIONS

3. This is a PARAGRAPH REFERENCE question. Re-read paragraph four and see what its purpose was.

    (A) The words "prove" and "any" are too extreme here.
    (B) Yes. The author shows how the middle class was affected as well.
    (C) This is discussed in paragraph five.
    (D) Understanding the political process is not mentioned in the paragraph.
    (E) This is discussed in paragraph five.

4. This is a GENERAL question. You have to read the choices and see which is closest to what the author thinks.

    (A) The author opposes redistributional retrenchment. Eliminate it.
    (B) Yes. See paragraph 4 and the last line of the passage.
    (C) The author's not talking about democracy, but about redistributional retrenchment.
    (D) The author never gives any examples of how it is a good thing anywhere.
    (E) No, the author says that the redistributional retrenchment school has "long argued" for it. See line 20.

SECTION II

QUESTIONS	EXPLANATIONS

5. The phrase "potent political opposition" (line 8) refers to

   (A) the ideology that favors taking wealth from the more fortunate and distributing it to the less fortunate
   (B) the political view that opposes redistribution on a large scale
   (C) the adverse effects of redistribution programs on international economic transactions
   (D) the large number of eligible voters who benefit from the existence of social welfare programs
   (E) the large number of political officials who support redistributional retrenchment

6. It can be inferred from the information in the passage that the author believes that redistributional retrenchment

   (A) has reduced profits for private industry
   (B) exerts its most serious effects on public employees
   (C) has produced only 20 percent of the savings its supporters expected
   (D) has left private industry unable to find qualified workers to fill its needs
   (E) has caused unemployment among some citizens who would otherwise have jobs

5. This is a LINE REFERENCE question. Read five lines above and five lines below the line reference.

   (A) An ideology isn't political opposition, people are.
   (B) This is the opposite of what you are looking for. "Potent political opposition" refers to those who oppose redistributional retrenchment.
   (C) An effect isn't political opposition, people are.
   (D) Bingo. Here are the people who support redistribution and make up the "political opposition" to it.
   (E) No, we learn that many officials don't support it. But it's continuing anyway.

6. This is a SPECIFIC question. Answer in your own words what the author thinks redistributional retrenchment has caused.

   (A) No, it has just not increased the number of jobs in private industry substantially.
   (B) No, "most serious effects" is too extreme.
   (C) This is not mentioned anywhere in the passage.
   (D) No, an inability to find qualified workers isn't mentioned.
   (E) Bingo. There are more middle-class people out of work because of it.

SECTION II

Questions 7–13 are based on the following passage:

A fundamental element of the American criminal justice system is trial by an impartial jury. This constitutionally protected guarantee is made meaningful by allowing the defendant to challenge and
(5) have removed from the panel those prospective jurors who are demonstrably prejudiced in the case. Such prejudice may be based on a juror's having some tangible interest in the case or on his relationship to the participants. Beyond this, a juror may be challenged if
(10) the defendant can show that the juror has preconceptions about the issues or parties that would prevent him from rendering a verdict based solely on the law and the evidence put forth at trial. In order to enable the defendant to discover these disqualifying factors,
(15) prospective jurors are subjected to questioning by the court or counsel or both. This interrogation is known as the *voir dire* examination.

Generally, the courts have recognized that any prejudice affecting the ability of a juror to decide a
(20) case fairly is a sufficient ground for a challenge. Such prejudices can be categorized in two basic ways: as a bias implied as a matter of law and as actual bias. The former may include such objective factors as a juror's relationship to a participant in the trial, whereas the
(25) latter may involve such subjective characteristics as racial, religious, economic, social, or political prejudices that would prevent the juror from trying the case fairly.

There is, however, a fundamental disagreement as to
(30) the extent to which the *voir dire* examination does, in fact, uncover juror prejudice. It has been suggested that once the prospective jurors are in the courtroom, they feel that disqualification for bias would impugn their integrity and may, therefore, be willing to lie to avoid
(35) removal from the panel.

While it may be true that people will not invariably answer truthfully on *voir dire*, the same may be said of other stages of the trial. That witnesses do not always testify truthfully at trial compels neither the conclusion
(40) that it is useless to examine or cross-examine them nor the conclusion that the trial process itself is invalid. Similarly, the recognition that prospective jurors may at times suppress what they know to be their own weaknesses need not lead to the determination that the
(45) *voir dire* process itself is worthless.

There is, for the most part, an absence of both explicit statutory guidelines and clear Supreme Court rulings indicating what specific inquiries must be made if *voir dire* is to fulfill its constitutional function. What
(50) the Constitution requires, and will be held to require, of juror interrogation as to, for example, racial prejudice is unclear. Recent case law suggests, however, that policy considerations and perhaps the Constitution itself call for some degree of direct and specific
(55) questioning as to not only racial bias, but also as to other common sources of prejudice as well.

SECTION II

QUESTIONS

7. The primary purpose of this passage is to

   (A) criticize a constitutionally guaranteed right
   (B) show how the Constitution fails to protect racial minorities
   (C) examine the problems inherent in a legal process
   (D) illustrate the weakness that qualifies an otherwise flawless process
   (E) compare two criteria that define a legal process

8. The passage suggests that *voir dire* fails in regard to which one of the following issues?

   (A) whether counsel or the court should conduct interrogations
   (B) determining whether a juror is actually prejudiced with regard to a certain case
   (C) the lack of specific statutory guidelines that designate when inquiries should be made
   (D) the need to keep issues of law free of social, religious, racial, or economic issues
   (E) the objectivity of counsel when interrogating potential jurors

9. The author states that "witnesses do not always testify truthfully" (lines 38–39) in order to highlight the fact that

   (A) lying on the part of trial participants is inevitable
   (B) distinguishing what is true from what is false is one of a juror's duties
   (C) *voir dire* is yet another opportunity for citizens to suppress their prejudices
   (D) witness testimony should not represent the exclusive premise upon which a defendant rests his case
   (E) many levels of the judicial process can be marred by suppression of the truth

EXPLANATIONS

7. This is a PRIMARY PURPOSE question. Answer in your own words first and then look at the choices.

   (A) No, overall the author thinks the *voir dire* process is a good one.
   (B) No, the correct answer should reference the *voir dire* process.
   (C) Yes. "A legal process" is referring to the *voir dire* process.
   (D) "Flawless process" is a bit too enthusiastic for this passage, which primarily discussed its problems.
   (E) What two criteria? The *voir dire* process is more complex than that.

8. This is a SPECIFIC question. Find a part of the passage that talks about when *voir dire* doesn't work.

   (A) No, it doesn't matter who conducts the investigations.
   (B) Yes, see lines 29–31. It doesn't always work.
   (C) Not *when* inquiries should be made, but *what* inquiries should be made. See line 48.
   (D) This is way too general; we're only talking about *voir dire* here.
   (E) Counsel objectivity is not an issue that was raised in the passage. Eliminate it.

9. This is a LINE REFERENCE question. Read five lines above and five lines below the line reference.

   (A) This is a bit too extreme. Is it really inevitable? In all cases?
   (B) The author's not talking about jurors' duties in this passage. Eliminate it.
   (C) This answer choice was written by a conspiracy theorist. Eliminate it.
   (D) This is true but that's not why it was mentioned. It is an example used to illustrate something about the *voir dire* process.
   (E) Yes—suppression of the truth affects both the testimony of witnesses on the stand AND the claims of prospective jurors during the *voir dire* process.

SECTION II

10. It can be inferred from the passage that *voir dire*, while possessing specific flaws, is designed to

   (A) aid the defendant by providing him with a trial by an impartial jury

   (B) weed out jurors who do not support the defendant's point of view

   (C) reveal a potential juror's racist inclinations

   (D) convince a prospective juror that his or her duty is to reach a verdict based on the law

   (E) interrogate potential jurors and make them testify to their own prejudices

10. This is a SPECIFIC question asking about the purpose of the *voir dire* process. Find the part about the *voir dire* process in the passage.

   (A) This is right. We're using the *voir dire* process to weed out prejudiced people. Re-read the first paragraph.

   (B) No, the process is to find impartial people. Eliminate it.

   (C) The purpose of the *voir dire* process is a bit broader than this. Eliminate it.

   (D) The *voir dire* process is not related to convincing anybody. Eliminate it.

   (E) This is a bit harsh. We don't want to torture these people. Eliminate it.

11. With which one of the following statements would the author be most likely to agree?

   (A) Prospective jurors should be subjected to rigorous questioning regarding their feelings towards specific social, ethnic, and economic groups.

   (B) The virtues of *voir dire* need to be carefully weighed against the limitations before the process is constitutionally mandated.

   (C) Because people can be depended upon to lie during a *voir dire* interrogation, the process itself should be deemed unconstitutional by the Supreme Court.

   (D) Courts should clarify which prejudices constitute sufficient grounds for a challenge.

   (E) While a trial by an impartial jury is a fundamental element of the criminal justice system, the *voir dire* process is the most limited way of approaching the idea.

11. This is a GENERAL question. Find the choice that is most in line with the main idea of the author and the primary purpose of the passage.

   (A) Yes, this should be done to make sure that the jurors aren't prejudiced.

   (B) There's nothing in the passage about whether or not the author thinks the *voir dire* process should be constitutionally mandated. Eliminate it.

   (C) Remember, the author likes the process overall. This is too extreme.

   (D) Which courts? You can't prove this choice with information from the passage. Eliminate it.

   (E) Remember, the author likes the process and doesn't think it's all that limiting.

SECTION II

QUESTIONS	EXPLANATIONS

12. Based on the information in the passage, in which one of the following circumstances might a defendant effectively challenge a prospective juror?

    (A) the prosecutor and the juror share the same racial background

    (B) the juror is ignorant of the laws applicable to the case

    (C) the juror is shown to be a habitual liar

    (D) the juror is casually acquainted with the prosecuting party

    (E) the juror has been disqualified from previous *voir dire* examinations

12. This is a SPECIFIC question. Find the part of the passage that talks about challenges.

    (A) Nope. The issue is racial bias, not racial similarity.

    (B) No, that's what the trial is for. The *voir dire* process is not an educational one.

    (C) This looks good, but it's a bit extreme and you can't find it in the passage.

    (D) Bingo. See lines 8–9. A juror shouldn't have a relationship with anyone involved in the trial.

    (E) This is not mentioned in the passage as grounds for a challenge. Eliminate it.

13. The author states that which one of the following might be a prospective juror's reason for suppressing information that might prejudice him or her from participating in a trial?

    (A) the prospective juror's actual bias with regard to issues such as race, economics, and religion

    (B) the desire to avoid maligning one's own reputation as an objective, bias-free citizen

    (C) the need to feel accepted by an institution of the U.S. government

    (D) the truth is considered less dangerous outside of an actual trial situation

    (E) the prospective juror's desire to mask his or her relationship to trial participants

13. This is a SPECIFIC question. Find the part of the passage that talks about the ulterior motives of a juror.

    (A) This was not mentioned as the reason. See lines 33–35.

    (B) Bingo. See lines 33–35. This is a paraphrase of "impugn their integrity." It's the answer.

    (C) This was not mentioned as the reason. See lines 33–35.

    (D) This was not mentioned as the reason. See lines 33–35.

    (E) This was not mentioned as the reason. See lines 33–35.

Questions 14–20 are based on the following passage:

Late in the nineteenth century, land reform emerged as a dominant concern of the Liberal Party in England. During this time, many prominent thinkers dissented from mainstream liberal ideology by questioning the
(5) justification of individual ownership. To John Stuart Mill, Henry George, and Herbert Spencer, for example, land represented something unique among ownable goods as "a thing not made by man, a thing necessary to life, and of which there is not enough for all." With
(10) these attributes—naturalness of origin, absolute scarcity, and centrality to all productive life-sustaining activity—land and land ownership, it was asserted, could be considered indefensible rights based upon personal labor or achievement.
(15) Prior to the emergence of these political analysts, the *laissez-faire* views of Adam Smith were the dominant liberal position. Smith asserted that "the interests of the state require that land should be as much in commerce as any other good." The "new liberal" thinking,
(20) however, rejected this traditional notion and attacked the institutions of primogeniture and strict family settlement that enabled the landed class to maintain their estates from one generation to the next. The new liberal ideology encompassed both economic and
(25) social goals. They envisioned a break with the static conditions of primogeniture and its replacement with a more egalitarian and morally vigorous society of peasant proprietors.

In addressing the dilemma of land ownership,
(30) proponents of the new liberal thinking offered several different strategies. Herbert Spencer's proposal sought to make land the joint property of society in which all land would be confiscated by the (democratic) state. Individuals might then lease parts of it through
(35) competitive bidding. By paying rent, tenants would thus compensate all non-owners for having relinquished their claim.

John Stuart Mill employed the law of rent to show that increased land values cannot be attributed to the
(40) exertions undertaken by owners; most often, rather, such increases are the function of the "mere progress of wealth and population." In his *Political Economy*, Mill held that private property is justified only insofar as the proprietor of land is its improver. Some policies
(45) advocated by Mill included a special tax on rent, the protection of tenants' rights, state land purchases, and the prohibition of any further enclosures of common lands. While supporting some land reform measures, however, Mill insisted that present owners were owed
(50) compensation. His proposal of a special tax on land pertained to future unearned income without disturbing past acquisitions.

According to Henry George, another prominent new liberal, virtually all social and moral ills of modern
(55) society could be traced to private ownership of land. In

Progress and Poverty, George rejects the inevitability of poverty and deprivation as remedial defects of society. In his view, rent represented not only unearned income, but a deleterious drain on much of
(60) society's earned income that absorbed the disposable surplus created by society's cooperative efforts. George's solution lay in the socialization of rent. He proposed that the community recapture its entitlement through a special tax on the rental value of land; a
(65) levy—known as the "single tax"—would eliminate the need for taxing productive enterprises and would eventually replace all other taxes.

SECTION II

Main idea: Nineteenth century liberals dissent from mainstream ideology of land ownership and move to ideas of rent to help non-owners.

14. The primary purpose of the passage is to

   (A) discuss contrasting views on land reform among nineteenth-century English liberals
   (B) trace the development of land ownership laws in England
   (C) describe a current debate on land ownership
   (D) prove that Adam Smith was not truly a *laissez-faire* liberal
   (E) suggest a new political approach to the problem of land scarcity

14. This is a PRIMARY PURPOSE question. Answer in your own words first and then look at the choices.

   (A) This looks pretty good. There are a bunch of liberals, and they are talking about land reform.
   (B) This would take several pages, if not several books, to accomplish. Too broad; eliminate it.
   (C) No, the passage is talking about the debate during the nineteenth century.
   (D) The question is about the entire passage. This is way too specific, not to mention wrong.
   (E) He's talking nineteenth century, which is hardly new. Eliminate it.

15. According to the passage, all of the following characteristics were ascribed to land as justification for its special treatment EXCEPT

   (A) the limited availability of land as a resource
   (B) its non-artificial essence
   (C) the integral nature of the commodity to human existence
   (D) the effort required to increase its value
   (E) the historical precedent for private property

15. This is a SPECIFIC question. Go and find the four things that were mentioned and eliminate the one that was not.

   (A) Mentioned in line 9. Eliminate it.
   (B) Mentioned in line 10. Eliminate it.
   (C) Mentioned in line 11. Eliminate it.
   (D) Mentioned in lines 13–14. Eliminate it.
   (E) This is referring to a different part of the passage, so it's our answer.

16. According to the passage, Henry George considered economic deprivation to be

   (A) an unfortunate but necessary global condition
   (B) a temporary state that would inevitably be reversed
   (C) a condition that varied according to the policies of the ruling elites
   (D) a situation that could be rectified by employing certain policies
   (E) a condition that was unlikely to be alleviated

16. This is a SPECIFIC question. Read the paragraph on Henry George and then answer the question.

   (A) He thinks we can beat it. See lines 56–57.
   (B) He thinks we *can* beat it, not that we *will* beat it. See lines 56–57.
   (C) Never mentioned anywhere. Eliminate it.
   (D) Yes. See lines 56–57.
   (E) We don't really know how likely he thought it was, just that he thought it was possible. Not as good as (D).

QUESTIONS	EXPLANATIONS

17. In addressing the issue of land reform, Mill prescribed that the unearned benefits accrued to landowners from prior transactions should be

(A) unlike future transactions in that they should not be taxed

(B) considered invalid and used for the benefits of all citizens

(C) left undisturbed by the society at large

(D) confiscated and distributed to the neediest members of society

(E) dealt with on a case-by-case basis in determining their disposal

17. This is a SPECIFIC question. Read the paragraph on John Stuart Mill and then answer the question.

(A) Yes. See lines 51–52.
(B) He never said this. Eliminate it.
(C) He never said this. Eliminate it.
(D) He never said this. Eliminate it.
(E) He never said this. Eliminate it.

18. The author introduces the term "new liberal" (lines 19–20) in order to

(A) delineate the dominant political parties of the time

(B) compare the views of Adam Smith to conservative land theories

(C) present a view that differed from traditional liberal thinking

(D) differentiate between U.S. liberals and English liberals

(E) explain the traditional opposition to the institution of primogeniture

18. This is a LINE REFERENCE question. Read five lines above and five lines below the line reference.

(A) We're not talking about parties but ideologies. Eliminate it.

(B) No, Adam Smith is not a new liberal—he's an old one.

(C) Yes, guys like Mill and George and Spencer were coming up with new theories. This is the answer.

(D) "U.S. liberals" is totally out of the scope of this passage, orbiting Pluto somewhere.

(E) This is not why he mentions new liberals. Eliminate it.

SECTION II

<table>
<tr><th>QUESTIONS</th><th>EXPLANATIONS</th></tr>
</table>

19. According to the passage, Mill believed that a landowner would be entitled to profit from his holdings as long as he

   (A) did so without taking unfair advantage of the less fortunate
   (B) offered some of the profits to be used for the public betterment
   (C) was prepared to pay substantial taxes on his past and present holdings
   (D) was directly responsible for improving the condition of the land
   (E) supplied parts of the land for communal use

19. This is a SPECIFIC question. Read the paragraph on John Stuart Mill and then answer the question.

   (A) He never said this. Eliminate it.
   (B) He never said this. Eliminate it.
   (C) He never said past holdings, only present ones. Eliminate it.
   (D) Yes. See lines 43–44. It's the answer.
   (E) He never said this. Eliminate it.

20. Based on the content of the passage, one can infer that, according to the traditional liberal outlook prior to the late nineteenth century, land was viewed as

   (A) an entity that should be used for the benefit of the entire society
   (B) a means by which wealth could be redistributed
   (C) a valid, but potentially deleterious, means of producing wealth
   (D) a private commodity to be bought and sold without outside interference
   (E) an area that developed mysteriously even without human interference

20. This is a SPECIFIC question. Go back to where the passage talked about what was happening before these dudes.

   (A) Nope. That's the radical view of the new guys.
   (B) Nope. Same problem as (A).
   (C) Hardly. No one before these guys thought that owning a lot of land was deleterious.
   (D) Bingo. Pure Adam Smith—it's pretty much exactly what he said. See lines 16–19.
   (E) Ah, yes, the mysterious nature of land ownership. Consult your local Psychic Friends Network representative. Eliminate it.

SECTION II

Questions 21–27 are based on the following passage:

[This passage was written in 1983.]

In both developed and developing nations, governments finance, produce, and distribute various goods and services. In recent years, the range of goods provided by the government has extended broadly,
(5) encompassing many goods that do not meet the economic purist's definition of "public goods." As the size of the public sector has increased steadily, there has been a growing concern about the effectiveness of the public sector's performance as producer.

(10) Critics argue that the public provision of certain goods is inefficient and have proposed that the private sector should replace many current public sector activities, that is, these services should be privatized. During the Reagan administration, greater privatization efforts have
(15) been pursued in the United States. Concurrent with this trend has been a strong endorsement by international bilateral donor agencies for heavier reliance on the private sector in developing countries. The underlying claim is that the private sector can improve the quality of
(20) outputs and deliver goods more quickly and less expensively than the public sector in these countries.

This claim, however, has mixed theoretical support and little empirical verification in the Third World. The political, institutional, and economic environments of
(25) developing nations are markedly different from those of developed countries. It is not clear that the theories and empirical evidence that purport to justify privatization in developed countries are applicable to developing countries. Often policy makers in
(30) developing nations do not have sufficient information to design effective policy shifts to increase efficiency of providing goods through private initiatives. Additionally, there is a lack of basic understanding about what policy variables need to be altered to attain
(35) desired outcomes of privatization in developing countries.

A recent study of privatization in Honduras examined the policy shift from "direct administration" to "contracting out" for three construction activities:
(40) urban upgrading for housing projects, rural primary schools, and rural roads. It tested key hypotheses pertaining to the effectiveness of privatization, focusing on three aspects: cost, time, and quality.

The main finding was that contracting out in
(45) Honduras did not lead to the common expectations of its proponents because institutional barriers and limited competitiveness in the marketplace have prevented private contractors from improving quality and reducing the time and cost required for construction.
(50) Privatization in developing countries cannot produce goods and services efficiently without substantial reform in the market and regulatory procedures. Policy makers interested in privatization as a policy measure should consider carefully the multiple objectives at the
(55) national level.

SECTION II

QUESTIONS	EXPLANATIONS

Main idea: The Reagan Administration pushed for privatization in the Third World, but some evidence suggests it hasn't worked.

21. The author's primary purpose in the passage is to

   (A) outline some of the shortcomings of privatization in developing nations

   (B) contrast the public sector's performance as producer in the United States and Honduras

   (C) explain the conditions that are necessary for privatization in Third World nations

   (D) justify heavier reliance on the private sector in developing countries

   (E) offer a solution for the future course of Honduran economic policy

21. This is a PRIMARY PURPOSE question. Answer in your own words first and then look at the choices.

   (A) This looks pretty good. Privatization might be okay, but so far we've had no evidence that it's good for developing countries. That's why the author uses the Honduras example.

   (B) Too specific. And it should say something about privatization. Eliminate it.

   (C) This looks good, but it's a bit too broad. He talks more about why it fails than about what is necessary for it to succeed. It would take more space than this paragraph if this were to be done. Eliminate it.

   (D) Hardly. The author doesn't think it works in developing countries.

   (E) Too specific. The author's only using Honduras as an example here. Eliminate it.

22. It can be inferred by the author's assessment of the Honduras study that a problem with introducing privatization in developing nations is that

   (A) most leaders of developing nations do not concur with the policies of the Reagan administration

   (B) the direct administration of services requires more capital than contracting out does

   (C) many developing nations lack the necessary competition between contractors in the marketplace

   (D) privatization of services is not politically acceptable in the struggling economies of Third World nations

   (E) contracting out is limited to upgrading facilities and most developing nations need to concentrate on constructing new facilities

22. This is a SPECIFIC question. Read the stuff about Honduras. Now.

   (A) We have no idea what these people think. Eliminate it.

   (B) The passage never says anything about more capital. Eliminate it.

   (C) Yes. See lines 47–48. This is our answer.

   (D) The author never says this. Eliminate it.

   (E) The author never says anything about new facilities. Eliminate it.

SECTION II

23. Which one of the following would weaken the author's statements about privatization in developing nations?

(A) The leading industrial nations have all benefited from the improved efficiency of privatization.

(B) International bilateral donor agencies have endorsed privatization efforts in developing nations.

(C) Many international economists favor the policies of the Reagan administration.

(D) A recent study of ten Third World nations found evidence contrary to the Honduran example.

(E) The citizens of developing nations use the term "public goods" differently than Americans.

23. This is a WEAKEN question. We know the author thinks privatization in developing countries isn't a good thing. What would weaken that?

(A) This has no impact because it's talking about industrialized nations.

(B) We know they like it, but the author already disagreed with them. Opinions don't matter—facts do.

(C) See (B). Same problem. We need an actual fact.

(D) Oops. Some evidence that it's working somewhere, which would weaken the author's argument. It's the answer.

(E) Huh? This doesn't give us any evidence that privatization is working somewhere. Eliminate it.

24. It could be inferred from the passage that which one of the following groups would most likely have an increased role in the privatized Honduran economy?

(A) U.S. banks
(B) Honduran entrepreneurs
(C) U.S. corporations
(D) international bilateral donor agencies
(E) Honduran economists

24. This is a SPECIFIC question. Read the stuff about Honduras. Now.

(A) Not mentioned.

(B) These people would be examples of private sector people in Honduras. It's the answer.

(C) Not mentioned.

(D) Mentioned, but we're looking for Honduran people here.

(E) We're looking for contractors, not economists. Eliminate it.

25. Based on the passage, it can be inferred that economic purists

(A) have a strict interpretation of what constitutes public goods

(B) endorse privatization only in developed nations

(C) are proponents of Honduran efforts to privatize

(D) feel that contracting out in Honduras has not led to diminished expectations

(E) disapprove of the shifting of responsibility for providing public services from the public to the private sector

25. This is a SPECIFIC question. Find the part of the passage that mentions what the economic purists would think.

(A) This looks good. See lines 3–6. They have a definition, and it's more strict than the government's definition.

(B) No, that's what the author does. Eliminate it.

(C) No, the author says that the claim has "mixed theoretical support." Eliminate it.

(D) We don't know what they think about Honduras. Eliminate it.

(E) We have no idea what they think about this. Eliminate it.

SECTION II

26. "Desired outcomes" (line 35) partially refers to which one of the following?

    (A) effective policy shifts
    (B) urban upgrading
    (C) political stability
    (D) improved quality of outputs
    (E) greater reliance on the public sectors

26. This is a LINE REFERENCE question. Read five lines above and five lines below the line reference.

    (A) No, we're looking for a positive outcome of privatization. Eliminate it.
    (B) This refers to Honduras, which is later in the passage. Eliminate it.
    (C) Not an outcome of privatization. Eliminate it.
    (D) Yes, see line 19–20. This is a pretty tricky line reference because the answer is so far above the reference. But this is a desired outcome of privatization.
    (E) Not a desired outcome of privatization—in fact, it's the opposite.

27. According to the passage, since the Reagan Administration, there has been

    (A) broad international support for privatization
    (B) demand from U.S. banks for diversification of Third World debt
    (C) encouragement for privatization of international donor agencies
    (D) a greater privatization effort pursued in Honduras
    (E) much evidence justifying privatization in developing nations

27. This is a SPECIFIC question. Find the part of the passage that mentions the Reagan administration.

    (A) Sure. Look at all those bilateral donor agencies in line 17.
    (B) Banks are never mentioned in the passage. Eliminate it.
    (C) No, the agencies are encouraging governments to privatize, not the other way around.
    (D) We don't know when exactly the Honduras effort took place.
    (E) There isn't any, which is why the author is against it.

SECTION III

QUESTIONS	EXPLANATIONS

1. The best professors never tell their students what to write. They strive instead to establish an intellectually critical environment conducive to thorough and creative scholarship, because training a student through indoctrination is never as effective as encouraging a student to develop his faculties independently. Truly impressive scholarly work can be produced only by the student who feels that he is breaking new ground, or at least treating familiar ground in a fresh and original manner.

Which one of the following statements is assumed by the argument above?

(A) Most students who are not told what to write produce great scholarly work.

(B) Professors who do not enjoy the security of tenure have no incentive to teach in the fashion described above.

(C) A student cannot create impressive scholarly work if he has been instructed on what he should write.

(D) Many great professors do not use an authoritative and dogmatic style of teaching.

(E) Many good students prefer being told what to write to the pressure of being encouraged to formulate their own, however original, ideas.

1. This is an ASSUMPTION question. The correct answer will be something necessary for the conclusion to be true, and, if made false, will make the argument fall apart.

(A) The amount or percentage of students who produce great scholarly work is not necessary for the author's conclusion to be true.

(B) Tenure is totally out of the scope of this argument.

(C) Yes. The argument says that independent thinking is what's important. If you make this choice false, the argument will totally fall apart.

(D) Authoritative and dogmatic styles are outside the scope of the argument.

(E) What the students would actually prefer is outside the scope of the argument.

SECTION III

QUESTIONS	EXPLANATIONS

2. Although all prisons have some system of social hierarchy among prisoners, there are some social hierarchies in prisons that are based neither on physical strength nor on length of incarceration. However, there is no such thing as a system of social hierarchy in which no distinction is made between those who have influence over the actions of others and those who do not.

Which one of the following can be inferred from the passage above?

- (A) The ability to measure personal influence is derived from the need for social hierarchy.
- (B) All prison hierarchies have a system with which to identify whether a given individual has influence over the actions of another.
- (C) Each individual prison community has its own unique set of criteria by which to measure social status.
- (D) There are certain aspects of social status that are common among all social hierarchies.
- (E) There are certain aspects of social status that are common among all hierarchies.

2. This is an INFERENCE question. Your goal is to find the one choice that must be true based on the information in the passage.

- (A) We have no idea whether the connection between these two ideas must be true.
- (B) The language of this answer choice is extreme, plus it seems to be confusing what exactly is a "system" and what is a "distinction." Let's eliminate it.
- (C) The argument doesn't say whether or not each prison system is "unique."
- (D) We are only concerned with social hierarchies, not all hierarchies.
- (E) What could this be referring to? The fact that in every hierarchy, a distinction of some sort is made in social status. Therefore, that's an aspect common among all hierarchies, and it's the answer.

3. Early in this century Heisenberg stated that it is impossible to know with certainty both the position and the velocity of an electron at any specific instant. Initially, this theory was rejected by the scientific community because there was no accurate way to measure the movement of electrons. Now, however, the theory is accepted as true, not because we can measure the movement of electrons, but because no other theory of merit has been able to explain the myriad observable inconsistencies of electron behavior.

The author appeals to which one of the following principles in establishing his conclusion?

- (A) The goal of science is to conscribe the vast variation apparent in nature in one comprehensive theory.
- (B) Through the acceptance of mathematical models that describe observable phenomena, scientists have come to a greater understanding of the uncertainties of nature.
- (C) Standard scientific method is to accept the best known explanation for an observable phenomenon regardless of its inconsistencies.
- (D) Science, through the study of probabilistic phenomena, transforms the complexities of nature into easily quantifiable terms.
- (E) A theory need not be supported by observational data to be accepted by the scientific community.

3. This is a PRINCIPLE question. We are given five principles in the answer choices for this specific question, so we should come up with our own principle for the actions in the argument and match it to the answer choices.

- (A) The goal of science is much too vast for this argument.
- (B) This is also too general a principle—remember, we're looking for something that says that sometimes the best theory is the only theory that just simply can't be refuted, even though there's no evidence for it.
- (C) While it's true that no one's come up with anything better than Heisenberg, we don't know one way or the other whether his theory contains inconsistencies or not.
- (D) If this were true, then Heisenberg would have already figured everything out to the last detail.
- (E) This is nice and basic, because it merely states that we can accept something even though we can't measure it, just like the current state of Heisenberg's theory. It's the answer.

SECTION III

QUESTIONS	EXPLANATIONS

4. Concerned citizen: The county government's new ordinance limiting the types of materials that can be disposed of in trash fires violates our rights as citizens. The fact that local environmental damage results from the burning of certain inorganic materials is not the primary issue. The real concern is the government's flagrant disregard for the right of the individual to establish what is acceptable on his or her own property.

Which one of the following principles, if accepted, would enable the concerned citizen's conclusion to be properly drawn?

(A) Legislative violation of an individual's right to privacy is not justifiable unless the actions of that individual put others at risk.

(B) The right of an individual to live in a safe environment takes precedence over the right of an individual to be exempt from legislative intrusion.

(C) An individual's personal rights supersede any right or responsibility the government may have to protect a community from harm.

(D) An individual has a moral obligation to act in the best interest of the community as a whole.

(E) A compromise must be found when the right of an individual to act independently conflicts with the responsibility of the government to provide protection for the local environment.

4. This is a PRINCIPLE question. We are given five principles in the answer choices for this specific question, so we should come up with our own principle for the actions in the argument and match it to the answer choices.

(A) If this were true, it would not match with the actions in the argument, since the argument says the local environmentenal risk isn't as important as individual rights.

(B) This has the same problem as answer choice (A). It's the opposite of what the argument is saying.

(C) Bingo. An individual's rights (such as privacy) are more important than environmental rights.

(D) This would also go in the opposite direction from the argument.

(E) This is nice, but it's not something that would strengthen the citizen's viewpoint. This is the politically correct response. Watch out—it's a trap.

SECTION III

QUESTIONS	EXPLANATIONS

5. As part of a new commitment to customer satisfaction, an electronics company sent a survey to all customers who had purchased its electronic personal organizer in the previous month. The survey, which was sent through the mail, asked customers to give personal information and to rate their satisfaction with the product. Of customers who returned the survey, more indicated that they had a negative opinion of the product's performance than indicated a neutral or positive opinion. On the basis of these results, the company, hoping to increase customer satisfaction, decided to allocate a large amount of capital to redesigning the product.

Which one of the following, if true, indicates the most serious flaw in the method of research used by the company?

(A) The company relied on a numerical system of rating responses rather than on open-ended questions that allow for more detailed feedback.

(B) Customers who were dissatisfied with the information display of the organizer outnumbered customers who were dissatisfied with the variety of functions offered by the organizer.

(C) Studies show that customer dissatisfaction with a new product is highest during the first year of the product's release and gradually decreases over the following years.

(D) The marketing division has found that responses to their mail-in surveys are generally accurate.

(E) People who are satisfied with a product or have no strong opinion about it are less likely to be motivated to return a mail-in questionnaire.

5. This is a WEAKEN question. Try and see which answer choice has the most negative impact on the conclusion of the argument. Remember to assume the hypothetical truth of each choice and apply it to the argument.

(A) We have no idea whether a numerical system or an open-ended system would be more appropriate for this survey.

(B) We're not concerned with what exactly about the product these customers didn't like. We're looking for something that would show why the conclusion might be wrong.

(C) This looks okay, but it doesn't really show that we should ignore the dissatisfaction of the customers. Let's eliminate it.

(D) This would strengthen the argument by showing how the survey was representative. It's the opposite of what we want in this case.

(E) This shows how the survey was not representative because there's a lot of happy, or at least not unhappy, people who aren't sending back the questionnaires, thereby skewing the data. It's the answer.

QUESTIONS	EXPLANATIONS

6. In an attempt to restructure the city's transit system, the head of the Mass Transit Authority has announced plans to cut services substantially and to increase fares on the subway and bus systems. He stated that the proposed changes represent the only means available to increase revenue and allow the Transit Authority to serve citizens better.

Opponents of the head of the Mass Transit Authority's plan would be best served if which one of the following were shown to be true?

(A) The installation of a new, more efficient turnstile system would eliminate fare evasion, saving more money than the proposed changes would raise.

(B) The revenue from the proposed changes would not be sufficient to prevent further fare increases in the future.

(C) The financial problems faced by the Mass Transit Authority were caused by a variety of factors, many of them legal as well as financial.

(D) A planned conversion from old, heavy steel cars to newer, lighter alloy cars has been factored into the Mass Transit Authority's budget, but has yet to be approved by the city council.

(E) The citizens of the city would be better served if people relied more on other means of transportation such as walking and biking.

6. This is a WEAKEN question. Try and see which answer choice has the most negative impact on the conclusion of the argument. Remember to assume the hypothetical truth of each choice and apply it to the argument.

(A) Here's an alternate solution to the problem of insubstantial revenue. Let's leave it.

(B) What happens in the future has no impact one way or another on the argument. Eliminate it.

(C) The causes of the lack of revenue have no impact on whether the head of the Mass Transit Authority's plan is good or bad. Eliminate it.

(D) The issue of the weight of the subway cars has no impact on the plan. Eliminate it.

(E) Here's another politically correct response for you tree-huggers out there. It tells us nothing about whether or not the plan is a good one though. Therefore, our answer is (A).

SECTION III

QUESTIONS	EXPLANATIONS

7. If the water level of the reservoir falls below the "safe line," then either the amount of water being consumed has increased or the amount of rainfall in the area has been below normal. If the amount of rainfall has been below normal, then the native plant life cannot be perfectly healthy.

Assume that the reservoir level falls below the safe line. According to the passage, which one of the following statements cannot be true?

(A) The amount of water being consumed has decreased.

(B) The amount of rainfall has been below normal, and the native plant life is not perfectly healthy.

(C) The amount of water being consumed has increased, the amount of rainfall has been below normal, and some of the native plant life is perfectly healthy.

(D) The amount of water being consumed has decreased, the amount of rainfall has been below normal, and the native plant life is perfectly healthy.

(E) The amount of water being consumed has increased, the amount of rainfall has been higher than normal, and the native plant life is not perfectly healthy.

7. This is an INFERENCE question. Your goal is to find the one choice that can't be true based on the information in the passage.

(A) This can be true, because the amount of rainfall could still be very far below normal, thereby making the reservoir level fall below a safe level even though the amount of water being consumed has decreased. So we eliminate this choice, since we're looking for what can't be true.

(B) This can be true, since the amount of rainfall decreasing leads to native plant life not being perfectly healthy.

(C) The first two parts of this three-part answer choice are fine, but we can't have perfectly healthy plant life if the amount of rainfall has been below normal, according to the argument. Therefore this answer choice might not be able to be true, although the last part of the answer choice is pretty wishy-washy because of the use of "some." Let's see if there's something better.

(D) There's no way that this answer choice can be true, because we are told in the argument that "if the amount of rainfall has been below normal, then the native plant life cannot be perfectly healthy," and this choice says the opposite. It's much worse than (C), so it's the answer.

(E) This can be true, since it's possible that the plant life is not healthy for some other reason.

8. If we are to improve the status of our college in the public's perception, our next promotional campaign should appear in the form of full-page advertisements placed in nationally circulated magazines, rather than in radio advertisements broadcast to a variety of stations. Although advertising fees for both campaigns are roughly equivalent, the production costs of the print advertisement campaign are nearly half those of the radio campaign. Therefore, our next promotional campaign should be a print advertisement campaign.

Which one of the following, if true, would most help to explain the difference in production costs of the two campaigns?

(A) More man-hours would be required in the preparation of the magazine advertisement than in the preparation of the radio advertisement.

(B) The number of people involved in the creation of a national ad campaign is greater than the number of people involved in the creation of a local ad campaign.

(C) The layout of the print ad campaign could potentially be reused in another campaign at a later date.

(D) The perceived impact of a magazine advertisement is greater than that of a radio advertisement.

(E) The creation of the layout for the magazine advertisement can be done in house at no extra cost to the college, whereas the creation of a radio advertisement requires scheduling many hours of expensive time at a recording studio.

8. This is a PARADOX question. Look for an answer choice that allows both parts of the argument to be true, and remember to assume the hypothetical truth of each of the answer choices.

(A) This choice would exacerbate the paradox. It's the opposite of what we want. Eliminate it.

(B) This has no impact on the argument because we're not talking about local campaigns.

(C) While this is nice, it doesn't explain why it's cheaper to create a print campaign than a radio campaign.

(D) This also doesn't explain why it's cheaper to produce a print campaign than a radio campaign.

(E) This explains the difference in cost pretty clearly. It's the answer.

SECTION III

9. Schools that train students in technical skills for a specific field of work are more successful, as measured by the percentage of students that gain employment in full-time jobs in the six-month period following graduation, than are institutions that teach a liberal arts curriculum. Technical schools have a student employment rate of approximately 65 percent, whereas liberal arts schools have a rate of only 56 percent. This difference reveals that technical schools are more effectively meeting the challenge of providing education than are liberal arts schools.

   Which one of the following is an assumption on which the above argument rests?

   (A) Schools will not accurately report information if they believe that information will reflect poorly on them.
   (B) The curriculum of a school can be evaluated by examining the number and types of job placements achieved by its students.
   (C) The percent of students that gain employment following graduation is a measurement of that school's ability to provide education.
   (D) The sole function of education is to help students gain employment.
   (E) Technical schools and liberal arts schools serve different educational purposes.

9. This is an ASSUMPTION question. The correct answer will be something necessary for the conclusion to be true, and, if made false, will make the argument fall apart.

   (A) This means that perhaps someone is lying, but we don't know who. It's certainly not an assumption of the argument. Eliminate it.
   (B) We're not concerned with evaluating the curriculum of a school—we're looking to see how getting a full-time job is linked with education. Eliminate it.
   (C) Bingo. This provides the link between having a full-time job and being educated. If this were false, then there would be no evidence that the technical schools are providing a better education than liberal arts schools.
   (D) This is too extreme. Education can still have other functions—it's just that the most relevant one is to get a job.
   (E) If this were true, it would weaken the argument. Eliminate it.

10. Scientists have long dreamed of the technological possibilities of nuclear fusion, a process in which the nuclei of two atoms are fused together. The energy that would be generated by this process would far surpass that of nuclear fission. However, years of research have failed to produce any tangible results and, as a result, funding for fusion projects has been drastically reduced. Nonetheless, some scientists continue to believe that fusion is possible. Unfortunately, the one team that claimed to have achieved "cold" fusion failed to replicate its experimental results, and scientists believe that other explanations can be found for the results the team initially observed. Therefore, it is unwise to conclude that nuclear fusion will be achieved in the immediate future.

   In the passage above, the author reaches his conclusion by

   (A) criticizing the premises on which the opposing side bases its view
   (B) basing his conclusion upon experimental results
   (C) drawing a conclusion based on a lack of evidence for the opposing view
   (D) questioning the opposing view's use of the indefinite term "cold"
   (E) reaching a conclusion that is incompatible with his premises

10. This is a REASONING question. Come up with your own description of how the author reaches his conclusion before you go to the answer choices, and then match your description to the choices.

   (A) The author is not saying that fusion isn't possible ever, just not soon. Eliminate it.
   (B) No, it was those wacky cold fusion scientists who based their conclusions on experimental results, not the author.
   (C) The opposing view states that we can achieve fusion soon, so by showing how everything up to this point has failed, the author feels he's supported his conclusion. This is pretty much what happened in the argument. It's the answer.
   (D) The author doesn't really care about the "cold" issue. It's certainly not a basis for his conclusion.
   (E) No, he's pretty solid here. Plus, if it were flawed reasoning, the question would've tipped us off to that in advance. Eliminate it.

SECTION III

11. At one time, nutritionists fervently advocated the consumption of large quantities of vitamins to correct certain minor health problems. They justified these claims by citing the negative effects of vitamin deficiency and by pointing out that the Recommended Daily Allowance specifies only the minimum amount of a vitamin required for normal health rather than the amount that would lead to optimal health. Recent studies, however, have discredited those recommendations by showing that high dosages can have detrimental effects.

The argument above best supports which one of the following claims?

(A) A person suffering from a minor ailment will always benefit from medical attention.

(B) Ingesting large doses of vitamins is the best way to treat minor ailments.

(C) A person suffering from a minor health problem would probably do best to avoid excessive doses of vitamins.

(D) Nutritionists were more motivated by their opposition to the Recommended Daily Allowance than by evidence of medical benefit.

(E) All minor health problems should be treated promptly, regardless of the method by which they are treated.

11. This is an INFERENCE question. Your goal is to find the one choice that must be true based on the information in the passage.

(A) Too extreme and out of the scope of the argument. Eliminate it.

(B) No, that's the opposite of what the author is saying.

(C) Nice and wishy-washy, and it's pretty much a restatement of the last sentence. It's the answer.

(D) We have no idea about the true motivations of the nutritionists, or anyone else for that matter.

(E) Too extreme. Eliminate it.

12. Recent studies of preventive dental care have clearly established the positive effects of regular dental care. While the frequency of visits to the dentist varies throughout the population, a general trend has emerged: Those who visit the dentist at least twice a year have significantly fewer dental problems than those who do not.

Which one of the following is most clearly implied in the argument above?

(A) An individual with few dental problems is likely to have recently visited the dentist.

(B) If one has a significant number of dental problems, it is likely that one has visited the dentist fewer than two times a year.

(C) Most people visit their dentists semiannually, and thus have little reason to worry about cavities.

(D) In order to have fewer dental problems, one need only visit the dentist twice a year.

(E) Frequency of dental care can affect the number of dental problems experienced by an individual.

12. This is an INFERENCE question. Your goal is to find the one choice that must be true based on the information in the passage.

(A) Not necessarily. Eliminate it.

(B) Not necessarily. Eliminate it.

(C) Cavities and patient worry are outside the scope of the argument. Eliminate it.

(D) The word "only" is too extreme. For a given individual other steps might be needed to reduce dental problems.

(E) Nice and wishy-washy again, right? ("…can affect the number…") It's the answer.

SECTION III

13. In recent years, the number of reported cases of ethical misconduct in the telemarketing of stocks, securities, and other investments has risen dramatically. In answer to the growing demand for regulation of this industry, federal agencies are formulating an approach to the problem that would entail close supervision of the activities of the investment houses that use telemarketing. Such government involvement in private industry is, however, antithetical to private industry and would surely dampen the spirit of free enterprise. Clearly, in order to prevent government interference, investment houses should cease the practice of paying telemarketers on commission.

Which one of the following is an assumption upon which the argument above is based?

(A) Successful capitalism is dependent upon a governmental policy of noninterference and furthered by pro-business regulations.

(B) The government's ability to detect misconduct, even with close supervision, is minimal, and therefore useless.

(C) If judged by contemporary standards, many of these so-called violations are considered ethical.

(D) Earning a high commission as a telemarketer is not proof of one's abilities as an investment broker.

(E) The incidence of ethical misconduct is directly related to the telemarketers' desire for larger commissions.

13. This is an ASSUMPTION question. The correct answer will be something necessary for the conclusion to be true, and, if made false, will make the argument fall apart.

(A) This doesn't address the gap in the argument between ethical misconduct and paying telemarketers on commission. Also, successful capitalism is out of the scope here. Eliminate it.

(B) This is not necessary for the conclusion to be true—the author's saying that the government shouldn't interfere whether or not they'd be successful.

(C) This is also not necessary for the conclusion to be true—the author's admitting that there is some ethical misconduct, and just saying that government control isn't the answer on how to stop it.

(D) Whether or not you can prove you're a good broker is totally out of the scope of this argument.

(E) If there were no link between the ethical misconduct and the desire for large commissions, the argument would totally fall apart. This is our answer.

SECTION III

QUESTIONS	EXPLANATIONS

14. A study of former college athletes revealed that, as a group, they are five times less likely to die before the age of fifty than are members of the population at large. The advice to derive from this is clear: colleges should vastly expand their athletic departments so as to allow a greater proportion of all students to participate in athletics, thereby increasing the overall life expectancy of their student population.

Which one of the following, if true, most seriously weakens the argument above?

(A) Since participation in college athletics requires tremendous academic discipline, college athletes are better suited to succeed in society than are students who do not participate in college athletics.

(B) The students who voluntarily compete in college athletics are more predisposed to good health than are those who do not.

(C) Few colleges have the resources to increase spending on athletics, a nonessential university program.

(D) People who become active after leading sedentary lives can remarkably decrease their chances of contracting heart disease.

(E) Women, whose average life expectancies exceed men's by seven years, have traditionally had fewer opportunities to participate in college athletics than have men.

14. This is a WEAKEN question. Figure out which answer choice has the most negative impact on the conclusion of the argument. Remember to assume the hypothetical truth of each choice and apply it to the argument.

(A) Succeeding in society has no impact on this argument. Eliminate this choice.

(B) Let's leave this choice, because it seems to be saying that the existing athlete population is different health-wise than the college population at large, which would weaken the argument that if we included more people in the program, more people would be healthy.

(C) This doesn't impact the argument that if colleges were able to expand athletic departments, people would be healthier.

(D) This would strengthen the argument, if anything, if we made non-athletes into athletes when they entered college.

(E) Comparing women to men is not relevant. There could be biological (or other) reasons why women live longer than men that are compleately unrelated to athletics. For this answer to be relevant, it would need to compare women athletes to women nonathletetes.

SECTION III

QUESTIONS	EXPLANATIONS

Questions 15–16

Dear Sirs,

In your letter, which detailed the many reasons you were not able to offer me the position at this time, you mentioned that my color-blindness was the central factor in your decision. In the hope that you may reconsider, I am writing to explain that my overall vision is actually quite good. Enclosed you will find three different optometrists' records confirming that I have never required any kind of corrective eyewear whatsoever.

Mark Furnace

15. Which one of the following would best highlight the flaw in Mr. Furnace's logic?

(A) Mr. Furnace had not been administered a complete eye examination before he wrote the letter.
(B) The evidence that Mr. Furnace mentions is not relevant to the decision made.
(C) In addressing only one of the many reasons why he was rejected, Mr. Furnace undermines his own intentions.
(D) The extent to which his color-blindness was responsible for his being rejected is not made clear.
(E) Doctors' records are not considered official documentation of a person's well-being.

16. Which one of the following is an assumption upon which Mr. Furnace's letter is based?

(A) A deal can be struck with his potential employers.
(B) A person wearing corrective eyewear should not be hired for certain positions.
(C) Color-blindness is not a fair criterion upon which to base hiring decisions.
(D) A note from a doctor can be sufficient to change a potential employers' opinion.
(E) His color-blindness is not affected by corrective eyewear.

15. This is a REASONING question. Come up with your own description of why the author's conclusion is flawed before you go to the answer choices, and then match your description to the choices.

(A) We have no idea whether he was administered one or not. Eliminate it.
(B) It sure looks that way. The company only cares about whether he can distinguish colors. It's the answer.
(C) While he should have addressed all the points, that's not why this one point is wrong. Eliminate it.
(D) That might be a reason why the company's decision is bad, but not a reason for why Furnace's logic is bad. Eliminate it.
(E) A person's "well-being" is outside the scope of this argument. Eliminate it.

16. This is an ASSUMPTION question. The correct answer will be something necessary for the conclusion to be true, and, if made false, will make the argument fall apart.

(A) What is this? Vegas? A "deal" is outside the scope of the argument.
(B) This would weaken his argument, if anything. Eliminate it.
(C) He's not saying that it's not a valid criticism, just that the good points of his vision outweigh this one detriment. Eliminate it.
(D) This looks pretty good. That's the whole point of his writing this letter—if this weren't true, the letter would have no purpose. It's the answer.
(E) We have no information about this. Eliminate it.

SECTION III

QUESTIONS	EXPLANATIONS

17. An airline representative announced the introduction of a new pricing system that uses sophisticated computer technology. Based on up-to-the-minute information on sales, the system identifies and continually updates peak times of high demand and off-peak times of low demand, keeping prices high when demand is high and lowering prices to attract customers when demand is low. As a result, the airline anticipates that large numbers of customers will choose to travel off-peak in order to experience savings, while those who wish to travel at peak times will enjoy greater availability due to higher prices. The airline therefore anticipates that the majority of customers will experience significant benefits as a result of the new system.

Which one of the following indicates an error in the reasoning on the part of the airline?

(A) The airline's conclusion is based on an unproven premise.
(B) The airline displays a naive trust in the possibilities of technology.
(C) The airline fails to factor in the cost of implementing the new system.
(D) The airline's conclusion rests on a result that would necessarily cancel out the anticipated benefit.
(E) The airline fails to establish the percentage of customers who would benefit from the change.

17. This is a REASONING question. Come up with your own description of why the author's conclusion is flawed before you go to the answer choices, and then match your description to the choices.

(A) No, the reason that this argument is flawed is actually much worse than this—the fact that the argument makes no sense, perhaps. Eliminate it.
(B) Assuming that the technology will work is not what's wrong with this line of reasoning. Eliminate it.
(C) This has no impact on the goal of the airline—to pass savings on to its customers. Eliminate it.
(D) Yes. The result, that a large number of people would choose to travel at off-peak times, would cancel the benefit that off-peak times would be cheaper since the system would increase the number of flights as a larger number of people sought to buy tickets.
(E) We're not concerned with the overall percentages here. Eliminate it.

SECTION III

Question 18

Kristen: Compared to a direct business tax cut, a personal income tax cut is a better way to stimulate our state's economy. A personal income tax cut would give residents greater in-pocket income. With this increase in income, individuals will be encouraged to start their own businesses. In addition, individuals will be more likely to spend more money at existing businesses.

Mark: A personal income tax cut is not the most effective way to help business. There is no guarantee that individuals will in fact start new businesses, and the additional income may be used to purchase products from a different state or even a different country.

18.   Mark objects to Kristen's argument by

(A)   suggesting that a personal income tax cut is no more important than a direct business tax cut
(B)   claiming that Kristen has reached a premature conclusion based on an inadequate understanding of the consequences of a business tax cut
(C)   demonstrating that the negative impact of a personal income tax outweighs the positive effects
(D)   questioning Kristen's use of the ambiguous phrase "in-pocket income"
(E)   indicating that the positive consequences that Kristen predicts may not occur

18.   This is a REASONING question. Come up with your own description of how Mark objects to Kristen before you go to the answer choices, and then match your description to the choices.

(A)   Importance is not the issue here—effectiveness is. Eliminate it.
(B)   No, she's making a mistake with regard to the personal income tax cut—not the business one. Eliminate it.
(C)   He doesn't point out any negative impacts of the personal income tax. He just shows that Kristen's positive points may not be so positive.
(D)   He doesn't ever question that.
(E)   Exactly. He shows how it's possible that neither of Kristen's good outcomes could occur. It's the answer.

QUESTIONS	EXPLANATIONS

19. Observation reveals that as children become physically exhausted, they become more prone to crying and temper tantrums. Thus, an occurrence of screaming or yelling in a small child is best remedied by providing physical rest.

Which one of the following uses the same pattern of reasoning as the argument above?

(A) People who feel insecure often compensate by acting in an aggressive manner. A person who is not acting in an aggressive manner is therefore unlikely to be insecure.

(B) Scientists establish the validity of their theories by conducting meticulously controlled experiments. Thus, a scientist who is conducting a meticulously controlled experiment is well on his way to establishing the validity of his theory.

(C) Completion of a four-year college program leads to an improvement in standard of living. A person who has not attended a four-year college program will not experience a comparable improvement in standard of living.

(D) The best way to avoid the common cold is to observe simple rules of hygiene, like washing one's hands. After all, people who don't wash their hands are far more likely to contract a cold.

(E) Habitual lack of sleep leads to a condition known as "chronic exhaustion." A person who is not chronically exhausted is likely to get regular and sufficient sleep.

19. This is a PARALLEL-THE-REASONING question. Try to get the theme or diagram of the logic and then match it to each answer choice.

(A) We need something that says you can stop a behavior by preventing its cause, since that's what the original argument says.

(B) We need something that says you can stop a behavior by preventing its cause, since that's what the original argument says.

(C) We need something that says you can stop a behavior by preventing its cause, since that's what the original argument says.

(D) This is closest (though not fabulously close) to the logic in the argument. It's the answer.

(E) We need something that says you can stop a behavior by preventing its cause, since that's what the original argument says.

SECTION III

QUESTIONS	EXPLANATIONS

20. Statistics show that there is a direct correlation between the ammonia content and the cleaning power of industrial-strength floor and tile cleaners; simply stated, the more ammonia, the better the cleaner. However, in a nationwide survey of commercial food services, cleaning supervisors uniformly replied that in order for any floor and tile cleaner to be effective, it must be used on a given surface twice a day with the right proportion of cleaner to water, and must be applied with well-maintained mops. The survey thus proves that ammonia content is not relevant to the efficacy of floor and tile cleaners after all.

Which one of the following best identifies the flawed reasoning in the passage above?

(A) There is no reason to assume that effective floor and tile cleaning is the only use for floor and tile cleaner.

(B) It cannot be assumed that industrial-strength floor and tile cleaners contain comparable levels of ammonia.

(C) It is unreasonable to conclude that the ammonia content is not relevant to a cleaner's efficacy just because there are requirements for the proper use of industrial-strength floor and tile cleaners.

(D) It cannot be assumed that the efficacy of all industrial-strength floor and tile cleaners depends on the same procedures for use.

(E) It is unreasonable to assume that the makers of industrial-strength floor and tile cleaners are unaware that food services don't always use them properly.

20. This is a REASONING question. Come up with your own description of why the author's conclusion is flawed before you go to the answer choices, and then match your description to the choices.

(A) This answer choice is an excellent example of LSAT gibberish. Eliminate it.

(B) Why not? Because you know that's true in life? We're talking about the argument. Eliminate it.

(C) That's right. The other requirements don't just make the ammonia issue evaporate. No pun intended.

(D) The author is flawed in assuming that ammonia content isn't relevant, not in discussing procedure.

(E) The awareness of the cleaner makers is out of the scope of this argument.

21. Products containing naproxen sodium produce relief from pain and fever by blocking prostaglandins. As a consequence of recent technological advances, production costs for pain and fever medications containing naproxen sodium, allowing for both packaging and marketing costs, are one-fifth of what they were ten years ago, while the corresponding cost for medications using the ingredient ibuprofen, which is produced by different means, has increased. Therefore, naproxen sodium is a less costly ingredient to use in medication for the prevention of pain and fever relief than ibuprofen.

The conclusion of the argument is properly drawn if which one of the following is assumed?

(A) The cost of producing pain and fever medication containing ibuprofen has increased over the past ten years.

(B) Ten years ago, ibuprofen was used more than five times as often as naproxen sodium.

(C) None of the recent technological advances in producing pain and fever medication with naproxen sodium can be applied to the production of medication using ibuprofen.

(D) Ten years ago, the cost of producing pain and fever medication with the ingredient naproxen sodium was less than five times the cost of producing medications with ibuprofen.

(E) The cost of producing pain and fever medication with naproxen sodium is expected to decrease further, while the cost of producing similar medications using ibuprofen is not expected to decrease.

21. This is a STRENGTHEN question. Figure out which answer choice has the most positive impact on the conclusion of the argument. Remember to assume the hypothetical truth of each choice and apply it to the argument.

(A) Nope. We need something that links the price of naproxen and ibuprofen. Eliminate it.

(B) The frequency of use of either product is outside the scope of the argument.

(C) Bummer, but we're not trying to help the ibuprofen makers here anyway. Eliminate it.

(D) Bingo. If you work out the math, you'll see that it's now a certainty that naproxen is less costly than ibuprofen.

(E) But if naproxen were *really* expensive as compared to the possibly super-cheap ibuprofen originally, this wouldn't necessarily make the conclusion work.

SECTION III

22. Below is an excerpt from a letter that a medical school sent to an applicant:

We regret that we will not be offering you a position at our school. The committee has been forced to reject many highly qualified applicants because we must restrict our class size to fewer than two hundered students.

Which one of the following can be logically inferred from the information in the letter above?

(A) Only highly qualified applicants were accepted by the medical school.
(B) The applicant was considered to be highly qualified.
(C) The school had already taken its maximum number of students.
(D) Most of the applicants were highly qualified.
(E) The qualifications of applicants were not the only factor affecting admissions.

22. This is an INFERENCE question. Your goal is to find the one choice that must be true based on the information in the passage.

(A) This does not necessarily have to be true. They could have admitted two hundered boneheads. The others that weren't admitted were just bigger boneheads.
(B) This does not necessarily have to be true. The letter doesn't specifically say that this particular applicant was highly qualified.
(C) We don't know this for sure. It could be that this guy was a major moron and was rejected for that.
(D) We have no idea how many were qualified out of the total pool of applicants.
(E) Obviously not, since it said right in the letter that class size was also an issue. Thus, it's the answer.

23. Many Americans are required to spend at least two years studying a foreign language as part of their high school or college education. As a result of this classroom study, students are usually able to conjugate verbs, define words, and write simple sentences. Yet since even those students who received good grades during their foreign language training find themselves unable to hold a brief, unrehearsed conversation in that language, classroom training is clearly insufficient in transmitting the essential principles of another language.

Which one of the following principles, if accepted, would provide the most justification for the conclusion?

(A) If a student cannot adequately conjugate verbs or write simple sentences in a foreign language, he has not grasped the essential principles of that language.
(B) Anyone who can converse fluently in another language is likely to have the ability to conjugate verbs and define words in that language.
(C) Students grasp the essential principles of a foreign language by living in the country where that language is spoken, not by studying it in the classroom.
(D) Someone can be said to understand the basic principles of a foreign language only when he is able to converse spontaneously in that language.
(E) Any person who has not grown up speaking a given language will never truly grasp the essential principles of that language.

23. This is a PRINCIPLE question. We are given five principles in the answer choices for this specific question, so we should come up with our own principle for the actions in the argument and match it to the answer choices.

(A) No, all the argument is saying is that conversation is an essential part of knowing another language.
(B) Probably, but this doesn't help the conclusion out any. Eliminate it.
(C) This looks pretty good, but it actually doesn't talk at all about conversation, which is a key element to the author's argument. Eliminate it.
(D) If this is true, then it helps strengthen the author's claim that classroom training is insufficient. It's the answer.
(E) Bummer, but then there's no solution, which is not the author's point. Eliminate it.

SECTION III

QUESTIONS

24. Jane Anne: Feeling frightened and delighted are mutually exclusive. Therefore, a person's behavior cannot both strike fear and evoke delight simultaneously.

    Clive: That's not true. Many people love to go to horror movies. The movies frighten them and amuse them. They simultaneously cringe and laugh.

    Clive has weakened Jane Anne's argument by

    (A) showing that Jane Anne's argument is based on circular reasoning
    (B) demonstrating that two feelings are not mutually exclusive
    (C) qualifying Jane Anne's usage of the term "simultaneously"
    (D) pointing out the inherent ambiguity in the relationship between "fear" and "delight"
    (E) changing an argument by analogy into one based on a more reliable sample

EXPLANATIONS

24. This is a REASONING question. Come up with your own description of how Clive weakened Jane Anne's argument before you go to the answer choices, and then match your description to the choices.

    (A) Jane Anne's argument, while inane, is not circular. Eliminate it.
    (B) Yep. Clive actually provides an example of this—people who go to horror movies.
    (C) He doesn't qualify or expand or do anything else to Jane Anne's use of that term. Eliminate it.
    (D) He does not see these things as ambiguous. Eliminate it.
    (E) No, he's the one who made the analogy, not Jane Anne. Eliminate it.

SECTION III

QUESTIONS	EXPLANATIONS

25. Journalistic criticism of literature is falling victim to its own efforts to justify its existence. Critics believe that they garner respect from their readers by ignoring objective description in favor of opinionated commentary. Any new work is given the briefest of summaries and then mercilessly carved up in an effort to divine its deeper meaning. But the best journalist simply presents facts and allows his audience to decide their meanings independently. Critics should convey the truest possible form of the works in question; let the art, and not the art critic, speak to us.

Which one of the following statements best lends support to the argument presented above?

(A) Libraries make all new work available to the interested public without regard to critical opinions.

(B) Because space is limited, it is not practical to reproduce completely every work that is criticized in print.

(C) Writers would likely alter their style if they knew that their works would simply be read rather than criticized.

(D) Since most people have the capacity to appreciate art to some degree, it is superfluous to criticize art and a mistake not to allow people to decide for themselves.

(E) In the context described, only parts of a work could be presented, and this would lead to an increased role for the critic, who would have to decide which parts would be shown.

25. This is a STRENGTHEN question. Figure out which answer choice has the most positive impact on the conclusion of the argument. Remember to assume the hypothetical truth of each choice and apply it to the argument.

(A) Libraries have no impact on this argument either way. Eliminate it.

(B) This, if anything, would weaken the argument, although it really has no impact either. Eliminate it.

(C) This choice makes no sense and has no impact. Eliminate it.

(D) This statement lends support to the argument that criticism isn't the point, merely presenting the work is. It's the answer.

(E) Giving the critic an increased role wouldn't help strengthen the conclusion. Eliminate it.

SECTION IV

1. In France, children in preschool programs spend a portion of each day engaged in a program of stretching and exercise. Preschool programs in the United States, however, seldom devote time to a daily stretching and exercise program. In tests designed to measure cardiovascular fitness, children in the United States were outperformed by their French counterparts. It can therefore be determined that children attending preschool programs in the United States can achieve cardiovascular fitness only by engaging in a daily school program of stretching and exercise.

    Which one of the following is an assumption on which the argument depends?

    (A) A daily program of stretching and exercise will allow all children to achieve cardiovascular fitness.

    (B) Cardiovascular fitness is integral to one's overall health.

    (C) It has been proven that children who participate in stretching and exercise programs in preschool have better cardiovascular fitness as adults.

    (D) Stretching and exercise are necessary components of French children's superior cardiovascular fitness programs.

    (E) United States preschool children could make healthful dietary changes as well as changes to their daily fitness regimens.

1. This is an ASSUMPTION question. The correct answer will be something necessary for the conclusion to be true, and, if made false, will make the argument fall apart.

    (A) This certainly strengthens the conclusion that stretching and fitness, applied to children anywhere, will help them achieve cardiovascular nirvana. Is it necessary though? We're only concerned with kids in the United States, so "all" is too extreme.

    (B) We're not concerned with the overall health of the children in this argument. Eliminate it.

    (C) We're not concerned with how fit the children will become when they are adults. Eliminate it.

    (D) If stretching *weren't* a necessary part of the French children's fitness, then the argument that doing the same thing in the United States would have the same result would fall apart. So (D) is the answer.

    (E) Dietary changes are outside the scope of the argument. Eliminate it.

SECTION IV

2. In an effort to lessen the risk of liability, fertility clinics are seeking new methods of record keeping and storage that would help avoid donor sperm that might contain dangerous genes. Towards this end, a database is being developed to aid the clients in their screening of donor sperm. The database is exhaustively thorough, containing the medical histories of more than twenty thousand people, approximately half of them men.

Which one of the following, if true, best explains why the database contains the records of almost ten thousand women?

(A) Small fertility clinics, located in remote areas, wish to have access to a large selection of donor sperm.

(B) Keeping genetic information on women is a standard procedure for many scientific clinics.

(C) Some genetic disorders are not expressed until the onset of puberty.

(D) Some genetic disorders may be carried by, but not manifested in, men who inherited the dangerous gene from their mothers.

(E) Some genetic disorders are due to the effects of drugs and alcohol during puberty.

2. This is a PARADOX question. Look for an answer choice that allows both parts of the argument to be true, and remember to assume the hypothetical truth of each of the answer choices.

(A) This doesn't explain why half the records are of women. Eliminate it.

(B) This looks pretty good, but it doesn't actually explain why this is "standard procedure." Also, it's a bit too general, because it says "scientific clinics," and we're talking specifically about fertility clinics. Eliminate it.

(C) Puberty is outside the scope of the argument. Eliminate it.

(D) Ah, so we have an example of why the records of the same number of women are kept as of men. It's the answer.

(E) Puberty is outside the scope of the argument. Eliminate it.

3. If the Food and Drug Administration (FDA) does not relax some of its regulations governing the testing of experimental drugs, tens of thousands of U.S. citizens are sure to die as a result of certain diseases before an effective treatment is found and made generally available.

It follows logically from the statement above that if the FDA does relax some of its regulations governing the testing of experimental drugs, then tens of thousands of U.S. citizens

(A) will definitely die of certain diseases
(B) will probably die of certain diseases
(C) will probably not die of certain diseases
(D) will not die of certain diseases
(E) may still die of certain diseases

3. This is an INFERENCE question. Your goal is to find the one choice that must be true based on the information in the passage.

(A) We don't know for sure what will happen if they do relax regulations, only what will happen if they don't. Therefore, look for a wishy-washy answer. This is too extreme.

(B) This is less extreme than (A), so let's leave it in for right now.

(C) This has a similar structure to (B), so we now have to eliminate both (B) and (C).

(D) Too extreme. Eliminate.

(E) This is the most wishy-washy choice, and therefore, it's the answer.

SECTION IV

4. The level of blood sugar for many patients suffering from disease Q is slightly higher than the level of blood sugar in the general population. Nonetheless, most medical professionals believe that slightly increasing blood sugar levels is a successful means by which to treat disease Q.

This apparently contradictory argument can best be resolved by which one of the following statements?

(A) Blood sugar levels for patients who have been cured of disease Q are virtually identical to the levels of blood sugar found in the general population.

(B) Many of the symptoms associated with severe cases of disease Q have been recognized in laboratory animals with experimentally induced high blood pressure, but none of the animals developed disease Q.

(C) The movement from inactive to advanced states of disease Q often occurs because the virus that causes Q flourishes during periods when blood sugar levels are slightly low.

(D) The blood sugar level in patients with disease Q fluctuates abnormally in response to changes in blood chemistry.

(E) Low levels of blood sugar are symptomatic of many other diseases that are even more serious than disease Q.

4. This is a PARADOX question. Look for an answer choice that allows both parts of the argument to be true, and remember to assume the hypothetical truth of each of the answer choices.

(A) This would exacerbate the paradox, if anything. Eliminate it.

(B) This doesn't do anything to explain the paradox, and blood pressure is out of the scope here. Eliminate it.

(C) So if we are always making sure to keep blood sugar levels high, then we won't ever have these slightly low periods where the virus will flourish. It's the answer.

(D) We don't care why the blood sugar fluctuates. We just want to know why we should keep it high.

(E) Other diseases are outside the scope of the argument.

SECTION IV

QUESTIONS	EXPLANATIONS

Questions 5–6

Many people, in the wake of an exceedingly large number of deaths in the United States caused by handguns, have argued for a federal law making handguns illegal for ordinary citizens anywhere in the United States. However, it is clear that any such proposal would be completely counterproductive. For instance, when handguns were outlawed in the city of Clarksville in 1990, the number of handgun deaths actually increased by 10 percent by 1991. Furthermore, such a proposal clearly violates the Second Amendment, which ensures every citizen's right to bear arms.

5. The above argument is vulnerable to criticism on the grounds that it

   (A) fails to consider the fact that other cities may have had different results with handgun bans
   (B) fails to define precisely the ambiguous term "handgun"
   (C) assumes that the aim of the Clarksville handgun ban was to reduce the number of handgun deaths
   (D) assumes that the Clarksville police were not responsible for a larger number of handgun deaths in 1991 than in previous years
   (E) fails to cite a legitimate authority in support of its interpretation of the Second Amendment

5. This is a REASONING question. Come up with your own description of why the author's conclusion is flawed before you go to the answer choices, and then match your description to the choices.

   (A) What's happened in other cities doesn't necessarily have an impact on why the Clarksville example is a bad one. Eliminate it.
   (B) "Handgun" is *not* an ambiguous term.
   (C) The argument does make this assumption but that's not why the argument is bad. Eliminate it.
   (D) Bingo—this points out that the author has failed to consider a possible alternate cause.
   (E) We don't need experts to prove anything about the Second Amendment. These types of answer choices are almost always wrong on the LSAT—choices that say an argument is bad because the author doesn't bring in an expert to validate assumptions. Eliminate it.

SECTION IV

6. Which one of the following, if true, would most strongly support the conclusion above?

    (A) The number of handgun deaths in Clarksville increased by 20 percent from 1989 to 1990.

    (B) The number of handgun deaths in the United States increased by 2 percent from 1990 to 1991.

    (C) The number of handgun deaths in Clarksville in 1991 was not as great as the number of handgun deaths in the entire country.

    (D) The attempt to ban handguns in Brazil in 1985 also led to a drastically increased number of handgun deaths.

    (E) Canada, which has a handgun ban, has a faster growing rate of deaths from firearms than does the United States.

6. This is a STRENGTHEN question. Figure out which answer choice has the most positive impact on the conclusion of the argument. Remember to assume the hypothetical truth of each choice and apply it to the argument.

    (A) This would weaken the conclusion by showing that after the law was passed in Clarksville, the rate of handgun deaths was actually increasing at a greater rate than before the law was passed.

    (B) So there's something seriously wrong in Clarksville, which is why the Monkees waited to take the last train there. Thus, the law had the opposite effect than what was intended. This is the answer.

    (C) The number of deaths in Clarksville as compared to everywhere else isn't the point—we want to look for something that shows us the law isn't effective.

    (D) What happened in Brazil, while interesting, is outside the scope of the argument.

    (E) "Firearms" is too general here. Our argument is only talking about handguns. Eliminate it.

SECTION IV

QUESTIONS	EXPLANATIONS

7. For our protein needs, sea plankton has none of the drawbacks that meat has. Plankton contains neither the high levels of saturated animal fat nor the dangerous hormones that commercially available meats do, and its harvest does not require the massive waste of natural and agricultural resources that meat production does. In light of these facts, it is clear that people must stop getting their protein from meat and start getting it from plankton.

Which one of the following statements, if true, most seriously weakens the argument above?

(A) Relatively few scientific studies have been done on people's willingness to make radical changes in their dietary habits.

(B) The only reports containing information on the drawbacks of plankton as a meat substitute have been funded by the United States Department of Agriculture.

(C) Greater governmental regulation of the meat industry could significantly reduce the use of dangerous chemicals and hormones in meat production.

(D) The costs incurred in the harvest of sea plankton in amounts large enough to meet the average person's annual protein needs exceed the costs incurred in the production of a similar amount of meat.

(E) As of yet, no effective means of making sea plankton commercially available for consumption have been developed.

7. This is a WEAKEN question. Figure out which answer choice has the most negative impact on the conclusion of the argument. Remember to assume the hypothetical truth of each choice and apply it to the argument.

(A) People's willingness to start eating plankton burgers has no impact on the argument, which merely says it would be a good thing to do, and makes no claims as to whether people would actually like it.

(B) So what's in these reports? We don't know, so how can we see if they would weaken the argument? Eliminate it.

(C) Better government regulation of the meat industry wouldn't weaken the argument that we should be eating plankton. Eliminate it.

(D) This is one piece of negative information about switching to plankton. You still don't know how wasteful it is. Also, how much more expensive? One penny? One million dollars? Let's see if (E) is better.

(E) Well, if it's not available to the people, the whole argument is pretty moot. This is the answer.

SECTION IV

8. Tenant Representative: Residents of units in the West Building of the Fife Arms apartment complex were recently subjected to rent increases averaging 12.5 percent, while residents of identical apartments in the East Building were given increases of, on the average, only 7 percent. Do our landlords really think that the residents of Fife Arms will believe that the maintenance costs on units in the West Building have risen more than one and a half times as quickly as the maintenance costs on units in the East Building? It seems to us that these identical units, which were built at the same time, have deteriorated equally, and we certainly haven't seen any better service here in the West Building than they have in the East Building.

Which one of the following statements would most seriously weaken the tenant representative's argument that the recent rent increases are inequitable?

(A) Before the recent increases were announced, residents of units in the West Building, who were the first to occupy Fife Arms, were not sharing the burden of the cost of maintenance of the entire complex equally with the residents of units in the East Building.

(B) Before the recent increases were announced, residents of units in the West Building, who were the first to occupy Fife Arms, were paying substantially less for the cost of the maintenance of the entire complex than were the residents of the units of the East Building.

(C) Although the units are identical in age, the rate of occupancy for units in the West Building has been higher than that for units in the East Building, resulting in more wear and tear on units in the West Building.

(D) The increases in rent were not determined by the landlords, but imposed by changes in the city regulations regarding landlord-owned residences.

(E) An independent appraiser judged units in the West Building in the Fife Arms to be one and a half times more valuable than units in the East Building.

8. This is a WEAKEN question. Figure out which answer choice has the most negative impact on the conclusion of the argument. Remember to assume the hypothetical truth of each choice and apply it to the argument.

(A) This looks pretty good, because it gives us a reason why the West Building people are now asked to pay a higher rate of maintenance than the East Building people do. Let's leave it.

(B) This would only weaken it if you knew that both sets of tenants were paying the same amount before the East Building got an increase.

(C) This looks pretty good too, but just because we've got more wear and tear in the West Building doesn't mean that those people should necessarily have to pay more. Besides, the argument says the units have deteriorated equally. Therefore, (A) is better.

(D) We don't care who actually determined the increases. Eliminate it.

(E) The value of the apartments is outside the scope of the argument.

QUESTIONS	EXPLANATIONS

9. It has long been thought that the ancestors of the human race who lived prior to the Ice Age did not have the aid of the many useful inventions characteristic of post–Ice Age humans. In particular, it has long been believed that they did not have the advantages of sharp cutting tools. Such people supposedly had to manage by tearing things, such as the animal skins that they needed for warmth, with their teeth and fingernails. However, the recent discovery of the well-preserved remains of a pre–Ice Age woman has shown this to be false. The woman was wearing a number of animal skins and carried in her hand a number of sharp-edged stones, which scientists discovered could cut through animal skins remarkably well.

A flaw in the above argument is that it

(A)   makes an appeal to the authority of scientists, without giving sufficient justification for that appeal

(B)   assumes that the stones were sharpened by the woman herself

(C)   assumes that if a thing can be used for a certain purpose, then that purpose must be what the thing in fact was used for

(D)   ignores the fact that many pre–Ice Age people used skins for other reasons besides warmth

(E)   assumes that any object that could be used for cutting animal skins would be good for cutting all kinds of things

9. This is a REASONING question. Try to come up with your own description why the author's conclusion is flawed before you go to the answer choices, and then try to match your description to the choices.

(A)   If the scientists have something valuable to contribute, then it's a good thing. That's not why the argument is flawed. Eliminate it.

(B)   No, the question is whether or not she actually used the stones for cutting things. Eliminate it.

(C)   This is the answer, because the arguer and the scientists have no proof that the woman was actually using the stones to cut things—she might have been using them for a game of pre-Ice Age ping pong, for instance.

(D)   The skins aren't the issue here; the sharp stones are. Eliminate it.

(E)   He didn't claim that the stones were used to cut everything. Be wary of the extreme language of the choice here. Eliminate it.

QUESTIONS	EXPLANATIONS

10. The accountant for a large retail store warned that over half of the accounts receivable for the previous quarter were delinquent. He suggested that the store hire a collection agency to collect the debt immediately. His suggestion was not followed, however, when it was noted that the store had already received over two-thirds of the total dollar amount of the outstanding accounts.

If the statements above are true, they most strongly support which one of the following?

(A) The store had already collected on twice as many accounts as remained unpaid.

(B) At least one-third of the accounts had been paid before the beginning of the last quarter.

(C) Two-thirds of the total number of delinquent accounts must have been collected by the store.

(D) The total dollar amount and the total number of delinquent accounts are not necessarily proportional.

(E) If each account paid in installments, then all the accounts paid at least two-thirds of the individual bill.

10. This is an INFERENCE question. Your goal is to find the one choice that must be true based on the information in the passage.

(A) We have no idea as to the actual number of accounts collected. Eliminate it.

(B) We have no idea as to the actual number of accounts at the beginning of the last quarter. Eliminate it.

(C) We have no idea as to the actual number of accounts collected. Eliminate it.

(D) Nice and wishy-washy. They could be proportional, they could not be proportional. This statement must be true even independently of the information provided in the argument, it's so wishy-washy. It's the answer.

(E) We have no idea about the percentage of installment payments as related to each person's account balance as a whole. Eliminate it.

SECTION IV

11. Statistics recently compiled from Fortune 500 companies seem to suggest that, in the top levels of management, those with a Masters in Business Administration (MBA) face fewer obstacles than do non-MBAs in becoming vice presidents and thus positioning themselves for further advancement. Fully 7 percent of all MBAs within the companies surveyed are vice presidents, while only 2 percent of all non-MBAs have achieved that status. Anyone planning a career in top-level management would be wise to go to graduate school for an MBA.

Information about which one of the following would be most helpful in evaluating the validity of the argument above?

(A) the percentages of eligible MBAs and eligible non-MBAs who have recently become corporate vice presidents

(B) the percentage of vice president positions in non–Fortune 500 companies that are held by non-MBAs

(C) whether other opportunities for advancement below the rank of vice president exist in Fortune 500 companies

(D) the actual number of non-MBAs who have recently become vice presidents in Fortune 500 companies versus the actual number of MBAs who have recently become vice presidents in those companies

(E) the percentage of people with MBAs versus the percentage of people without MBAs who seek employment in Fortune 500 companies

11. This is most like an ASSUMPTION question, because you are looking for a fact that will help you to evaluate the validity of the assumption.

(A) This looks good—if all MBAs were vice presidents before going to business school it weakens the argument; if not, it strengthens it.

(B) Remember, we're concerned with Fortune 500 companies. Let's eliminate this.

(C) We're concerned with top-level management only. Eliminate it.

(D) The numbers don't matter if the percentages are already established, which they are. Eliminate it.

(E) The number of prospective candidates in each group won't help us to find out whether they get top-level managerial positions. Eliminate it.

QUESTIONS	EXPLANATIONS

12. Concerns about the quality of domestic cars drove many consumers to purchase foreign cars in the 1970s through the late 1980s. But here is a car that will change all that. According to the J.P.R. Glowers customer satisfaction survey, a survey that asks car owners how they feel about their car after the first year of ownership, the Acme Roadster scored highest of all cars in quality for the second year in a row. It also scored very high in safety features, look and feel, and overall driveability. It is clear that this is a car that represents the new domestic standard: high quality for many years of enjoyable driving.

Which one of the following arguments contains a flaw that is most similar to the one in the argument above?

(A) There is no doubt that these are the finest roses in the country. Eight out of nine growers surveyed rated these the most colorful in their class.

(B) This house paint will last for decades. When it was tested on several houses it showed barely a crack after 10 years.

(C) This new skyscraper will be one of the sturdiest buildings ever built. It has three separate stabilization systems, which will allow it to withstand even significant earthquakes.

(D) Even though the domestic tea market has been depressed for years, it should be coming out with some better teas soon, which will increase its market share dramatically.

(E) The best boats in the world are built by domestic boat manufacturers. We know they are the best because they last the longest of any boats in the world.

12. This is a PARALLEL-THE-REASONING question. Figure out the theme or diagram of the logic and then match it to each answer choice.

(A) We need to find something that shows that good performance in the short run proves good performance in the long run. This choice doesn't do that.

(B) This says ten years is equal to "decades," which does the same thing as the argument. It's the answer.

(C) The skyscraper as yet hasn't been proven to be sturdy at all because it's new. Therefore, it's not parallel to the argument.

(D) This has no relevance to the theme in the argument. Eliminate it.

(E) We have proof of long-standing performance here, so eliminate it.

SECTION IV

Questions 13–14

For many years, skeptics scoffed at the idea that plants respond to environmental stimuli other than those that directly affect the process of photosynthesis. Recent studies, however, offer contradictory evidence that seems to suggest that music, for instance, can have a direct and positive effect on plant development. Plants that were kept in the presence of music during the first six weeks of development grew considerably faster and showed fewer signs of disease than those plants developed in silence. The "music-advantaged" plants were also 35 percent more likely to survive the process of transplantation initially than were the "music-disadvantaged" plants.

13. Which one of the following is an assumption upon which the above argument is based?

   (A) Many skeptics still do not believe that music is beneficial to plant development.
   (B) Plants that do not thrive have been deprived of music during the first six weeks of their development.
   (C) Plants that were exposed to music for longer periods of time were healthier and grew faster than those with less exposure.
   (D) Some kinds of music are more beneficial to plants than others.
   (E) Music does not significantly damage a plant's ability to photosynthesize.

14. A logical critique of the study cited above would most likely raise which one of the following questions?

   (A) Was the type of music used during the experiment consistent over time?
   (B) Were both plant groups raised in the same quality soil?
   (C) Did the "music-advantaged" plants that survived transplantation live longer than the "music-disadvantaged" plants that survived transplantation?
   (D) Is the idea that plants respond to environmental stimuli other than those traditionally accepted as aiding growth now accepted by the scientific community?
   (E) What types of plants were used in the experiment?

13. This is an ASSUMPTION question. The correct answer will be something necessary for the conclusion to be true, and, if made false, will make the argument fall apart.

   (A) What skeptics believe or don't believe is outside the scope of the argument.
   (B) This is not essential to the argument—we're just looking to see something that strengthens the fact that music helps.
   (C) This is nice, but it's not an underlying assumption of the argument. We don't know anything about longer periods of time.
   (D) A specific type of music isn't the issue.
   (E) This is definitely an assumption. Make this choice false—what would happen to the argument if music damaged the photosynthetic ability of plants? The argument would crumble. So it's the answer.

14. This is a REASONING question. Come up with your own description of why the author's conclusion is flawed before you go to the answer choices, and then match your description to the choices.

   (A) A specific type of music isn't the issue.
   (B) Exactly. Do we know for sure that all the conditions of the experiment other than music were identical? If not, the results are garbage. This is a classic LSAT issue—learn it well!
   (C) The life expectancy of the plants isn't the issue here; their healthfulness and ability to survive transplantation is.
   (D) What the scientific community thinks is irrelevant if we actually have proof of something. A classic LSAT trap. Eliminate it.
   (E) The types of plants used aren't important as long as the same types were used for both the control and experimental groups. Eliminate it.

15. Max: It's a travesty that our government gives away billions of dollars every year to foreign countries while people in this country are poor, starving, and living in inadequate housing. Many foreigners now live far better than the majority of our own people, courtesy of our leaders. This is clearly wrong. A government is obligated to serve its own citizens' interests first, before trying to further the interests of other people in other countries.

Alex: But that is precisely what our government is doing in giving large amounts of foreign aid. Giving such money to foreign countries ensures their loyalty to us, so that we will have their help in furthering our international goals. Thus, even though the poor people in this country may not believe that the government is serving them, it most certainly is.

Which one of the following is the point at issue between Max and Alex?

(A)   whether or not foreign governments ought to give money away to other countries

(B)   what should be considered in the citizens' interests, when judging the actions of a government

(C)   whether or not the government should consider the interests of foreign people before the interests of its own citizens

(D)   whether or not providing food and adequate housing are important functions of a government

(E)   how much of the government's money should be allowed to go to foreign aid

15.   This is a REASONING question. Come up with your own description of what they're arguing about before you go to the answer choices, and then match your description to the choices.

(A)   Foreign government isn't what they're talking about. Eliminate it.

(B)   Right. Max is claiming foreign aid isn't in the interest of citizens, and Alex is claiming that it is.

(C)   No, because both are claiming that the government should care more about its own citizens.

(D)   No, because we have no idea whether Alex thinks this is important or not.

(E)   Not how much, but whether they should be giving any money at all. Eliminate it.

SECTION IV

QUESTIONS	EXPLANATIONS

16. Excessive logging has led to a sharp drop in the available supply and an increase in the price of hardwood lumber such as oak and maple. This same pattern has occurred with far too many of our scarce and vital natural resources, resulting in high prices for many products. It is likely, then, that the prices of new hardwood furniture will rise in the near future.

In making the argument above, the author relies on all of the following assumptions EXCEPT:

(A) The price of raw materials is a determining factor in the cost of new furniture.

(B) An increase in the price of lumber usually leads to an increase in the price of newly produced furniture.

(C) There will not be any substantial decrease in other costs to furniture producers that could keep the price of newly produced furniture from increasing.

(D) The cost of new hardwood furniture is affected by an increase in the price of hardwood lumber.

(E) Logging practices can substantially influence the demand for wooden manufactured goods.

16. This is an ASSUMPTION question. Four answers will be something necessary for the conclusion to be true, and, if made false, will make the argument fall apart.

(A) This is an assumption, because if the price of the raw materials weren't a factor, then the price of the furniture wouldn't necessarily rise. Eliminate it.

(B) This is an assumption, because if this weren't true, the price wouldn't necessarily rise. Eliminate it.

(C) This is an assumption, because if prices of things like glue and screws and saws all decreased a lot, then the price of newly produced furniture wouldn't necessarily rise. Eliminate it.

(D) This is an assumption; it says the same thing as (B). Eliminate it.

(E) The demand for furniture isn't an issue here; the price is. This isn't a necessary assumption and therefore it's the answer.

SECTION IV

QUESTIONS

Questions 17–18

Dr. Ronson: These animal tracks exhibit some interesting and strange characteristics. This first footprint appears to have two toes, whereas this second footprint appears to have three. And while this first footprint is facing north, this second footprint is facing east. Due to the weight of this evidence, we can safely conclude that these prints were made by two different animals.

Dr. Martinson: These tracks may indeed have been made by two different animals, but your evidence does not conclusively demonstrate that fact. A slight twist of the foot can make a print that seems to have extra toes. And some animals have feet that are oriented at right angles to one another, such that when they walk, their footprints face different directions. Now, if one footprint had claws while the other one did not, I would find your case more persuasive.

17. Drs. Ronson and Martinson disagree about which of the following?

   (A) Any group of tracks can be determined as having been made by a single animal or more than one animal, based on the shapes of the footprints and the directions that they are facing.
   (B) Any group of tracks made by a single individual would have similarly shaped footprints and would be facing in the same direction.
   (C) Each kind of animal leaves a distinct kind of footprint by which it can be uniquely identified.
   (D) The shapes and directions of the footprints in groups of tracks can be used to determine the number of animals who made them.
   (E) It is not possible for a single animal to leave both a two-toed and a three-toed footprint.

18. Dr. Martinson does which one of the following?

   (A) argues that one can never conclusively determine how many animals made a given group of tracks
   (B) criticizes Ronson's conclusion based on other known facts about footprints and the properties of some animals' feet
   (C) attacks Ronson's authority as a scientist
   (D) disputes Ronson's reasoning by giving an explanation of the facts
   (E) states an alternative criterion that would conclusively determine whether one or more animals made a given group of tracks

EXPLANATIONS

17. This is a REASONING question. Come up with your own idea of what they're arguing about before you go to the answer choices, and then match your description to the choices.

   (A) Ronson says it's possible in this case; Martinson says it isn't. Therefore, they would disagree about this statement. It's the answer.
   (B) They're not disagreeing about this.
   (C) That's not what they are arguing about. Eliminate it.
   (D) In all cases? They're only talking about this one specific instance.
   (E) They're not arguing about whether the animal is a freak. Eliminate it.

18. This is a REASONING question. Come up with your own description of what Dr. Martinson does before you go to the answer choices, and then match your description to the choices.

   (A) "Never" is too extreme here. We're only talking about one specific set of tracks. Eliminate it.
   (B) Bingo. He calls into question the two pieces of evidence Ronson brings up. It's the answer.
   (C) He doesn't do this. Eliminate it.
   (D) He gives an *alternative* explanation. Eliminate it.
   (E) "Conclusively" is too extreme here. (B) is the better answer; it's more wishy-washy and therefore more easily provable.

SECTION IV

QUESTIONS	EXPLANATIONS

19. At current rates of emission, a tax of one cent per pound of pollutant released into the air or water would raise $15 billion. This seems to be an ideal way to pay for the new environmental cleanup program that was recently instituted by the government. Not only that, but this tax would also help prevent further need for such cleanup efforts by encouraging companies to install more modern, less environmentally damaging equipment, and in the future, the money collected from the tax could support programs such as the National Park Service.

Which one of the following most clearly identifies a flaw in the author's reasoning?

(A) The author makes a generalization based on insufficient data.

(B) The author fails to consider other possible ways to accomplish the same end.

(C) The author mistakes an effect for a cause.

(D) The author makes incompatible assumptions.

(E) The author fails to consider a possible result of his plan.

19. This is a REASONING question. Come up with your own description of what's wrong with the argument before you go to the answer choices, and then match your description to the choices.

(A) There's no generalization here. He's actually talking about a specific plan. Eliminate it.

(B) This isn't necessarily bad as long as his plan is a good one. Eliminate it.

(C) He's not confused to this degree. Eliminate it.

(D) The argument isn't contradictory, just weak. Eliminate it.

(E) Yep—the result that if companies don't pollute much any more by installing less damaging equipment, there won't *be* any tax money with which to fund the National Park Service. Oops. It's the answer.

QUESTIONS	EXPLANATIONS

20. Vaccines have allowed us to eradicate diseases such as smallpox, polio, and diptheria. Vaccines work by the injection of a weak or harmless version of a certain virus or bacteria in order to allow the body to learn to recognize it and build a defense against it, so that if a full-strength version of the virus ever enters the body, it will be recognized and attacked before it can do serious damage. In the last 10 years, vaccine therapy itself has undergone a major change. The old polio vaccine, for instance, actually required the injection of live (although severely weakened) polio virus into the subject, thereby causing polio in about 3 percent of the subjects. However, today's more modern polio vaccine works by administering a completely crippled polio vaccine: one that has had its genetic information removed so that it can never reproduce itself or cause polio. This new vaccine is at least as effective as the old one, and it has not caused polio in a single patient since it began to be used nearly a decade ago.

If all of the above statements are true, which one of the following must also be true?

(A) Aside from the few cases of polio caused by the administration of the old vaccine, the old vaccine was completely effective in preventing polio.

(B) The body must learn to recognize viruses by some other factor than their genetic information.

(C) Once we are able to manufacture a vaccine for a certain virus, the disease caused by that virus will be eradicated within a period of years.

(D) Vaccines will only work if your body's own immune system is in perfect shape.

(E) Except for cases of polio caused by the administration of the old vaccine, the old polio vaccine was no less effective than the new one.

20. This is an INFERENCE question. Your goal is to find the one choice that must be true based on the information in the passage.

(A) We don't know if this must be true or not. Eliminate it.

(B) This must be true, because if the body recognized viruses by their genetic information, then there's no way that the new genetic-information–free virus would be recognized by the body. It's the answer.

(C) This is too extreme. Eliminate it.

(D) This is too extreme. Eliminate it.

(E) This is the opposite of what the argument said, which was that the new one is at least as effective as the old one, not the other way around.

SECTION IV

QUESTIONS	EXPLANATIONS

21. In order to lose body fat, you have to raise your metabolism. If you run six hours per week, you'll be able to lose body fat. Therefore, if you lose body fat, you must be running six hours per week.

Which one of the following best describes the flaw in the argument?

(A) Some people might not want to run six hours per week.

(B) Although running six hours per week may be sufficient to raise your metabolism, it may not be necessary.

(C) If you don't run at least six hours per week, you will not raise your metabolism.

(D) Some people may want to run more than six hours per week in order to get in shape more quickly.

(E) Some people are not marathon runners and may take years to lose a significant amount of body fat.

21. This is a REASONING question. Come up with your own description of what's wrong with the argument before you go to the answer choices, and then match your description to the choices.

(A) The desire of people to run is not what's wrong with the argument. Eliminate it.

(B) Exactly. The argument flip-flops the logic on itself, saying that the only way to lose body fat is to run six hours a week, eliminating all other possibilities.

(C) This is merely repeating the mistake the argument makes. Eliminate it.

(D) Once again, desire isn't the issue, and we don't know what happens if you run more than six hours.

(E) Marathon runners aren't the issue here. Eliminate it.

22. The current notion of corporate liability holds that no corporate head can be sued unless criminal misconduct is established. Thus the corporate head cannot be held individually responsible but is viewed simply as a part of the corporate body, rather than as a distinct entity. This makes it difficult to recover compensation for corporate negligence from corporate heads who may ultimately have been responsible for their company's negligence, and may very well be directly responsible for implementation of the negligent act.

Which one of the following best supports the argument that corporate liability should be extended to corporate heads?

(A) The assets of negligent small corporations are often sufficient to compensate for damages awarded in negligence suits.

(B) The assets of heads of small corporations are often insufficient to compensate for damages awarded in negligence suits.

(C) The threat of personal liability will dissuade corporate heads from discharging their duties improperly.

(D) Threats of corporate liability are necessary in order to recover compensation for corporate negligence.

(E) Statistics indicate that where threats of personal liability are present, corporations are more likely to violate regulations that could lead to liability disputes.

22. This is a STRENGTHEN question. Figure out which answer choice has the most positive impact on the conclusion of the argument. Remember to assume the hypothetical truth of each choice and apply it to the argument.

(A) This, if anything, would weaken the argument. Eliminate it.

(B) This would also weaken the argument because it says you wouldn't get any money even if you were able to sue corporate heads directly. Eliminate it.

(C) This would definitely help the conclusion that making corporate heads personally responsible would be a good thing. Let's keep it.

(D) If this choice said *personal* liability, then it might make sense. As of now, it doesn't. Eliminate it.

(E) This would also weaken the argument since it would have the opposite effect desired. Eliminate it.

QUESTIONS	EXPLANATIONS

23. Sarah, a surgeon at a large hospital, asked a hospital administrator for permission to take the vital organs from a man who had just died in an accident, in order to use his organs to save the lives of several other people who needed immediate organ transplants to survive. The man carried neither identification with which to attempt to contact his family, nor anything that specifically authorized the use of his organs, such as an organ donor card. But the man did have a Goose Lodge lapel pin, and the Goose Lodge had long been in favor of encouraging its members to be organ donors.

Which one of the following principles, if accepted, would determine either that the man's organs should be used or that they should not be used?

(A) If using parts of a dead body can save people's lives, and if members of the dead person's family are notified and do not object, then those parts can be used.

(B) The fact that someone belongs to a group that encourages organ donations does not constitute consent on the part of that person to have his organs used.

(C) Authorization from a person's family, an organ donor card, or other authorizing document signed by that person is always sufficient to give permission to take that person's vital organs.

(D) If no relatives can be found after a period of 30 days, then a dead body can be used for whatever purposes its possessors see fit.

(E) Only if members of a dead person's family consent can that person's organs be used to save other lives.

23. This is a PRINCIPLE question. We are given five principles in the answer choices for this specific question, so we should come up with our own principle for the actions in the argument and match it to the answer choices.

(A) This wouldn't work because we can't contact the family of the guy.

(B) All this tells us is that we can't make a decision based on the pin. This is no help in deciding whether we should or should not use the organs.

(C) Since we don't have any of this, it doesn't help make our decision for us.

(D) This answer just says that in 30 days, we can use the organs if we want to. But the question is *should* we use the organs or not, not *can* we use the organs.

(E) This is much more powerful than (B) because it says the *only* way for us to take the organs is through family consent. Therefore, it's the answer.

SECTION IV

24. A survey of urban middle-class citizens revealed some inconsistencies in their attitudes towards the homeless. Over 75 percent of those who responded said that they believed the general public to be sympathetic towards the plight of the homeless. Ironically, an overwhelming majority of the respondents confessed to going to great lengths to avoid homeless people on the street.

   Which one of the following, if true, would explain the apparent paradox in the results reported in the passage above?

   (A) Having sympathy for homeless people and wanting to avoid them on the street are not necessarily incompatible positions.
   (B) Sympathizing with one person who has no home is easier than dealing with homelessness as an abstract concept.
   (C) There was a wide variety of sentiment regarding homelessness among the respondents themselves.
   (D) Many of the respondents had once been homeless people themselves.
   (E) The general public is not aware of government programs designed to implement low-income housing.

24. This is a PARADOX question. Look for an answer choice that allows both parts of the argument to be true, and remember to assume the hypothetical truth of each of the answer choices.

   (A) Bingo. This allows both facts from the argument to be true.
   (B) We're not talking about an abstract concept here. This has no impact. Eliminate it.
   (C) That's nice, but it doesn't help to explain the seeming discrepancy. Eliminate it.
   (D) Wow. Interesting, but it doesn't help to explain the discrepancy. In fact, it would exacerbate it, if anything.
   (E) Government programs are really, really far outside the scope of this argument. Like, in Andromeda.

25. As a result of recent studies that successfully established that drinking a glass of red wine with dinner can reduce the risk of heart disease, doctors have begun to recommend that their patients consume red wine with their evening meals. Surprisingly, according to research intended to track the effectiveness of such recommendations, many patients who followed these recommendations continued to be vulnerable to heart disease.

   Which one of the following, if true, would explain the unexpected result described above?

   (A) Many patients ignore their doctors' recommendations to drink wine with meals.
   (B) A greater number of people are likely to drink red wine than did before the results of the study were known.
   (C) The high cost of red wine has discouraged many people from consuming it regularly.
   (D) Red wine is not believed to prevent all types of diseases, so it is to be expected that people will continue to have some types of diseases.
   (E) The beneficial effects of drinking red wine are incurred only when the wine is drunk in moderation, which many patients fail to do.

25. This is a PARADOX question. Look for an answer choice that allows both parts of the argument to be true, and remember to assume the hypothetical truth of each of the answer choices.

   (A) But we're told in the argument that these patients have actually followed the recommendations.
   (B) But we still have lots of people with heart disease.
   (C) This is the same problem as (A).
   (D) This is too general and therefore has no impact, because the argument is specifically talking about heart disease.
   (E) Oops. Everyone's boozing it up! Therefore, this can explain why the treatment isn't working. It's the answer.

10

The Princeton Review
LSAT Diagnostic Test II

THE
PRINCETON
REVIEW

L S A T

Law School Admission Test

SECTION I

Time—35 minutes

27 Questions

Directions: Each passage in this section is followed by a group of questions to be answered on the basis of what is <u>stated</u> or <u>implied</u> in the passage. For some questions, more than one of the choices could conceivably answer the question. However, you are to choose the <u>best</u> answer, that is, the response that most accurately and completely answers the question, and blacken the corresponding space on your answer sheet.

Conventionally, the landowner wishing to build on his land has the structure designed by one entity and then built by another; the design and build functions are viewed as separate. With the innovative "design-build"
(5) construction arrangement, however, a single entity performs both the design and construction functions. That single entity may be a joint venture between an architect or engineer and general contractor, a design-build firm that employs both professionals and contractors, or a
(10) general contracting firm subcontracting with an architectural or engineering firm. Design-build contracts appeal to owners because they require only one entity for performance; if a problem arises, the owner does not have to decide whether the architect or the contractor is
(15) the culprit. From the standpoint of the contractor, design-build contracts are advantageous because they secure both design fees and construction profits. In addition, many design-build contracts are calculated on a cost-plus basis and are therefore less risky than fixed-price work.
(20) A design-build job may be carried out like a traditional project, in which the contractor prepares design documents and obtains owner approval before construction commences, or as a series of tasks entailing the preparation of design documents in phases, with
(25) construction beginning as each phase of the design is completed. The process of starting construction before the overall design is complete is known as the "fast-track" construction plan. Often, the design-build and fast-track concepts are employed together.
(30) Fast-track construction appeals to owners because it reduces the time between a project's conception and its completion, thus minimizing finance costs and the often disastrous effects of inflation and increasing the likelihood that the budget will be adequate to complete
(35) the project. On the other hand, the fast-track approach presents problems to owners seeking construction changes. Normally, a builder is obliged to conform to designs and, with compensation for extra expense, to owner-requested changes when such changes are within
(40) the "scope of the project"; while in the traditional format, determining whether or not a change is within the scope of the project is relatively simple.
On a fast-track job, however, the finishing details of the job are defined after construction begins. Thus, there

(45) is more room for misunderstanding between the owner and the contractor as to whether design changes are within the scope of the project.
In this regard, a contractor should define the parameters of his obligations as early as possible. For example, the
(50) parties should be able to agree on the type and function of the structure, the number of stories, and the approximate area before any construction commences. Once building has begun, the keys to minimizing disputes are constant communication with the owner regarding what the
(55) contractor deems the scope of his work, and prompt notice if the contractor perceives that these bounds are being overstepped.

1. According to the passage, the design-build method of construction is attractive to a landowner who wishes to build on her land because

(A) she no longer needs to work with two separate entities
(B) it allows earlier marketing, thereby reducing finance costs
(C) its speed of construction protects her against inflation
(D) when problems develop, she has financial recourse
(E) it enables her to make changes even after the building has begun

GO ON TO THE NEXT PAGE.

2. Which one of the following would best serve as the concluding sentence of the last paragraph?

    (A) Close contact allows full benefit from fast-track construction and reduces the likelihood of disputes.
    (B) Since no communication is perfect, however, most owners choose conventional construction to avoid disputes.
    (C) Unfortunately, owners of multiple projects often cannot maintain such close contact.
    (D) Effective communication is ultimately the key to a productive work environment.
    (E) Inspection of the building on completion would verify that it continued to adhere to safety regulations.

3. It can be inferred from the passage that contractors find the design-build method advantageous because

    (A) it reduces the number of design documents that need to be prepared
    (B) design changes are easier to facilitate
    (C) owners are less likely to request costly changes in the scope of the project
    (D) the financial risks are less than for traditional construction projects
    (E) they need hire only one entity

4. Which one of the following best summarizes the main point of the author?

    (A) Fast-track programs represent a radical departure from the no-longer-effective traditional method of construction.
    (B) Conventional construction and design-build construction are both equally valid methods of construction, though each is best suited to different circumstances.
    (C) The combination of design-build and fast-track methods of construction creates financial risks that many landowners find unacceptable.
    (D) Contractors have begun to encourage their clients to explore new methods and systems of design and construction.
    (E) While the design-build and fast-track methods of construction provide advantages to both landowners and contractors, the fast-track method also carries some risks.

5. In mentioning the "disastrous effects of inflation" (line 33), the author is probably referring to the fact that

    (A) delayed completion inhibits renting or selling the building because of higher costs
    (B) lengthy construction time can put costs beyond the owner's ability to pay
    (C) financiers may, because of inflationary pressures, demand earlier returns
    (D) inflation can weaken the link between design-build and fast-track
    (E) the contractor may demand higher payment for design changes

6. Based on the information given in the passage, the author would consider each of the following good advice to an owner who has arranged for fast-track construction of a building on his land EXCEPT

    (A) After construction is complete, verify that changes have been made according to specifications.
    (B) Reach agreement on the major decisions concerning the project before construction begins.
    (C) Bring problems to the attention of the contractor as soon as they arise.
    (D) Confer with the contractor frequently during construction.
    (E) Prepare a list of important design details before the project begins so that misunderstandings are avoided.

GO ON TO THE NEXT PAGE.

In the early 1980s, a number of citizens established organizations devoted to preventing drivers from operating motor vehicles while under the influence of alcohol. These organizations represent a grassroots social
(5) movement that attacks the problem of drunk driving by calling for community awareness and stronger sanctions. Unlike the prohibitionist movements of the late nineteenth and early twentieth centuries, which identified drinking itself as inherently wrong, the anti-drunk-
(10) driving movements emphasize the issue of drinking while driving automobiles; the problem is not alcohol use (or abuse), but the irresponsibility of individuals using alcohol. In essence, these organizations have spawned a social movement against the evils caused by personal
(15) irresponsibility.

The Progressive reform movements around the turn of the century shared the same moral ethic. As Hofstadter has argued, the Progressive reform movements were strongly based on the "ethos of personal responsibility"
(20) and the basic morality of civic consciousness. That approach is reflected in the goals of today's movement and in its views on proposals to solve the drunk-driving problem. The two most important program goals of current-day organizations are public awareness activities
(25) designed to make drinkers understand that it is wrong to drive when under the influence of alcohol and youth education programs designed to convey this message to young drivers.

The "ethos of personal responsibility" for one's
(30) actions also has an impact in determining what actions are taken to solve the problem. Grassroots organizations call for punitive measures to be taken against drunk drivers. They perceive non-punitive programs—such as the safe-ride program—as ineffective. As one founding
(35) member of one organization put it: "Safe ride programs may help temporarily, but they cause people to ignore their part in the problem."

Rehabilitation programs are rejected on the same grounds. In addition to labeling these programs as
(40) ineffective, grassroots organizers perceive them as a minor inconvenience to offenders and as a means of avoiding stricter punishment. This punitive approach to "problem drinking" represents a departure from the trend of viewing drinking problems as a disease and thus a
(45) medical problem. The movement does not distinguish between the sick alcoholic and the irresponsible "problem drinker" in its desire to enforce sanctions against the drunk driver.

These opinions reflect the basic moral view that
(50) citizens should be aware of the dangers of driving while drunk and their individual responsibility to drive sober. As a result of this awareness, those individuals acting irresponsibly should face serious punishment. Society, on the other hand, should not take the responsibility for
(55) individual conduct by instituting prohibitionist measures, safe-ride programs, or programs for rehabilitation.

7. The main idea of the passage is that
   (A) centuries of anti-alcohol public awareness campaigns reflect the United States' focus on personal responsibility
   (B) present-day grassroots anti-drunk-driving organizations emphasize personal responsibility as the key to effecting change
   (C) Prohibition failed because it ignored the United States' ethic of responsibility
   (D) if non-punitive programs worked, there would be no grassroots anti-drunk-driving movement
   (E) no anti-drunk-driving campaign is likely to succeed without punishing the driver

8. According to the passage, the modern grassroots movement designed to prevent drunk driving
   (A) is largely unconcerned with the broader issue of alcohol abuse
   (B) is more concerned with protecting the lives of sober drivers than of drunk drivers
   (C) is less opposed to drunk driving than it is in favor of personal responsibility
   (D) is excessively punitive, and, therefore, not likely to be effective
   (E) views drunk driving narrowly, and, therefore, promises less success than the prohibition movement

9. The turn-of-the-century Progressive reform movements and the current grassroots movements share all of the following EXCEPT
   (A) a belief in personal responsibility
   (B) an emphasis on morality
   (C) a desire for behavior modification as it relates to civic consciousness
   (D) a disapproval of drinking
   (E) a commitment to altering certain conduct

GO ON TO THE NEXT PAGE.

10. As used in line 20 of the passage, a person who follows a "basic morality of civic consciousness" probably

    (A) abides by community standards for moral behavior

    (B) supports the work done by alcoholic-rehabilitation programs

    (C) advocates the adoption of severe penalties for driving while intoxicated

    (D) proposes that basic rules of moral behavior are essential to a just society

    (E) understands that drinking before driving wrongfully endangers the safety and welfare of others

11. According to the passage, grassroots organizations do not believe that prohibition is an effective solution to the drunk-driving problem because prohibition

    (A) is too punitive, especially for responsible drinkers

    (B) fails to recognize alcoholism as a disease

    (C) does not share the aims of the history of Progressive reform movements in the United States

    (D) makes society responsible for an individual's problems

    (E) does nothing to make citizens aware of the drunk-driving problem

12. In the third paragraph, the author's purpose is to

    (A) demonstrate the grassroots rejection of solutions that do not address driver accountability

    (B) explain why the safe-ride program is unlikely to eradicate drunk driving

    (C) present a view in opposition to that of the progressive reform movements

    (D) support his belief that non-punitive programs are ineffective

    (E) distinguish between punitive and non-punitive social reforms, favoring non-punitive reforms

13. Which one of the following best describes the organization of the passage?

    (A) A general philosophy of responsibility is presented, and specific approaches that do not adhere to that philosophy are rejected.

    (B) An ethos of personal responsibility is described, and then an alternate approach is described.

    (C) The history of a movement is outlined in chronological order.

    (D) A current political movement is analyzed, and the events that led to its creation are examined.

    (E) The historical approaches to a social problem are outlined and comparisons made.

14. The author of the passage would be most likely to agree with which one of the following statements about the "ethos of personal responsibility" and its relationship to grassroots campaigns against drunk driving?

    (A) Its impact on the organization of grassroots campaigns has been negligible, since these campaigns favor a more punitive approach.

    (B) It causes certain methods for dealing with drunk drivers to be favored over others that are perceived as ineffective or even dangerous.

    (C) It has been largely responsible for the introduction of public awareness campaigns involving both adults and teenagers.

    (D) It results in the belief that drinking is inherently wrong.

    (E) It establishes a general principle that provides a justification for acting irresponsibly while under the influence of alcohol.

GO ON TO THE NEXT PAGE.

In a representative democracy, legislatures exist to represent the public and to ensure that public issues are efficiently addressed by a group representative of the population as a whole. It is often written that a legislator (5) confronts a moral dilemma if, on a given issue upon which he must cast a vote, his view is decidedly different from that of the majority of his constituents. In such a circumstance, it is not clear whether voting citizens have chosen the legislator because of their faith in his personal (10) judgment or whether they have elected him in order to give direct effect to their own views.

But this dilemma is more apparent than real. A truly identifiable conflict between the legislator's opinion and that of his constituency is rare, since the legislator is (15) usually better informed than the public on the issue in question and his opinion, therefore, cannot fairly be compared to theirs. Indeed, this fact underscores the legislator's most important function: to gather broad-based information in order to make more considered (20) decisions than each citizen could reach individually and thus to serve the public interest better than the public could do on its own.

Let us suppose that a legislator opposes a very popular proposed public works project because he has studied its (25) financial ramifications and believes, over the long run, it is fiscally unsound. If the legislator's constituents write letters expressing their ardent support for the project, not having studied the relevant financial data, it is entirely too simplistic to view the legislator as having to confront (30) a moral dilemma. The truth is that the legislator does not know how his constituents would view the project if they truly understood its financial consequences. Without such knowledge, the legislator cannot actually conclude that his view differs from that of his constituents. To conclude (35) that their views should dictate his decision might foster his popularity, but would contravene his fundamental legislative responsibility.

The legislator's job is first to study the short-range and long-range goals of the people he represents, without (40) confusing these with his own. Then, using his knowledge and judgment, he is to promote the electorate's goals as he understands them. Consider, for instance, a legislator whose constituents wish to maintain the rural character of their district. If the legislator himself dislikes rural living and (45) would like to see the area undergo industrial development, or if he believes an industrial environment would offer greater benefit to the community than a rural environment, he must separate these viewpoints from his professional judgment. He is not to promote industrialization because he (50) personally favors it.

However, if the legislator's considered opinion is that his district needs to sponsor *some* industrial development in order to maintain its overall agricultural character, it is his duty to promote the industrial development, even if his

(55) constituents oppose it. So long as he honestly attempts to serve his electorate's objectives, the legislator should stand firm against the expressed opinions of his own constituents.

15. The author's purpose in the first paragraph is to

(A) explain that many legislative questions require economic as well as political understanding
(B) point out that a possible moral dilemma exists when a legislator disagrees with her constituents
(C) illustrate that the legislator's extra knowledge creates the gap between her views and those of her constituents
(D) argue that legislative decisions should not be made simplistically
(E) encourage the rejection of legislation that runs counter to the public interest

16. According to the passage, the differences between a legislator's view and the views expressed by the legislator's constituents

(A) do not actually create a moral dilemma in most cases
(B) create a moral dilemma only in a democracy
(C) only arise when constituents are ill-informed
(D) require that a legislator gather more information than he would otherwise have done
(E) usually reflect a difference not in opinion, but in long-range goals

GO ON TO THE NEXT PAGE.

17. It can be inferred from the passage that the author believes a legislator should

   (A) carry out her constituents' intentions if doing so conforms to her assessment

   (B) ignore her constituents' long-range objectives when they are morally incompatible with her own beliefs

   (C) take whatever actions her constituents recommend

   (D) determine what action will best serve her constituents, regardless of their stated position

   (E) put her own assessments aside and embody those of her electorate

18. Which one of the following would the author most likely believe to be true of a legislator who routinely reached legislative decisions by following constituents' instructions?

   (A) The legislator would probably not fully understand the public's goals.

   (B) The legislator would be acting in a manner contrary to her own interests.

   (C) The legislator would probably be unaware of the course of action most favorable to her constituency.

   (D) The legislator might not be fulfilling her proper role of defending the best interests of the electorate.

   (E) The legislator would be overly concerned with maintaining her own popularity, not carrying out her appropriate duties.

19. Which one of the following, if true, would most weaken the author's contention that a legislator can make "more considered decisions" than can his constituents?

   (A) A community should be allowed to make its own decisions, even if these are not the most informed decisions.

   (B) Because a legislator does not live in the same circumstances as do his constituents, he is more objective and less emotional in his decision-making.

   (C) Some constituents make a great effort to inform themselves on all aspects of proposed legislation.

   (D) The information provided to the legislator is occasionally biased or misleading.

   (E) Some legislators have difficulty separating their personal views from those of their constituents.

20. According to the author, the introduction of widespread industrialization into the rural community described in lines 42–50 represents

   (A) the failure of a legislator to understand the requirements of the region

   (B) an example of a legislator advancing his agenda at the expense of that of his constituents

   (C) the failure of representative democracy to address the needs of its constituents

   (D) the ability of a legislator to ignore the interests of the community he represents

   (E) the result of a legislator carrying through on the expressed views of his constituents

GO ON TO THE NEXT PAGE.

The KT boundary, as it is called, marks one of the most violent events ever to befall life on earth. Sixty-five million years ago, according to current theory, the Cretaceous period was brought to a sudden conclusion
(5) by the impact of an asteroid or a comet ten kilometers in diameter. It would be natural to suppose that the KT boundary is a fossil hunter's paradise. But it is nothing of the sort. In fact, no bones have been found at the KT boundary anywhere on earth.

(10) Some paleontologists find the situation frustrating, to put it mildly. Granted, they say, the record of life preserved in sedimentary rocks is far from perfect. But in this case the event of record is a cosmic catastrophe that killed all the dinosaurs in the world. Shouldn't the
(15) concentration of bones in the fossil record be, at very least, above average?

In some places the sedimentary rocks preserve detailed temporal signals with near-textbook fidelity, but such detailed windows into the past are relatively
(20) rare. More commonly, various natural forces like the wind and rain disrupt the chronological ordering of the fossils-to-be.

The first serious proposal for solving this sedimentary puzzle came in 1940, in a paper by the
(25) Soviet paleontologist Ivan A. Efremov. Paleontologists, Efremov said, were too inclined to take the fossil record at face value; instead, he advised, they ought to pay more attention to the processes whereby living organisms become, or fail to become,
(30) fossils. A better understanding of burial and fossilization might enable paleontologists to "back calculate" and reclaim lost data from the fossil record.

Paleontologists Alan Cutler and Anna Behrensmeyer have developed just such a model of fossil preservation.
(35) Starting with a hypothetical population of dinosaurs, they estimated normal annual mortality rates for dinosaurs from ecological data collected for large mammals in African wildlife preserves. Next, to estimate what fraction of the dinosaurs' bones would end up safely
(40) buried, they drew on data from Behrensmeyer's study of the decay of mammal carcasses in Ambeseli National Park, Kenya. Finally, they ran the model to see what sort of bone spike would result if the entire population of dinosaurs suddenly died. The answer, they discovered,
(45) was no bone spike at all.

In the mixed, or convoluted, record, spikes in the abundance of species are attenuated and tail off exponentially. The thicker the mixing layer, the greater the smearing. Thus, the sudden extinction of a
(50) species shows up not as an abrupt disappearance of fossils, but a gradual petering out.

Such research is still in its infancy, and there is no way of predicting exactly what further research may bring. However promising its results may be, though,
(55) one caveat is necessary: It will never be able to work miracles. The most sophisticated mathematics in the world cannot unscramble an egg or resurrect the dinosaurs.

21. Which of the following may be inferred about the KT boundary?

(A) The fossil record it contains is above average in both the quantity of fossils and their degree of preservation.
(B) It was destroyed by a large comet sixty-five million years ago.
(C) The fossil record it contains is, in some ways, inconsistent with the dominant theory of dinosaur extinction.
(D) Its significance was first described by paleontologist Ivan A. Efremov.
(E) Paleontologists consider it to be the single richest source in the fossil record.

22. Which of the following best describes the main idea of the passage?

(A) If paleontologists are to achieve significant results in the future, they must reject their older methods.
(B) Because it cannot be substantiated by the fossil record, the dominant theory of dinosaur extinction should be rejected.
(C) Because of the nature of the process by which bones become fossils, scientists should not be surprised by the relative absence of fossils at the KT boundary.
(D) Back-calculation indicates that the KT boundary should contain more fossils than more recent rock layers.
(E) More recent methods of modeling fossil preservation provide evidence that contradicts earlier findings made by paleontologists.

GO ON TO THE NEXT PAGE.

23. Which one of the following best describes the relationship between the work of Efremov and that of Cutler and Behrensmeyer?

(A) Efremov's work described the need for a significant shift in approach and Cutler and Behrensmeyer carried out research based in part on his approach.

(B) Efremov's work provided the data from which Cutler and Behrensmeyer were able to develop a model of fossil preservation.

(C) Whereas Efremov focused principally on why bones do not become fossils, Cutler and Behrensmeyer focused on why they do.

(D) Efremov's work was theoretically more complex than that carried out by Cutler and Behrensmeyer.

(E) Efremov focused on processes whereas Cutler and Behrensmeyer focused on data collection.

24. Which of the following best describes the organization of the passage?

(A) Data gathered from a broad range of sources is presented, inconsistencies among the data are described, then these inconsistencies are resolved.

(B) Research from two different groups of scientists is presented, a question about the research is posed, and an answer is offered.

(C) A new theoretical model is explained, problems with the model are pointed out, and possible explanations for the problem are suggested.

(D) A paradox is described, and both theoretical and empirical information is presented to help explain the paradox.

(E) A fundamental scientific failure is described, evidence substantiating this failure is presented, then a new approach to the problem is described.

25. The author would be most likely to agree with which of the following statements?

(A) Data from large mammal populations are essential in any attempt to model the process of dinosaur extinction.

(B) Fossil evidence indicates that the dinosaurs probably became extinct over a longer period of time than previously believed.

(C) The KT boundary provides a unique source of information about animal extinction.

(D) In most fossil layers, evidence of extinction trails off exponentially but contains an initial bone spike.

(E) Improvements in paleontological research, while useful, will not provide sufficient answers to all of the questions about dinosaur extinction.

26. The author states that, in their evaluation of the fossil record, Cutler and Behrensmeyer did all of the following EXCEPT

(A) conclude that the data from the fossil record was consistent with a mass extinction of dinosaurs

(B) work with paleontologist Ivan A. Efremov

(C) use data gathered from populations of large animals to estimate characteristics of dinosaur populations

(D) base their work on hypothetical information about dinosaur populations

(E) use data from studies of the decay of mammal carcasses in Africa

27. According to the passage, a segment of the fossil record in which paleontologists would LEAST expect to see a clear record of a period of sudden extinction would be one in which

(A) an abundance of bone spikes exist.

(B) an unusually large portion of the bones were safely buried before fossilization.

(C) "back calculation" would be difficult, but possible.

(D) drought occurred at the time of fossilization.

(E) a particularly thick mixing layer was present during fossil formation.

S T O P

IF YOU FINISH BEFORE TIME IS CALLED, YOU MAY CHECK YOUR WORK ON THIS SECTION ONLY.
DO NOT WORK ON ANY OTHER SECTION IN THE TEST.

SECTION II

Time—35 minutes

25 Questions

Directions: The questions in this section are based on the reasoning contained in brief statements or passages. For some questions, more than one of the choices could conceivably answer the question. However, you are to choose the best answer; that is, the response that most accurately and completely answers the question. You should not make assumptions that are by common sense standards implausible, superfluous, or incompatible with the passage. After you have chosen the best answer, blacken the corresponding space on your answer sheet.

1. The quality of our public schools is more likely to decline if people expect it to. The number of illiterate graduates and the level of administrative incompetence will increase as people's disrespect for public schools discourages more able people from pursuing careers in teaching.

The logical structure of the above statement is most consistent with which one of the following?

(A) If people believe that an eagerly anticipated event will take place, then it most likely will.

(B) When people believe that money grows on trees, then, for all practical purposes, money does grow on trees.

(C) When people expect the economy to flourish, they become willing to spend and invest more, thus helping the economy to flourish.

(D) When people expect world affairs to be tragic, they notice tragic events more than they do pleasant ones.

(E) If people enjoy sporting events, the stadiums and arenas will be full, thus encouraging high attendance at future sporting events.

2. In an experiment, first-year college students were asked to listen to a tape of someone speaking French. When asked to repeat the sounds they had heard, students who had studied French in high school could repeat more of the sounds than could students who had no knowledge of French. When asked to listen to a tape of only meaningless sounds, none of the students were able to repeat more than a few seconds' worth of the sounds made on the tape.

Which one of the following conclusions is best supported by the information above?

(A) Knowledge of a foreign language interferes with one's ability to repeat unfamiliar sounds.

(B) People who have a knowledge of French have better memories than do people who have no knowledge of French.

(C) The ability to repeat unrelated sounds is not improved by frequent practice.

(D) The ability to repeat sounds is influenced by one's ability to comprehend the meaning of the sounds.

(E) Learning a foreign language requires an ability to distinguish unfamiliar sounds from gibberish.

GO ON TO THE NEXT PAGE.

Questions 3–4

Many commercial pesticides, used primarily in indoor atriums, greenhouses, and solariums, release toxic levels of DDT and other potentially carcinogenic agents hazardous to the health of workers and other individuals who pass through the area. This problem can be avoided by providing adequate ventilation, but this becomes difficult during winter months when the area must maintain sufficient heat to ensure the survival of the plants. A recent study shows that certain tropical grasses will remove some of these toxins from the air, eliminating the danger to humans. In one winter trial, a four-foot-square patch of tropical grass eliminated the DDT in a solarium of average size.

3. Assume that a patch of tropical grass is introduced into a solarium of average size that contains toxic pesticide residue.

Which one of the following can be expected as a result?

(A) Occasional ventilation, even during the summer, will become unnecessary.
(B) The concentration of toxic pesticide residues will remain unchanged.
(C) The solarium will continue to maintain a constant level of toxicity and temperature.
(D) If there are toxic DDT residues in the solarium, these levels will decrease.
(E) If DDT and other potentially carcinogenic agents are being released in the solarium, the quantities of each agent will decrease.

4. The passage above is designed to lead to which one of the following conclusions?

(A) Tropical grass removes all carcinogenic agents from the air.
(B) Natural pesticides do not release toxins into greenhouses, solariums, or corporate atriums.
(C) Planting tropical grass is an effective means of maintaining a constant temperature in a greenhouse.
(D) Growing tropical grass can counteract some of the negative effects of a poorly ventilated atrium.
(E) The air in an atrium that contains tropical grass and maintains a constant temperature will contain fewer toxic residues than will the air in a similarly maintained atrium without tropical grass.

5. Medical Researcher: If I don't get another research grant soon, I'll never be able to discover a cure for phlebitis.

Assistant: But that's great. If your grant does come through, that dreaded disease will finally be eradicated.

Which one of the following statements best describes the flaw in the assistant's reasoning?

(A) The assistant believes the researcher will be unable to cure phlebitis unless the grant comes through.
(B) The assistant thinks the researcher will use the grant to find a cure for phlebitis, rather than for some other purpose.
(C) The assistant believes it is more important to cure phlebitis than to eradicate other, more deadly conditions.
(D) The assistant believes that all the researcher needs in order to cure phlebitis is another research grant.
(E) The assistant thinks the researcher will cure phlebitis even if the grant does not come through.

6. Economist: The keys to a growth economy are low interest rates and a high number of investments; as there cannot be investments without low interest rates, it can be concluded that where there are low interest rates there are investments.

Which one of the following, if true, would most weaken the argument above?

(A) Many growth economies with high interest rates have few investments.
(B) Stagnant economies with high interest rates have few investments.
(C) Stagnant economies with low interest rates have few investments.
(D) A high number of investments is adequate to guarantee low interest rates.
(E) Some stagnant economies have low interest rates.

GO ON TO THE NEXT PAGE.

7. A study commissioned by the National Association of Women Professors seems to indicate that women face greater obstacles in becoming tenured professors than do men. Whereas more than 70 percent of the male professors in this country have tenure, fewer than half of the female professors have achieved that rank.

    Which one of the following statistics would be most relevant to an assessment of the accuracy of the study mentioned above?

    (A) the respective percentages of eligible women and men who have earned tenure in each of the past ten years
    (B) the percentage of all tenured positions that have gone to women in each of the past ten years
    (C) an analysis of the bias faced by women in other professional fields
    (D) the number of men who have been appointed to tenured positions, and the number of women who have not been appointed to tenured positions
    (E) the number of professional women who cite the difficulty of achieving tenure when asked to explain why they decided against entering academia

8. Sheet for sheet, Brand A paper towels cost less than Brand B paper towels and are more absorbent. Yet a roll of Brand A paper towels costs more than a roll of Brand B paper towels.

    Which one of the following, if true, explains how the statements above can both be true?

    (A) Both Brand A and Brand B towels are manufactured by the same company, which often creates artificial competition for its expensive products.
    (B) A roll of Brand B paper towels is more absorbent than a roll of Brand A paper towels.
    (C) A roll of Brand A paper towels is more absorbent than a roll of Brand B paper towels.
    (D) The cost of a roll of Brand A towels has risen every year for the last five years.
    (E) A roll of Brand A paper towels has more sheets than a roll of Brand B paper towels.

9. State agricultural officials are hoping to save California's $30 billion-a-year fruit industry from destruction by the Mediterranean fruit fly by releasing nearly one billion sterile female fruit flies throughout the state. This has, in the past, been shown to be the only effective means of limiting the spread of this destructive pest, outside of large-scale pesticide spraying.

    Which one of the following best explains the intended effect of the program described above?

    (A) To drastically increase the number of potential mates for the male fruit flies, requiring them to devote more of their energies to mating rather than eating fruit.
    (B) To saturate a given area with fruit flies, creating greater competition for food and thereby containing the damage done by the fruit fly to a smaller area.
    (C) To ensure that a large number of fruit flies in succeeding generations are born infertile.
    (D) To limit the growth of the population by reducing the number of successful matings between fruit flies.
    (E) To encourage overpopulation of the fruit fly in the hopes that nature will correct the situation itself.

10. A fit, well-tuned body is essential to good health because exercise acts to improve circulation and helps to eliminate toxins from the body. If one is to remain healthy, one must get regular exercise.

    Which one of the following conclusions can most logically be drawn from the passage above?

    (A) If one exercises, one will be healthy.
    (B) Only exercise acts to improve the circulation and eliminate toxins from the body.
    (C) A healthy person must have eliminated all toxins from his or her body.
    (D) If one does not exercise regularly, one will not remain healthy.
    (E) A person who is not healthy must not exercise.

GO ON TO THE NEXT PAGE.

11. Marie: I just found out that it is cheaper for me to heat my home with gas or oil than for me to use any of the alternative methods available. I don't understand why environmentalists insist that the cost of fossil fuels is so high.

Louise: That's because you are confusing the price of fossil fuels with their cost. Gas and oil release tremendous amounts of pollution into the water and air, causing great damage to the environment. Not only does this pose a threat to the ecological balance that will affect the quality of life for future generations, but it also causes health problems that may be related to the consumption of these fuels. Once you add in these factors, it is clear that there are many alternatives that are actually cheaper than gas or oil, and consumers should adopt them.

According to her argument above, if an alternative energy source were to be found, under which one of the following conditions would Louise definitely object to its use?

(A) if its price and cost were equal
(B) if its cost were higher than the price of fossil fuels
(C) if its cost were higher than the cost of fossil fuels
(D) if the price of fossil fuels were to fall
(E) if it were less efficient than fossil fuels

12. An office equipment rental firm made the following claim:

Owning your office equipment is actually more expensive than renting it. Over a three-year period, a mid-sized copier, for example, costs $23,000 per year to own, based on the average purchase price of the machine and the cost of its maintenance. The cost of renting a comparable copier is $22,000 per year.

Which one of the following statements, if true, provides the most effective criticism of the argument above?

(A) The average lifespan of a copier is between five and six years.
(B) The figures cited above remain proportionally the same even when more expensive copiers are considered.
(C) The price of copiers actually has decreased in the last ten years.
(D) The price of copier paper and electricity may soon rise sharply.
(E) Buying used copiers can save money, even though such machines need more maintenance.

GO ON TO THE NEXT PAGE.

Questions 13–14

Despite advances in geothermal technology and equipment, experts rarely agree which method is the best indicator of a likely source of oil. Some believe the cycle of environmental changes determines the primary sources for crude oil, while others look to the evolution of organic matter as the most significant indicator. What they do agree on, however, is where oil won't be found. They agree that in areas that were scraped clean of organic sedimentary deposits by glaciers during the last million years or so, the biological "ingredients" that they believe are necessary for the formation of oil and gas are not present. That is, where glaciers have scoured a landmass, oil and gas will not be found.

13. If all of the information above is true, which one of the following can be reasonably inferred?

(A) Geologists understand some of the physical conditions necessary for the formation of deposits of oil.

(B) Scientists leave open the possibility that oil may have been formed during the last million years in some regions that were covered by glaciers during the same period.

(C) Geologists can, with a fairly high degree of accuracy, predict whether an area that meets the necessary preconditions for the formation of oil will, in fact, yield oil.

(D) Geologists can, with a fairly high degree of accuracy, predict whether oil can be found in a particular landmass that was not scoured by glaciers.

(E) If geologists can determine the biological "ingredients" necessary for the formation of oil, they can determine the locations of the most promising oil fields.

14. Which one of the following, if true, would most seriously weaken the geologists' view?

(A) Relatively little of the Earth's surface is known to rest above the sort of organic sedimentary deposits described above.

(B) Despite the existence of permanent glaciers, oil has been found at both the North and South Poles.

(C) There are too many variables involved for experts to be able to identify what does and does not need to be present for the formation of oil.

(D) The glacier theory cannot help locate oil in the ocean since ocean beds went untouched by glaciers.

(E) Oil deposits exist below the crust of the entire Earth, and are brought nearer to the surface by cracks in the crust.

15. Although all societies have some form of class system, there are systems that are based on neither wealth nor power. Still, there is no society that does not divide its population into the privileged and the common.

If the above statements are correct, it can be properly concluded that

(A) making distinctions between haves and have-nots is a part of human nature

(B) there are some people in all cultures who are considered privileged

(C) every society has its own unique hierarchy

(D) privileged people must have money

(E) all societies have a tradition of seeing themselves as either privileged or common

16. One can predict that the number of people in the nation's labor force will diminish in the next 20 years. Population growth in our country reached its apex in 1961, and by the late 1960s there were more employed heads of households in this country than ever before. The growth has slackened significantly, and by 1997 the total number of households will be reduced, thus limiting the number of potential employees in the work force.

Which one of the following, if true, would most seriously damage the conclusion of the above argument?

(A) The urge to acquire wealth contributed to the growth of the labor force in the 1960s.

(B) There will be greater competition among employers to attract employees from a shrinking population base in the 1990s.

(C) In the 1990s there will be more people who are not the heads of household entering the labor force than there were in the 1960s.

(D) Employers fared well in the 1950s with fewer potential employees than exist today.

(E) By 1997 there will be far more people running their own businesses than there are today.

GO ON TO THE NEXT PAGE.

Questions 17–18

A controversy recently erupted at College X after the student newspaper printed several letters to the editor that attacked the college's affirmative action program in offensive, racially charged language. Two psychologists at the school took advantage of the controversy by conducting an experiment on campus. Psychologist #1, posing as a reporter, stopped a student at random, ostensibly to solicit his or her opinion of the controversy. At the same time, psychologist #2, posing as a student, also stopped, joined the discussion, and made the first reply to the questions of the "reporter." The experiment showed that when psychologist #2 expressed support for the racist sentiments expressed in the letters, 75 percent of the subjects responded similarly. When psychologist #2 expressed strong disapproval of the language and substance of the letters, 90 percent of the subjects responded similarly.

17. Which one of the following represents the most reasonable conclusion that can be drawn from the information in the passage above?

   (A) People are more likely to voice their opposition to racism if they hear others doing the same.
   (B) People are less likely to hide their sympathy for certain racist attitudes if they feel that others share the same feelings.
   (C) People's willingness to voice their racist sentiments is proportional to the percentage of all people who share such sentiments.
   (D) People may be influenced by the opinions of others when they express their opinions of racist sentiments.
   (E) The extent to which popular opinion molds the opinions of individuals is significant, though not easily quantifiable.

18. If the psychologists described above were to conclude from their data that some people are more willing to speak up against racism if they hear others doing so, their conclusion would depend on the validity of which one of the following assumptions?

   (A) The students at College X are no more racist than are students at other colleges.
   (B) The students at College X are more likely to have experienced racism personally.
   (C) Some of the subjects in the experiment knew that the psychologists were posing as a reporter and a student.
   (D) Some of the subjects in their experiment would have changed their response to psychologist #1's questions if psychologist #2 had responded differently.
   (E) All of the subjects in the experiment stated their heartfelt, uninfluenced opinion of the incident in question.

19. Evidence seems to indicate that people's faith in some mystical practices increases when these practices offer relief in frightening or challenging situations. One significant piece of evidence is the observation that the use of "healing crystals" is more prevalent among people who suffer from life-threatening diseases such as cancer than it is among people who have minor health problems such as colds or the flu.

Which one of the following, if true, would most seriously weaken the conclusion drawn in the passage above?

   (A) Rapid social change has alienated people and has led to an overall increase in people's adoption of mystical practices.
   (B) Many mystical practices are never used by more than a small number of extremely ill people.
   (C) If someone has a life-threatening disease, he may try nontraditional cures without necessarily believing that they will work.
   (D) Psychics and mediums do not experience a surge in business after the occurrence of earthquakes and plane crashes.
   (E) The use of crystals is one of the most ancient methods utilized for healing.

GO ON TO THE NEXT PAGE.

20. Lithotripsy is a relatively new procedure for the treatment of kidney stones. The patient is suspended in a tub of water and sound waves are aimed at his kidneys. Upon impact, the waves shatter the stones. Recovery time from this procedure is shorter than that of surgery, which is the conventional method of treatment. Lithotripsy is also less expensive than surgery. Therefore, physicians should stop performing invasive surgery for kidney stones soon.

    Which one of the following statements, if true, most seriously weakens the argument in the passage above?

    (A) There has been little research done on the effect of lithotripsy on senior citizens.
    (B) It will be many years before lithotripsy equipment can be produced in sufficient quantity to meet demand.
    (C) Many doctors do not know much about lithotripsy, as it is a relatively new procedure.
    (D) Some insurance companies do not cover treatments such as lithotripsy.
    (E) Lithotripsy is not an available option for children.

21. The human body changes a great deal over the course of a lifetime. As people enter middle age, for instance, they tend to become overweight, regardless of their body type as young adults. Though this weight gain has long been blamed on the tendency of middle-aged people to consume an excess of calories daily, recent evidence suggests that it is instead attributable to the body's decreased demand for calories. This decreased demand means that a maintenance of prior caloric consumption will provide an excess of calories, most of which will simply be stored as body fat.

    A logical critique of the passage above would likely emphasize the fact that the author fails to

    (A) establish definitively the connection between caloric intake and weight gain
    (B) offer any hard evidence of the percentage of middle-aged people who are actually overweight
    (C) give detailed information as to the causes of the body's decreased demand for calories in middle age
    (D) offer a consistent definition of the term "excess" as it relates to caloric consumption
    (E) discuss the causes of obesity in the population at large

22. If a candidate is to win an election easily, that candidate must respond to the electorate's emotional demands—demands that the opponent either does not see or cannot act upon. Though these emotional demands are often not directly articulated by the electorate or by the candidate responding to them, they are an integral part of any landslide victory.

    Which one of the following conclusions can most logically be drawn from the passage above?

    (A) If neither candidate responds to the emotional demands of the electorate, either candidate might win in a landslide.
    (B) If an election was close, the emotional demands of the electorate were conflicting.
    (C) If a candidate responds to the emotional demands of the electorate, that candidate will have a landslide victory.
    (D) An election during which neither candidate responds to the emotional demands of the electorate will not result in a landslide.
    (E) Emotional demands are the only inarticulated issues in an election.

23. Commodities analysts maintain that if the price of soybeans decreases by more than half, the consumer's purchase price for milk produced by livestock fed these soybeans will also decrease by more than half.

    Which one of the following, if true, casts the most doubt on the prediction made by the commodities analysts?

    (A) New genetic strains of livestock and improvements in feed lot procedures have enabled some cows to increase their milk output while decreasing their soybean intake.
    (B) Dairy farmers cannot expand their profit margins any further without compromising the health of their livestock.
    (C) Many different dairy suppliers compete with each other, forcing a consumer-driven market.
    (D) Studies in other dairy-producing countries show that the amount of milk purchased by consumers usually rises after an initial decrease in milk prices.
    (E) Pasteurization and distribution costs, neither of which varies with the price of soybeans, constitute the major portion of the price of milk.

GO ON TO THE NEXT PAGE.

24. The more dairy products a person consumes, the higher his cholesterol level is. More than half of the people in this country eat in excess of four dairy products each day, whereas in Germany the figure is only 10 percent. Accordingly, more than 65 percent of the people in this country have cholesterol levels that are considered too high and only 2 percent of Germans have similarly excessive levels. Therefore, if the cholesterol levels of Americans are to be brought down, we must eat fewer dairy products.

Which one of the following, if established, could strengthen the author's argument?

(A) Citizens of the United States are less concerned with cholesterol levels than citizens of Germany.

(B) Germans are more disciplined about watching their diets than Americans.

(C) People who are concerned about their cholesterol levels will eat fewer dairy products.

(D) A person's cholesterol level is reduced significantly when he or she consumes fewer than two dairy products per day.

(E) Dairy products, and not any other food items, are the critical factors in determining cholesterol levels.

25. The introduction of new technologies and equipment into the marketplace can significantly alter the quality of life for the members of a society. The automatic dishwasher, for example, eased the housekeeping burdens traditionally borne by women. At the same time, the convenience of an automatic dishwasher has fostered a dependence upon its time-saving qualities. It has become increasingly difficult to find a household with an automatic dishwasher where small numbers of dishes are washed by hand. In the long run, the environmental cost of such behavior is scarcely worth the amount of time saved.

Which one of the following principles is best illustrated by the example presented in the passage?

(A) The significance of a benefit should be weighed in terms of its overall effect.

(B) People should make a unified effort to reduce their negative impact upon the environment.

(C) Some new technologies offer no perceptible benefit to society.

(D) The acquisition of leisure time is not worth the destruction of the biosphere.

(E) Most new machinery makes our lives more streamlined and economical.

S T O P

IF YOU FINISH BEFORE TIME IS CALLED, YOU MAY CHECK YOUR WORK ON THIS SECTION ONLY.
DO NOT WORK ON ANY OTHER SECTION IN THE TEST.

SECTION III

Time—35 minutes

25 Questions

Directions: The questions in this section are based on the reasoning contained in brief statements or passages. For some questions, more than one of the choices could conceivably answer the question. However, you are to choose the best answer; that is, the response that most accurately and completely answers the question. You should not make assumptions that are by common sense standards implausible, superfluous, or incompatible with the passage. After you have chosen the best answer, blacken the corresponding space on your answer sheet.

1. Senator: For economic issues, I base my responses on logic. For political issues, I base my responses either on logic or gut instinct. For moral issues, I never base my responses on logic.

    Which one of the following can be correctly inferred from the statements above ?

    (A) If the senator relies on logic, he may be responding to a moral issue.
    (B) If the senator relies on logic, he is not responding to an economic issue.
    (C) If the senator does not rely on logic, he is responding to a political issue.
    (D) If the senator does not rely on logic, he must be responding to an economic issue.
    (E) If the senator does not rely on logic, he might be responding to a political issue.

2. Concern about the environmental and health problems associated with nuclear energy has compelled activist groups to join forces in an attempt to shut down nuclear power plants. However, a survey of nuclear power plants across the United States showed that there have only been two accidents in the past ten years, both minor in nature, and in both cases, the danger was quickly contained. If the United States is to produce enough energy to become completely independent from foreign sources of energy, more nuclear power plants must be built, and the misinformation being distributed by activist groups must be countered by the statistics found in the study.

    All of the following are assumptions of the above argument EXCEPT:

    (A) Using nuclear power is the only way for the United States to produce enough energy that no fuel needs to be imported.
    (B) Some people think nuclear power plants are dangerous.
    (C) The accidents caused little harm.
    (D) Other methods of producing energy are also considered dangerous.
    (E) The United States needs to be completely self-sufficient in the production of energy.

3. Rather than learn about Senate hearings by listening to word-of-mouth accounts or by sitting in on the sessions themselves, people now depend mainly on newspapers and television for information about important investigative and confirmation hearings conducted by Senate committees. Thus, the media serve as a surrogate for the millions of people who care deeply about such proceedings but could never attend them themselves.

    The above passage is most likely part of an argument in favor of

    (A) reserving more seats for ordinary citizens at important Senate hearings
    (B) imposing secrecy rules on the Senate committee hearings not already covered by the media
    (C) expanding media coverage of important Senate hearings
    (D) enacting a law that would prohibit any censorship of press coverage of the Senate
    (E) widening the scope of Senate inquiry of press censorship

GO ON TO THE NEXT PAGE.

4. Advertisement: Professional exterminators will tell you that in order to rid your home of roaches, you must do more than kill all the roaches you see. This is why the system that professional exterminators use most includes a poison that inhibits the development of roach eggs already laid, as well as a chemical that kills all adult roaches. This same combination is now available to the nonprofessional in new Extirm. When you're ready to get rid of roaches once and for all, get Extirm in your corner.

All of the following are implied by the advertisement above EXCEPT:

(A) Professional exterminators asked about roach extermination recommended Extirm.
(B) Extirm contains a chemical that inhibits the development of roach eggs.
(C) More than one chemical is required to rid a home of roaches.
(D) Inhibiting the development of roach eggs may not eliminate roaches from the home.
(E) Roaches reproduce by laying eggs.

5. In congressional hearings the question arises: "Which side knows best the potential benefits and dangers involved in the drilling of new offshore oil wells within U.S. territorial waters?" Oil companies' advice must certainly be taken with a grain of salt, since they are concerned only with profit and will oppose any legislation that would reduce such profit. Environmentalists' dire warnings must also be questioned, since many environmentalists' opposition to such drilling is purely reflexive, and without basis in scientific fact. This is why, in order to understand fully the costs and benefits that must be weighed in deciding whether to drill oil wells in U.S. coastal waters, Congress should rely primarily on the advice of academic research geologists, who are both informed and objective on the issue.

Which one of the following, if true, would most seriously weaken the author's conclusion in the passage above?

(A) Environmentalists are more knowledgeable about the dangers associated with drilling oil wells than is the average congressperson.
(B) Most academic research geologists rely heavily on income earned from consulting fees paid by oil companies.
(C) Oil companies have responded to public outcry over environmental damage caused by offshore oil drilling by developing technology that makes offshore oil drilling much safer than it used to be.
(D) The oil industry lobby is responsible each year for significant campaign contributions to legislators.
(E) Academic research geologists are not unanimous in their support of or opposition to new offshore oil drilling in U.S. coastal waters.

GO ON TO THE NEXT PAGE.

Questions 6–7

Throughout the twentieth century, anthropologists studying the myths and ceremonies of a particular group indigenous to the Amazon rain forest in Brazil have maintained that their presence and the questions they asked were not influencing the group's culture. Researchers now note, however, that the earliest recorded observations, made in 1919, of the group's ceremonies marking the onset of the rainy season made no reference to a creation myth. The first mention of a creation myth's appearance in the ceremony is found in 1933, and by 1986, nearly twenty minutes of the seventy-minute ceremony were devoted to a myth explaining the rains in relation to a "First Great Storm," during which the world was supposed to have been created.

6.   Which one of the following is most strongly implied by the argument above?

   (A)   The observations of the ceremonies in 1919 were either incomplete or inaccurate.
   (B)   After the anthropologists explained the importance of creation myths to their subjects, the group developed myths of its own.
   (C)   The anthropologists' interests in particular cultural beliefs, such as creation myths, may have induced a gradual change in the group's ceremonies.
   (D)   If the anthropologists had been more conscientious, their records would not reflect apparent discrepancies in their accounts of the group's beliefs.
   (E)   The subjects of study, trying to secure the benefits of the industrial world enjoyed by anthropologists, changed their ceremonies to correspond to the ideas of the anthropologists.

7.   Which one of the following represents an illustration of the same phenomenon that the author describes in the passage above?

   (A)   A sociologist notes that a wave of immigration invariably results in changes in some religious practices of the dominant culture.
   (B)   A psychologist discovers that patients who originally reported few or no dreams consistently acknowledge frequent and vivid dreams after eight months of dream-analysis therapy.
   (C)   An economist studying a Third World country finds an increasing reliance on Western technology rather than on indigenous agricultural methods.
   (D)   An astronomer, using two different telescopes to measure the distance to a nearby star, gets two different results.
   (E)   An historian of religion finds that the creation myths of several cultures have changed over time.

GO ON TO THE NEXT PAGE.

8. Mayor: An across-the-board increase of just twenty cents on all the city's toll bridges and tunnels would raise close to a hundred thousand dollars a year at the current bridge and tunnel traffic levels. Because a toll increase of three dollars would therefore raise more than a million dollars a year, such an increase seems like the ideal solution to our persistent school-budget shortfalls. The toll increase would offer further savings by lessening the volume of traffic over our bridges and tunnels, which would result in reduced maintenance costs for those structures.

Which one of the following identifies most accurately the error in the mayor's reasoning?

(A) She incorrectly assumes that two different causes are necessarily related.
(B) She bases her argument on erroneous figures for the current traffic flow.
(C) She makes assumptions that are mutually exclusive.
(D) She takes as a given what should instead first be established as evidence.
(E) She bases her argument on political considerations rather than logical analysis.

9. Dale: The city can't possibly have budget problems this quarter because of the heavier than normal snows this winter. A recent article mentioned that Haline, a substance used to de-ice roads and sidewalks, costs three cents a pound, which is quite cheap considering how effective it is.

Glenn: In actuality the cost of Haline is closer to eighty cents a pound. When you factor in the destructive effect of Haline on the infrastructure, and its deleterious effects on groundwater and vegetation, the cost of Haline clearly exceeds its price.

If a substance performs as effectively as Haline and has no harmful side effects (but its price is higher than that of Haline), Glenn would be most likely to oppose its use if

(A) its price fluctuates seasonally
(B) its price and its cost are similar
(C) it must be handled in the same manner as Haline
(D) its cost is higher than the price of Haline
(E) its price is higher than the cost of Haline

10. Since mandatory water conservation measures were enacted by the state of California in response to the drought of 1990–1992, water consumption in the state has increased by nearly 10 percent. Clearly, the state's water conservation measures have been counterproductive, and California's water situation is more dire now than it was in 1992, the year of the last drought.

All of the following facts, if true, would be useful in evaluating the validity of the argument above EXCEPT:

(A) The population of California has increased by 15 percent since 1992.
(B) The average California resident now uses less water on an annual basis than he or she did in 1992.
(C) The water conservation measures did not apply to agricultural usage.
(D) In accordance with the conservation measures, nonessential water use in private homes has declined by 50 percent since 1992.
(E) In the years since 1992, water collection technology has developed to such a point that state and municipal water districts have an increased capacity to gather and store water.

GO ON TO THE NEXT PAGE.

11. Netta: A recent study revealed that while the overall
          crime rate has gone down, crimes committed by
          youths have increased dramatically. The irony
          is that our own judicial system is fostering this
          situation. By treating young people who
          commit crimes less severely than adults who
          commit similar crimes, the courts allow these
          young criminals to go free, and they then
          commit more crimes. The message that "crime
          is wrong, but not as bad if you're not of age" is
          being communicated. A person who is
          convicted of a crime should be sufficiently
          punished regardless of age, otherwise the
          number of crimes committed by youths will
          continue to increase.

     Trey: Netta, you are being extremely shortsighted.
          The alternative to allowing young criminals to
          go free is incarcerating them in a youth facility
          or penitentiary. But sociologists have found that
          the social environment in such facilities
          encourages and condones delinquent behavior
          within the facility, and by extension, outside the
          facility. When the youth returns to society after
          having been incarcerated for even a short
          period, recidivism occurs within three to four
          weeks.

     The point at issue between Netta and Trey is

     (A) the extent to which the judicial system is
          contributing to the increase in the crime rate
     (B) whether the leniency shown towards
          adolescents can be cited as the sole cause of
          the increase in crimes committed by young
          people
     (C) what types of judicial reform could affect the
          rise in youth crime
     (D) how most effectively to stop the increase in
          crime by examining which cause is most often
          to blame
     (E) whether incarceration as an alternative to
          leniency for convicted youths will in fact help
          to solve the problem

12. Computer Technician: This system has either a
          software problem or a hardware problem. None
          of the available diagnostic tests has been able to
          determine where the problem lies. The software
          can be replaced, but the hardware cannot be
          altered in any way, which means that if the
          problem lies in the hardware, the entire system
          will have to be scrapped. We must begin work
          to solve the problem by presupposing that the
          problem is with the software.

     On which one of the following principles could the
     technician's reasoning be based?

     (A) In fixing a problem that has two possible
          causes, it makes more sense to deal with both
          causes rather than spend time trying to
          determine which is the actual cause of the
          problem.
     (B) If events outside one's control bear on a
          decision, the best course of action is to assume
          the "worst-case" scenario.
     (C) When the soundness of an approach depends on
          the validity of an assumption, one's first task
          must be to test that assumption's validity.
     (D) When circumstances must be favorable in order
          for a strategy to succeed, the strategy must be
          based on the assumption that conditions are
          indeed favorable until proved otherwise.
     (E) When only one strategy can be successful, the
          circumstances affecting that strategy must be
          altered so that strategy may be employed.

GO ON TO THE NEXT PAGE.

13. To become a master at chess, a person must play. If a person plays for at least four hours a day, that person will inevitably become a master of the game. Thus, if a person is a master at the game of chess, that person must have played each day for at least four hours.

The error in the logic of the argument above is most accurately described by which one of the following?

(A) The conclusion is inadequate because it fails to acknowledge that people who play for four hours each day might not develop a degree of skill for the game that others view as masterful.

(B) The conclusion is inadequate because it fails to acknowledge that playing one hour a day might be sufficient for some people to become masters.

(C) The conclusion is inadequate because it fails to acknowledge that if a person has not played four hours a day, that person has not become a master.

(D) The conclusion is inadequate because it fails to acknowledge that four hours of playing time each day is not a strategy recommended by any world-champion chess players.

(E) The conclusion is inadequate because it fails to acknowledge that most people are not in a position to devote four hours each day to playing chess.

14. Libraries are eliminating many subscriptions to highly specialized periodicals due to budget cuts. Yet without these reference materials, many subjects cannot be researched effectively. Therefore, efforts must be made to provide better funding so as to ensure the maintenance of at least those periodicals that will be most used by researchers in the future.

Which one of the following can be inferred from the author's argument for the maintenance of funding for the periodicals?

(A) If a periodical is highly specialized, the maintenance of its subscription is more important than any financial considerations.

(B) Research performed with periodicals is not a valid consideration in determining funding.

(C) Research should be the focus of a library's funding.

(D) It can be predicted which periodicals will be of value for researchers in the future.

(E) The elimination of periodicals is simply an inevitable part of library organization.

15. Last year, Marcel enjoyed a high income from exactly two places: his sporting goods store and his stock market investments. Although Marcel earns far more from his store than from his investments, the money he earns from the stock market is an important part of his income. Because of a series of drops in the stock market, Marcel will not earn as much from his investments this year. It follows then that Marcel will make less money this year than he did last year.

Which one of the following is an assumption necessary to the author's argument?

(A) Increased profits at Marcel's sporting goods store will not offset any loss in stock market income.

(B) Sporting goods stores earn lower profits when the stock market drops.

(C) Drops in the stock market do not always affect all of a particular investor's stocks.

(D) Marcel's stock market investments will be subject to increased volatility.

(E) If his income is lower, Marcel will not be able to meet his expenses.

GO ON TO THE NEXT PAGE.

16. **Johanna:** Quinto admits that because of his governmental post he can select which companies are awarded municipal contracts. He further admits that he awarded a contract to a company owned by a member of the town council who offered to support Quinto in his mayoral bid in exchange for the contract. There is no excuse for this kind of unethical behavior.

Iya: I don't see his actions as unethical. The company awarded the contract is known to produce the highest quality work at a comparatively competitive price. So in getting support for his mayoral bid, Quinto has ensured the city will get quality work, and thus has saved the taxpayers thousands of dollars.

Iya disagrees with Johanna by

(A) insisting that ethical behavior can only be viewed in the context in which it takes place
(B) countering that the result of Quinto's actions determines whether those activities are ethical
(C) comparing Quinto's actions to the actions of the company and finding both behaviors to be ethical
(D) applying a different definition of the word "ethical" to two situations
(E) defining ethical behavior as being formed by personal, religious, or spiritual philosophies

17. One of the criticisms of recent political campaigns is that the candidate with the greater financial resources usually wins. A long presidential election campaign is more equitable than is the quick and expedient process recommended by some. A longer campaign, however, decreases the likelihood that a candidate with tremendous resources can control the campaign through a barrage of high-priced media campaigns. In a long campaign, a candidate is forced to speak substantively on the issues, and the voters have more complete access to the candidate. Thus, a long campaign creates parity among candidates who may not be equally financed by permitting the less popular, less well-funded candidates to invest time rather than money in their campaigns, thereby gaining recognition for themselves through the use of speeches, debates, and other media-oriented forums.

Which one of the following statements most seriously weakens the argument made above in favor of long presidential campaigns?

(A) Voters who lose interest during a long campaign are less likely to show up at the polls, thus contributing to the already significant problem of voter apathy.
(B) A long campaign requires candidates to divide their attention between public matters and the needs of their parties.
(C) A long campaign weakens the general public's interest in the process of global democracy.
(D) Candidates depend on volunteers, whose sense of commitment is frayed by a long campaign.
(E) A long campaign precludes participation by many able candidates who cannot afford to take time off from their private occupations for extended lengths of time.

GO ON TO THE NEXT PAGE.

18. Some botanists have found it extremely difficult to save certain species of elm tree from fungal infection. Even the most potent fungicide has been unsuccessful in preventing its growth on such trees. However, researchers have managed to control the growth and spread of the fungus by spraying the fungus with a 0.2% saline solution.

Which one of the following, if true, offers the strongest explanation as to why the saline spray has been successful?

(A) The cell walls of the fungus cannot filter out the salt compounds, which, once inside the cell, interfere with reproduction.

(B) The presence of salt creates an electrolyte imbalance within living cells, ultimately killing each cell it comes in contact with.

(C) When salt is used in combination with strong fungicide, the fungicide becomes potent enough to kill any fungus.

(D) It has been on record that farmers have used salt to kill destructive plant fungi since the late eighteenth century.

(E) Fungicides have generally been unsuccessful because any fungicide strong enough to destroy a fungus would be strong enough to destroy the roots as well.

19. In concluding that there has been a shift in the sense of parental responsibility in America since the 1960s, researchers point to the increase in the frequency with which fathers tend to the daily needs of their children. However, this increase cannot be attributed exclusively to a shift in parental mores, for during the same period there has been an increase in the percentage of mothers who have jobs. With this in mind, the increased participation of fathers in child-rearing may well be only a symptom of a more fundamental change in society.

The author of the passage criticizes the conclusion of the researchers by

(A) offering a clearer definition of the researchers' premises, thereby compromising their argument

(B) attacking the integrity of the researchers rather than their reasoning

(C) showing that the researchers have reversed cause and effect in making their argument

(D) pointing out that their criteria for "parental responsibility" are not a logical basis for their argument

(E) suggesting an alternative cause for the effect cited by the researchers

GO ON TO THE NEXT PAGE.

Questions 20–21

Upon exiting an exhibit, some visitors to art museums find it difficult to describe what it was that they liked and didn't like about the paintings. Yet since these visitors feel strongly about which art they believed to be good and which art they believed to be bad, appreciating a work of art obviously does not require the ability to articulate what, specifically, was perceived to be good or bad.

20. The argument above assumes which one of the following?

    (A) The fact that some people find it difficult to articulate what they like about a work of art does not mean that no one can.
    (B) If an individual feels strongly about a work of art, then he or she is capable of appreciating that work of art.
    (C) The vocabulary of visual art is not a part of common knowledge, but rather is known only to those who study the arts.
    (D) When a person can articulate what he or she likes about a particular painting, he or she is able to appreciate that work of art.
    (E) Paintings can be discussed only in general terms of good and bad.

21. According to the passage above, all of the following could be true EXCEPT:

    (A) Some museum visitors can explain with great precision what they liked and didn't like about a certain painting.
    (B) If a person studies art, then that person will be able to articulate her opinion about paintings.
    (C) If a person can't say why she likes a piece of art, it doesn't necessarily mean that she doesn't appreciate that piece.
    (D) Some visitors can explain what they liked about a piece, but are unable to explain what they didn't like.
    (E) The inability to articulate always indicates the inability to appreciate.

22. Evan: Earlier this year, the *Stockton Free Press* reported that residents consider Mayor Dalton more concerned with his image than with advancing the cause of the less fortunate of Stockton.

    Dalia: But the mayor appointed a new director of the public television station, and almost immediately the station began running a documentary series promoting the mayor's antipoverty program.

    Evan: Clearly the mayor has, by this appointment, attempted to manipulate public opinion through the media.

    Evan's second statement counters Dalia's argument by

    (A) disputing the relevancy of her statement
    (B) suggesting that Dalia is less informed about the issue than he
    (C) confusing the argument she presents with his own
    (D) appealing to popular opinion that the mayor should not misuse his access to the media
    (E) claiming that Dalia's argument is an example that actually strengthens his own argument

GO ON TO THE NEXT PAGE.

23. Naturalist: Every year, thousands of animals already on the endangered species list are killed for their hides, furs, or horns. These illegal and often cruel deaths serve to push these species further toward the brink of extinction. The products made from these animals, such as articles of clothing and quack medical remedies, are goods no one really needs. What is needed is a large-scale media campaign to make the facts of the killings known and lessen the demand for these animal products. Such a campaign would be a good start in the effort to save endangered species from extinction.

Environmentalist: For the overwhelming majority of currently endangered species, the true threat of extinction comes not from hunting and poaching, but from continually shrinking habitats. Concentrating attention on the dangers of poaching for a very few high-visibility species would be counterproductive, leading people to believe that a boycott of a few frivolous items is enough to protect endangered species, when what is needed is a truly global environmental policy.

The point at issue between the naturalist and the environmentalist is which one of the following?

(A) whether the poaching of some endangered species actually increases that species' chances of becoming extinct

(B) whether a large-scale media campaign can affect the demand for some products

(C) whether more endangered species are threatened by poaching and hunting or shrinking of habitat

(D) whether some species could be saved from extinction by eliminating all commercial demand for that species

(E) whether a large-scale media campaign that lessens the demand for products made from endangered species is a good strategy for saving endangered species

24. Deborah: If one-third of the people who do not recycle would start recycling their paper products, approximately 150,000 fewer trees would be destroyed each year.

Lee: That is unlikely. It would then follow that in the next ten years, the forests will increase by more than 1.5 million trees, more than there is room for.

Which one of the following statements could Deborah offer Lee to clarify her own position and address the point that Lee makes?

(A) It is possible for forests to increase by 150,000 trees per year if the growth rate of the previous year was unusually low.

(B) The 150,000 trees that are saved would still be subject to forest fires and other destructive natural phenomena.

(C) If the number of recyclers was increased by more than a third, the number of trees saved would be more than 150,000.

(D) Any prediction of tree growth always presumes a constant growth and death rate.

(E) For the number of nonrecyclers to be reduced by a third, the number of recycling materials, special recyclable trash bins, for example, would have to be increased by much more than a third.

GO ON TO THE NEXT PAGE.

25. Adoption Agent: Although my view runs counter to the trend in public sentiment, I believe a proposed new law granting adoptive parents access to the birth records of children to be adopted should not be passed. My experience as an adoption agent has supplied me with two reasons for holding this view. First, granting adoptive parents access to the records will result in wasted hours on the part of the adoption agency employees, who will be forced to spend time finding and subsequently returning files, when that time could be better spent out in the field. Second, based upon my agency experience, no adoptive parents are going to request the children's records anyway.

Which one of the following, if true, establishes that the adoption agent's second reason does not negate the first?

(A)   The new law would necessitate that adoption agents, when reviewing the adoption agreement with prospective adoptive parents, have at hand the birth record of the child to be adopted, not simply have access to them.

(B)   The task of retrieving and explaining birth records would fall to the least experienced member of the adoption agency's staff.

(C)   Any children who asked to see their birth records would also insist on having details they did not understand explained to them.

(D)   The new law does not exclude adoption agencies from charging adoptive parents for extra expenses incurred in order to comply with the new law.

(E)   Some adoption agencies have always had a policy of allowing children access to their birth records, but none of those agency's children took advantage of that policy.

S T O P

IF YOU FINISH BEFORE TIME IS CALLED, YOU MAY CHECK YOUR WORK ON THIS SECTION ONLY.
DO NOT WORK ON ANY OTHER SECTION IN THE TEST.

SECTION IV

Time—35 minutes

24 Questions

Directions: Each group of questions in this section is based on a set of conditions. In answering some of the questions, it may be useful to draw a rough diagram. Choose the response that most accurately and completely answers each question and blacken the corresponding space on your answer sheet.

Questions 1–6

A bakery is making exactly three birthday cakes: A, B, and C. Each cake is to be composed of two different layers, a top layer and a bottom layer, consistent with the following guidelines:
   Each layer is exactly one of the following flavors: vanilla, chocolate, strawberry, or lemon.
   For each cake, the flavor of the top layer is different from that of the bottom layer.
   Of the three cakes, no two bottom layers are the same flavor.
   Of the three cakes, no two top layers are the same flavor.
   Exactly one top layer is strawberry.
   In cake C, either the top layer or the bottom layer, but not both, is vanilla.
   The top layer of cake B is chocolate.
   None of the bottom layers is chocolate.

1. If the top layer of cake C is strawberry, then which one of the following statements must be true?

   (A)   The top layer of cake A is vanilla.
   (B)   The top layer of cake A is lemon.
   (C)   The bottom layer of cake A is strawberry.
   (D)   The bottom layer of cake B is lemon.
   (E)   The bottom layer of cake C is vanilla.

2. If the bottom layer of cake B is vanilla, then which one of the following statements must be true?

   (A)   The bottom layer of cake C is strawberry.
   (B)   The top layer of cake C is strawberry.
   (C)   The bottom layer of cake A is strawberry.
   (D)   The bottom layer of cake C is vanilla.
   (E)   The bottom layer of cake C is lemon.

3. Which one of the following statements could be true?

   (A)   No top layer of any cake is vanilla.
   (B)   No bottom layer of any cake is vanilla.
   (C)   Only cake B has a strawberry layer.
   (D)   Of the three cakes, one top layer is vanilla and one top layer is lemon.
   (E)   The top layer of cake B is the same flavor as the bottom layer of cake A.

4. Which one of the following statements could be true?

   (A)   Both the top layer of cake A and the bottom layer of cake B are vanilla.
   (B)   Both the top layer of cake A and the bottom layer of cake B are lemon.
   (C)   Both the top layer of cake A and the bottom layer of cake C are lemon.
   (D)   The top layer of cake A is vanilla, and the bottom layer of cake C is strawberry.
   (E)   The top layer of cake C is lemon, and the bottom layer of cake A is strawberry.

5. If the bottom layer of cake C is lemon, then each of the following statements must be true EXCEPT:

   (A)   One top layer is vanilla.
   (B)   One layer of cake A is strawberry.
   (C)   One layer of cake B is strawberry.
   (D)   Two of the six layers are strawberry.
   (E)   Two of the six layers are lemon.

6. Suppose that none of the layers is chocolate. If all of the other conditions remain the same, then which one of the following statements could be true?

   (A)   None of the top layers is vanilla.
   (B)   None of the bottom layers is vanilla.
   (C)   Cake B has no vanilla layer.
   (D)   Neither cake A nor cake B has a lemon layer.
   (E)   Neither cake B nor cake C has a strawberry layer.

GO ON TO THE NEXT PAGE.

Questions 7–11

An independent automobile magazine is trying to determine the four best-selling automobiles from among J, K, L, M, N, P. The information that follows is available:

There are no ties among the cars.
Each car is either a sports car or a luxury car, but not both.
Two of the six cars are imported and four are domestic.
Both imported cars are among the four best-sellers, exactly one of which is a luxury car.
Exactly one luxury car is among the four best-selling.
Cars J and L sold better than car M, and car M sold better than cars K and N.
Cars J and L are sports cars.
Cars M and P are luxury cars.

7. Which of the following is a complete and accurate list of the cars that can be sports cars?

   (A) J, K
   (B) J, L
   (C) J, K, L
   (D) J, L, N
   (E) J, K, L, N

8. Which of the following cars must be a domestic car?

   (A) Car J
   (B) Car L
   (C) Car M
   (D) Car N
   (E) Car P

9. Which of the following could be false?

   (A) Car J had higher sales than L.
   (B) Car J had higher sales than N.
   (C) Car L had higher sales than P.
   (D) Car L had higher sales than N.
   (E) Car M had higher sales than P.

10. If car K is imported, which of the following can be false?

   (A) Car J is domestic.
   (B) Car L is domestic.
   (C) Car K is the fourth best-seller.
   (D) Car K is a sports car.
   (E) Car N is a sports car.

11. If car N is the fourth best-selling car, which of the following must be true?

   (A) Car J is domestic.
   (B) Car K is domestic.
   (C) Car N is domestic.
   (D) Car K is luxury.
   (E) Car N is luxury.

GO ON TO THE NEXT PAGE.

Questions 12–18

In a certain computer language, an acceptable sequence of five words forms a command. A command must meet the following requirements:

Each word must contain at least five letters, no more than two of which can be vowels (a, e, i, o, u).

A word may not begin with c, o, or y.

The first letters of the five words of a command must be in consecutive alphabetical order.

12. Which one of the following is an acceptable command?

   (A) ankle, baker, dentist, enter, finger
   (B) jingle, killer, lentil, metal, nicer
   (C) nexus, optic, paint, quince, raked
   (D) oafish, plate, quake, ringer, table
   (E) single, taker, soaked, under, venture

13. If the third word in a command is "hinder," the first letter of the first word and the first letter of the last word of that command, respectively, must be

   (A) c, g
   (B) d, k
   (C) e, j
   (D) f, j
   (E) g, l

14. The last word in a command CANNOT begin with the letter

   (A) j
   (B) n
   (C) r
   (D) t
   (E) u

15. The first word in a command CANNOT begin with the letter

   (A) f
   (B) h
   (C) r
   (D) t
   (E) u

16. Which one of the following is an acceptable word with which a command can begin?

   (A) apple
   (B) major
   (C) quint
   (D) uncle
   (E) white

17. If "xenon" is the last word in a command, it is possible for the first word in that command to be

   (A) tailor
   (B) talk
   (C) treacle
   (D) tale
   (E) tactic

18. Each of the following could be the last word in a command EXCEPT

   (A) hamper
   (B) jumble
   (C) scatter
   (D) tamper
   (E) units

GO ON TO THE NEXT PAGE.

Questions 19–24

A florist is arranging eight flowers—A, B, C, F, G, J, K, and L—in the shape of a circle as shown:

The following is known about the arrangement of the flowers:

A, B, and C are lilies; F and G are mums; J, K, and L are irises.

The lilies must all be next to each other.

The irises must all be next to each other.

No lily can be next to an iris.

Flower 5 is F.

Flower 2 is A.

If F is next to J, then F cannot also be next to C.

19. Which one of the following flowers could be flower 3?

 (A) L
 (B) K
 (C) J
 (D) F
 (E) C

20. Each one of the following statements must be true EXCEPT:

 (A) Flower 1 is an iris.
 (B) Flower 3 is a lily.
 (C) Flower 7 is an iris.
 (D) Flower 4 is a lily.
 (E) Flower 8 is an iris.

21. Which one of the following flowers must be next to A?

 (A) B
 (B) C
 (C) F
 (D) G
 (E) J

22. If L is flower 8, and K is next to L, which one of the following statements must be true?

 (A) A is directly to the left of B.
 (B) B is directly to the right of G.
 (C) G is directly across from J.
 (D) J is directly across from A.
 (E) L is directly across from A.

23. If K is flower 8, then which one of the following pairs of flowers could NOT be directly across from each other?

 (A) B and J
 (B) B and K
 (C) B and L
 (D) C and J
 (E) C and L

24. If K is flower 8 and C is flower 3, then each of the following is a pair of flowers that must be next to each other EXCEPT

 (A) A and C
 (B) B and F
 (C) F and J
 (D) G and K
 (E) J and L

S T O P

IF YOU FINISH BEFORE TIME IS CALLED, YOU MAY CHECK YOUR WORK ON THIS SECTION ONLY.
DO NOT WORK ON ANY OTHER SECTION IN THE TEST.

THE PRINCETON REVIEW

1. YOUR NAME:
(Print)   Last   First   M.I.

SIGNATURE: _____   DATE: ___ / ___ / ___

HOME ADDRESS: _____
(Print)   Number

_____
City   State   Zip Code

PHONE NO.: _____
(Print)

IMPORTANT: Please fill in these boxes exactly as shown on the back cover of your test book.

2. TEST

_____

6. DATE OF

Month	Day	Year
○ JAN		
○ FEB		
○ MAR	○ ○	○ ○
○ APR	○ ○	○ ○
○ MAY	○ ○	○ ○
○ JUN	○ ○	○ ○
○ JUL	○ ○	○ ○
○ AUG	○ ○	○ ○
○ SEP	○ ○	○ ○
○ OCT	○ ○	○ ○
○ NOV	○ ○	○ ○
○ DEC		

3. TEST CODE   4. REGISTRATION

7. SEX

○ MALE
○ FEMALE

THE PRINCETON REVIEW

© 1996 Princeton Review L.L.C.
FORM NO. 00001-PR

5. YOUR NAME

| First 4 letters of last name | | | | FIRST INIT | MID INIT |

(bubble grid A–Z)

Section 1

Start with number 1 for each new section.
If a section has fewer questions than answer spaces, leave the extra answer spaces blank.

Column 1
1. A B C D E
2. A B C D E
3. A B C D E
4. A B C D E
5. A B C D E
6. A B C D E
7. A B C D E
8. A B C D E
9. A B C D E
10. A B C D E
11. A B C D E
12. A B C D E
13. A B C D E
14. A B C D E
15. A B C D E
16. A B C D E
17. A B C D E
18. A B C D E
19. A B C D E
20. A B C D E
21. A B C D E
22. A B C D E
23. A B C D E
24. A B C D E
25. A B C D E
26. A B C D E
27. A B C D E
28. A B C D E
29. A B C D E
30. A B C D E

Column 2
1. A B C D E
2. A B C D E
3. A B C D E
4. A B C D E
5. A B C D E
6. A B C D E
7. A B C D E
8. A B C D E
9. A B C D E
10. A B C D E
11. A B C D E
12. A B C D E
13. A B C D E
14. A B C D E
15. A B C D E
16. A B C D E
17. A B C D E
18. A B C D E
19. A B C D E
20. A B C D E
21. A B C D E
22. A B C D E
23. A B C D E
24. A B C D E
25. A B C D E
26. A B C D E
27. A B C D E
28. A B C D E
29. A B C D E
30. A B C D E

Column 3
1. A B C D E
2. A B C D E
3. A B C D E
4. A B C D E
5. A B C D E
6. A B C D E
7. A B C D E
8. A B C D E
9. A B C D E
10. A B C D E
11. A B C D E
12. A B C D E
13. A B C D E
14. A B C D E
15. A B C D E
16. A B C D E
17. A B C D E
18. A B C D E
19. A B C D E
20. A B C D E
21. A B C D E
22. A B C D E
23. A B C D E
24. A B C D E
25. A B C D E
26. A B C D E
27. A B C D E
28. A B C D E
29. A B C D E
30. A B C D E

Column 4
1. A B C D E
2. A B C D E
3. A B C D E
4. A B C D E
5. A B C D E
6. A B C D E
7. A B C D E
8. A B C D E
9. A B C D E
10. A B C D E
11. A B C D E
12. A B C D E
13. A B C D E
14. A B C D E
15. A B C D E
16. A B C D E
17. A B C D E
18. A B C D E
19. A B C D E
20. A B C D E
21. A B C D E
22. A B C D E
23. A B C D E
24. A B C D E
25. A B C D E
26. A B C D E
27. A B C D E
28. A B C D E
29. A B C D E
30. A B C D E

2
1   14   cont
23

14⌐ Para   ⌈21 — Para
20.5   ⌊16

10   16

Computing Your Score

Directions

1. Use the Answer Key on the next page to check your answers.

2. Use the Scoring Worksheet below to compute your raw score.

3. Use the Score Conversion Chart to convert your raw score into the 120–180 LSAT scale.

Your scaled score on this virtual test is for general guidance only.

Scores obtained by using the Score Conversion Chart can only approximate the score you would receive if this virtual test were an actual LSAT. Your score on an actual LSAT may differ from the score obtained on this virtual test.

In an actual test, final scores are computed using an equating method that makes scores earned on different editions of the LSAT comparable to one another. This virtual test has been constructed to reflect an actual LSAT as closely as possible, and the conversion of raw scores to the LSAT scale has been approximated.

What this means is that the Conversion Chart reflects only an estimate of how raw scores would translate into final LSAT scores. Your score on an actual LSAT may differ from the score range obtained on this virtual test.

Scoring Worksheet

1. Enter the number of questions you answered correctly in each section.

	Number Correct
Section I	19
Section II	21
Section III	16
Section IV	16

2. Enter the sum here: 72

This is your raw score.

SCORE CONVERSION CHART

For Converting Raw Scores to the 120–180 LSAT Scaled Score

Reported Score	Raw Score Lowest	Raw Score Highest
180	99	101
179	—*	—*
178	98	98
177	97	97
176	96	96
175	95	95
174	94	94
173	93	93
172	92	92
171	91	91
170	90	90
169	89	89
168	88	88
167	86	87
166	85	85
165	84	84
164	82	83
163	81	81
162	79	80
161	77	78
160	76	76
159	74	75
158	72	73
157	71	71
156	69	70
155	67	68
154	65	66
153	63	64
152	61	62
151	59	60
150	58	58
149	56	57
148	54	55
147	52	53
146	50	51
145	48	49
144	46	47
143	44	45
142	43	43
141	41	42
140	39	40
139	37	38
138	36	36
137	34	35
136	32	33
135	30	31
134	29	29
133	27	28
132	26	26
131	24	25
130	23	23
129	22	22
128	20	21
127	19	19
126	18	18
125	17	17
124	16	16
123	15	15
122	14	14
121	13	13
120	0	12

*There is no raw score that will produce this scaled score for this form.

SECTION I

1.	A	7.	B	14.	C	21.	C
2.	A	8.	A	15.	B	22.	C
3.	D	9.	D	16.	A	23.	A
4.	E	10.	E	17.	D	24.	D
5.	B	11.	D	18.	D	25.	E
6.	A	12.	A	19.	D	26.	B
		13.	E	20.	B	27.	E

SECTION II

1.	C	8.	E	15.	B	22.	D
2.	D	9.	D	16.	C	23.	E
3.	D	10.	D	17.	D	24.	E
4.	D	11.	C	18.	D	25.	A
5.	D	12.	A	19.	C		
6.	C	13.	A	20.	B		
7.	A	14.	E	21.	D		

SECTION III

1.	E	8.	C	15.	A	22.	E
2.	D	9.	E	16.	B	23.	E
3.	C	10.	E	17.	E	24.	B
4.	A	11.	E	18.	A	25.	A
5.	B	12.	D	19.	E		
6.	C	13.	B	20.	B		
7.	B	14.	D	21.	E		

SECTION IV

1.	E	8.	E	15.	E	22.	D
2.	A	9.	A	16.	C	23.	C
3.	A	10.	E	17.	E	24.	C
4.	B	11.	B	18.	C		
5.	E	12.	B	19.	E		
6.	C	13.	D	20.	A		
7.	E	14.	C	21.	D		

11

Answers and Explanations
to Diagnostic Test II

SECTION I

Questions 1–6 are based on the following passage:

Conventionally, the landowner wishing to build on his
land has the structure designed by one entity and then
built by another; the design and build functions are
viewed as separate. With the innovative "design-build"
(5) construction arrangement, however, a single entity
performs both the design and construction functions. That
single entity may be a joint venture between an architect
or engineer and general contractor, a design-build firm
which employs both professionals and contractors, or a
(10) general contracting firm subcontracting with an
architectural or engineering firm. Design-build contracts
appeal to owners because they require only one entity for
performance; if a problem arises, the owner does not
have to decide whether the architect or the contractor is
(15) the culprit. From the standpoint of the contractor, design-
build contracts are advantageous because they secure
both design fees and construction profits. In addition,
many design-build contracts are calculated on a cost-plus
basis and are therefore less risky than fixed-price work.
(20) A design-build job may be carried out like a traditional
project, in which the contractor prepares design
documents and obtains owner approval before
construction commences, or as a series of tasks entailing
the preparation of design documents in phases, with
(25) construction beginning as each phase of the design is
completed. The process of starting construction before
the overall design is complete is known as the "fast-
track" construction plan. Often, the design-build and fast-
track concepts are employed together.
(30) Fast-track construction appeals to owners because it
reduces the time between a project's conception and its
completion, thus minimizing finance costs and the often
disastrous effects of inflation and increasing the
likelihood that the budget will be adequate to complete
(35) the project. On the other hand, the fast-track approach
presents problems to owners seeking construction
changes. Normally, a builder is obliged to conform to
designs and, with compensation for extra expense, to
owner-requested changes when such changes are within
(40) the "scope of the project"; while in the traditional format,
determining whether or not a change is within the scope
of the project is relatively simple.
On a fast-track job, however, the finishing details of
the job are defined after construction begins. Thus, there
(45) is more room for misunderstanding between the owner
and the contractor as to whether design changes are
within the scope of the project.

In this regard, a contractor should define the parameters of
his obligations as early as possible. For example, the
(50) parties should be able to agree on the type and function of
the structure, the number of stories, and the approximate
area before any construction commences. Once building
has begun, the keys to minimizing disputes are constant
communication with the owner regarding what the
(55) contractor deems the scope of his work, and prompt notice
if the contractor perceives that these bounds are being
overstepped.

SECTION I

QUESTIONS	EXPLANATIONS

Main idea: Design-build and fast-track construction are both good, but fast-track has potential problems.

1. According to the passage, the design-build method of construction is attractive to a landowner who wishes to build on her land because

(A) she no longer needs to work with two separate entities

(B) it allows earlier marketing, thereby reducing finance costs

(C) its speed of construction protects her against inflation

(D) when problems develop, she has financial recourse

(E) it enables her to make changes even after the building has begun

1. This is a SPECIFIC question. Find the part of the passage that talks about the benefits for landowners.

(A) Yes, take a look at lines 11–13.

(B) Marketing isn't mentioned in the passage.

(C) Inflation is an issue for fast-track construction, not design-build.

(D) The passage does not mention financial recourse.

(E) This is a fast-track construction issue.

2. Which one of the following would best serve as the concluding sentence of the last paragraph?

(A) Close contact allows full benefit from fast-track construction and reduces the likelihood of disputes.

(B) Since no communication is perfect, however, most owners choose conventional construction to avoid disputes.

(C) Unfortunately, owners of multiple projects often cannot maintain such close contact.

(D) Effective communication is ultimately the key to a productive work environment.

(E) Inspection of the building on completion would verify that it continued to adhere to safety regulations.

2. This is a MAIN IDEA question. Come up with what you think is the main point of the last paragraph before you go to the answer choices.

(A) Yes, the paragraph is talking about how close contact between the owner and contractor during fast-track construction is necessary. This choice summarizes that thought.

(B) We don't know the percentages of conventional vs. design-build construction projects.

(C) The passage never mentions owners of multiple projects.

(D) This is too general an answer choice—we're talking construction projects in the passage, and this choice merely says "a productive work environment."

(E) Safety regulations were never mentioned in the passage—it's out of scope.

SECTION I

QUESTIONS	EXPLANATIONS

3. It can be inferred from the passage that contractors find the design-build method advantageous because

   (A) it reduces the number of design documents that need to be prepared

   (B) design changes are easier to facilitate

   (C) owners are less likely to request costly changes in the scope of the project

   (D) the financial risks are less than for traditional construction projects

   (E) they need hire only one entity

3. This is a SPECIFIC question. Find the part of the passage that talks about the benefits for design-build contractors.

   (A) The number of design documents was never mentioned in the passage.

   (B) Easier to facilitate than what? Design changes are talked about later in the passage.

   (C) This has the same problem as (B). This is talked about later in the passage.

   (D) See line 19. This is the answer.

   (E) No, this is a benefit for landowners.

4. Which one of the following best summarizes the main point of the author?

   (A) Fast-track programs represent a radical departure from the no-longer-effective traditional method of construction.

   (B) Conventional construction and design-build construction are both equally valid methods of construction, though each is best suited to different circumstances.

   (C) The combination of design-build and fast-track methods of construction creates financial risks that many landowners find unacceptable.

   (D) Contractors have begun to encourage their clients to explore new methods and systems of design and construction.

   (E) While the design-build and fast-track methods of construction provide advantages to both landowners and contractors, the fast-track method also carries some risks.

4. This is a MAIN IDEA question. Come up with your own main idea before you go to the answer choices.

   (A) This doesn't talk about the design-build arrangement, which is also a key element of the passage. Eliminate it.

   (B) The author seems to like design-build better, and this choice doesn't talk about fast-track construction, which is also a key element of the passage.

   (C) No, the only financial risks that are talked about in the passage are those of the fast-track method.

   (D) This isn't specific enough—what are the new methods?

   (E) Bingo, it mentions both things and even says that there are both advantages and disadvantages to fast-track.

SECTION I

QUESTIONS	EXPLANATIONS

5. In mentioning the "disastrous effects of inflation" (line 33), the author is probably referring to the fact that

(A) delayed completion inhibits renting or selling the building because of higher costs

(B) lengthy construction time can put costs beyond the owner's ability to pay them

(C) financiers may, because of inflationary pressures, demand earlier returns

(D) inflation can weaken the link between design-build and fast-track

(E) the contractor may demand higher payment for design changes

6. Based on the information given in the passage, the author would consider each of the following good advice to an owner who has arranged for fast-track construction of a building on his land EXCEPT

(A) after construction is complete, verify that changes have been made according to specifications

(B) reach agreement on the major decisions concerning the project before construction begins

(C) bring problems to the attention of the contractor as soon as they arise

(D) confer with the contractor frequently during construction

(E) prepare a list of important design details before the project begins so that misunderstandings are avoided

---

5. This is a LINE REFERENCE question. Read five lines above and five lines below the line reference.

(A) The renting or selling of the building is never mentioned in the passage.

(B) This is the answer—see line 34, which mentions concerns about the adequacy of the budget.

(C) Earlier returns were never mentioned in the passage.

(D) The passage never says this. This portion of the passage is not really concerned with the design-build approach, either.

(E) Design changes are an issue of fast-track building, just not an inflationary one.

6. This is a SPECIFIC question. Find out what the important issues are surrounding fast-track building. Remember that this is an EXCEPT question, so we're looking for the one thing not mentioned in the passage.

(A) We don't know anything about what happens after the building is completed—there is no mention of this in the passage. It's the answer.

(B) No, because this is mentioned in lines 50–52.

(C) No, because this is mentioned in lines 56–57.

(D) No, because this is mentioned in lines 54–55.

(E) No, because this is mentioned in lines 43–45.

SECTION I

Questions 7–14 are based on the following passage:

In the early 1980s, a number of citizens established organizations devoted to preventing drivers from operating motor vehicles while under the influence of alcohol. These organizations represent a grassroots social
(5) movement that attacks the problem of drunk driving by calling for community awareness and stronger sanctions. Unlike the prohibitionist movements of the late nineteenth and early twentieth centuries, which identified drinking itself as inherently wrong, the anti-drunk-
(10) driving movements emphasize the issue of drinking while driving automobiles; the problem is not alcohol use (or abuse), but the irresponsibility of individuals using alcohol. In essence, these organizations have spawned a social movement against the evils caused by personal
(15) irresponsibility.

The Progressive reform movements around the turn of the century shared the same moral ethic. As Hofstadter has argued, the Progressive reform movements were strongly based on the "ethos of personal responsibility"
(20) and the basic morality of civic consciousness. That approach is reflected in the goals of today's movement and in its views on proposals to solve the drunk-driving problem. The two most important program goals of current-day organizations are public awareness activities
(25) designed to make drinkers understand that it is wrong to drive when under the influence of alcohol and youth education programs designed to convey this message to young drivers.

The "ethos of personal responsibility" for one's
(30) actions also has an impact in determining what actions are taken to solve the problem. Grassroots organizations call for punitive measures to be taken against drunk drivers. They perceive non-punitive programs—such as the safe-ride program—as ineffective. As one founding
(35) member of one organization put it: "Safe ride programs may help temporarily, but they cause people to ignore their part in the problem."

Rehabilitation programs are rejected on the same grounds. In addition to labeling these programs as
(40) ineffective, grassroots organizers perceive them as a minor inconvenience to offenders and as a means of avoiding stricter punishment. This punitive approach to "problem drinking" represents a departure from the trend of viewing drinking problems as a disease and thus a
(45) medical problem. The movement does not distinguish between the sick alcoholic and the irresponsible "problem drinker" in its desire to enforce sanctions against the drunk driver.

These opinions reflect the basic moral view that
(50) citizens should be aware of the dangers of driving while drunk and their individual responsibility to drive sober. As a result of this awareness, those individuals acting irresponsibly should face serious punishment. Society, on the other hand, should not take the responsibility for
(55) individual conduct by instituting prohibitionist measures, safe-ride programs, or programs for rehabilitation.

SECTION I

QUESTIONS	EXPLANATIONS

7. The main idea of the passage is that

   (A) centuries of anti-alcohol public awareness campaigns reflect the United States' focus on personal responsibility
   (B) present-day grassroots anti-drunk-driving organizations emphasize personal responsibility as the key to effecting change
   (C) Prohibition failed because it ignored the United States' ethic of responsibility
   (D) if non-punitive programs worked, there would be no grassroots anti-drunk-driving movement
   (E) no anti-drunk-driving campaign is likely to succeed without punishing the driver

7. This is a MAIN IDEA question. Come up with your own main idea before you go to the answer choices.

   (A) This is too broad—we're talking about grassroots organizations of the present day for most of the passage. Eliminate it.
   (B) Bingo. It mentions the new grassroots organizations and what their philosophy is based on.
   (C) Doesn't mention the all-important grassroots folks.
   (D) We have no idea whether this is true and this is not what the author is interested in talking about.
   (E) Possibly true, but this is too specific an issue for it to be the main idea of the whole passage.

8. According to the passage, the modern grassroots movement designed to prevent drunk driving

   (A) is largely unconcerned with the broader issue of alcohol abuse
   (B) is more concerned with protecting the lives of sober drivers than of drunk drivers
   (C) is less opposed to drunk driving than it is in favor of personal responsibility
   (D) is excessively punitive, and, therefore, not likely to be effective
   (E) views drunk driving narrowly, and, therefore, promises less success than the prohibition movements

8. This is a SPECIFIC question. Find the part of the passage that talks about the grassroots folks.

   (A) This looks pretty good. Take a look at lines 9–12.
   (B) No, they care about all drivers. Eliminate it.
   (C) No, they really hate drunk driving. Eliminate it.
   (D) The movement isn't punitive; their recommendations are. Eliminate it.
   (E) No, the author thinks that they've got a good idea here and will be more successful than the prohibition movements. Eliminate it.

9. The turn-of-the-century Progressive reform movements and the current grassroots movements share all of the following EXCEPT

   (A) a belief in personal responsibility
   (B) an emphasis on morality
   (C) a desire for behavior modification as it relates to civic consciousness
   (D) a disapproval of drinking
   (E) a commitment to altering certain conduct

9. This is a SPECIFIC question. Find the part of the passage that talks about the grassroots folks AND the prohibition folks. That this is an EXCEPT question, too.

   (A) They both believe in this. See lines 18–21.
   (B) They both believe in this. See line 17.
   (C) They both believe in this. See line 20.
   (D) Here's the answer—see lines 7–9. The grassroots people of today don't condemn drinking altogether.
   (E) They both tried to do this with various initiatives.

SECTION I

QUESTIONS	EXPLANATIONS

10. As used in line 20 of the passage, a person who follows a "basic morality of civic consciousness" probably

   (A) abides by community standards for moral behavior

   (B) supports the work done by alcoholic rehabilitation programs

   (C) advocates the adoption of severe penalties for driving while intoxicated

   (D) proposes that basic rules of moral behavior are essential to a just society

   (E) understands that drinking before driving wrongfully endangers the safety and welfare of others

10. This is a LINE REFERENCE question. Read five lines above and five lines below the line reference.

   (A) This is a bit general because we're talking about drinking and driving in the passage. Moral behavior is a pretty big topic.

   (B) We don't like rehab programs. This answer choice is crossing its signals. Eliminate it.

   (C) This is what the grassroots people think should happen, but we don't know about the community at large. Let's see if there is anything better than this.

   (D) As in answer choice (A), this is too general. We're talking about drinking and driving.

   (E) Bingo. Grassroots people see civic consciousness and education as going hand-in-hand. See lines 23–28.

11. According to the passage, grassroots organizations do not believe that prohibition is an effective solution to the drunk-driving problem because prohibition

   (A) is too punitive, especially for responsible drinkers

   (B) fails to recognize alcoholism as a disease

   (C) does not share the aims of the history of Progressive reform movements in the United States

   (D) makes society responsible for an individual's problems

   (E) does nothing to make citizens aware of the drunk-driving problem

11. This is a SPECIFIC question. Find the part of the passage that talks about the grassroots and prohibition.

   (A) Not that it's too punitive, just that it's not the point. Eliminate it.

   (B) Not the point here. Eliminate it.

   (C) No, that's what the old progressive reforms were pushing for.

   (D) This looks good, because the grassroots people think it's about each person individually. It's the answer.

   (E) That's not why they think it's a bad idea. They can still educate people.

12. In the third paragraph, the author's purpose is to

   (A) demonstrate the grassroots rejection of solutions that do not address driver accountability

   (B) explain why the safe-ride program is unlikely to eradicate drunk driving

   (C) present a view in opposition to that of the Progressive reform movements

   (D) support his belief that non-punitive programs are ineffective

   (E) distinguish between punitive and non-punitive social reforms, favoring non-punitive reforms

12. This is a PARAGRAPH REFERENCE question. Re-read the third paragraph to see what its purpose was.

   (A) Yes, this paragraph's purpose is to show how non-punitive solutions aren't very good. It's the answer.

   (B) This is something that the paragraph does, but it's not the overall goal of the paragraph. Too specific.

   (C) No, we don't even know what those people thought about rehab or safe-ride programs. Eliminate it.

   (D) No, we don't know what the author thinks about these programs yet. The author is telling us what the grassroots people think.

   (E) No, we don't learn this until the following paragraph.

SECTION I

QUESTIONS	EXPLANATIONS

13. Which one of the following best describes the organization of the passage?

   (A) A general philosophy of responsibility is presented, and specific approaches that do not adhere to that philosophy are rejected.

   (B) An ethos of personal responsibility is described, and then an alternate approach is described.

   (C) The history of a movement is outlined in chronological order.

   (D) A current political movement is analyzed, and the events that led to its creation are examined.

   (E) The historical approaches to a social problem are outlined and comparisons made.

14. The author of the passage would be most likely to agree with which one of the following statements about the "ethos of personal responsibility" and its relationship to grassroots campaigns against drunk driving?

   (A) Its impact on the organization of grassroots campaigns has been negligible, since these campaigns favor a more punitive approach.

   (B) It causes certain methods for dealing with drunk drivers to be favored over others that are perceived as ineffective or even dangerous.

   (C) It has been largely responsible for the introduction of public awareness campaigns involving both adults and teenagers.

   (D) It results in the belief that drinking is inherently wrong.

   (E) It establishes a general principle that provides a justification for acting irresponsibly while under the influence of alcohol.

13. This is a STRUCTURE question. Go back to the passage and find out how the passage flowed from paragraph to paragraph.

   (A) No, the passage starts off talking historically, not philosophically. Eliminate it.

   (B) Same problem as (A). We don't get this personal responsibility stuff until later.

   (C) No, because the author mentions the old progressive people throughout the passage.

   (D) Is it a political movement? Not really.

   (E) The social problem is drinking, and the approaches between the old and the new are indeed contrasted. This is our answer.

14. This is a SPECIFIC question. Find the part of the passage that talks about the ethos of personal responsibility.

   (A) Negligible impact? Hardly. It's one of their basic tenets. Eliminate it.

   (B) Dangerous methods? Never mentioned in the passage.

   (C) Bingo—it's a basic part of their philosophy. This is our answer.

   (D) No, because then the grassroots people would have contradicted themselves.

   (E) Acting *irresponsibly*? It's the opposite of what we want here. Eliminate it.

SECTION I

Questions 15–20 are based on the following passage:

In a representative democracy, legislatures exist to represent the public and to ensure that public issues are efficiently addressed by a group representative of the population as a whole. It is often written that a legislator
(5) confronts a moral dilemma if, on a given issue upon which he must cast a vote, his view is decidedly different from that of the majority of his constituents. In such a circumstance, it is not clear whether voting citizens have chosen the legislator because of their faith in his personal
(10) judgment or whether they have elected him in order to give direct effect to their own views.

But this dilemma is more apparent than real. A truly identifiable conflict between the legislator's opinion and that of his constituency is rare, since the legislator is
(15) usually better informed than the public on the issue in question and his opinion, therefore, cannot fairly be compared to theirs. Indeed, this fact underscores the legislator's most important function: to gather broad-based information in order to make more considered
(20) decisions than each citizen could reach individually and thus to serve the public interest better than the public could do on its own.

Let us suppose that a legislator opposes a very popular proposed public works project because he has studied its
(25) financial ramifications and believes, over the long run, it is fiscally unsound. If the legislator's constituents write letters expressing their ardent support for the project, not having studied the relevant financial data, it is entirely too simplistic to view the legislator as having to confront
(30) a moral dilemma. The truth is that the legislator does not know how his constituents would view the project if they truly understood its financial consequences. Without such knowledge, the legislator cannot actually conclude that his view differs from that of his constituents. To conclude
(35) that their views should dictate his decision might foster his popularity but would contravene his fundamental legislative responsibility.

The legislator's job is first to study the short-range and long-range goals of the people he represents, without
(40) confusing these with his own. Then, using his knowledge and judgment, he is to promote the electorate's goals as he understands them. Consider, for instance, a legislator whose constituents wish to maintain the rural character of their district. If the legislator himself dislikes rural living and
(45) would like to see the area undergo industrial development, or if he believes an industrial environment would offer greater benefit to the community than a rural environment, he must separate these viewpoints from his professional judgment. He is not to promote industrialization because
(50) he personally favors it.

However, if the legislator's considered opinion is that his district needs to sponsor *some* industrial development in order to maintain its overall agricultural character, it is his duty to promote the industrial development, even if his
(55) constituents oppose it. So long as he honestly attempts to serve his electorate's objectives, the legislator should stand firm against the expressed opinions of his own constituents.

SECTION I

QUESTIONS	EXPLANATIONS

15. The author's purpose in the first paragraph is to

  (A) explain that many legislative questions require economic as well as political understanding

  (B) point out that a possible moral dilemma exists when a legislator disagrees with her constituents

  (C) illustrate that the legislator's extra knowledge creates the gap between her views and those of her constituents

  (D) argue that legislative decisions should not be made simplistically

  (E) encourage the rejection of legislation that runs counter to the public interest

15. This is a PARAGRAPH REFERENCE question. Re-read the first paragraph and see what its purpose was.

  (A) Economic issues weren't mentioned in paragraph one. Eliminate it.

  (B) Looks pretty good. See lines 4–11. This is the answer.

  (C) This isn't mentioned until later in the passage. Eliminate it.

  (D) This is true but this isn't the purpose of the first paragraph. The first paragraph is talking about a dilemma.

  (E) The author is not talking about rejection of legislation here.

16. According to the passage, the differences between a legislator's view and the views expressed by the legislator's constituents

  (A) do not actually create a moral dilemma in most cases

  (B) create a moral dilemma only in a democracy

  (C) only arise when constituents are ill-informed

  (D) require that a legislator gather more information than he would otherwise have done

  (E) usually reflect a difference not in opinion, but in long-range goals

16. This is a SPECIFIC question. Find the part of the passage that talks about the two views.

  (A) Yep. See line 12. It doesn't really exist.

  (B) The passage isn't talking about any specific types of government.

  (C) No, they can still disagree even when everyone has the same information.

  (D) The differences don't require this—his job does.

  (E) No, the passage says they should have the same goals.

17. It can be inferred from the passage that the author believes a legislator should

  (A) carry out her constituents' intentions if doing so conforms to her assessment

  (B) ignore her constituents' long-range objectives when they are morally incompatible with her own beliefs

  (C) take whatever actions her constituents recommend

  (D) determine what action will best serve her constituents, regardless of their stated position

  (E) put her own assessments aside and embody those of her electorate

17. This is a SPECIFIC question. Find the part of the passage that talks about legislators.

  (A) This isn't specific enough. Only if their intentions are also in line with the short- and long-range goals of the community.

  (B) No, the community's goals need to drive the process. See lines 38–40.

  (C) No, it's bad for the legislator to just be a rubber stamp. See lines 34–38.

  (D) Bingo. See lines 17–23.

  (E) No, she needs to do both.

SECTION I

18. Which one of the following would the author most likely believe to be true of a legislator who routinely reached legislative decisions by following constituents' instructions?

    (A) The legislator would probably not fully understand the public's goals.

    (B) The legislator would be acting in a manner contrary to her own interests.

    (C) The legislator would probably be unaware of the course of action most favorable to her constituency.

    (D) The legislator might not be fulfilling her proper role of defending the best interests of the electorate.

    (E) The legislator would be overly concerned with maintaining her own popularity, not carrying out her appropriate duties.

18. This is a SPECIFIC question. Find the part of the passage that talks about a legislator merely following instructions.

    (A) Maybe she would, maybe she wouldn't. We don't know. Eliminate it.

    (B) Same problem as (A). We don't know.

    (C) She might know but just want to be more popular than honest. Eliminate it.

    (D) Exactly. The passage states that the legislator has to look further than the wishes of her electorate.

    (E) Maybe, or maybe she can't think for herself. We don't know either way. Eliminate it.

19. Which one of the following, if true, would most weaken the author's contention that a legislator can make "more considered decisions" than can his constituents?

    (A) A community should be allowed to make its own decisions, even if these are not the most informed decisions.

    (B) Because a legislator does not live in the same circumstances as do his constituents, he is more objective and less emotional in his decision-making.

    (C) Some constituents make a great effort to inform themselves on all aspects of proposed legislation.

    (D) The information provided to the legislator is occasionally biased or misleading.

    (E) Some legislators have difficulty separating their personal views from those of their constituents.

19. This is a WEAKEN question. See which choice will weaken the author's point that a legislator is in a better position to make decisions.

    (A) Permission isn't the issue—ability is.

    (B) This would strengthen the author's point, not weaken it.

    (C) This looks pretty good, but "some" constituents isn't very strong. "Some" could be two, or five. Let's look for something stronger.

    (D) This is it. If the legislator's information is bad, he won't make better decisions. (D) is better than (C).

    (E) Same problem as (C). Not strong enough. (D) is the best choice here.

SECTION I

20. According to the author, the introduction of widespread industrialization into the rural community described in lines 42–50 represents

    (A) the failure of a legislator to understand the requirements of the region
    (B) an example of a legislator advancing his agenda at the expense of that of his constituents
    (C) the failure of representative democracy to address the needs of its constituents
    (D) the ability of a legislator to ignore the interests of the community he represents
    (E) the result of a legislator carrying through on the expressed views of his constituents

20. This is a LINE REFERENCE question. Read five lines above and five lines below the line reference.

    (A) No, because he might have understood them but just blown them off.
    (B) Bingo—he knows what they want but since he has the power, he can do what he thinks is best.
    (C) Way out of the scope of the passage here.
    (D) This sounds okay, but compare it to (B). The lines are more about advancing his own position than ignoring others.
    (E) Nope—they wanted to remain as rural as possible.

SECTION I

Questions 21–27 are based on the following passage:

The KT boundary, as it is called, marks one of the most violent events ever to befall life on earth. Sixty-five million years ago, according to current theory, the Cretaceous period was brought to a sudden conclusion
(5) by the impact of an asteroid or a comet ten kilometers in diameter. It would be natural to suppose that the KT boundary is a fossil hunter's paradise. But it is nothing of the sort. In fact, no bones have been found at the KT boundary anywhere on earth.

(10) Some paleontologists find the situation frustrating, to put it mildly. Granted, they say, the record of life preserved in sedimentary rocks is far from perfect. But in this case the event of record is a cosmic catastrophe that killed all the dinosaurs in the world. Shouldn't the
(15) concentration of bones in the fossil record be, at the very least, above average?

In some places the sedimentary rocks preserve detailed temporal signals with near-textbook fidelity, but such detailed windows into the past are relatively
(20) rare. More commonly, various natural forces like the wind and rain disrupt the chronological ordering of the fossils-to-be.

The first serious proposal for solving this sedimentary puzzle came in 1940, in a paper by the
(25) Soviet paleontologist Ivan A. Efremov. Paleontologists, Efremov said, were too inclined to take the fossil record at face value; instead, he advised, they ought to pay more attention to the processes whereby living organisms become, or fail to become,
(30) fossils. A better understanding of burial and fossilization might enable paleontologists to "back calculate" and reclaim lost data from the fossil record.

Paleontologists Alan Cutler and Anna Behrensmeyer have developed just such a model of fossil preservation.
(35) Starting with a hypothetical population of dinosaurs, they estimated normal annual mortality rates for dinosaurs from ecological data collected for large mammals in African wildlife preserves. Next, to estimate what fraction of the dinosaurs' bones would end up safely
(40) buried, they drew on data from Behrensmeyer's study of the decay of mammal carcasses in Ambesoli National Park, Kenya. Finally, they ran the model to see what sort of bone spike would result if the entire population of dinosaurs suddenly died. The answer, they discovered,
(45) was no bone spike at all.

In the mixed, or convoluted, record, spikes in the abundance of species are attenuated and tail off exponentially. The thicker the mixing layer, the greater the smearing. Thus, the sudden extinction of a
(50) species shows up not as an abrupt disappearance of fossils, but a gradual petering out.

Such research is still in its infancy, and there is no way of predicting exactly what further research may bring. However promising its results may be, though,
(55) one caveat is necessary: It will never be able to work miracles. The most sophisticated mathematics in the world cannot unscramble an egg or resurrect the dinosaurs.

SECTION I

21. Which of the following may be inferred about the KT boundary?

    (A) The fossil record it contains is above average in both the quantity of fossils and their degree of preservation.

    (B) It was destroyed by a large comet sixty-five million years ago.

    (C) The fossil record it contains is, in some ways, inconsistent with the dominant theory of dinosaur extinction.

    (D) Its significance was first described by paleontologist Ivan A. Efremov.

    (E) Paleontologists consider it to be the single richest source in the fossil record.

22. Which of the following best describes the main idea of the passage?

    (A) If paleontologists are to achieve significant results in the future, they must reject their older methods.

    (B) Because it cannot be substantiated by the fossil record, the dominant theory of dinosaur extinction should be rejected.

    (C) Because of the nature of the process by which bones become fossils, scientists should not be surprised by the relative absence of fossils at the KT boundary.

    (D) Back-calculation indicates that the KT boundary should contain more fossils than more recent rock layers.

    (E) More recent methods of modeling fossil preservation provide evidence that contradicts earlier findings made by paleontologists.

21. This is a SPECIFIC question. Find the part of the passage that first talks about the KT boundary.

    (A) No, it's the opposite. There should be more fossils, but there aren't. Eliminate it.

    (B) The boundary wasn't destroyed; the dinosaurs were.

    (C) Yep—we've got a bunch of dead dinosaurs but no fossils showing that.

    (D) Wrong part of the passage on this one.

    (E) No, it's got few fossils considering what happened.

22. This is a MAIN IDEA question. Come up with your own main idea before you go to the answer choices.

    (A) This is way too general—we're talking about this one specific event, the KT thing.

    (B) Too extreme! We don't know enough about this stuff to pass a judgment like this.

    (C) Yes—we've got some inconsistencies, but there seems to be an explanation for them. Bingo.

    (D) Too specific, way too specific. This was only mentioned once.

    (E) No, there still aren't a lot of fossils, no matter how you slice it.

SECTION I

23. Which one of the following best describes the relationship between the work of Efremov and that of Cutler and Behrensmeyer?

   (A) Efremov's work described the need for a significant shift in approach and Cutler and Behrensmeyer carried out research based in part on his approach.

   (B) Efremov's work provided the data from which Cutler and Behrensmeyer were able to develop a model of fossil preservation.

   (C) Whereas Efremov focused principally on why bones do not become fossils, Cutler and Behrensmeyer focused on why they do.

   (D) Efremov's work was theoretically more complex than that carried out by Cutler and Behrensmeyer.

   (E) Efremov focused on processes whereas Cutler and Behrensmeyer focused on data collection.

23. This is a SPECIFIC question. Find the part of the passage that talks about these folks.

   (A) Yup. He had the idea, and they proved it was pretty accurate.

   (B) Nope, this has the facts switched. Efremov came up with the idea, not the data.

   (C) No, they worked around the same ideas.

   (D) We have no idea whether Efremov was more complex.

   (E) Close, but not as good as (A). This just talks about how they're different from each other. (A) is a better description of how they both fit into the KT discussion.

24. Which of the following best describes the organization of the passage?

   (A) Data gathered from a broad range of sources is presented, inconsistencies among the data are described, then these inconsistencies are resolved.

   (B) Research from two different groups of scientists is presented, a question about the research is posed, and an answer is offered.

   (C) A new theoretical model is explained, problems with the model are pointed out, and possible explanations for the problem are suggested.

   (D) A paradox is described, and both theoretical and empirical information is presented to help explain the paradox.

   (E) A fundamental scientific failure is described, evidence substantiating this failure is presented, then a new approach to the problem is described.

24. This is a STRUCTURE question. Go back to the passage and find out how the passage flowed from paragraph to paragraph.

   (A) Broad range of sources? Where? We're only talking about the KT boundary.

   (B) No, we only get research from one group.

   (C) No, the new theory is pretty good.

   (D) Yes—the fact that we have lots of dead dinosaurs but no evidence. That's the paradox. This is the answer.

   (E) Is this a failure of science? It's just a failure to obtain evidence.

SECTION I

QUESTIONS	EXPLANATIONS

25. The author would be most likely to agree with which of the following statements?

(A) Data from large mammal populations are essential in any attempt to model the process of dinosaur extinction.

(B) Fossil evidence indicates that the dinosaurs probably became extinct over a longer period of time than previously believed.

(C) The KT boundary provides a unique source of information about animal extinction.

(D) In most fossil layers, evidence of extinction trails off exponentially but contains an initial bone spike.

(E) Improvements in paleontological research, while useful, will not provide sufficient answers to all of the questions about dinosaur extinction.

25. This is a GENERAL INFERENCE question. Go to the answer choices and see which statement must be true given the information in the passage.

(A) Data are useful, but "essential" may be a bit too strong here. Let's look for something more wishy-washy.

(B) We have no idea. We've got no evidence. We're clueless.

(C) No, it doesn't provide enough information. That's the problem with it—it should, but it doesn't. Also, we don't know that it is unique.

(D) We have no idea about this.

(E) Nice and wishy-washy—we'll find out some answers, but just not all of them. That's what lines 56–58 are implicating.

26. The author states that in their evaluation of the fossil record, Cutler and Behrensmeyer did all of the following EXCEPT:

(A) conclude that the data from the fossil record was consistent with a mass extinction of dinosaurs

(B) work with paleontologist Ivan A. Efremov

(C) use data gathered from populations of large animals to estimate characteristics of dinosaur populations

(D) base their work on hypothetical information about dinosaur populations

(E) use data from studies of the decay of mammal carcasses in Africa

26. This is a SPECIFIC question. Find the part of the passage that talks about these folks. Remember that it's an EXCEPT question.

(A) Yes, see lines 44–45. No bone spike occurred. Eliminate it.

(B) No, they just used his idea. This is the answer.

(C) Yes, see lines 37–38. Eliminate it.

(D) Yes, see lines 35–36. Eliminate it.

(E) Yes, see lines 41–42. Eliminate it.

27. According to the passage, a segment of the fossil record in which paleontologists would LEAST expect to see a clear record of a period of sudden extinction would be one in which

(A) an abundance of bone spikes exist

(B) an unusually large portion of the bones were safely buried before fossilization

(C) "back calculation" would be difficult, but possible

(D) drought occurred at the time of fossilization

(E) a particularly thick mixing layer was present during fossil formation

27. This is a SPECIFIC question. But make sure you're looking for the thing we'd LEAST expect to see.

(A) We'd expect this, because where there is mass extinction, there are no spikes.

(B) We'd expect this, since we haven't found a lot of fossilized bones.

(C) We'd expect this, because there isn't all that much information with which to calculate.

(D) We'd expect this, since there would be more evidence.

(E) We wouldn't expect this, because it would indicate a gradual extinction, not a sudden one. This is the answer.

QUESTIONS	EXPLANATIONS

1. The quality of our public schools is more likely to decline if people expect it to. The number of illiterate graduates and the level of administrative incompetence will increase as people's disrespect for public schools discourages more able people from pursuing careers in teaching.

   The logical structure of the above statement is most consistent with which one of the following?

   (A) If people believe that an eagerly anticipated event will take place, then it most likely will.

   (B) When people believe that money grows on trees, then, for all practical purposes, money does grow on trees.

   (C) When people expect the economy to flourish, they become willing to spend and invest more, thus helping the economy to flourish.

   (D) When people expect world affairs to be tragic, they notice tragic events more than they do pleasant ones.

   (E) If people enjoy sporting events, the stadiums and arenas will be full, thus encouraging high attendance at future sporting events.

1. This is a PARALLEL-THE-REASONING question. Try to get the theme or diagram of the logic and then match it to each answer choice.

   (A) No, we're looking for something where people have an expectation, and then the expected result occurs. This leaves out the middle step.

   (B) This is silly. It's expectation, not belief.

   (C) Yep. We need that middle step that they are "willing to spend and invest more." This is the same construction as the argument, i.e., having an expectation, an action, and a result.

   (D) It's not noticing what meets expectations. It's that the expectation causes the action.

   (E) There is no expectation here.

2. In an experiment, first-year college students were asked to listen to a tape of someone speaking French. When asked to repeat the sounds they had heard, students who had studied French in high school could repeat more of the sounds than could students who had no knowledge of French. When asked to listen to a tape of only meaningless sounds, none of the students were able to repeat more than a few seconds' worth of the sounds made on the tape.

   Which one of the following conclusions is best supported by the information above?

   (A) Knowledge of a foreign language interferes with one's ability to repeat unfamiliar sounds.

   (B) People who have a knowledge of French have better memories than do people who have no knowledge of French.

   (C) The ability to repeat unrelated sounds is not improved by frequent practice.

   (D) The ability to repeat sounds is influenced by one's ability to comprehend the meaning of the sounds.

   (E) Learning a foreign language requires an ability to distinguish unfamiliar sounds from gibberish.

2. This is an INFERENCE question. Your goal is to find the one choice that must be true based on the information in the passage.

   (A) No, because none of the students was able to repeat the sounds for more than a few seconds.

   (B) General memory is not related to an ability to speak French.

   (C) Maybe, but we don't know about practice.

   (D) Do we have proof of this? Yes—the French-speaking students remembered more of the sounds that were the French language than they did of the gibberish language. Plus, it's nice and wishy-washy—"is influenced by." This is the answer.

   (E) Maybe, but we don't know about learning a foreign language.

SECTION II

| QUESTIONS | EXPLANATIONS |

Questions 3–4

Many commercial pesticides, used primarily in indoor atriums, greenhouses, and solariums, release toxic levels of DDT and other potentially carcinogenic agents hazardous to the health of workers and other individuals who pass through the area. This problem can be avoided by providing adequate ventilation, but this becomes difficult during winter months when the area must maintain sufficient heat to ensure the survival of the plants. A recent study shows that certain tropical grasses will remove some of these toxins from the air, eliminating the danger to humans. In one winter trial, a four-foot-square patch of tropical grass eliminated the DDT in a solarium of average size.

3. Assume that a patch of tropical grass is introduced into a solarium of average size that contains toxic pesticide residue.

   Which one of the following can be expected as a result?

   (A) Occasional ventilation, even during the summer, will become unnecessary.
   (B) The concentration of toxic pesticide residues will remain unchanged.
   (C) The solarium will continue to maintain a constant level of toxicity and temperature.
   (D) If there are toxic DDT residues in the solarium, these levels will decrease.
   (E) If DDT and other potentially carcinogenic agents are being released in the solarium, the quantities of each agent will decrease.

3. This is an INFERENCE question. Your goal is to find the one choice that must be true based on the information in the passage.

   (A) "Unnecessary" is too extreme.
   (B) We don't know—is there DDT in this residue or not? If so, they should decrease.
   (C) No, the grass should reduce toxic DDT.
   (D) This is extreme, but it's the right answer. We know that the grass reduces the level of DDT, so this is our answer.
   (E) Too far out there—we know about the DDT, but "each agent" is too extreme.

4. The passage above is designed to lead to which one of the following conclusions?

   (A) Tropical grass removes all carcinogenic agents from the air.
   (B) Natural pesticides do not release toxins into greenhouses, solariums, or corporate atriums.
   (C) Planting tropical grass is an effective means of maintaining a constant temperature in a greenhouse.
   (D) Growing tropical grass can counteract some of the negative effects of a poorly ventilated atrium.
   (E) The air in an atrium that contains tropical grass and maintains a constant temperature will contain fewer toxic residues than will the air in a similarly maintained atrium without tropical grass.

4. This is an INFERENCE question. Your goal is to find the one choice that must be true based on the information in the passage.

   (A) "All" is too extreme. We only know that the grass removes the DDT.
   (B) We have no idea about natural pesticides. Eliminate it.
   (C) No, the grass is there to counteract pesticides, not regulate temperature. Eliminate it.
   (D) Nice and wishy-washy. "Some" negative effects (i.e., DDT) can be counteracted. This is our answer.
   (E) "Will" is too extreme here. And we don't know this—unless the atrium definitively contained DDT, the residues might not decrease.

SECTION II

5.   Medical Researcher: If I don't get another research grant soon, I'll never be able to discover a cure for phlebitis.

Assistant: But that's great. If your grant does come through, that dreaded disease will finally be eradicated.

Which one of the following statements best describes the flaw in the assistant's reasoning?

(A)   The assistant believes the researcher will be unable to cure phlebitis unless the grant comes through.

(B)   The assistant thinks the researcher will use the grant to find a cure for phlebitis, rather than for some other purpose.

(C)   The assistant believes it is more important to cure phlebitis than to eradicate other, more deadly conditions.

(D)   The assistant believes that all the researcher needs in order to cure phlebitis is another research grant.

(E)   The assistant thinks the researcher will cure phlebitis even if the grant does not come through.

5.   This is a REASONING question. Come up with your own description of how the assistant made a mistake before you go to the answer choices, and then match your description to the choices.

(A)   No, this is what the medical researcher said. Look for something that mentions how the assistant thinks the researcher said that the grant was sufficient to ensure success.

(B)   This isn't a flaw in the argument—it's accurate.

(C)   Other diseases weren't mentioned by anyone.

(D)   Yes, he confused *necessary* with *sufficient* in this case—the researcher said it was necessary for him to get the grant, the assistant assumed that the grant will be sufficient to effect the cure.

(E)   No, neither person said this.

6.   Economist: The keys to a growth economy are low interest rates and a high number of investments; as there cannot be investments without low interest rates, it can be concluded that where there are low interest rates there are investments.

Which one of the following, if true, would most weaken the argument above?

(A)   Many growth economies with high interest rates have few investments.

(B)   Stagnant economies with high interest rates have few investments.

(C)   Stagnant economies with low interest rates have few investments.

(D)   A high number of investments is adequate to guarantee low interest rates.

(E)   Some stagnant economies have low interest rates.

6.   This is a WEAKEN question. Figure out which answer choice has the most negative impact on the conclusion of the argument. Remember to assume the hypothetical truth of each choice and apply it to the argument.

(A)   This would strengthen the argument.

(B)   This would strengthen the argument.

(C)   Here's a situation where low interest rates have NOT produced investments, which is what the argument said would happen. This is the answer.

(D)   This is saying the causality can flow the other way, but it doesn't preclude it from happening in the way the argument says it does. (C) is a better answer.

(E)   What about the number of investments?

SECTION II

QUESTIONS	EXPLANATIONS

7. A study commissioned by the National Association of Women Professors seems to indicate that women face greater obstacles in becoming tenured professors than do men. Whereas more than 70 percent of the male professors in this country have tenure, fewer than half of the female professors have achieved that rank.

Which one of the following statistics would be most relevant to an assessment of the accuracy of the study mentioned above?

(A) the respective percentages of eligible women and men who have earned tenure in each of the past ten years

(B) the percentage of all tenured positions that have gone to women in each of the past ten years

(C) an analysis of the bias faced by women in other professional fields

(D) the number of men who have been appointed to tenured positions, and the number of women who have not been appointed to tenured positions

(E) the number of professional women who cite the difficulty of achieving tenure when asked to explain why they decided against entering academia

7. This is most like an ASSUMPTION question because you are looking for a fact that will help you to evaluate the validity of the assumption.

(A) This would definitely have impact. If the percentages were equal, the argument would be weakened. This is our answer.

(B) What about men? This doesn't help as much as (A).

(C) What about men? This doesn't help as much as (A).

(D) Without the overall percentages, the numbers themselves are useless.

(E) What about men? This doesn't help as much as (A).

8. Sheet for sheet, Brand A paper towels cost less than Brand B paper towels and are more absorbent. Yet a roll of Brand A paper towels costs more than a roll of Brand B paper towels.

Which one of the following, if true, explains how the statements above can both be true?

(A) Both Brand A and Brand B towels are manufactured by the same company, which often creates artificial competition for its expensive products.

(B) A roll of Brand B paper towels is more absorbent than a roll of Brand A paper towels.

(C) A roll of Brand A paper towels is more absorbent than a roll of Brand B paper towels.

(D) The cost of a roll of Brand A towels has risen every year for the last five years.

(E) A roll of Brand A paper towels has more sheets than a roll of Brand B paper towels.

8. This is a PARADOX question. Look for an answer choice that allows both parts of the argument to be true, and remember to assume the hypothetical truth of each of the answer choices.

(A) This doesn't explain the discrepancy in the per sheet vs. overall price issue.

(B) Absorbency is totally out of the scope here. Eliminate it.

(C) Same problem as (B). Eliminate it.

(D) What about Brand B? Without anything to compare this information to, it's useless. Eliminate it.

(E) Can this explain why the overall price is higher? Yes—there are more sheets on Brand A. It's the answer.

QUESTIONS	EXPLANATIONS

9. State agricultural officials are hoping to save California's $30 billion-a-year fruit industry from destruction by the Mediterranean fruit fly by releasing nearly one billion sterile female fruit flies throughout the state. This has, in the past, been shown to be the only effective means of limiting the spread of this destructive pest, outside of large-scale pesticide spraying.

Which one of the following best explains the intended effect of the program described above?

(A) To drastically increase the number of potential mates for the male fruit flies, requiring them to devote more of their energies to mating rather than eating fruit.

(B) To saturate a given area with fruit flies, creating greater competition for food and thereby containing the damage done by the fruit fly to a smaller area.

(C) To ensure that a large number of fruit flies in succeeding generations are born infertile.

(D) To limit the growth of the population by reducing the number of successful matings between fruit flies.

(E) To encourage overpopulation of the fruit fly in the hopes that nature will correct the situation itself.

---

9. This is a CONCLUSION question. Look for the answer that is the goal of the agricultural officials. What are they trying to do here?

(A) This looks okay, but they're still going to eat some fruit. Let's see if there is something better.

(B) Still not all that great, is it? At least part of the state isn't going to have any fruit left at all. Let's keep looking.

(C) But if we're releasing sterile flies, there won't be succeeding generations. Eliminate it.

(D) This looks really good. By releasing sterile flies, we should be able to reduce the population of fruit flies. It's the answer.

(E) Overpopulation is the opposite of what we want here. Eliminate it.

---

10. A fit, well-tuned body is essential to good health because exercise acts to improve circulation and helps to eliminate toxins from the body. If one is to remain healthy, one must get regular exercise.

Which one of the following conclusions can most logically be drawn from the passage above?

(A) If one exercises, one will be healthy.

(B) Only exercise acts to improve the circulation and eliminate toxins from the body.

(C) A healthy person must have eliminated all toxins from his or her body.

(D) If one does not exercise regularly, one will not remain healthy.

(E) A person who is not healthy must not exercise.

---

10. This is an INFERENCE question. Your goal is to find the one choice that must be true based on the information in the passage.

(A) This does not necessarily have to be true—it's an invalid contrapositive of what is in the argument.

(B) We don't know this to be true—exercise is necessary, but is it the only thing that is necessary?

(C) "All" is too extreme here. Eliminate it.

(D) Bingo! This is the contrapositive of the last sentence of the argument.

(E) This is another invalid contrapositive. You could exercise but still have some unhealthy genetic defect. Eliminate it.

SECTION II

QUESTIONS	EXPLANATIONS

11. Marie: I just found out that it is cheaper for me to heat my home with gas or oil than for me to use any of the alternative methods available. I don't understand why environmentalists insist that the cost of fossil fuels is so high.

   Louise: That's because you are confusing the price of fossil fuels with their cost. Gas and oil release tremendous amounts of pollution into the water and air, causing great damage to the environment. Not only does this pose a threat to the ecological balance that will affect the quality of life for future generations, but it also causes health problems that may be related to the consumption of these fuels. Once you add in these factors, it is clear that there are many alternatives that are actually cheaper than gas or oil, and consumers should adopt them.

   According to her argument above, if an alternative energy source were to be found, under which one of the following conditions would Louise definitely object to its use?

   (A)   if its price and cost were equal
   (B)   if its cost were higher than the price of fossil fuels
   (C)   if its cost were higher than the cost of fossil fuels
   (D)   if the price of fossil fuels were to fall
   (E)   if it were less efficient than fossil fuels

11. This is most like a WEAKEN or STRENGTHEN or PARADOX question, because you're looking for the one thing in the answer choices that, if known, will have the most IMPACT on the argument. So let's go looking for that.

   (A)   It depends. If they were equal at current cost levels? No. At current price levels? Maybe. Eliminate it.
   (B)   This confuses "cost" and "price." Eliminate it.
   (C)   Yep. We know she doesn't like the current situation, and this would make it worse. She would object to this.
   (D)   This would have no impact on the argument either way. Eliminate it.
   (E)   Efficiency is not the issue—cost is.

12. An office equipment rental firm made the following claim:

   Owning your office equipment is actually more expensive than renting it. Over a three-year period, a mid-sized copier, for example, costs $23,000 per year to own, based on the average purchase price of the machine and the cost of its maintenance. The cost of renting a comparable copier is $22,000 per year.

   Which one of the following statements, if true, provides the most effective criticism of the argument above?

   (A)   The average lifespan of a copier is between five and six years.
   (B)   The figures cited above remain proportionally the same even when more expensive copiers are considered.
   (C)   The price of copiers actually has decreased in the last ten years.
   (D)   The price of copier paper and electricity may soon rise sharply.
   (E)   Buying used copiers can save money, even though such machines need more maintenance.

12. This is a WEAKEN question. Figure out which answer choice has the most negative impact on the conclusion of the argument. Remember to assume the hypothetical truth of each choice and apply it to the argument.

   (A)   So if this were true, it would be better to buy because the price would be lower than $23,000 since we're now spreading it out over five or six years rather than just three. It's the answer.
   (B)   This would strengthen the argument.
   (C)   This has no relevance to the argument because it affects renting and leasing equally.
   (D)   Same problem as (C)—there is no relevance.
   (E)   This just says that it can save money, not that it will—so it doesn't have as much impact as (A).

SECTION II

Questions 13–14

Despite advances in geothermal technology and equipment, experts rarely agree which method is the best indicator of a likely source of oil. Some believe the cycle of environmental changes determines the primary sources for crude oil, while others look to the evolution of organic matter as the most significant indicator. What they do agree on, however, is where oil won't be found. They agree that in areas that were scraped clean of organic sedimentary deposits by glaciers during the last million years or so, the biological "ingredients" that they believe are necessary for the formation of oil and gas are not present. That is, where glaciers have scoured a landmass, oil and gas will not be found.

13. If all of the information above is true, which one of the following can be reasonably inferred?

(A) Geologists understand some of the physical conditions necessary for the formation of deposits of oil.

(B) Scientists leave open the possibility that oil may have been formed during the last million years in some regions that were covered by glaciers during the same period.

(C) Geologists can, with a fairly high degree of accuracy, predict whether an area that meets the necessary preconditions for the formation of oil will, in fact, yield oil.

(D) Geologists can, with a fairly high degree of accuracy, predict whether oil can be found in a particular landmass that was not scoured by glaciers.

(E) If geologists can determine the biological "ingredients" necessary for the formation of oil, they can determine the locations of the most promising oil fields.

13. This is an INFERENCE question. Your goal is to find the one choice that must be true based on the information in the passage.

(A) This is nice and wishy-washy—they understand "some" of the conditions. Let's leave it.

(B) No, they said that there shouldn't be any. Eliminate it.

(C) We have no idea about their accuracy. They're still arguing methodology. Eliminate it.

(D) Same problem as (C). Eliminate it.

(E) We don't know this for sure. (A) is by far our safest choice here.

14. Which one of the following, if true, would most seriously weaken the geologists' view?

(A) Relatively little of the Earth's surface is known to rest above the sort of organic sedimentary deposits described above.

(B) Despite the existence of permanent glaciers, oil has been found at both the North and South Poles.

(C) There are too many variables involved for experts to be able to identify what does and does not need to be present for the formation of oil.

(D) The glacier theory cannot help locate oil in the ocean since ocean beds went untouched by glaciers.

(E) Oil deposits exist below the crust of the entire Earth, and are brought nearer to the surface by cracks in the crust.

14. This is a WEAKEN question. Try and see which answer choice has the most negative impact on the conclusion of the argument. Remember to assume the hypothetical truth of each choice and apply it to the argument.

(A) This has no impact on the argument either way—eliminate it.

(B) This choice doesn't say whether the glaciers have actually scoured the landmasses in these places. Let's see if there is anything better.

(C) Remember, the geologists are trying to say what the conditions are for it not happening, not the other way around. This has no impact.

(D) This also has no impact on the argument. Eliminate it.

(E) Oops—the geologists are boneheads because oil exists below the "entire earth." Thus, there are no places it doesn't exist, which totally destroys their argument. It's the answer.

SECTION II

15. Although all societies have some form of class system, there are systems that are based on neither wealth nor power. Still, there is no society that does not divide its population into the privileged and the common.

If the above statements are correct, it can be properly concluded that

(A) making distinctions between haves and have-nots is a part of human nature
(B) there are some people in all cultures who are considered privileged
(C) every society has its own unique hierarchy
(D) privileged people must have money
(E) all societies have a tradition of seeing themselves as either privileged or common

15. This is an INFERENCE question. Your goal is to find the one choice that must be true based on the information in the passage.

(A) "Human nature" is a little too general here. Eliminate it.
(B) "Some" is nice and wishy-washy. Let's leave it.
(C) It doesn't have to be true that every society's hierarchy is "unique." Eliminate it.
(D) Money is out of the scope of the argument. Eliminate it.
(E) Each society has BOTH privileged and common categories. (B) is our best answer here.

16. One can predict that the number of people in the nation's labor force will diminish in the next 20 years. Population growth in our country reached its apex in 1961, and by the late 1960s there were more employed heads of households in this country than ever before. The growth has slackened significantly, and by 1997 the total number of households will be reduced, thus limiting the number of potential employees in the work force.

Which one of the following, if true, would most seriously damage the conclusion of the above argument?

(A) The urge to acquire wealth contributed to the growth of the labor force in the 1960s.
(B) There will be greater competition among employers to attract employees from a shrinking population base in the 1990s.
(C) In the 1990s there will be more people who are not the heads of household entering the labor force than there were in the 1960s.
(D) Employers fared well in the 1950s with fewer potential employees than exist today.
(E) By 1997 there will be far more people running their own businesses than there are today.

16. This is a WEAKEN question. Figure out which answer choice has the most negative impact on the conclusion of the argument. Remember to assume the hypothetical truth of each choice and apply it to the argument.

(A) This has no impact—we're looking to weaken the conclusion that there will be fewer people in the workforce.
(B) This would strengthen the argument that there will be fewer people.
(C) So we've got this second whole group of people—this would weaken the argument. It's the answer.
(D) The 1950s are totally out of the scope here.
(E) Running your own business is out of scope.

SECTION II

| QUESTIONS | EXPLANATIONS |

Questions 17–18

A controversy recently erupted at College X after the student newspaper printed several letters to the editor that attacked the college's affirmative action program in offensive, racially charged language. Two psychologists at the school took advantage of the controversy by conducting an experiment on campus. Psychologist #1, posing as a reporter, stopped a student at random, ostensibly to solicit his or her opinion of the controversy. At the same time, psychologist #2, posing as a student, also stopped, joined the discussion, and made the first reply to the questions of the "reporter." The experiment showed that when psychologist #2 expressed support for the racist sentiments expressed in the letters, 75 percent of the subjects responded similarly. When psychologist #2 expressed strong disapproval of the language and substance of the letters, 90 percent of the subjects responded similarly.

17. Which one of the following represents the most reasonable conclusion that can be drawn from the information in the passage above?

   (A) People are more likely to voice their opposition to racism if they hear others doing the same.
   (B) People are less likely to hide their sympathy for certain racist attitudes if they feel that others share the same feelings.
   (C) People's willingness to voice their racist sentiments is proportional to the percentage of all people who share such sentiments.
   (D) People may be influenced by the opinions of others when they express their opinions of racist sentiments.
   (E) The extent to which popular opinion molds the opinions of individuals is significant, though not easily quantifiable.

18. If the psychologists described above were to conclude from their data that some people are more willing to speak up against racism if they hear others doing so, their conclusion would depend on the validity of which one of the following assumptions?

   (A) The students at College X are no more racist than are students at other colleges.
   (B) The students at College X are more likely to have experienced racism personally.
   (C) Some of the subjects in the experiment knew that the psychologists were posing as a reporter and a student.
   (D) Some of the subjects in their experiment would have changed their response to psychologist #1's questions if psychologist #2 had responded differently.
   (E) All of the subjects in the experiment stated their heartfelt, uninfluenced opinion of the incident in question.

17. This is an INFERENCE question. Your goal is to find the one choice that must be true based on the information in the passage.

   (A) This just focuses on the opponents of racism, and the argument is about both opponents and supporters.
   (B) Same problem as (A), so they are both wrong.
   (C) Same problem as (A)—we're only focusing on half of the people.
   (D) Nice and wishy-washy, and this is talking about both groups of people.
   (E) "Popular opinion" is too general a term here. (D) is the best answer.

18. This is an ASSUMPTION question. The correct answer will be something necessary for the conclusion to be true, and, if made false, will make the argument fall apart.

   (A) Racism per se is not the issue. The issue is students' willingness to express an opinion on racism.
   (B) Personal experiences are outside the scope of the argument.
   (C) If this were true, it would probably destroy the argument. Eliminate it.
   (D) Otherwise, the whole experiment would have had no impact—this is the answer.
   (E) We're interested in the willingness of people to express themselves, not in whether their opinions were heartfelt or uninfluenced.

SECTION II

19. Evidence seems to indicate that people's faith in some mystical practices increases when these practices offer relief in frightening or challenging situations. One significant piece of evidence is the observation that the use of "healing crystals" is more prevalent among people who suffer from life-threatening diseases such as cancer than it is among people who have minor health problems such as colds or the flu.

Which one of the following, if true, would most seriously weaken the conclusion drawn in the passage above?

(A) Rapid social change has alienated people and has led to an overall increase in people's adoption of mystical practices.

(B) Many mystical practices are never used by more than a small number of extremely ill people.

(C) If someone has a life-threatening disease, he may try nontraditional cures without necessarily believing that they will work.

(D) Psychics and mediums do not experience a surge in business after the occurrence of earthquakes and plane crashes.

(E) The use of crystals is one of the most ancient methods utilized for healing.

19. This is a WEAKEN question. Figure out which answer choice has the most negative impact on the conclusion of the argument. Remember to assume the hypothetical truth of each choice and apply it to the argument.

(A) We're concerned more with crystals and specific diseases—this is a little too general.

(B) Mystical practices that are not used are not the issue.

(C) Ah, so while they are trying these cures, their faith in them hasn't necessarily increased—this would weaken the argument.

(D) None of this is talking about anything in the argument. Eliminate it.

(E) The ancientness of crystals has no impact on the argument. Eliminate it.

20. Lithotripsy is a relatively new procedure for the treatment of kidney stones. The patient is suspended in a tub of water and sound waves are aimed at his kidneys. Upon impact, the waves shatter the stones. Recovery time from this procedure is shorter than that of surgery, which is the conventional method of treatment. Lithotripsy is also less expensive than surgery. Therefore, physicians should stop performing invasive surgery for kidney stones soon.

Which one of the following statements, if true, most seriously weakens the argument in the passage above?

(A) There has been little research done on the effect of lithotripsy on senior citizens.

(B) It will be many years before lithotripsy equipment can be produced in sufficient quantity to meet demand.

(C) Many doctors do not know much about lithotripsy, as it is a relatively new procedure.

(D) Some insurance companies do not cover treatments such as lithotripsy.

(E) Lithotripsy is not an available option for children.

20. This is a WEAKEN question. Figure out which answer choice has the most negative impact on the conclusion of the argument. Remember to assume the hypothetical truth of each choice and apply it to the argument.

(A) Bummer, but we don't know if kidney stone operations are performed on senior citizens to begin with. Eliminate it.

(B) So the fact that surgery will stop "soon" is not going to happen. This is the answer.

(C) The fact that they don't know doesn't mean that they can't find out quickly. Eliminate it.

(D) Bummer, but maybe they will soon.

(E) Same problem as (A)—we don't know if children ever need kidney stone operations.

SECTION II

QUESTIONS	EXPLANATIONS

21. The human body changes a great deal over the course of a lifetime. As people enter middle age, for instance, they tend to become overweight, regardless of their body type as young adults. Though this weight gain has long been blamed on the tendency of middle-aged people to consume an excess of calories daily, recent evidence suggests that it is instead attributable to the body's decreased demand for calories. This decreased demand means that a maintenance of prior caloric consumption will provide an excess of calories, most of which will simply be stored as body fat.

A logical critique of the passage above would likely emphasize the fact that the author fails to

(A) establish definitively the connection between caloric intake and weight gain

(B) offer any hard evidence of the percentage of middle-aged people who are actually overweight

(C) give detailed information as to the causes of the body's decreased demand for calories in middle age

(D) offer a consistent definition of the term "excess" as it relates to caloric consumption

(E) discuss the causes of obesity in the population at large

21. This is a REASONING question. Come up with your own description of why the author's conclusion is flawed before you go to the answer choices, and then match your description to the choices.

(A) No, the author does establish the connection, just not exactly how it works.

(B) Lack of hard evidence is almost never the correct answer. Just because the author doesn't provide statistics is not why the argument is internally bad. Eliminate it.

(C) Same problem as (B).

(D) This is the biggest problem here. The author never tells us that a certain amount isn't in excess when you're younger but then is later on—that's why the argument is bad.

(E) Obesity was never mentioned. (D) is the best answer here.

22. If a candidate is to win an election easily, that candidate must respond to the electorate's emotional demands—demands that the opponent either does not see or cannot act upon. Though these emotional demands are often not directly articulated by the electorate or by the candidate responding to them, they are an integral part of any landslide victory.

Which one of the following conclusions can most logically be drawn from the passage above?

(A) If neither candidate responds to the emotional demands of the electorate, either candidate might win in a landslide.

(B) If an election was close, the emotional demands of the electorate were conflicting.

(C) If a candidate responds to the emotional demands of the electorate, that candidate will have a landslide victory.

(D) An election during which neither candidate responds to the emotional demands of the electorate will not result in a landslide.

(E) Emotional demands are the only inarticulated issues in an election.

22. This is an INFERENCE question. Your goal is to find the one choice that must be true based on the information in the passage.

(A) No, because if candidates don't respond, there can't be a landslide.

(B) We have no idea what would happen if the election were close. Eliminate it.

(C) This is the invalid contrapositive of the first sentence. Eliminate it.

(D) Bingo—it's the contrapositive of the first sentence—that if you don't respond, you can't have a landslide.

(E) "Only" is too extreme here. Eliminate it.

SECTION II

23. Commodities analysts maintain that if the price of soybeans decreases by more than half, the consumer's purchase price for milk produced by livestock fed these soybeans will also decrease by more than half.

Which one of the following, if true, casts the most doubt on the prediction made by the commodities analysts?

(A) New genetic strains of livestock and improvements in feed lot procedures have enabled some cows to increase their milk output while decreasing their soybean intake.

(B) Dairy farmers cannot expand their profit margins any further without compromising the health of their livestock.

(C) Many different dairy suppliers compete with each other, forcing a consumer-driven market.

(D) Studies in other dairy-producing countries show that the amount of milk purchased by consumers usually rises after an initial decrease in milk prices.

(E) Pasteurization and distribution costs, neither of which varies with the price of soybeans, constitute the major portion of the price of milk.

23. This is a WEAKEN question. Figure out which answer choice has the most negative impact on the conclusion of the argument. Remember to assume the hypothetical truth of each choice and apply it to the argument.

(A) Great! Unfortunately, we're interested in the price of milk. No impact here.

(B) Bummer for them. However, no impact on the argument again.

(C) One would assume that people in the same business compete with each other. No impact.

(D) Other countries really won't help us here. No impact.

(E) Yes—this would show that the price of milk won't change because the soybean component of it is small. It's the answer.

24. The more dairy products a person consumes, the higher his cholesterol level is. More than half of the people in this country eat in excess of four dairy products each day, whereas in Germany the figure is only 10 percent. Accordingly, more than 65 percent of the people in this country have cholesterol levels that are considered too high and only 2 percent of Germans have similarly excessive levels. Therefore, if the cholesterol levels of Americans are to be brought down, we must eat fewer dairy products.

Which one of the following, if established, could strengthen the author's argument?

(A) Citizens of the United States are less concerned with cholesterol levels than citizens of Germany.

(B) Germans are more disciplined about watching their diets than Americans.

(C) People who are concerned about their cholesterol levels will eat fewer dairy products.

(D) A person's cholesterol level is reduced significantly when he or she consumes fewer than two dairy products per day.

(E) Dairy products, and not any other food items, are the critical factors in determining cholesterol levels.

24. This is a STRENGTHEN question. Figure out which answer choice has the most positive impact on the conclusion of the argument. Remember to assume the hypothetical truth of each choice and apply it to the argument.

(A) We need something about dairy products here—level of concern has no impact.

(B) Discipline has no impact—we're looking for dairy products.

(C) This is the same problem as (A). Eliminate it.

(D) This looks pretty good, but we don't know exactly how many dairy products the Germans consume, just that they don't consume "in excess of four." Let's see if there is something better.

(E) Bingo—this shows a necessary causality, because the author's conclusion doesn't allow for any other explanations. Therefore, dairy has to be the critical factor.

SECTION II

| QUESTIONS | EXPLANATIONS |

25. The introduction of new technologies and equipment into the marketplace can significantly alter the quality of life for the members of a society. The automatic dishwasher, for example, eased the housekeeping burdens traditionally borne by women. At the same time, the convenience of an automatic dishwasher has fostered a dependence upon its time-saving qualities. It has become increasingly difficult to find a household with an automatic dishwasher where small numbers of dishes are washed by hand. In the long run, the environmental cost of such behavior is scarcely worth the amount of time saved.

Which one of the following principles is best illustrated by the example presented in the passage?

(A) The significance of a benefit should be weighed in terms of its overall effect.
(B) People should make a unified effort to reduce their negative impact upon the environment.
(C) Some new technologies offer no perceptible benefit to society.
(D) The acquisition of leisure time is not worth the destruction of the biosphere.
(E) Most new machinery makes our lives more streamlined and economical.

25. This is a PRINCIPLE question. We are given five principles in the answer choices for this specific question, so we should come up with our own principle for the actions in the argument and match it to the answer choices.

(A) This looks good. Even though dishwashers are cool, their overall impact is negative. Let's leave this one.
(B) The argument is about dishwashers, not people.
(C) But dishwashers do—it's just that they also offer a perceptible downside, too.
(D) This is good, but it is a bit extreme—will dishwashers really destroy the biosphere? (A) is a more balanced response here.
(E) True, but this doesn't talk about the downside at all—(A) is the answer.

SECTION III

QUESTIONS	EXPLANATIONS

1. Senator: For economic issues, I base my responses on logic. For political issues, I base my responses either on logic or gut instinct. For moral issues, I never base my responses on logic.

   Which one of the following can be correctly inferred from the statements above ?

   (A) If the senator relies on logic, he may be responding to a moral issue.
   (B) If the senator relies on logic, he is not responding to an economic issue.
   (C) If the senator does not rely on logic, he is responding to a political issue.
   (D) If the senator does not rely on logic, he must be responding to an economic issue.
   (E) If the senator does not rely on logic, he might be responding to a political issue.

1. This is an INFERENCE question. Your goal is to find the one choice that must be true based on the information in the passage.

   (A) No, the senator never bases moral issue responses on logic. Eliminate it.
   (B) No, the senator may very well be responding to an economic issue. Eliminate it.
   (C) No, the senator could be responding to a moral issue. Eliminate it.
   (D) No, the senator always uses logic to respond to economic issues. Eliminate it.
   (E) Bingo. Nice and wishy-washy, and accurate. With political issues, the senator might respond with a gut instinct. This is the answer.

2. Concern about the environmental and health problems associated with nuclear energy has compelled activist groups to join forces in an attempt to shut down nuclear power plants. However, a survey of nuclear power plants across the United States showed that there have only been two accidents in the past ten years, both minor in nature, and in both cases, the danger was quickly contained. If the United States is to produce enough energy to become completely independent from foreign sources of energy, more nuclear power plants must be built, and the misinformation being distributed by activist groups must be countered by the statistics found in the study.

   All of the following are assumptions of the above argument EXCEPT:

   (A) Using nuclear power is the only way for the United States to produce enough energy that no fuel needs to be imported.
   (B) Some people think nuclear power plants are dangerous.
   (C) The accidents caused little harm.
   (D) Other methods of producing energy are also considered dangerous.
   (E) The United States needs to be completely self-sufficient in the production of energy.

2. This is an ASSUMPTION question. Since this is an EXCEPT question, the correct answer will be the one thing that is NOT necessary for the conclusion to be true, and, if made false, will NOT make the argument fall apart.

   (A) If there were another method, the argument would fall apart. This is a necessary assumption—eliminate it.
   (B) If no one thought they were dangerous, then what are they worrying about? Eliminate it.
   (C) If they caused a lot of harm, it would weaken the argument. Eliminate it.
   (D) Bummer, but it isn't necessary for the conclusion to be true that nuclear power is the ONLY way. Let's leave it.
   (E) If we didn't need to be self-sufficient, then why bother with building more nuclear power plants? This is also necessary, so the answer here is (D).

SECTION III

3. Rather than learn about Senate hearings by listening to word-of-mouth accounts or by sitting in on the sessions themselves, people now depend mainly on newspapers and television for information about important investigative and confirmation hearings conducted by Senate committees. Thus, the media serve as a surrogate for the millions of people who care deeply about such proceedings but could never attend them themselves.

The above passage is most likely part of an argument in favor of

(A) reserving more seats for ordinary citizens at important Senate hearings
(B) imposing secrecy rules on the Senate committee hearings not already covered by the media
(C) expanding media coverage of important Senate hearings
(D) enacting a law that would prohibit any censorship of press coverage of the Senate
(E) widening the scope of Senate inquiry of press censorship

3. This is a CONCLUSION question. Look for the answer that is the goal of the passage. What is it trying to do here?

(A) No, we want to look for something about how the media is so good for us.
(B) This would go against what the argument is saying—we want more, not less, coverage.
(C) Bingo—they're doing such a great job, let's expand their coverage. This is the answer.
(D) We're not concerned in the argument with anyone taking away the media's power or coverage rights. Eliminate it.
(E) We don't care about Senate inquiries. We like the press. Eliminate it.

4. Advertisement: Professional exterminators will tell you that in order to rid your home of roaches, you must do more than kill all the roaches you see. This is why the system that professional exterminators use most includes a poison that inhibits the development of roach eggs already laid, as well as a chemical that kills all adult roaches. This same combination is now available to the nonprofessional in new Extirm. When you're ready to get rid of roaches once and for all, get Extirm in your corner.

All of the following are implied by the advertisement above EXCEPT:

(A) Professional exterminators asked about roach extermination recommended Extirm.
(B) Extirm contains a chemical that inhibits the development of roach eggs.
(C) More than one chemical is required to rid a home of roaches.
(D) Inhibiting the development of roach eggs may not eliminate roaches from the home.
(E) Roaches reproduce by laying eggs.

4. This is an INFERENCE question. It is also an EXCEPT question, so your goal is to find the one choice that doesn't have to be true based on the information in the passage.

(A) We have no idea what they recommend. It's never mentioned in the passage. This is the answer.
(B) Yes, this is mentioned in the second sentence. Eliminate it.
(C) Yes, this is mentioned in the second sentence. One for eggs, one for adults. Eliminate it.
(D) Which is why we need two chemicals—see the second sentence again.
(E) This is a major part of sentence two. Eliminate it.

SECTION III

| QUESTIONS | EXPLANATIONS |

5. In congressional hearings the question arises: "Which side knows best the potential benefits and dangers involved in the drilling of new offshore oil wells within U.S. territorial waters?" Oil companies' advice must certainly be taken with a grain of salt, since they are concerned only with profit and will oppose any legislation that would reduce such profit. Environmentalists' dire warnings must also be questioned, since many environmentalists' opposition to such drilling is purely reflexive, and without basis in scientific fact. This is why, in order to understand fully the costs and benefits that must be weighed in deciding whether to drill oil wells in U.S. coastal waters, Congress should rely primarily on the advice of academic research geologists, who are both informed and objective on the issue.

Which one of the following, if true, would most seriously weaken the author's conclusion in the passage above?

(A) Environmentalists are more knowledgeable about the dangers associated with drilling oil wells than is the average congressperson.

(B) Most academic research geologists rely heavily on income earned from consulting fees paid by oil companies.

(C) Oil companies have responded to public outcry over environmental damage caused by offshore oil drilling by developing technology that makes offshore oil drilling much safer than it used to be.

(D) The oil industry lobby is responsible each year for significant campaign contributions to legislators.

(E) Academic research geologists are not unanimous in their support of or opposition to new offshore oil drilling in U.S. coastal waters.

5. This is a WEAKEN question. Figure out which answer choice has the most negative impact on the conclusion of the argument. Remember to assume the hypothetical truth of each choice and apply it to the argument.

(A) We want something that shows how the geologists are biased. This doesn't do that. Eliminate it.

(B) Oops! So the geologists may not be objective. This is the answer.

(C) It's nice that it's safer than it used to be, but this doesn't call into question the geologists' suitability.

(D) Doesn't say anything about how the geologists would be biased. Eliminate it.

(E) This would strengthen the argument that the geologists would be unbiased. Eliminate it.

Questions 6–7

Throughout the twentieth century, anthropologists studying the myths and ceremonies of a particular group indigenous to the Amazon rain forest in Brazil have maintained that their presence and the questions they asked were not influencing the group's culture. Researchers now note, however, that the earliest recorded observations, made in 1919, of the group's ceremonies marking the onset of the rainy season made no reference to a creation myth. The first mention of a creation myth's appearance in the ceremony is found in 1933, and by 1986, nearly twenty minutes of the seventy-minute ceremony were devoted to a myth explaining the rains in relation to a "First Great Storm," during which the world was supposed to have been created.

6. Which one of the following is most strongly implied by the argument above?

(A) The observations of the ceremonies in 1919 were either incomplete or inaccurate.

(B) After the anthropologists explained the importance of creation myths to their subjects, the group developed myths of its own.

(C) The anthropologists' interests in particular cultural beliefs, such as creation myths, may have induced a gradual change in the group's ceremonies.

(D) If the anthropologists had been more conscientious, their records would not reflect apparent discrepancies in their accounts of the group's beliefs.

(E) The subjects of study, trying to secure the benefits of the industrial world enjoyed by anthropologists, changed their ceremonies to correspond to the ideas of the anthropologists.

7. Which one of the following represents an illustration of the same phenomenon that the author describes in the passage above?

(A) A sociologist notes that a wave of immigration invariably results in changes in some religious practices of the dominant culture.

(B) A psychologist discovers that patients who originally reported few or no dreams consistently acknowledge frequent and vivid dreams after eight months of dream-analysis therapy.

(C) An economist studying a Third World country finds an increasing reliance on Western technology rather than on indigenous agricultural methods.

(D) An astronomer, using two different telescopes to measure the distance to a nearby star, gets two different results.

(E) An historian of religion finds that the creation myths of several cultures have changed over time.

6. This is an INFERENCE question. Your goal is to find the one choice that must be true based on the information in the passage.

(A) We have no evidence for this. Eliminate it.

(B) We have no evidence that they explained anything, just that they asked questions. Eliminate it.

(C) The anthropologists asked questions. That could have been how they showed their interest in the creation myths. Let's leave this in.

(D) We have no evidence that they weren't conscientious. Eliminate it.

(E) We have no evidence that the subjects had any knowledge of the benefits of the industrial world. Eliminate it. (C) is the best answer here.

7. This is a PARALLEL-THE-REASONING question. Try to get the theme or diagram of the logic and then match it to each answer choice.

(A) They didn't add people to the group in the passage—they just observed them. Eliminate it.

(B) This looks pretty good. The argument had people starting out without finding anything they were looking for, and then later on, what they were looking for developed. This is the answer.

(C) The people in the passage weren't relying on anything. Eliminate it.

(D) Two telescopes? Two results? Huh?

(E) Yes, but was there any observation or questioning of these cultures along the way? We have no idea. Eliminate it.

SECTION III

QUESTIONS	EXPLANATIONS

8. Mayor: An across-the-board increase of just twenty cents on all the city's toll bridges and tunnels would raise close to a hundred thousand dollars a year at the current bridge and tunnel traffic levels. Because a toll increase of three dollars would therefore raise more than a million dollars a year, such an increase seems like the ideal solution to our persistent school budget shortfalls. The toll increase would offer further savings by lessening the volume of traffic over our bridges and tunnels, which would result in reduced maintenance costs for those structures.

Which one of the following identifies most accurately the error in the mayor's reasoning?

(A) She incorrectly assumes that two different causes are necessarily related.

(B) She bases her argument on erroneous figures for the current traffic flow.

(C) She makes assumptions that are mutually exclusive.

(D) She takes as a given what should instead first be established as evidence.

(E) She bases her argument on political considerations rather than logical analysis.

8. This is a REASONING question. Come up with your own description of why the author's conclusion is flawed before you go to the answer choices, and then match your description to the choices.

(A) No, we're looking for some sort of contradiction here. This doesn't say that. Eliminate it.

(B) We have no idea whether or not the figures are erroneous. Eliminate it.

(C) Bingo. If both assumptions are true, the argument makes no sense. You can't simultaneously generate the same sort of money and have fewer people paying the tolls.

(D) Same problem as (A). Eliminate it.

(E) There is no mention of political considerations. Eliminate it.

9. Dale: The city can't possibly have budget problems this quarter because of the heavier than normal snows this winter. A recent article mentioned that Haline, a substance used to de-ice roads and sidewalks, costs three cents a pound, which is quite cheap considering how effective it is.

Glenn: In actuality the cost of Haline is closer to eighty cents a pound. When you factor in the destructive effect of Haline on the infrastructure, and its deleterious effects on ground water and vegetation, the cost of Haline clearly exceeds its price.

If a substance performs as effectively as Haline and has no harmful side effects (but its price is higher than that of Haline), Glenn would be most likely to oppose its use if

(A) its price fluctuates seasonally
(B) its price and its cost are similar
(C) it must be handled in the same manner as Haline
(D) its cost is higher than the price of Haline
(E) its price is higher than the cost of Haline

9. This is most like a WEAKEN or STRENGTHEN or PARADOX question, because you're looking for the one thing in the answer choices that, if known, will have the most IMPACT on the argument. So let's go looking for that.

(A) By how much? Eliminate it.

(B) Similar to what? Each other or to Haline? Eliminate it.

(C) We're more interested in cost and price, not handling. Eliminate it.

(D) Close, but actually we want the opposite of this.

(E) Bingo. If this were the case, the new substance would be even worse than Haline, so Glenn would oppose it. This is the answer.

SECTION III

QUESTIONS	EXPLANATIONS

10. Since mandatory water conservation measures were enacted by the state of California in response to the drought of 1990–1992, water consumption in the state has increased by nearly 10 percent. Clearly, the state's water conservation measures have been counterproductive, and California's water situation is more dire now than it was in 1992, the year of the last drought.

All of the following facts, if true, would be useful in evaluating the validity of the argument above EXCEPT:

(A) The population of California has increased by 15 percent since 1992.

(B) The average California resident now uses less water on an annual basis than he or she did in 1992.

(C) The water conservation measures did not apply to agricultural usage.

(D) In accordance with the conservation measures, nonessential water use in private homes has declined by 50 percent since 1992.

(E) In the years since 1992, water collection technology has developed to such a point that state and municipal water districts have an increased capacity to gather and store water.

10. This is most like an ASSUMPTION question because you are looking for a fact that will help you to evaluate the validity of the assumption.

(A) This would be useful because, if true, it would tell us that the conservation measures actually are working. Eliminate it.

(B) This would also tell us that the conservation measures are working, so eliminate this too.

(C) So maybe there is more agriculture happening, so this information would be useful too. Eliminate it.

(D) Same thing as in (A), (B), and (C). It would tell us that the conservation is actually working. Eliminate it.

(E) This is nice, but it doesn't let us know whether or not the conservation measures are working or not—it tells us that we won't have to worry about it, which isn't the point of the argument. So this is the answer.

SECTION III

QUESTIONS	EXPLANATIONS

11.   Netta: A recent study revealed that while the overall crime rate has gone down, crimes committed by youths have increased dramatically. The irony is that our own judicial system is fostering this situation. By treating young people who commit crimes less severely than adults who commit similar crimes, the courts allow these young criminals to go free, and they then commit more crimes. The message that "crime is wrong, but not as bad if you're not of age" is being communicated. A person who is convicted of a crime should be sufficiently punished regardless of age, otherwise the number of crimes committed by youths will continue to increase.

Trey: Netta, you are being extremely shortsighted. The alternative to allowing young criminals to go free is incarcerating them in a youth facility or penitentiary. But sociologists have found that the social environment in such facilities encourages and condones delinquent behavior within the facility, and by extension, outside the facility. When the youth returns to society after having been incarcerated for even a short period, recidivism occurs within three to four weeks.

The point at issue between Netta and Trey is

(A)   the extent to which the judicial system is contributing to the increase in the crime rate

(B)   whether the leniency shown towards adolescents can be cited as the sole cause of the increase in crimes committed by young people

(C)   what types of judicial reform could affect the rise in youth crime

(D)   how most effectively to stop the increase in crime by examining which cause is most often to blame

(E)   whether incarceration as an alternative to leniency for convicted youths will in fact help to solve the problem

11.   This is a REASONING question. Come up with your own description of what they're arguing about, and then match your description to the choices.

(A)   No, because it just says "crime rate," which is too general. We're talking juvenile crimes here. Eliminate it.

(B)   "Sole cause" is a bit extreme here. They're not arguing absolutes. Eliminate it.

(C)   We're arguing about what would cause decreases, not increases. Eliminate it.

(D)   Same problem as (A). It only talks about crime generally. Eliminate it.

(E)   Bingo—Netta thinks incarceration would be a deterrent; Trey thinks it would cause even greater recidivism. This is the answer.

QUESTIONS	EXPLANATIONS

12. Computer Technician: This system has either a software problem or a hardware problem. None of the available diagnostic tests has been able to determine where the problem lies. The software can be replaced, but the hardware cannot be altered in any way, which means that if the problem lies in the hardware, the entire system will have to be scrapped. We must begin work to solve the problem by presupposing that the problem is with the software.

On which one of the following principles could the technician's reasoning be based?

(A) In fixing a problem that has two possible causes, it makes more sense to deal with both causes rather than spend time trying to determine which is the actual cause of the problem.

(B) If events outside one's control bear on a decision, the best course of action is to assume the "worst-case" scenario.

(C) When the soundness of an approach depends on the validity of an assumption, one's first task must be to test that assumption's validity.

(D) When circumstances must be favorable in order for a strategy to succeed, the strategy must be based on the assumption that conditions are indeed favorable until proved otherwise.

(E) When only one strategy can be successful, the circumstances affecting that strategy must be altered so that strategy may be employed.

12. This is a PRINCIPLE question. We are given five principles in the answer choices for this specific question, so we should come up with our own principle for the actions in the argument and match it to the answer choices.

(A) But they're not dealing with both causes— only the software cause. Eliminate it.

(B) They're not assuming that—if they were, they'd go out and replace the hardware. Eliminate it.

(C) They're not testing assumptions; they can't test anything. They just have to hope it's the problem that's cheaper to fix. Eliminate it.

(D) They're hoping that it's the software until it's really obvious it's not. This is the answer.

(E) They're not altering any strategy in the argument. Eliminate it.

SECTION III

QUESTIONS	EXPLANATIONS

13. To become a master at chess, a person must play. If a person plays for at least four hours a day, that person will inevitably become a master of the game. Thus, if a person is a master at the game of chess, that person must have played each day for at least four hours.

The error in the logic of the argument above is most accurately described by which one of the following?

(A) The conclusion is inadequate because it fails to acknowledge that people who play for four hours each day might not develop a degree of skill for the game that others view as masterful.

(B) The conclusion is inadequate because it fails to acknowledge that playing one hour a day might be sufficient for some people to become masters.

(C) The conclusion is inadequate because it fails to acknowledge that if a person has not played four hours a day, that person has not become a master.

(D) The conclusion is inadequate because it fails to acknowledge that four hours of playing time each day is not a strategy recommended by any world-champion chess players.

(E) The conclusion is inadequate because it fails to acknowledge that most people are not in a position to devote four hours each day to playing chess.

13. This is a REASONING question. Try to come up with your own description of why the author's conclusion is flawed before you go to the answer choices, and then match your description to the choices.

(A) Whether other people think the player is a master is irrelevant. According to the argument, anyone who plays at least four hours a day "will inevitably become a master."

(B) Bingo. The author makes an invalid contrapositive in the argument. This is the answer.

(C) We have no idea whether this is true. Eliminate it.

(D) We don't care about chess champion recommendations. Eliminate it.

(E) We don't care about most people. The argument doesn't say everyone. Eliminate it.

14. Libraries are eliminating many subscriptions to highly specialized periodicals due to budget cuts. Yet without these reference materials, many subjects cannot be researched effectively. Therefore, efforts must be made to provide better funding so as to ensure the maintenance of at least those periodicals that will be most used by researchers in the future.

Which one of the following can be inferred from the author's argument for the maintenance of funding for the periodicals?

(A) If a periodical is highly specialized, the maintenance of its subscription is more important than any financial considerations.

(B) Research performed with periodicals is not a valid consideration in determining funding.

(C) Research should be the focus of a library's funding.

(D) It can be predicted which periodicals will be of value for researchers in the future.

(E) The elimination of periodicals is simply an inevitable part of library organization.

14. This is an INFERENCE question. Your goal is to find the one choice that must be true based on the information in the passage.

(A) This is a little too extreme. What if the periodical cost more than the library itself? Eliminate it.

(B) The argument says it is. Eliminate it.

(C) Should it be the focus of their funding or of their subscription policies? Eliminate it.

(D) See the last sentence of the passage. If we can't predict this, the argument falls apart. This is the answer.

(E) We have no idea whether or not this is true. Eliminate it.

15. Last year, Marcel enjoyed a high income from exactly two places: his sporting goods store and his stock market investments. Although Marcel earns far more from his store than from his investments, the money he earns from the stock market is an important part of his income. Because of a series of drops in the stock market, Marcel will not earn as much from his investments this year. It follows then that Marcel will make less money this year than he did last year.

Which one of the following is an assumption necessary to the author's argument?

(A) Increased profits at Marcel's sporting goods store will not offset any loss in stock market income.

(B) Sporting goods stores earn lower profits when the stock market drops.

(C) Drops in the stock market do not always affect all of a particular investor's stocks.

(D) Marcel's stock market investments will be subject to increased volatility.

(E) If his income is lower, Marcel will not be able to meet his expenses.

15. This is an ASSUMPTION question. The correct answer will be something necessary for the conclusion to be true, and, if made false, will make the argument fall apart.

(A) If they did offset, then Marcel could make just as much, which would make the argument fall apart. This is the answer.

(B) There is no connection between these two things except for the fact that Marcel is interested in both of them. Eliminate it.

(C) But we are specifically told in the argument that his portfolio WILL be affected. Eliminate it.

(D) Bummer, but we already know he's not going to make as much. Eliminate it.

(E) Bummer, but the argument never mentions his expenses. This is out of scope.

SECTION III

QUESTIONS	EXPLANATIONS

16. Johanna: Quinto admits that because of his governmental post he can select which companies are awarded municipal contracts. He further admits that he awarded a contract to a company owned by a member of the town council who offered to support Quinto in his mayoral bid in exchange for the contract. There is no excuse for this kind of unethical behavior.

Iya: I don't see his actions as unethical. The company awarded the contract is known to produce the highest-quality work at a comparatively competitive price. So in getting support for his mayoral bid, Quinto has ensured the city will get quality work, and thus has saved the taxpayers thousands of dollars.

Iya disagrees with Johanna by

(A) insisting that ethical behavior can only be viewed in the context in which it takes place

(B) countering that the result of Quinto's actions determines whether those activities are ethical

(C) comparing Quinto's actions to the actions of the company and finding both behaviors to be ethical

(D) applying a different definition of the word "ethical" to two situations

(E) defining ethical behavior as being formed by personal, religious, or spiritual philosophies

16. This is a REASONING question. Come up with your own description of how Iya disagrees with Johanna, and then match your description to the choices.

(A) This choice is too general; she's talking about one instance, not ethical behavior in general.

(B) Iya claims that everything's all right because the results will all be good. This is the answer.

(C) Iya is not comparing actions; she's commenting on the actions of the mayor.

(D) The definition remains the same—Iya just thinks everything is cool and Johanna doesn't.

(E) This is all out of the scope of the argument. Eliminate it.

SECTION III

17. One of the criticisms of recent political campaigns is that the candidate with the greater financial resources usually wins. A long presidential election campaign is more equitable than is the quick and expedient process recommended by some. A longer campaign, however, decreases the likelihood that a candidate with tremendous resources can control the campaign through a barrage of high-priced media campaigns. In a long campaign, a candidate is forced to speak substantively on the issues, and the voters have more complete access to the candidate. Thus, a long campaign creates parity among candidates who may not be equally financed by permitting the less popular, less well-funded candidates to invest time rather than money in their campaigns, thereby gaining recognition for themselves through the use of speeches, debates, and other media-oriented forums.

Which one of the following statements most seriously weakens the argument made above in favor of long presidential campaigns?

(A) Voters who lose interest during a long campaign are less likely to show up at the polls, thus contributing to the already significant problem of voter apathy.

(B) A long campaign requires candidates to divide their attention between public matters and the needs of their parties.

(C) A long campaign weakens the general public's interest in the process of global democracy.

(D) Candidates depend on volunteers, whose sense of commitment is frayed by a long campaign.

(E) A long campaign precludes participation by many able candidates who cannot afford to take time off from their private occupations for extended lengths of time.

17. This is a WEAKEN question. Figure out which answer choice has the most negative impact on the conclusion of the argument. Remember to assume the hypothetical truth of each choice and apply it to the argument.

(A) We don't care about the percentage of people voting. We're talking candidates here, not voter turnout. No impact.

(B) This would have impact on both the well-funded and non-funded people equally, so eliminate it.

(C) Global democracy isn't the point here. Eliminate it.

(D) This looks good, but it actually has the same problem as (B)—it would affect both groups equally.

(E) Yes. So a long campaign isn't going to create parity, because the people with money will be able to stick with it longer. This is the answer.

SECTION III

18. Some botanists have found it extremely difficult to save certain species of elm tree from fungal infection. Even the most potent fungicide has been unsuccessful in preventing its growth on such trees. However, researchers have managed to control the growth and spread of the fungus by spraying the fungus with a 0.2% saline solution.

Which one of the following, if true, offers the strongest explanation as to why the saline spray has been successful?

(A) The cell walls of the fungus cannot filter out the salt compounds, which, once inside the cell, interfere with reproduction.

(B) The presence of salt creates an electrolyte imbalance within living cells, ultimately killing each cell it comes in contact with.

(C) When salt is used in combination with strong fungicide, the fungicide becomes potent enough to kill any fungus.

(D) It has been on record that farmers have used salt to kill destructive plant fungi since the late eighteenth century.

(E) Fungicides have generally been unsuccessful because any fungicide strong enough to destroy a fungus would be strong enough to destroy the roots as well.

18. This is a STRENGTHEN question. Figure out which answer choice has the most positive impact on the conclusion of the argument. Remember to assume the hypothetical truth of each choice and apply it to the argument.

(A) This would explain why the growth and spread of the fungus would be stopped—it couldn't reproduce. This is the answer.

(B) If this were true, the saline would actually kill the fungus—but the argument says it controls the fungus. Eliminate it.

(C) The argument doesn't say we're using the saline in conjunction with the fungicide. Eliminate it.

(D) This is a nice bit of history, but it doesn't explain WHY the salt is effective—just that it was effective in the past. Eliminate it.

(E) Right. Which is why we're using the saline. But this doesn't explain why the saline works. Eliminate it.

SECTION III

QUESTIONS	EXPLANATIONS

19. In concluding that there has been a shift in the sense of parental responsibility in America since the 1960s, researchers point to the increase in the frequency with which fathers tend to the daily needs of their children. However, this increase cannot be attributed exclusively to a shift in parental mores, for during the same period there has been an increase in the percentage of mothers who have jobs. With this in mind, the increased participation of fathers in child-rearing may well be only a symptom of a more fundamental change in society.

The author of the passage criticizes the conclusion of the researchers by

(A) offering a clearer definition of the researchers' premises, thereby compromising their argument

(B) attacking the integrity of the researchers rather than their reasoning

(C) showing that the researchers have reversed cause and effect in making their argument

(D) pointing out that their criteria for "parental responsibility" are not a logical basis for their argument

(E) suggesting an alternative cause for the effect cited by the researchers

19. This is a REASONING question. Come up with your own description of how the author makes the argument and then match your description to the choices.

(A) Their argument is clear; it's their conclusion that stinks. Eliminate it.

(B) The author doesn't say that they are liars, just that their conclusion is wrong.

(C) No, the author is saying that there is a different cause. Eliminate it.

(D) Their criteria and premises are fine; it's their conclusion that is bad. Eliminate it.

(E) Yes—that it's not that fathers care more, it's just that they are exposed more to their children because mothers now work. This is the answer.

SECTION III

Questions 20–21

Upon exiting an exhibit, some visitors to art museums find it difficult to describe what it was that they liked and didn't like about the paintings. Yet since these visitors feel strongly about which art they believed to be good and which art they believed to be bad, appreciating a work of art obviously does not require the ability to articulate what, specifically, was perceived to be good or bad.

20. The argument above assumes which one of the following?

(A) The fact that some people find it difficult to articulate what they like about a work of art does not mean that no one can.

(B) If an individual feels strongly about a work of art, then he or she is capable of appreciating that work of art.

(C) The vocabulary of visual art is not a part of common knowledge, but rather is known only to those who study the arts.

(D) When a person can articulate what he or she likes about a particular painting, he or she is able to appreciate that work of art.

(E) Paintings can be discussed only in general terms of good and bad.

20. This is an ASSUMPTION question. The correct answer will be something necessary for the conclusion to be true, and, if made false, will make the argument fall apart.

(A) We're looking for a connection between articulation and appreciation. This isn't it.

(B) Bingo. If it were not true that strong feelings can lead to appreciation, the argument would totally fall apart. This is the answer.

(C) This is classic LSAT babble. Vocabulary of visual art? Eliminate it.

(D) Always? What if the person hates it? Is that appreciation?

(E) We're not talking specific or general here, we're more concerned with whether or not we merely can or can't say anything at all. (B) is the best choice.

21. According to the passage above, all of the following could be true EXCEPT:

(A) Some museum visitors can explain with great precision what they liked and didn't like about a certain painting.

(B) If a person studies art, then that person will be able to articulate her opinion about paintings.

(C) If a person can't say why she likes a piece of art, it doesn't necessarily mean that she doesn't appreciate that piece.

(D) Some visitors can explain what they liked about a piece, but are unable to explain what they didn't like.

(E) The inability to articulate always indicates the inability to appreciate.

21. This is an INFERENCE question. Since it is also an EXCEPT question, your goal is to find the one choice that can't be true based on the information in the passage.

(A) This can be true—the argument only says that some can't. Eliminate it.

(B) This can be true—there could be some people who can do this. Eliminate it.

(C) Yes—as long as they feel strongly about it, they can still appreciate it. Articulation isn't necessary.

(D) This can be true also—there is no contradiction in the argument.

(E) This is the opposite of the argument, which says you can feel strongly and appreciate. This is the answer.

SECTION III

22. Evan: Earlier this year, the *Stockton Free Press* reported that residents consider Mayor Dalton more concerned with his image than with advancing the cause of the less fortunate of Stockton.

Dalia: But the mayor appointed a new director of the public television station, and almost immediately the station began running a documentary series promoting the mayor's antipoverty program.

Evan: Clearly the mayor has, by this appointment, attempted to manipulate public opinion through the media.

Evan's second statement counters Dalia's argument by

(A) disputing the relevancy of her statement
(B) suggesting that Dalia is less informed about the issue than he
(C) confusing the argument she presents with his own
(D) appealing to popular opinion that the mayor should not misuse his access to the media
(E) claiming that Dalia's argument is an example that actually strengthens his own argument

22. This is a REASONING question. Come up with your own description of how Evan's second statement counters Dalia, and then match your description to the choices.

(A) No, he attacks it directly, so he does think it's relevant. Eliminate it.
(B) He doesn't call into question the amount of information she possesses, but rather her interpretation of that information. Eliminate it.
(C) No, he's not confused at all. He's actually saying that her argument supports his argument.
(D) He doesn't appeal to anyone. Eliminate it.
(E) Bingo. He twists it around so it supports his argument. This is the answer.

QUESTIONS	EXPLANATIONS

23. Naturalist: Every year, thousands of animals already on the endangered species list are killed for their hides, furs, or horns. These illegal and often cruel deaths serve to push these species further toward the brink of extinction. The products made from these animals, such as articles of clothing and quack medical remedies, are goods no one really needs. What is needed is a large-scale media campaign to make the facts of the killings known and lessen the demand for these animal products. Such a campaign would be a good start in the effort to save endangered species from extinction.

Environmentalist: For the overwhelming majority of currently endangered species, the true threat of extinction comes not from hunting and poaching, but from continually shrinking habitats. Concentrating attention on the dangers of poaching for a very few high-visibility species would be counterproductive, leading people to believe that a boycott of a few frivolous items is enough to protect endangered species, when what is needed is a truly global environmental policy.

The point at issue between the naturalist and the environmentalist is which one of the following?

(A) whether the poaching of some endangered species actually increases that species' chances of becoming extinct

(B) whether a large-scale media campaign can affect the demand for some products

(C) whether more endangered species are threatened by poaching and hunting or shrinking of habitat

(D) whether some species could be saved from extinction by eliminating all commercial demand for that species

(E) whether a large-scale media campaign that lessens the demand for products made from endangered species is a good strategy for saving endangered species

---

23. This is a REASONING question. Come up with your own description of what they're arguing about, and then match your description to the choices.

(A) They both agree poaching is bad; they're arguing about whether or not it's the primary cause of extinction.

(B) Not whether this campaign will affect the demand, but whether it will affect extinction.

(C) We don't know the numbers. Eliminate it.

(D) They're arguing over the best method for saving as many species as possible.

(E) Yes—the environmentalist thinks that the strategy of saving habitats is more important than the naturalist's strategy of a media campaign. This is the answer.

SECTION III

24. Deborah: If one-third of the people who do not recycle would start recycling their paper products, approximately 150,000 fewer trees would be destroyed each year.

    Lee: That is unlikely. It would then follow that in the next ten years, the forests will increase by more than 1.5 million trees, more than there is room for.

    Which one of the following statements could Deborah offer Lee to clarify her own position and address the point that Lee makes?

    (A) It is possible for forests to increase by 150,000 trees per year if the growth rate of the previous year was unusually low.

    (B) The 150,000 trees that are saved would still be subject to forest fires and other destructive natural phenomena.

    (C) If the number of recyclers was increased by more than a third, the number of trees saved would be more than 150,000.

    (D) Any prediction of tree growth always presumes a constant growth and death rate.

    (E) For the number of nonrecyclers to be reduced by a third, the number of recycling materials, special recyclable trash bins, for example, would have to be increased by much more than a third.

24. This is a STRENGTHEN question. Figure out which answer choice has the most positive impact on the conclusion of Deborah's argument. Remember to assume the hypothetical truth of each choice and apply it to the argument.

    (A) We're not talking about increasing trees, just saving already existing ones. This has no impact. Eliminate it.

    (B) So the forest wouldn't really expand more than there is room for, since natural phenomena will regulate it. This is the answer.

    (C) We've already scared Lee enough. This wouldn't answer her issue at all. Eliminate it.

    (D) There is no prediction of tree growth in Deborah's argument.

    (E) The discussion about recycling bins, while fascinating, is outside the scope of the argument. Eliminate it.

SECTION III

QUESTIONS	EXPLANATIONS

25. Adoption Agent: Although my view runs counter to the trend in public sentiment, I believe a proposed new law granting adoptive parents access to the birth records of children to be adopted should not be passed. My experience as an adoption agent has supplied me with two reasons for holding this view. First, granting adoptive parents access to the records will result in wasted hours on the part of the adoption agency employees, who will be forced to spend time finding and subsequently returning files, when that time could be better spent out in the field. Second, based upon my agency experience, no adoptive parents are going to request the children's records anyway.

Which one of the following, if true, establishes that the adoption agent's second reason does not negate the first?

(A) The new law would necessitate that adoption agents, when reviewing the adoption agreement with prospective adoptive parents, have at hand the birth record of the child to be adopted, not simply have access to them.

(B) The task of retrieving and explaining birth records would fall to the least experienced member of the adoption agency's staff.

(C) Any children who asked to see their birth records would also insist on having details they did not understand explained to them.

(D) The new law does not exclude adoption agencies from charging adoptive parents for extra expenses incurred in order to comply with the new law.

(E) Some adoption agencies have always had a policy of allowing children access to their birth records, but none of those agency's children took advantage of that policy.

25. This is a PARADOX question. Look for an answer choice that allows both parts of the argument to be true, and remember to assume the hypothetical truth of each of the answer choices.

(A) Bingo. So we're going to spend the time of the employees anyway, whether or not anyone walks in the door and actually asks for the records. This is the answer.

(B) If no one asks for the records, it doesn't matter.

(C) Children requesting records is out of the scope of the argument.

(D) Money isn't the issue—time is the issue.

(E) This is the same problem as (C). Eliminate it.

SECTION IV

Questions 1-6

A bakery is making exactly three birthday cakes: A, B, and C. Each cake is to be composed of two different layers, a top layer and a bottom layer, consistent with the following guidelines:

Each layer is exactly one of the following flavors: vanilla, chocolate, strawberry, or lemon.

For each cake, the flavor of the top layer is different from that of the bottom layer.

Of the three cakes, no two bottom layers are the same flavor.

Of the three cakes, no two top layers are the same flavor.

Exactly one top layer is strawberry.

In cake C, either the top layer or the bottom layer, but not both, is vanilla.

The top layer of cake B is chocolate.

None of the bottom layers is chocolate.

		A	B	C
VCSL				one V
T ≠ B	① S Top		Ⓒ	S
B ≠ B	~C Bottom			V
T ≠ T	② S Top	S	Ⓒ	V
	~C Bottom	L	V	S
	⑤ S Top	S	Ⓒ	V
	~C Bottom	V	S	L
	③ S Top	L	Ⓒ	S
	~C Bottom	S	L	V
	S Top		Ⓒ	
	~C Bottom			

1. If the top layer of cake C is strawberry, then which one of the following statements must be true?

    (A) The top layer of cake A is vanilla.
    (B) The top layer of cake A is lemon.
    (C) The bottom layer of cake A is strawberry.
    (D) The bottom layer of cake B is lemon.
    (E) The bottom layer of cake C is vanilla.

1. (A) Not necessarily. We don't know anything about cake A.
    (B) Not necessarily. We don't know anything about cake A.
    (C) Not necessarily. We don't know anything about cake A.
    (D) Not necessarily. We don't know anything about the bottom layer of cake B.
    (E) Right. One of the layers in cake C must be vanilla.

2. If the bottom layer of cake B is vanilla, then which one of the following statements must be true?

    (A) The bottom layer of cake C is strawberry.
    (B) The top layer of cake C is strawberry.
    (C) The bottom layer of cake A is strawberry.
    (D) The bottom layer of cake C is vanilla.
    (E) The bottom layer of cake C is lemon.

2. (A) Right. Since the bottom of cake B is vanilla, the top of C is vanilla, and so the top of A is strawberry. Since strawberry must be used in the bottom and the top and the bottom of a cake cannot be the same flavor, strawberry must be the bottom layer of cake C.
    (B) The top layer of cake C must be vanilla, since the bottom can't be.
    (C) The top layer of A must be strawberry, so the bottom can't be.
    (D) It can't be if the bottom layer of cake B is.
    (E) The bottom layer of C must be strawberry.

3. Which one of the following statements could be true?

    (A) No top layer of any cake is vanilla.
    (B) No bottom layer of any cake is vanilla.
    (C) Only cake B has a strawberry layer.
    (D) Of the three cakes, one top layer is vanilla and one top layer is lemon.
    (E) The top layer of cake B is the same flavor as the bottom layer of cake A.

3. (A) Right. See the setup.
    (B) This isn't possible. Try it.
    (C) This isn't possible. Try it.
    (D) This isn't possible. Try it.
    (E) This isn't possible. Try it.

SECTION IV

QUESTIONS	EXPLANATIONS

4. Which one of the following statements could be true?

(A) Both the top layer of cake A and the bottom layer of cake B are vanilla.

(B) Both the top layer of cake A and the bottom layer of cake B are lemon.

(C) Both the top layer of cake A and the bottom layer of cake C are lemon.

(D) The top layer of cake A is vanilla, and the bottom layer of cake C is strawberry.

(E) The top layer of cake C is lemon, and the bottom layer of cake A is strawberry.

4.
(A) This isn't possible. Try it.
(B) Right. See the setup for question 3.
(C) This isn't possible. Try it.
(D) This isn't possible. Try it.
(E) This isn't possible. Try it.

5. If the bottom layer of cake C is lemon, then each of the following statements must be true EXCEPT:

(A) One top layer is vanilla.

(B) One layer of cake A is strawberry.

(C) One layer of cake B is strawberry.

(D) Two of the six layers are strawberry.

(E) Two of the six layers are lemon.

5.
(A) If the bottom of C is lemon, the top has to be vanilla.

(B) If the bottom of C is lemon, the top has to be vanilla. There has to be one top layer that's strawberry, so it has to be on cake A.

(C) If the bottom of C is lemon, the top has to be vanilla. There has to be one top layer that's strawberry, so it has to be on cake A. That forces vanilla on the bottom of A, and strawberry on the bottom of B.

(D) If the bottom of C is lemon, the top has to be vanilla. There has to be one top layer that's strawberry, so it has to be on cake A. That forces vanilla on the bottom of A, and strawberry on the bottom of B. That's two strawberries.

(E) Right. If the bottom of C is lemon, the top has to be vanilla. There has to be one top layer that's strawberry, so it has to be on cake A. That forces vanilla on the bottom of A, and strawberry on the bottom of B.

6. Suppose that none of the layers is chocolate. If all of the other conditions remain the same, then which one of the following statements could be true?

(A) None of the top layers is vanilla.

(B) None of the bottom layers is vanilla.

(C) Cake B has no vanilla layer.

(D) Neither cake A nor cake B has a lemon layer.

(E) Neither cake B nor cake C has a strawberry

6.
(A) With only three flavors to work with, this isn't possible.

(B) With only three flavors to work with, this isn't possible.

(C) Right. No chocolate anywhere means we only have three flavors to use: vanilla, lemon and strawberry. One of C's layers has to be vanilla, so only one other cake can have a vanilla layer. So it's possible for cake B not to have one.

(D) With only three flavors to work with, this isn't possible.

(E) With only three flavors to work with, this isn't possible.

Questions 7–11

An independent automobile magazine is trying to determine the four best-selling automobiles from among J, K, L, M, N, P. The information that follows is available:

There are no ties among the cars.

Each car is either a sports car or a luxury car, but not both.

Two of the six cars are imported and four are domestic.

Both imported cars are among the four best-sellers, exactly one of which is a luxury car.

Exactly one luxury car is among the four best-selling.

Cars J and L sold better than car M, and car M sold better than cars K and N.

Cars J and L are sports cars.

Cars M and P are luxury cars.

		1	2	3	4	5 (P)	6 (L)
(10)	car	J/L	I/J	(M)	K	N/P	P/N
	S/L	(S)	(S)	(L)	(S)		
	D/I	D	D	(I)	I	(D)	(D)
(11)	car	J/L	L/J	(M)	N	K/P	P/K
	S/L	(S)	(S)	(L)	(S)		
	D/I			(I)		(D)	(D)
	car			(M)			
	S/L	(S)	(S)	(L)	(S)		
	D/I			(I)		(D)	(D)

J_S K L_S M_L N P_L

I I D D D D

J_S K
 \   /
  M_L
 /   \
L   N

M is third. We know this because, first, it must come after J and L; second, it must come before K and N (which means it must be one of the cars selected); and finally, because only one luxury car can be selected, P cannot be selected, and so M must also come before P. So there must be two spaces before M and three spaces after M, making the third space the only possible space.

7. Which of the following is a complete and accurate list of the cars that can be sports cars?

(A) J, K
(B) J, L
(C) J, K, L
(D) J, L, N
(E) J, K, L, N

7. (A) The only cars that definitely can't be sports cars are M and P, so everything else can be.
(B) The only cars that definitely can't be sports cars are M and P, so everything else can be.
(C) The only cars that definitely can't be sports cars are M and P, so everything else can be.
(D) The only cars that definitely can't be sports cars are M and P, so everything else can be.
(E) Right. The only cars that definitely can't be sports cars are M and P, so that leaves everything else.

8. Which of the following cars must be a domestic car?

(A) Car J
(B) Car L
(C) Car M
(D) Car N
(E) Car P

8. (A) J could be imported.
(B) L could be imported.
(C) M must be third, and is a luxury car, so it must be the imported one.
(D) N could be imported.
(E) Right. P is a luxury car and is not one of the top four sellers, so it must be the domestic one.

SECTION IV

QUESTIONS	EXPLANATIONS

9. Which of the following could be false?

   (A) Car J had higher sales than L.
   (B) Car J had higher sales than N
   (C) Car L had higher sales than P.
   (D) Car L had higher sales than N.
   (E) Car M had higher sales than P.

9. (A) Right. J could be first and L could be second, or vice versa.
   (B) This must be true, since J is either first or second, and the highest N could be is fourth.
   (C) This must be true, since L is either first or second, and the highest P could be is fifth.
   (D) This must be true, since L is either first or second, and the highest N could be is fourth.
   (E) This must be true, since M is third, and the highest P could be is fifth.

10. If car K is imported, which of the following can be false?

   (A) Car J is domestic.
   (B) Car L is domestic.
   (C) Car K is the fourth best-seller.
   (D) Car K is a sports car.
   (E) Car N is a sports car.

10. (A) If K and M are imported, J must be domestic.
   (B) If K and M are imported, L must be domestic.
   (C) If K is imported, it must be fourth.
   (D) Only one luxury car can be among the top four, and we already know it's M.
   (E) Right. K must be fourth, so N is fifth or sixth, and could be sports or luxury.

11. If car N is the fourth best-selling car, which of the following must be true?

   (A) Car J is domestic.
   (B) Car K is domestic.
   (C) Car N is domestic.
   (D) Car K is luxury.
   (E) Car N is luxury.

11. (A) J could be imported.
   (B) Right. N is fourth, so K is either fifth or sixth, and both the fifth and sixth cars are domestic.
   (C) N could be imported.
   (D) K could be a sports car.
   (E) N must be a sports car if it's fourth, since only one luxury car can be among the top four, and we already know it's M.

SECTION IV

Questions 12–18

In a certain computer language, an acceptable sequence of five words forms a command. A command must meet the following requirements:

Each word must contain at least five letters, no more than two of which can be vowels (a, e, i, o, u).

A word may not begin with c, o, or y.

The first letters of the five words of a command must be in consecutive alphabetical order.

12. Which one of the following is an acceptable command?

(A) ankle, baker, dentist, enter, finger
(B) jingle, killer, lentil, metal, nicer
(C) nexus, optic, paint, quince, raked
(D) oafish, plate, quake, ringer, table
(E) single, taker, soaked, under, venture

12. (A) This is not consecutive.
(B) Right.
(C) No word can begin with o.
(D) No word can begin with o.
(E) This is not in alphabetical order.

13. If the third word in a command is "hinder," the first letter of the first word and the first letter of the last word of that command, respectively, must be

(A) c, g
(B) d, k
(C) e, j
(D) f, j
(E) g, l

13. (A) If the third word is hinder, the words start with f, g, h, i, and j, in that order.
(B) If the third word is hinder, the words start with f, g, h, i, and j, in that order.
(C) If the third word is hinder, the words start with f, g, h, i, and j, in that order.
(D) Right. If the third word is hinder, the words start with f, g, h, i, and j, in that order.
(E) If the third word is hinder, the words start with f, g, h, i, and j, in that order.

14. The last word in a command CANNOT begin with the letter

(A) j
(B) n
(C) r
(D) t
(E) u

14. (A) Sure, f, g, h, i, j is fine.
(B) Sure, j, k, l, m, n is fine.
(C) Right. This would mean the first letters are n, o, p, q, and r, and no word can begin with o.
(D) Sure, p, q, r, s, t is fine.
(E) Sure, q, r, s, t, u is fine.

SECTION IV

QUESTIONS	EXPLANATIONS

15. The first word in a command CANNOT begin with the letter

    (A) f
    (B) h
    (C) r
    (D) t
    (E) u

15. (A) Sure, f, g, h, i, j is fine.
      (B) Sure, h, i, j, k, l is fine.
      (C) Sure, r, s, t, u, v is fine.
      (D) Sure, t, u, v, w, x is fine.
      (E) Right. This would mean the first letters are u, v, w, x, and y, and no word can begin with y.

16. Which one of the following is an acceptable word with which a command can begin?

    (A) apple
    (B) major
    (C) quint
    (D) uncle
    (E) white

16. (A) This would mean the first letters are a, b, c, d, and e, and no word can begin with c.
      (B) This would mean the first letters are m, n, o, p, and q, and no word can begin with o.
      (C) Right. Q, r, s, t, u is fine.
      (D) This would mean the first letters are u, v, w, x, and y, and no word can begin with y.
      (E) This would mean the first letters are w, x, y, z, and that's it, and no word can begin with y.

17. If "xenon" is the last word in a command, it is possible for the first word in that command to be

    (A) tailor
    (B) talk
    (C) treacle
    (D) tale
    (E) tactic

17. (A) This word has more than two vowels.
      (B) This word has only four letters.
      (C) This word has more than two vowels.
      (D) This word has only four letters.
      (E) Right. If the last word starts with x, the first word starts with t, and must be at least five letters and contain at most two vowels.

18. Each of the following could be the last word in a command EXCEPT

    (A) hamper
    (B) jumble
    (C) scatter
    (D) tamper
    (E) units

18. (A) Sure. D, e, f, g, h is fine.
      (B) Sure. F, g, h, i, j is fine.
      (C) Right. This would mean the first letters are o, p, q, r, and s, and no word can begin with o.
      (D) Sure. P, q, r, s, t is fine.
      (E) Sure. Q, r, s, t, u is fine.

QUESTIONS	EXPLANATIONS

Questions 19–24

A florist is arranging eight flowers—A, B, C, F, G, J, K, and L—in the shape of a circle as shown:

```
        1
   8         2

 7             3

   6         4
        5
```

The following is known about the arrangement of the flowers:

A, B, and C are lilies; F and G are mums; J, K, and L are irises.
The lilies must all be next to each other.
The irises must all be next to each other.
No lily can be next to an iris.
Flower 5 is F.
Flower 2 is A.
If F is next to J, then F cannot also be next to C.

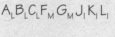

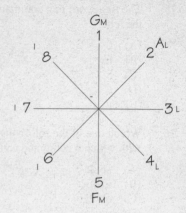

Deduction: G must be in 1. We know this because, first, F is in 5; second, the lilies all have to be together and the irises all have to be together (which means in both cases they take up blocks of three consecutive spaces); and, finally, no lily can be next to an iris. The only way you can have two blocks of three that are not next to each other if F is in 5 is if one block is in 2, 3, and 4 and the other is in 6, 7, and 8. Therefore, G must be in 1, the only remaining space.

19. Which one of the following flowers could be flower 3?

   (A) L
   (B) K
   (C) J
   (D) F
   (E) C

19. (A) Flower 3 has to be a lily, and we already know that A is in 2, so 3 is either B or C.
   (B) Flower 3 has to be a lily, and we already know that A is in 2, so 3 is either B or C.
   (C) Flower 3 has to be a lily, and we already know that A is in 2, so 3 is either B or C.
   (D) Flower 3 has to be a lily, and we already know that A is in 2, so 3 is either B or C.
   (E) Right. Flower 3 has to be a lily, and we already know that A is in 2, so 3 is either B or C.

20. Each one of the following statements must be true EXCEPT:

   (A) Flower 1 is an iris.
   (B) Flower 3 is a lily.
   (C) Flower 7 is an iris.
   (D) Flower 4 is a lily.
   (E) Flower 8 is an iris.

20. (A) Right. We know that flower 1 is a mum; in fact, it's G.
   (B) This must be true. Be careful; this is an EXCEPT question.
   (C) This must be true. Be careful; this is an EXCEPT question.
   (D) This must be true. Be careful; this is an EXCEPT question.
   (E) This must be true. Be careful; this is an EXCEPT question.

SECTION IV

QUESTIONS	EXPLANATIONS

21. Which one of the following flowers must be next to A?

   (A) B
   (B) C
   (C) F
   (D) G
   (E) J

21.
   (A) B could be next to A, but doesn't have to be.
   (B) C could be next to A, but doesn't have to be.
   (C) A is 2 and F is 5.
   (D) Right. We know A is 2, and because 5 is F, 1 must be G.
   (E) A is 2 and J is either 6, 7, or 8.

22. If L is flower 8, and K is next to L, which one of the following statements must be true?

   (A) A is directly to the left of B.
   (B) B is directly to the right of G.
   (C) G is directly across from J.
   (D) J is directly across from A.
   (E) L is directly across from A.

22.
   (A) F ends up next to J, which puts B on the other side of F, so C is to the left of A.
   (B) F ends up next to J, which puts B on the other side of F, in 4. G is in 1.
   (C) G is always across from F.
   (D) Right. A is 2 and J is 6.
   (E) L is 8 and A is 2.

23. If K is flower 8, then which one of the following pairs of flowers could NOT be directly across from each other?

   (A) B and J
   (B) B and K
   (C) B and L
   (D) C and J
   (E) C and L

23.
   (A) This is possible.
   (B) This is possible.
   (C) Right. If B and L are across from each other (in 3 and 7), F ends up being next to both J and C, which is a violation of the rules.
   (D) This is possible.
   (E) This is possible.

24. If K is flower 8 and C is flower 3, then each of the following is a pair of flowers that must be next to each other EXCEPT

   (A) A and C
   (B) B and F
   (C) F and J
   (D) G and K
   (E) J and L

24.
   (A) A is 2 and C is 3, so they must be next to each other.
   (B) B must be 4 if C is 3, and F is always 5, so they must be next to each other.
   (C) Right. F could be next to L.
   (D) K is 8 and G is always 1, so they must be next to each other.
   (E) J is either in 6 or 7, and so is L, so they must be next to each other.

Afterword

The Princeton Review was founded in New York City in 1981 to prepare students for the SAT. Our SAT students improved their scores by an average of 150 points, so in a few years we became the largest SAT course in the country. In 1985 we started our courses for the graduate exams.

At most locations, LSAT courses consist of between thirty and forty hours of classroom instruction. To ensure plenty of individual attention, class size is strictly limited—never more than fifteen students. Moreover, classes are arranged according to ability, so your fellow students will be at the same level of achievement. At least once a week, workshops meet to provide an even more thorough review. If you want still more practice, you can arrange for tutoring with your instructor at *no additional cost*. (By the way, in addition to our LSAT course, The Princeton Review also offers private tutoring.)

Each student is assigned to a class on the basis of his or her score on the first of our four diagnostic LSATs. These diagnostic tests are actual LSATs to give students accurate feedback about their performance and improvement. Within a few days of each test, we'll provide you with a detailed computerized analysis of your responses. This personalized assessment will pinpoint your test-taking strengths and weaknesses. Armed with this evaluation, you will be able to study with maximum efficiency.

All the practice tests used by the Princeton Review are actual LSATs. The materials you will use throughout the course have been prepared by our research staff to reflect the most up-to-date techniques we have developed to crack the LSAT. For example, when the LSAC contracted with new test developers in 1986 (and again in 1989, and again in 1991), Princeton Review students were prepared for the subtle changes in test design.

If you'd like more information about The Princeton Review and its courses, you can reach us at our toll-free number, 800-995-5585, or on the web at www.review.com.

ABOUT THE AUTHORS

Adam Robinson was born in 1955. He graduated from the Wharton School at the University of Pennsylvania before earning a law degree at Oxford University in England. Robinson, a rated chess master, devised and perfected the now famous "Joe Bloggs" approach to beating standardized tests in 1980, as well as numerous other core Princeton Review techniques. A freelance author of many books, Robinson has collaborated with The Princeton Review to develop a number of its courses. He lives in New York City.

Rob Tallia has been a teacher and trainer with the Princeton Review since 1990. Most recently he was the Research and Development Director of the LSAT Program, a job which he held from 1994–1997. Rob has published fiction, magazine articles, and, in 1997, he contributed three chapters to The Princeton Review's *Best Law Schools*. He lives in New York City with seven million of his very close friends.

NOTES

NOTES

your study break...

www.review.com

Expert Advice

Talk About It

Pop Surveys

Paying for it

www.review.com

THE
PRINCETON
REVIEW

Getting in

Word du Jour

Find-O-Rama School & Career Search

www.review.com

Best Schools

Finding it

FIND US...

International

Hong Kong
4/F Sun Hung Kai Centre
30 Harbour Road, Wan Chai,
Hong Kong
Tel: (011)85-2-517-3016

Japan
Fuji Building 40, 15-14
Sakuragaokacho, Shibuya Ku,
Tokyo 150, Japan
Tel: (011)81-3-3463-1343

Korea
Tae Young Bldg, 944-24,
Daechi- Dong, Kangnam-Ku
The Princeton Review- ANC
Seoul, Korea 135-280,
South Korea
Tel: (011)82-2-554-7763

Mexico City
PR Mex S De RL De Cv
Guanajuato 228 Col. Roma
06700 Mexico D.F., Mexico
Tel: 525-564-9468

Montreal
666 Sherbrooke St.
West, Suite 202
Montreal, QC H3A 1E7 Canada
Tel: (514) 499-0870

Pakistan
1 Bawa Park - 90 Upper Mall
Lahore, Pakistan
Tel: (011)92-42-571-2315

Spain
Pza. Castilla, 3 - 5° A, 28046
Madrid, Spain
Tel: (011)341-323-4212

Taiwan
155 Chung Hsiao East Road
Section 4 - 4th Floor,
Taipei R.O.C., Taiwan
Tel: (011)886-2-751-1243

Thailand
Building One, 99 Wireless Road
Bangkok, Thailand 10330
Tel: (662) 256-7080

Toronto
1240 Bay Street, Suite 300
Toronto M5R 2A7 Canada
Tel: (800) 495-7737
Tel: (716) 839-4391

Vancouver
4212 University Way NE,
Suite 204
Seattle, WA 98105
Tel: (206) 548-1100

locations

National (U.S.)

We have over 60 offices around the U.S. and
run courses in over 400 sites. For courses and locations
within the U.S. call 1 (800) 2/Review and you will be
routed to the nearest office.